A FEAST
OF FRUITS

A FEAST OF FRUITS

Elizabeth Riely

Color Photography by Ellen Silverman

MACMILLAN PUBLISHING COMPANY   NEW YORK
MAXWELL MACMILLAN CANADA   TORONTO
MAXWELL MACMILLAN INTERNATIONAL
NEW YORK   OXFORD   SINGAPORE   SYDNEY

Macmillan Publishing Company
866 Third Avenue
New York, NY 10022

Maxwell Macmillan Canada, Inc.
1200 Eglinton Avenue East
Suite 200
Don Mills, Ontario M3C 3N1

Macmillan Publishing Company is part of the Maxwell Communication Group of Companies.

The recipes for Strawberry Sablés, Apricot Orange Pavé, and Chocolate Pecan Tulipes copyright © 1986 by Bon Appétit Publishing Corp. Reprinted with permission.

The recipes for Italian Prune Plum and Port Sherbet, Lemon Butter Cookies, Shrimp Seviche with Creme Fraiche, and Apricot Rum Sauce copyright © 1985 by Bon Appétit Publishing Corp. Reprinted with permission.

Library of Congress Cataloging-in-Publication Data
Riely, Elizabeth.
  A feast of fruits / Elizabeth Riely.
    p.   cm.
  Includes bibliographical references and index.
  ISBN 0-02-601961-2
  1. Cookery (Fruit)   I. Title.
TX811.R54   1993
641.6′4—dc20   92-46080   CIP

Macmillan books are available at special discounts for bulk purchases for sales promotions, premiums, fund-raising, or educational use. For details, contact:

Special Sales Director
Macmillan Publishing Company
866 Third Avenue
New York, NY 10022
Design by Janet Tingey

Food stylist: Deborah Mintcheff
Prop stylist: Christine McCabe

10 9 8 7 6 5 4 3 2 1

Printed in the United States of America

For John

CONTENTS

ACKNOWLEDGMENTS

Many people have helped me more than they can know in the writing of this book, and it gives me great pleasure to thank them for their kindness. Friends who have shared their recipes with me are mentioned in the headnotes for those dishes. Let me add that responsibility for any mistakes is mine alone.

The United Fresh Fruit and Vegetable Association and the individual fruit associations have sent me detailed information on their produce. In addition, they have answered my countless questions quickly and efficiently. Janet Christensen of the Massachusetts Department of Food and Agriculture has shown patience and ingenuity in fielding my queries and putting me in touch with just the right person. Nancy Stutzman of the Cooperative Extension of the University of Massachusetts, USDA, assisted me with directions for sterilizing preserves and pickles. Marc Gonick, Joe Rigoli, and Peter Connolly of Blacker Brothers Inc., in Newton Centre, Massachusetts, have graciously responded to my constant requests for information and produce in and sometimes out of season.

From their firsthand knowledge of life in China, Nina Simonds and Celia Riely Lewis provided background on peaches in Chinese cuisine and culture. Steven Cohen helped me to fathom the mysteries of the computer. My good friend Sarah Boardman, through her experience in the sometimes disparate worlds of food and publishing, gave wise advice on matters great and small. Her independent point of view proved invaluable in offering ideas that were always fresh, provocative, and thoughtful in the truest sense.

I owe a special debt to Evelynne Kramer of *The Boston Globe* for reminding me that I write not only for food writers but for busy people with full lives outside the kitchen. Thanks also go to Cynthia Dockrell of the *Globe* for her keen eye. Members of the Culinary Historians of Boston have broadened and deepened my awareness of food history.

My agent, Susan Lescher, has given crucial support not only with with her understanding and judgment, but also with her enthusiasm and warmth. Pam Hoenig, my editor at Macmillan, has amply demonstrated her patience, tact, discrimination, and common sense. My gratitude extends to her assistant, Justin Schwartz, for following through cheerfully on countless details. I also wish to thank Mary Flower for saving me from errors and Janet Tingey for designing this handsome book. Ellen Silverman's photographs capture the inherent beauty of fruit.

Particular thanks go to my family for their essential part in this venture. My husband John, a true teacher and scholar, gave me my voice as a writer. From the beginning, he has encouraged and inspired me to do more than I ever could have imagined. My son Christopher revealed his discerning palate, often telling me after a taste or two exactly what a dish did—or did not—need. My son Andrew, a voracious reader, led me to passages about fruit in his library. As for my father, Robert Gawthrop, his appetite for food and history sparked my own interest in those subjects. My mother, Elizabeth Gawthrop, who died just as the manuscript reached completion, shared with all of us her great exuberance for life. May the book reflect her spirit of generosity.

INTRODUCTION

Ripening in a bowl on the kitchen table, fruit becomes a still life centerpiece that fills the room with its subtle shadings and inviting fragrance. We all know that fruit is beautiful, delicious, and nourishing. Lending itself to simple but stylish cooking, it also goes with every other type of food—vegetables, grains, fish, poultry, meat, and dairy products. Yet we often overlook fruit's versatility in the kitchen, especially in savory cooking, where its ambiguous balance of sweetness and acidity can mellow or spark a dish. This book tries to draw attention to a class of food that combines all these excellent qualities while easily within our reach.

To make the book as useful as possible, each section is devoted to a single fruit, arranged alphabetically for easy access. Background on each fruit's history and cultivation provides some understanding of its cultural traditions. To guide the reader through the supermarket and greengrocer's, the book suggests how to choose fruit, with descriptions of the varieties available in season. Once home, there are suggestions on how to use the fruit in the kitchen—ripening, storing, preparing, and cooking—followed by up-to-date nutritional information.

A Feast of Fruits emphasizes fruits that we find and eat most commonly. Apples and oranges, for instance, have many more recipes than quinces and mangoes. But with the arrival of many new immigrants from all corners of the globe, markets now offer a vastly wider diversity of fruits than only a few years ago. A final chapter gathers information on the selection and handling of the more exotic fruits that are quickly changing the look of our grocery markets. Readers who would like to know more than could be given in these pages should see Elizabeth Schneider's and Alan Davidson's admirable books listed in the bibliography.

Since this is primarily a cookbook, recipes make up its bulk: savory and sweet, simple and sophisticated, familiar and exotic, classic and contemporary. They draw on a wide range of traditions and techniques that are updated and lightened without compromising quality. They include preparations of all kinds throughout the meal, highlighting healthy and uncomplicated dishes that work so well with fruit. Then there are some recipes for more leisurely occasions when we want to explore an idea in the kitchen or to prepare something truly extraordinary for friends and family.

To help the busy cook, the recipes point out what can be made ahead and suggest ways to serve a dish, taking advantage of a fruit's natural beauty. They also recommend variations with other fruits that are suitable, to encourage the cook to experiment further. Most of the recipes call for fresh fruit, but consideration is given to frozen, and numerous dried fruit dishes allow welcome variety in the winter months. Since a fruit's season can be fleeting and our windfall unexpected, these recipes offer some dishes to be enjoyed right away and others, such as jams, pickles, and chutneys, to be preserved and set on a cupboard shelf for pleasures yet to come.

APPLES

A is for apple, begins many an abecedarium, or fruit book, for that matter. But at the beginning of the Bible, in the Book of Genesis, the forbidden fruit in the Garden of Eden was not an apple. It was the fruit of the tree of the knowledge of good and evil, even though we may picture the apple as that legendary fruit.

The apple originated in the Caucasus in the form of a small and sour crab apple; cultivation since the beginning of the Stone Age has vastly improved it. The technique of grafting rootstock to produce consistent fruit, rather than relying on cross-fertilization of the blossom, was an important advance during the classical period. Today's apple, *Malus pumila* of the rose family, is large, sweet, juicy, and cultivated in many thousands of varieties, making it the most important fruit in the temperate world.

All apples have their primary season, which is September through February unless otherwise indicated. In the past, many were dried as an important method of preservation. Today fresh apples are kept just above freezing in "controlled storage," where the high nitrogen and low oxygen levels extend their natural season virtually throughout the year.

American apples are different from European varieties because they were grown from seeds brought by early immigrants on long voyages, and thus developed differently from those grown by graft in Europe. Crossbreeding with native American crab apples differentiated them further. Of the more than seven thousand apple varieties grown in the United States, only a couple of handfuls have commercial significance. But recently there has been an encouraging revival of older "antique" varieties, where taste matters as much as looks and durability in shipping.

Of the main American commercial varieties and in order of popularity, Red Delicious provides nearly half the crop. It has crimson skin, five distinctive bumps around the blossom end (corresponding to the five star-shaped seed chambers in the core), and a large, fairly tall shape. Red Delicious is suitable for eating out of hand, but not for cooking. It is sweet, low in acid, and crisp in texture when fresh, but becomes insipid and mealy with age—which is how we too often find it in markets.

The Golden Delicious (no relation to Red) is pale green to yellow, large, firm, and tarter when grown in colder regions, otherwise tending toward blandness. It holds its shape in cooking. Because it is a heavy-bearing tree, this variety has become very popular with growers.

1

The Granny Smith has tart, crisp, firm flesh and bright green color. This apple has leapt in popularity in the United States. Like the Gravenstein, it grows well in warmer climates and is excellent for cooking as well as eating.

The McIntosh is juicy, sweet, spicy with plenty of acid, and medium to small in size. Its red-streaked green skin pulls off easily. This northern apple is excellent for both eating and cooking, but the flesh quickly discolors and softens. It ripens early, but does not keep especially well.

Among other varieties, Rome Beauty (available from late October on) is solid red and round, tart and firm, best for cooking. Jonathan (late October on) is yellow with red stripes superimposed. Small to medium in size, it is crisp, somewhat acid, rich in flavor, and fine for cooking, but keeps rather poorly. Empire, a recent cross between the Red Delicious and McIntosh varieties, is dark red, firm, juicy, fairly tart, and versatile. Newtown Pippin is green, firm, tart, versatile, and keeps exceptionally well. Winesap is medium-size, round, dark red, with a spicy flavor excellent for cider, cooking, and eating, and a good keeper (available October on).

Cortland, crisp and tart, is exceptional as a cooking or eating apple; it has the particular advantage of not darkening quickly when cut and exposed to oxygen. Macoun is large and red, similar to its McIntosh parent, but a better keeper. Stayman, Northern Spy, Ida Red, Empire, Baldwin, Criterion, Rhode Island Greening, Crispin (also called Mutsu), and Gala (eating only) are other good American varieties. Other countries have their particular favorites: in England, Cox's Orange Pippin, for example, especially with port, and in France, Reinette.

When choosing apples, select firm fruit with smooth skin well-colored for its variety, without bruises or soft spots; the occasional blemish or odd shape is trifling. In general, green apples are tarter. Americans tend to go for picture-perfect fruit, especially red, ignoring flavor, texture, and character. Since local farmers' markets are enjoying a resurgence, if you live in apple country, try some of the more unusual varieties they offer. Windfall apples, literally or figuratively, may bring you an unexpected good turn.

Apples will continue to ripen at room temperature. Unless you plan to use them right away, store small quantities in the refrigerator; if in a bag, poke a few holes through it to let the apples breathe. Large quantities should be kept in a cool, dry, dark, airy space. One bad apple, as the adage goes, will spoil the whole barrel, so check for spots. The natural ethylene gas that apples give off in ripening will mature other fruit as well. To hasten their ripening, enclose them together in a bag.

Apple flesh exposed to the air will discolor, a natural process called oxidation. To retard it, dip the cut apple flesh in lemon juice. Some varieties such as Cortland discolor slowly, making them convenient for certain recipes. If cooking apples lack character, you can heighten their flavor by adding a little lemon juice to the dish.

Cider originally designated the fermented juice of apples. Since water was often contaminated in the past, cider was an everyday drink in apple-growing regions, especially England's West Country and France's Normandy. When New England was settled and every farm had an orchard, adults and children alike drank hard cider the way we drink water until the temperance movement checked cider-making in the nineteenth century. Cider vinegar was important in preserving other foods.

To clarify the confusing terms of apple-juice products, in the United States sweet cider—that quintessential flavor of fall—means the juice of fresh-pressed apples of any variety, preferably unbruised. The slight fizz it develops in a few days is a sign of fermentation which can be checked with freezing. Hard cider can be dry or sweet, depending on the apple varieties used and whether fresh cider was added back after fermentation. The alcoholic content can range from 3 to 7 percent. In the past, homemade hard cider could be as rough as moonshine, but likewise it could be very fine. European cider is usually naturally sparkling, bottled before fermentation is complete, or perhaps with carbonation added afterward, as in lesser quality beer.

Apple wine means fresh apple cider with sugar added ("chaptalized," in wine terminology) to increase the alcoholic content to 10 to 14 percent, usually about 11 percent. Normandy's Calvados is a distilled and aged spirit made from apple pomace, the mash residue left after pressing. Its alcoholic content is much higher than that of cider or wine, about 40 percent. Applejack, with roots in New England, is the American equivalent of the brandy.

Apple juice is a vague term that for marketing purposes means a pasteurized apple product containing preservatives, often made from concentrate, and with sugar added. Compared to fresh cider, it has no "real *tang* nor *smack*," as Henry David Thoreau described bland cultivated apples in his essay "Wild Apples." Apple juice has its place, but not in cooking.

Sweet and hard cider have culinary uses similar to those of wine. For braising poultry, game, pork, and ham, cider's rich but tart taste is the perfect complement. Baste a stuffed roast with cider, especially when apples are in the stuffing. To make a quick sauce for sautéed meats, deglaze the pan with cider, a method that also works with fall vegetables. As in Normandy, where apple trees and dairy cows dot the landscape, try a dry cider and cream sauce with seafood as well as chicken. For desserts, cider's acidity can lighten baked dishes; homespun or sophisticated, they gain a resonant depth of flavor. Pair other fruits with apples, binding the marriage with cider: early fall raspberries or cranberries give a sparkle and brilliance to the muted apple.

Nutritionally, the apple is very healthful: an apple a day keeps the doctor away. It is not a major source of any particular nutrient, but gives small amounts of several important ones. The apple is very high in fiber (both pectin and cellulose) and a valuable source of vitamin C, with some A and several of the B complex, as well as potassium, iron, and phosphorus. An apple helps to aid digestion, quench thirst (85 percent water), and clean teeth. A medium-size apple contains virtually no sodium and relatively few calories, about eighty.

Stonewall

This is the perfect drink when fresh sweet cider comes into the market as the first nip of fall is in the air. Serve it if you can in a pewter tumbler.

1 jigger bourbon
Fresh sweet cider

Fill a glass or tumbler with ice cubes. Pour in the bourbon and fill with cider.

MAKES 1 DRINK

Mussels in Cider Cream Sauce

These mussels are cooked in the style of Normandy, in northern France, where cream is abundant and apple cider replaces wine in both cooking and drinking.

2 pounds mussels, scrubbed clean and beards removed
1 small leek, split, rinsed, and chopped (½ cup)
3 tablespoons chopped fresh parsley
1 cup hard dry cider
½ cup heavy cream
Salt and ground white pepper to taste
1 green apple, such as Granny Smith, cut into thin slices for garnish

Put the mussels in a wide, nonreactive (nonaluminum) pan, discarding any that are cracked or refuse to close when tapped. Add the leek, parsley, and cider. Cover tightly and simmer over low heat until the shells open, about 5 minutes. Remove the mussels with a slotted spoon and keep warm. Pour the contents of the pan through a sieve lined with a double layer of cheesecloth, moistened in cool water and squeezed dry, into a saucepan. Discard the solids and boil the liquid down until reduced by half. Add the cream and continue to boil until the sauce is thick and concentrated.

While the sauce is reducing, remove the mussels from their shells, reserving a few shells for garnish. Place the mussel meats on serving plates. Season the reduced sauce with salt and white pepper, and spoon it over or under the mussels. Garnish them with the reserved shells and a few thin slivers of apple with the green peel left on.

MAKES 2 FIRST-COURSE SERVINGS

Sliced Apples with Roquefort Spread

Blue cheese and apples go hand in hand before dinner as well as after. Use Cortland apples because their cut flesh keeps from turning dark much longer than that of other varieties.

6 ounces Roquefort, Stilton, or other strong blue cheese, crumbled
3 ounces cream cheese
2 scallions (green and white parts), chopped
1 clove garlic, minced (optional)
¼ cup chopped walnuts, lightly toasted (see page 179)
Cortland apples, cored and sliced

In a large bowl, mix together the Roquefort and cream cheeses with the scallion, garlic, and walnuts. A food processor will homogenize the cheeses, so mash them with a fork to keep some texture. Taste carefully for balance. (The cheese can be mixed a day or two before serving and kept covered and chilled.)

Mound the cheese on a serving plate and surround it with the apple slices. Serve with good crackers or bread, allowing your guests to take the cheese with either or both apple and bread.

MAKES ABOUT 2 CUPS

Waldorf Salad with Fennel

Traditional Waldorf salad uses celery and sometimes raisins, but fennel adds the subtle flavor of anise and transforms a boring luncheon staple into something more interesting. This salad goes well with smoked chicken or fish; or replace the mayonnaise with sour cream, and mix some flaked smoked fish right into the salad.

2 crisp, tart, firm apples, preferably 1 red and 1 green
Juice of ½ lemon
1 cup chopped fennel (stalks are fine)
2 tablespoons chopped fresh fennel leaves
½ cup chopped walnuts, lightly toasted (see page 179)
½ cup mayonnaise
Salt and freshly ground black pepper to taste
4 handfuls redleaf lettuce

Quarter, core, and dice the apples, leaving the skin on (about 1½ to 2 cups). Toss the apples in the lemon juice, coating all surfaces, to keep the flesh from darkening. Add the chopped fennel, fennel leaves, and walnuts. Toss with just enough mayonnaise to bind the

mixture, and season with several gratings of black pepper and salt (you may not need any). Make a bed of lettuce leaves on four serving plates and spoon the mixture on top.
MAKES 4 SERVINGS

Red Cabbage with Apples and Chestnuts

Redolent of wintry flavors, this sweet-and-sour cabbage dish goes perfectly with pork and game.

3 strips bacon or 2 tablespoons vegetable oil
2 tablespoons sugar
1 large onion, chopped
1 small head red cabbage (about 2 pounds), cored, cut into eighths, and shredded
2 large tart apples, peeled, cored, and chopped
½ cup red wine vinegar
½ cup sweet cider or water
½ cup shelled chestnuts (optional)
4 juniper berries, crushed (optional)

In a large frying pan, fry the bacon until it is brown and crisp; dry on a paper towel, then break it into pieces. Drain all but 2 tablespoons of the fat from the pan. Add the sugar and onion; stir to dissolve the sugar and cook the onion over moderate heat, letting it brown lightly. Add the cabbage, apples, vinegar, and cider, and cook over low heat for about 10 minutes, pressing the cabbage down and stirring from time to time. Add the chestnuts and juniper berries. With the cover askew, cook over low heat until the cabbage is tender and most of the liquid evaporated, 30 to 40 minutes. Taste carefully for the balance of sweet and sour: add a touch more sugar if necessary. Stir in the reserved bacon and serve.
MAKES 8 SERVINGS

Applesauce

Fresh applesauce is so delicious and easy to make that it's hard to understand why we don't bother more often. For an intense apple flavor, use cider instead of water. A combination of varieties gives complexity. Red skins impart a pink tinge; green apples should be peeled. For coarser texture, mash the chunks with the back of a slotted spoon rather than sieving them. Feel free to add your favorite spices to taste, perhaps a little grated lemon zest or preserved ginger too.

2 pounds tart apples, cored and coarsely chopped
½ cup water or fresh sweet cider
¼ cup sugar, or to taste
½ teaspoon ground spice, such as cinnamon, allspice, coriander, ginger, nutmeg, or mace, alone or in combination (optional)
1 tablespoon unsalted butter (optional, if to be served warm)

Put the apples into a large saucepan with the water. Cover and bring to a boil, then cook over low heat until the flesh turns soft, about 20 minutes, depending on the firmness of the apples. Put the contents of the pan through a sieve set over another pot or bowl, and press to purée the pulp and remove the apple skins. Season with sugar and spices, a little at a time to avoid overseasoning, and add the butter for richness. For a dessert sauce, rather than as a savory accompaniment, add more sugar. Serve warm or cold. Tightly covered and well chilled, applesauce will keep for a week or more.

MAKES ABOUT 3½ CUPS; 6 SERVINGS

VARIATION: For apple butter, make applesauce in greater quantity and with cider instead of water. Very slowly cook it down further than for applesauce. To tell when the fruit purée is thick enough to be apple butter, draw a spoon through the sauce across the bottom of the pot; if the bottom remains visible, it is ready. To avoid burning, add the sugar toward the end of cooking, cook slowly, and watch carefully. Apple butter can be put up in clean warm jars and sterilized (see page 321), to be stored on a cupboard shelf.

Spiced Crab Apples

These little apples are piquant and pretty as a garnish for meats, especially at holiday time. If you prefer, use half water and half vinegar.

2 cups sugar
1½ cups white distilled or red or white wine vinegar (at least 5% acidity)
1 pound unblemished whole crab apples, with stems (preferably red)
One 1-inch stick cinnamon
6 allspice berries
4 whole cloves

Combine the sugar and vinegar in a saucepan, bring to a boil, and let boil, covered, until the sugar has dissolved, about 5 minutes. Add the apples and poach over low heat just until they are tender, 3 to 5 minutes, depending on their size and firmness. Do not let them get mushy. Remove the apples from the syrup and place in a 1-quart jar. Add the spices to the syrup and cook over high heat until it is thickened and seasoned to your taste. When the syrup has cooled, strain it through a sieve and pour over the apples. Cover and refrigerate, or seal and sterilize in a hot water bath (see page 321). Sterilized and kept in a cool dark cupboard, they will keep for six months or longer.

MAKES ABOUT 1 QUART

Apple Chutney

A firm fall pear such as Kieffer also works well in this dark spicy chutney.

2½ cups cider vinegar (at least 5% acidity)
4 cups firmly packed light brown sugar
2 pounds tart, firm apples, peeled, cored, and sliced
1 medium-size to small onion, chopped
1 cup (6 ounces) raisins
2 cloves garlic, minced
3 tablespoons peeled and minced fresh ginger
1 small, fresh red chile, seeded and minced
6 allspice berries
1 tablespoon salt

Put the vinegar and sugar in a large nonreactive pot, bring to a boil, and let boil until the sugar is dissolved, about 5 minutes. Add the remaining ingredients and stir to combine. Return the liquid to a boil, reduce the heat to low, and simmer, stirring occasionally, until the liquid has thickened and the apples are tender but not mushy, about 30 minutes. Cool the chutney and put it up in jars to keep in the refrigerator or in hot sterilized jars (see page 321) to store on a cupboard shelf. The chutney should mellow for about a month before opening and will keep for a year. Refrigerate after opening.

MAKES 7 OR 8 HALF-PINT JARS

Apple Cranberry Onion Marmalade

The deep flavor and russet color of this side dish are quintessentially fall. It is at once sophisticated and homey. Serve it as a savory applesauce to accompany meats, especially poultry, game, pâté, or pork.

2 tablespoons vegetable oil
1 pound onions, sliced or chopped
1 pound tart apples, peeled, cored, and chopped

2 cups cranberries, picked over
2 cups fresh sweet cider
¼ cup firmly packed brown sugar, or to taste
1 teaspoon ground allspice, or to taste
½ teaspoon ground cinnamon, or to taste

Heat the vegetable oil in a very large skillet over high heat. Add the onions and cook them, stirring occasionally, until caramelized, 15 to 20 minutes. Do not let them burn, but allow them to turn a deep rich brown. Add the apples, cranberries, and cider, cover, and let simmer over low heat until the cranberries pop, about 5 minutes. Uncover and cook over low heat for a long time, about 1 hour, stirring once in a while, until the liquid evaporates and the pulp gets jammy. As it cooks down, mash the solids with the back of a slotted spoon. When the mixture has become thick, season it with the sugar and spices. Serve the marmalade warm.

This is a good dish to simmer on the back burner while you are attending to another. Refrigerated in a jar, it keeps well for several weeks. If you like, put it up in warm sterilized jars (see page 321) to keep on the pantry shelf for six months or longer. Refrigerate after opening.

MAKES 1 GENEROUS QUART

Fried Apples

This simple breakfast dish makes a nice change with biscuits and sausage. Or serve it as a supper side dish with ham, pork, or chicken. Aside from giving character and texture, the skins keep the slices from breaking apart.

4 large, firm, tart apples, cored, quartered, and cut into fairly thick slices
2 tablespoons butter
1 to 2 tablespoons firmly packed brown sugar, or to taste
¼ teaspoon ground cinnamon, or to taste
¼ teaspoon ground coriander, or to taste

Over medium-low heat, melt the butter in a large skillet. When it begins to foam, add the apple slices and cook, stirring occasionally. When they have started to color, stir in the sugar and spices. Cook the apples until they have caramelized, but do not let them turn mushy.

MAKES 4 SERVINGS

Whole-Wheat Apple Pancakes with Honey

The whole-wheat flour and apple give texture, while the buttermilk and honey lend their own subtle contrast.

> 1⅓ cups sifted all-purpose flour
> ⅔ cup whole-wheat flour
> 1 teaspoon baking soda
> ½ teaspoon salt
> ¾ teaspoon ground cinnamon, or to taste
> 2 large eggs, at room temperature
> 2 tablespoons honey
> 2 cups buttermilk, at room temperature
> 2 tablespoons butter, melted and cooled
> 1 medium-size tart apple, peeled, cored, and coarsely grated (1 cup)

In a medium-size bowl, combine the flours, baking soda, salt, and cinnamon. In another bowl beat the eggs lightly with the honey, then stir in the buttermilk. Make a well in the middle of the dry ingredients and pour in the buttermilk mixture. Stir to incorporate the flour into the milk gradually, smoothing the lumps as you go. When the batter is smooth, stir in the melted butter and grated apple.

Heat a griddle or large skillet, and lightly grease it with vegetable shortening or butter. Ladle the batter onto the griddle in 5-inch rounds, or whatever size you prefer, and cook them until golden on both sides, turning once. Keep the pancakes warm in a low oven. Continue until all the batter is used. Serve the pancakes as you like, with butter, maple syrup, honey, or molasses.

MAKES ABOUT 20 PANCAKES; 6 SERVINGS

Glazed Apple Rings

Serve these sugar-glazed apples at breakfast with sausages or bacon or as a garnish for roast chicken.

> 2 tablespoons butter
> 2 firm, tart apples, cored and cut into ⅜-inch slices
> 2 tablespoons sugar

Over medium-low heat melt the butter in a large skillet. When it begins to foam, add the apples in one layer and cook until they turn golden; gently turn with a spatula and cook the other side a few minutes more, depending on the firmness of the apple. Do not let them turn soft. To glaze them, especially if they are very tart, sprinkle a little sugar over the surface, put the top on the pan, and let sit until the sugar melts; keep warm.

MAKES ABOUT 4 BREAKFAST SERVINGS OR 8 GARNISH SERVINGS

Apple Crumb Cake

This fruity, crumbly cake is perfect for tailgate picnics and other autumn outings.

1½ cups all-purpose flour
1 teaspoon baking powder
½ teaspoon salt
¾ cup firmly packed brown sugar
½ teaspoon ground cinnamon
½ cup (1 stick; ¼ pound) butter, cut into pieces
1 large egg, lightly beaten
2 tablespoons rum, bourbon, or Scotch
½ cup chopped pecans, lightly toasted (see page 179)
½ cup raisins
1½ cups peeled, cored, and coarsely chopped apples (about 1½ apples)

Preheat the oven to 325°F. Butter and flour an 8-inch round cake pan, tapping out any excess.

In a large bowl sift together the flour, baking powder, and salt. Stir in the brown sugar, cinnamon, and butter. Using your fingertips or a pastry blender, rub the butter into the dry mixture until it has the texture of oatmeal. Mix together the egg and rum in a small bowl and blend into the batter. Combine the pecans, raisins, and apples, and stir evenly into the batter; it will be very heavy. Spoon the batter into the pan and smooth the surface. Bake until golden brown, about 1½ hours. When the cake is done, it should shrink from the sides of the pan and a skewer inserted in the middle will come out clean. Cool and slice into wedges to serve.

MAKES ONE 8-INCH CAKE; 8 SERVINGS

Apple Pie

This American standard has countless variations. To name a few, add chopped nuts or cranberries to the filling; substitute whiskey for the lemon juice; add more apples and use a top crust only for a deep-dish pie.

Pastry for a 9-inch double-crust pie (see page 35)
2½ pounds firm, tart apples
3 tablespoons fresh lemon juice
¼ to ½ cup white or firmly packed brown sugar, depending on the tartness of the apples
1 teaspoon ground spices, usually cinnamon and nutmeg, or another combination
1 tablespoon unsalted butter, cut into small pieces
Milk, cream, or 1 egg, lightly beaten

Preheat the oven to 400°F. Roll out half the pastry on a floured board and fit it into a 9-inch pie plate. Trim the edge and chill well.

Peel, quarter, core, and slice the apples. Toss them in a large bowl with the lemon juice. Add the sugar and spices and toss again. Pile the apples into the pie shell, dot the top with butter, and wet the pastry lip. Roll out the other half of the pastry, carefully fit it over the pie, and trim the edge, allowing a half-inch overhang. Tuck the extra pastry under the lower lip and crimp it to seal the crust. Cut vents into the top crust. Decorate the top of the pie with extra pastry cutouts or whatever design you may choose, plain or fancy. Brush the surface with a little milk or cream or with an egg thinned with water.

Bake the pie for 20 minutes, then lower the heat to 350°F and bake until the crust is golden brown and the apples are tender, 20 to 30 minutes longer. If the edge of the crust browns too much, cover it with aluminum foil. Serve the pie warm or at room temperature with a slice of cheddar cheese, a scoop of vanilla ice cream, or a dollop of whipped cream.

MAKES ONE 9-INCH PIE; 8 SERVINGS

Aunt Ora's Apple Pie

This shredded-apple pie, quickly made in a food processor, has a soft, loose texture quite unlike that of other apple pies. It comes from Ora Cottre, of Lexington, Alabama, the aunt of my editor, Pam Hoenig. In apple season Aunt Ora makes the pies in quantity, stacking them one on another in the freezer and pulling one out for company. It's even better with vanilla ice cream.

½ cup (1 stick; ¼ pound) unsalted butter
1 cup sugar
Pinch of salt
2 large eggs, lightly beaten
1 teaspoon ground cinnamon, or to taste
3 large, firm cooking apples, peeled, cored, and coarsely grated
Qne 8- or 9-inch pie crust (see page 35) unbaked and halve the recipe

Preheat the oven to 350° F. Cream the butter and sugar together until light and fluffy. Add the salt, eggs, and cinnamon and blend well. In a bowl, combine the butter and sugar mixture with the grated apples. Pat the filling into the pie crust and bake until the pie is golden and the center set, about 1 hour. Let it cool somewhat before serving.

MAKES ONE 8- OR 9-INCH PIE; 6 SERVINGS

French Apple Tart

This tart, as typically French as apple pie is American, is also delicious with peaches or pears in place of apples.

One 9-inch pâte sucrée (see page 35) or pâte brisée shell (see page 16), unbaked
¼ cup apricot jam, strained through a sieve
2 tablespoons fresh lemon juice
2 or 3 cooking apples, peeled, cored, and thinly sliced

Preheat the oven to 400°F. In a small nonreactive saucepan combine the apricot jam and lemon juice; stir over low heat until the jam is melted. Brush a thin layer over the bottom of the tart shell. Set the rest aside; rewarm it before the final glazing.

Arrange the apple slices overlapping each other in the tart shell in a pretty design, either like a pinwheel, each concentric circle reversing direction, or like a flower. Put a few slices in the center. Bake until the pastry is cooked and the apples are tinged with color, about 20 minutes. Take the tart out of the oven and brush the surface with the remaining apricot glaze, taking care not to dislodge the design. Serve warm or cold.

MAKES ONE 9-INCH TART; 6 SERVINGS

Cider Pie in Walnut Crust

Cider pie used to be very popular in New England when orchards were prolific. Old recipes often begin with the step of boiling down cider to reduce its volume and intensify its tang.

One 9-inch walnut pâte sucrée (see following recipe), baked for 20 minutes

FOR THE CIDER FILLING
1½ cups fresh sweet cider
¾ cup firmly packed dark brown sugar
3 tablespoons unsalted butter, cut into pieces
3 large eggs
⅜ teaspoon ground cinnamon
⅜ teaspoon ground ginger
⅜ teaspoon ground cloves

Preheat the oven to 400°F. Pour the cider into a saucepan, and over moderate heat boil to reduce its volume by half to ¾ cup (do not guess; measure it accurately), about 15 minutes. Add the brown sugar and stir to dissolve it. Add the butter and stir to melt. Let the mixture cool somewhat.

Lightly beat the eggs with the spices in a medium-size bowl until the eggs froth up. Pour the cider mixture into the eggs in a steady stream, beating continuously to incorporate them. Pour the mixture into the prepared pie shell and carefully put it in the oven. Immediately turn the heat down to 350°F and bake until the surface turns a caramel brown and the center is just set, like a custard, 30 to 35 minutes. Let the pie cool before serving.

MAKES ONE 9-INCH PIE; 6 SERVINGS

Walnut Pâte Sucrée

¼ cup walnuts (or blanched almonds)
2 tablespoons sugar
¾ cup plus 2 tablespoons all-purpose flour
6 tablespoons (¾ stick) unsalted butter, cut into pieces, very cold or even frozen
1 large egg
Pinch of salt

Put the walnuts in a food processor with the sugar and process until the nuts are coarsely—not finely—ground, about 10 seconds. Add the other ingredients and process just until a ball forms on the blades. You may need to moisten the dough with a little water so that it clings together. Wrap the ball in plastic and chill for an hour or more.

Roll the dough out thinly on a lightly floured board and fit it into a 9-inch tart pan. Trim the edges so that the dough extends slightly above the rim. Cover and chill again thoroughly.

Preheat the oven to 400° F. Prick the dough all over with the tines of a fork and line it with aluminum foil, shiny side down. Fill the tart with dried beans or pastry weights and bake it for 10 minutes to set the dough. Remove the pan from the oven and lift out the foil and weights. If the pastry has puffed up, prick those areas with a fork and press down with a spatula to deflate it. For a partially baked tart shell, put it back in the oven until the pastry loses its raw, translucent look and turns the palest beige, about 5 minutes more. Remember to press it down if it puffs up again. Cool the partially baked tart shell on a rack. If you are continuing directly with the recipe, lower the oven to 350° F.

For a completely baked tart shell, return the shell to the slightly cooler (350° F) oven and bake until the pastry is golden brown, another 10 to 15 minutes. Cool the finished shell on a rack.

Pie and tart pastry can be frozen at each stage: mixed in a ball, raw and fitted in a

tart shell, partially baked, and fully baked. Be sure it is tightly wrapped and clearly labeled.
MAKES ONE 9-INCH PASTRY SHELL

NOTE: If the partially baked pastry shell is to hold a moist or juicy filling, before it has cooled you can brush the bottom with an egg wash of 1 whole egg beaten with 1 tablespoon water, and bake an additional 5 minutes or so, to seal the crust and prevent it from becoming soggy.

Tarte des Demoiselles Tatin

This upside-down tart was devised by two sisters named Tatin who ran a small restaurant in provincial France. The apples cook in the bottom of the pan with the pastry baked on top, the whole flipped over before serving. Today there are many versions of the celebrated tart, but whichever method is used, the apples must give up their juices and caramelize to a deep rich color and flavor. To serve more people, rather than prepare a second tart, make a larger one using a wider pan and more apples.

¼ cup (½ stick) unsalted butter
1 tablespoon fresh lemon juice
¾ cup sugar
2½ pounds Granny Smith, Golden Delicious, or other firm, tart cooking apples, peeled,
    quartered, and cored
One 10-inch round pâte brisée (see page 16), unbaked and well chilled
Sweetened whipped cream or crème fraîche (see page 155) for garnish

In a 9-inch, heavy-bottomed frying pan with a sturdy nonplastic handle (cast iron is perfect), melt the butter with the lemon juice. Off the heat, distribute the sugar on top. Lay a circle of apple quarters close together around the circumference of the pan on top of the sugar. Fill the inside with more apple quarters, trimming them as needed to fit together toward the center. Cut the rest of the apples into thin slices and spread them on top. The pattern above the bottom level does not matter except that it be even.

Over medium-high heat, heat the pan to caramelize the sugar and apples, about 20 minutes total—keep an eye on it throughout. The sugar should turn a deep brown, and the apples should render their liquid and cook down, producing rich, dark, thick juices. Level the surface and set the pan aside to cool somewhat.

Preheat the oven to 400°F. Lay the round of pâte brisée over the apples, quickly tucking the edges in at the sides before the heat softens it too much. Bake until the pastry turns golden and is cooked through, about 30 minutes.

Let the tart sit for a few minutes. (At this point, you should securely cover the very hot handle with a mitt so that you don't forget its retained heat and burn your hand—all too easy to do.) Check to see how much moisture is in the bottom of the pan. If the apples are stuck to the bottom, free them with a spatula. If they are swimming in juice, evaporate most of it by cooking it off over medium-high heat.

To serve the tart, put a wide serving plate on top to catch the syrupy juices and quickly invert both, then lift off the pan. Tidy up any dislodged apples to make the top look attractive. Serve the tarte Tatin warm with whipped cream or crème fraîche.

MAKES ONE 9-INCH TART; 6 SERVINGS

Pâte Brisée

This same pie dough or short pastry, without the sugar, is suitable for savory tarts. You can mix it with your fingers as well as in a food processor, but handle it as little as possible.

    1 cup all-purpose flour
    1 tablespoon sugar
    Pinch salt
    6 tablespoons (¾ stick) unsalted butter, cut in pieces, very cold or even frozen
    3 to 4 tablespoons cold water

Put the flour, sugar, salt, and butter in the food processor, and process until the butter is in pieces the size of oatmeal. Don't let the butter be completely blended in. Add the water through the feedtube, only as much as needed, and process just until the dough barely starts to clump on the blade into a ball. Wrap the dough tightly in plastic wrap, shape it into a flattened ball, and refrigerate for at least an hour.

On a lightly floured board, roll the dough out to ⅛-inch thickness. For Tarte Tatin, trim the edges to 10 inches, wrap the dough again in plastic, and keep it ready in the refrigerator. For other tarts, fit it into the pan, trim, prick, and finish as for other tarts (see page 35).

This dough can be made a day or two ahead; you can also freeze it in a ball or after it has been rolled and fitted into the pan, and thaw it in the refrigerator before continuing.

MAKES ONE 10-INCH ROUND

Apple-Cranberry Charlotte

This is a variation on the traditional apple charlotte, which was popular in England after Princess Charlotte of Mecklenburg became the consort of George III. Here the purée—a rosy combination of apples and cranberries—fills individual molds, avoiding the problem of serving from one large pudding that collapses. You can bake the charlottes ahead and rewarm them before unmolding.

> 2½ pounds apples, peeled and cored (weighed before trimming)
> One 12-ounce bag fresh cranberries, picked over
> 1 cup fresh sweet cider or water
> 1 cup sugar
> ½ cup (1 stick; ¼ pound) unsalted butter
> ½ teaspoon ground coriander, or to taste
> Most of a loaf of thin-sliced bread, preferably an egg bread such as brioche or challah
> Crème anglaise (recipe follows)

Combine the apples, cranberries, and cider in a large pot, cover, and stew over low heat, stirring occasionally, until the apples are soft, 10 to 15 minutes. Press the contents through a fine sieve, discarding the solids. Cook the sieved fruit longer, uncovered, to reduce it to a thick purée. Stir the sugar and 2 tablespoons of the butter into the fruit. You should have about 6 or 7 cups. (This may be done several days ahead, covered, and chilled.)

Preheat the oven to 400°F. Line eight 6-ounce ramekins or soufflé dishes with aluminum foil and press it tightly to fit. Melt the remaining butter in a saucepan. Trim the crusts from the bread, and cut about 6 pieces to fit each mold, a circle for the bottom (which will become the top) and 5 near-rectangles for the sides. Dip one side of the bread into the butter and place the buttered side against the ramekin; fill any cracks with scraps.

Divide the fruit purée among the eight ramekins and fill to the top. Trim any extending pieces of bread; you do not need to cover the tops. Set the ramekins on a tray without touching each other and bake in the preheated oven until the bread is crisp and browned on the outside, about 25 minutes. If any of the pieces of bread have pushed up, gently press them down into place. Let the charlottes cool somewhat. They may be prepared a day ahead up to this point and rewarmed in a 325°F oven for 15 minutes.

To serve, loosen each mold by running the tip of a knife around between the toast and ramekin, set a serving plate on top, and invert. Surround the charlotte with crème anglaise.

MAKES 8 SERVINGS

Crème Anglaise

Crème anglaise is nothing but stovetop English custard, delicious by itself, as a dessert sauce, or as part of innumerable composite desserts. Richer milk or cream and more egg yolks make for a richer custard. Liqueurs, melted chocolate, or other flavorings can be added.

One 1-inch piece vanilla pod or 1 teaspoon pure vanilla extract
2 cups milk
4 or 5 large egg yolks
¼ cup sugar, or to taste

Put the vanilla bean and the milk in a saucepan and heat the milk over medium heat to scald it: heat it until little bubbles appear around the edges. Do not let it boil. Leave the vanilla pod to infuse for about 10 minutes.

Combine the egg yolks and sugar in a bowl and whisk them for 3 minutes or so, until the yolks turn pale and thick and fall from the whisk in ribbons. Slowly pour the hot milk into the yolk mixture, stirring constantly to keep the yolks from scrambling. Pour the mixture back into the pan and over low heat, stirring all the while, cook the custard until it coats the back of a spoon. When you run your finger across the back of the spoon, it will leave a clear trail. (On a thermometer the temperature should reach 170°F, so that the eggs are sufficiently cooked to avoid the danger of salmonella.) Do not let the eggs scramble.

Take the pan off the heat, pour the custard through a fine sieve into a bowl, and stir briefly to cool the custard. Remove the vanilla bean (rinse and dry it to use again) or, if you are using vanilla extract, stir it in now. Cover the bowl to prevent a skin from forming and serve warm or chilled.

MAKES ABOUT 2½ CUPS

Apple Strudel

Ready-made phyllo sheets, although not authentic, substitute well for strudel dough and make the traditional Austrian dessert possible without a long day's labor. Have all the filling ingredients ready before you take out the phyllo, and take care to keep the sheets from drying out by covering them with damp cloths.

½ cup golden raisins (sultanas), or chopped dried apricots, cherries, cranberries, or other
*   dried fruit, plumped in boiling water to cover and then drained*
⅓ chopped walnuts or other nuts, lightly toasted (see page 179)
1 pound tart apples, peeled, cored, and very thinly sliced
⅓ cup sugar
Juice and grated zest of ½ lemon
¼ teaspoon ground cinnamon
¼ teaspoon ground nutmeg
¼ teaspoon ground allspice
5 tablespoons unsalted butter, melted and cooled (use half vegetable oil if you like)
½ cup fresh bread crumbs

8 sheets frozen phyllo dough (18 x 14 inches), thawed and at room temperature
Confectioners' sugar for dusting

Mix together in a large bowl the raisins, nuts, apples, sugar, lemon juice and zest, and spices. Have the butter and bread crumbs ready. Preheat the oven to 400°F.

Spread a towel or a couple of sheets of waxed paper on a counter. Working quickly to keep the phyllo from drying out and keeping the remaining sheets covered with a damp towel, place one sheet at the top of the towel long side across. Quickly brush it with some of the melted butter, stroking in one direction to minimize inevitable tears. Place the second sheet about an inch below the first, and brush it with more butter. Continue to overlap the sheets of phyllo, brushing each with butter, to make a rectangle about 22 x 14 inches.

Scatter the bread crumbs over the phyllo, leaving a 3-inch border all around. Spread the apple mixture evenly over the bread crumbs. Fold over the border of two short sides on top of the filling, then fold over the longer sides. Lifting the towel to help you, roll up the filling along the long side to make a bundle about 16 x 4 x 2 inches. With spatulas, transfer it seam-side down to a buttered baking sheet or jelly-roll pan. Brush the top and ends with the remaining butter and bake until golden brown, 25 to 30 minutes. Let it cool somewhat on the sheet. Dust the strudel with confectioners' sugar, and serve still warm with lightly sweetened whipped cream.

MAKES 8 SERVINGS

Sautéed Apples in Phyllo Cups with Cider Sauce

This rich cider sauce is essentially a sweetened beurre blanc made with cider instead of wine.

4 sheets frozen phyllo dough (18 x 14 inches), thawed and at room temperature
¾ cup (1½ sticks; 6 ounces) unsalted butter
Confectioners' sugar for dusting
3 large cooking apples, peeled, cored, and sliced
3 tablespoons firmly packed dark brown sugar
½ cup fresh sweet cider
Dash of ground cinnamon

First make the phyllo cups. Preheat the oven to 350°F. Melt ¼ cup of the butter in a small pan (let the rest soften at room temperature), then brush a thin film of it inside four shallow custard cups (6-ounce Pyrex cups are ideal). Taking one sheet of phyllo at a time and keeping the rest wrapped in a damp towel to prevent them from drying out, cut the sheet into four rectangles. One at a time, press each into the bottom of a cup, making a container, and brush the surface with a little melted butter. Repeat with each of the three remaining sheets, brushing each layer with butter and making four layers in all for each cup. The corners should stick out in different places: fold, rumple, or ruffle the phyllo to make it look attractive. Bake the phyllo cups until the edges are golden, about 10 minutes. Let them cool, then dust a little confectioners' sugar on top. Gently lift the phyllo out of the custard cups and set each on a serving plate.

Spoon the remaining melted butter into a large skillet and heat it to bubbling. Cook the apple slices for about 5 minutes, stirring to coat them all over with butter. Sprinkle 1 tablespoon of the brown sugar over them and continue to cook over moderate heat until the apples give up their juices, turn tender, and start to color, about 5 minutes more. Spoon them into the prepared phyllo cups, dividing them evenly.

Pour the apple cider into the pan and deglaze it over high heat, stirring to dissolve the crust on the bottom. Reduce the cider to about 3 tablespoons. Off the heat, add the remaining brown sugar (more or less, according to the sweetness of the apples) and stir until dissolved. A tablespoon at a time, add the remaining butter, stirring constantly until absorbed into the cider. When all the butter is added, the sauce should be silky smooth and glossy. Season it to taste with a dash of cinnamon and spoon it over the apples. Serve at once.

MAKES 4 SERVINGS

Apple Turnovers

Turnovers can be made in squares or circles of any size and filled with any fruit alone or in combination, savory as well as sweet. They are a fine way to use up leftover bits of this and that, including pastry, and their handy self-packaging makes them excellent picnic fare.

½ cup dried fruit such as raisins, cherries, or diced apricots
2 cups peeled, cored, and diced apples (2 large apples)
¼ cup chopped pecans or other nuts
¼ cup sugar, or to taste
1 tablespoon fresh lemon juice
¼ teaspoon ground cinnamon or other spice
2 sheets frozen puff pastry, thawed and chilled, or enough pie dough for 1 double-crust pie,
   either rough puff, flaky, or another pastry (see Index)
1 large egg
1 tablespoon water
Confectioners' sugar for dusting

Plump the dried fruit in boiling water to cover while you prepare the apples. Combine the apples, nuts, sugar, lemon juice, and cinnamon in a bowl and toss well. Drain the plumped dried fruit, stir it in with the other ingredients, and let their flavors marry while you prepare the pastry.

On a lightly floured board, one at a time, roll the pastry sheets out to approximately 12 inches square. Trim the outer edges (this is essential for the puff pastry) and cut each sheet into four 6-inch squares, making eight in all. Place a generous ⅓ cup of fruit filling just off center in each square. Moisten the edges of two adjacent sides, fold the opposite sides over, and press to seal. Crimp the edges closed with the tines of a fork. Repeat with the remaining turnovers and chill thoroughly.

Preheat the oven to 425°F. Beat together the egg and water and brush lightly on top of the turnover without letting the egg wash drip down the cut sides. Place the turnovers on cookie sheets (for puff pastry, spread a little cold water on the sheets but do not grease; for flaky pie pastry, grease the sheets). Bake until they are puffed and golden, about 20 minutes. Serve them warm or at room temperature dusted, if you like, with confectioners' sugar.

MAKES 8 LARGE TURNOVERS

Apple Fritters

This batter also works well with banana and pineapple slices. You can add the egg whites unbeaten, but their airiness gives a lighter, crisper, more elegant fritter. For dessert, try mixing a spoonful of Calvados into the batter.

1 cup all-purpose flour
2 tablespoons sugar
1½ teaspoons baking powder
¼ teaspoon salt
⅔ cup milk
1 large egg yolk
1 tablespoon butter, melted and cooled
Juice of 1 lemon
4 large, firm apples
Vegetable oil for deep-frying
2 large egg whites, at room temperature
Confectioners' sugar or pure maple syrup

In a medium-size bowl, mix together the flour, sugar, baking powder, and salt. In another bowl, beat together the milk, egg yolk, and butter, then slowly stir them into the dry ingredients to make a smooth batter. Set aside to rest.

Pour the lemon juice into a wide shallow nonreactive pan or baking dish. Peel and core the apples, cut them into ¼-inch slices, and dip them on both sides in the juice to keep them from discoloring.

In a wide, heavy-bottomed saucepan or deep fryer, heat 3 inches of oil to 375°F. Whip the egg whites in a medium-size bowl until stiff peaks form, then fold them into the batter. A few apples slices at a time, shake off the lemon juice and dip them into the batter, letting the excess drip off. Immediately drop the slices into the hot fat and deep-fry, turning once, until golden brown and puffed. Drain the fritters on paper towels and keep warm in a low oven until all are finished. Serve the apple fritters dusted with confectioners' sugar or, better yet, drizzled with maple syrup.

MAKES ABOUT 6 SERVINGS

Apple Crêpes With Cider Sauce

These sautéed apples in their cider reduction sauce are rich and spicy. Lace the sauce with a little rum, bourbon, or applejack if you wish.

> 2 cups fresh sweet cider
> ¼ cup raisins
> ¼ cup (½ stick) unsalted butter
> 4 cups peeled, cored, and diced cooking apples
> ½ teaspoon ground cinnamon
> 2 tablespoons sugar
> 12 crêpes (recipe follows)

Bring ½ cup of the cider to a boil, pour it over the raisins, and allow them to steep until well plumped, about 30 minutes. Do not drain.

Over moderate heat, melt half the butter in a large pan. When it begins to foam, add the diced apples and cook about 5 minutes, stirring often. Do not let them brown. Add the raisins, cinnamon, sugar, and the rest of the cider, and simmer over low heat, uncovered, until the apples are tender but not mushy, about 10 minutes.

With a slotted spoon place the apples and raisins in a bowl, leaving the liquid behind. Put a spoonful of fruit on the edge of a crêpe and roll up. Place it seam-side down on a serving dish or dessert plates, two per serving. Repeat with the remaining fruit and crêpes; keep warm in a low oven.

Over high heat, boil down the liquid left in the pan until reduced to a thick, syrupy glaze. Swirl in the remaining butter until it is absorbed. Immediately spoon the sauce over the crêpes and serve. Pass some whipped cream on the side.

MAKES 6 SERVINGS

Crêpes

1 cup all-purpose flour
1 tablespoon sugar
Pinch of salt
3 large eggs, at room temperature
1 cup milk, at room temperature
½ cup lukewarm water
2 tablespoons butter, melted and cooled but still liquid

Mix together the dry ingredients in a bowl. Make a well in the center. Pour in the eggs and beat them together until combined; then little by little mix in the flour, keeping the batter smooth. When the flour is mostly combined, gradually add the milk, water, and finally the butter. If you prefer, combine the ingredients in a food processor or blender until smooth.

Heat a little oil in a 5-inch frying or crêpe pan. When hot, pour in a large spoonful of the batter and immediately tilt the pan to let it run over the entire surface: the thinner the better. Cook over medium-low heat until the bottom of the crêpe (the better side) turns light brown, then turn and cook the other side briefly.

Continue until all the crêpes are cooked, adding more oil as needed—as little as possible. Stack the finished crêpes, allow them to cool completely before wrapping, and refrigerate or freeze them before use. They will keep up to a week in the refrigerator and for several months in the freezer. Let them return to room temperature before filling them.

MAKES ABOUT 22 CRÊPES

Apple Plum Grasmere

This recipe is Sarah Boardman's version of Elizabeth David's shortbread pudding from the English Lake District. The plums give a rosy hue and depth of flavor.

3 pounds tart apples, peeled, cored, and coarsely chopped
1 pound blue, red, or purple plums, pitted and coarsely chopped
⅔ cup sugar
½ cup fresh sweet cider
½ cup (1 stick; ¼ pound) unsalted butter, softened and cut into pieces
2¼ cups sifted all-purpose flour
¼ cup firmly packed brown sugar
¼ cup sugar
¼ teaspoon baking soda
1 teaspoon ground ginger

Combine the apples, plums, sugar, and cider in a large pot. Cover and cook over low heat until the fruit softens, breaking up the chunks with a spoon. Remove the plum skins but leave some of the lumps of fruit; let it cool. (This much may be done well ahead.) Turn the fruit into a large shallow ovenproof pan that will hold 8 cups comfortably.

Preheat the oven to 350°F. In a large bowl, cut or rub the butter into the flour. Mix in the sugars, baking soda, and ginger. Scatter the topping over the fruit and lightly smooth it with the back of a spoon without pressing down. Bake until the surface is pale golden, like shortbread, 30 to 35 minutes. Let the pudding cool before serving it with fresh thick cream.

MAKES 8 SERVINGS

Apple Blackberry Crisp

The thin topping for this favorite is so simple that you may wish to make double, freezing half for another time. Blackberries grow wild in fall; or use more apples or another fruit.

> 1 pound tart apples, peeled, cored, and sliced
> 2 tablespoons fresh lemon juice
> 1 tablespoon white sugar
> ⅓ cup all-purpose flour
> ¼ cup firmly packed brown sugar
> ¼ cup (½ stick) unsalted butter, cut into small pieces
> ¼ teaspoon ground allspice
> ⅜ teaspoon ground cinnamon
> 6 ounces fresh blackberries (about ¾ cup)
> ¼ cup chopped blanched hazelnuts or other nuts

Preheat the oven to 375°F. In a large bowl, toss the apples with the lemon juice and the white sugar to coat the slices. Set aside while you prepare the topping.

Mix the flour, brown sugar, butter, and spices in a small bowl. Work the butter into the flour and sugar with your fingertips until the mixture is finely crumbled.

Add the blackberries to the apples and gently turn the fruit into a buttered 8-inch-square baking dish or 9-inch pie plate. Scatter the hazelnuts, then the butter-sugar topping over the fruit. Bake until the top is golden and crisp, about 35 minutes. Serve warm with cream or ice cream on the side.

MAKES 4 SERVINGS

Apple Oatmeal Crumble

The oatmeal in this version of an old favorite gives crunch; add nuts or not, as you like. Use peaches, pears, plums, or another fruit.

6 cups peeled, cored, and thinly sliced apples (about 7 apples)
2 tablespoons fresh lemon juice
½ cup white or firmly packed brown sugar
½ cup rolled ("old-fashioned") oats
¼ cup all-purpose flour
½ teaspoon ground cinnamon
6 tablespoons (¾ stick) butter, cut into pieces
½ cup chopped nuts, lightly toasted (optional; see page 179)

Preheat the oven to 350°F. Butter a shallow 8-cup ovenproof pan.

In a large bowl toss the apple slices with the lemon juice and 2 tablespoons of the sugar. Spread the slices in the buttered pan. In the same bowl mix the remaining sugar, oats, flour, and cinnamon. With your fingertips rub the butter into the dry ingredients until it sticks together in crumbles, then mix in the nuts. Scatter the topping over the apple slices. Put the pan in the oven and bake until the topping is brown and crisp and the apples tender, 30 to 40 minutes. Serve with vanilla ice cream or whipped cream.

MAKES 6 OR MORE SERVINGS

Baked Apples

Seemingly simple, baked apples are surprisingly hard to do well. The most important thing is to choose an apple variety that is firm, tart, and full of character. Seasonings can vary widely: for contrast, any nut or dried fruit; ginger in any of its forms; white sugar, maple syrup, honey, or preserves for sweetening. Experiment to suit your own taste, plain or fancy.

4 large or 6 small, firm, tart, flavorful apples
⅓ cup firmly packed brown sugar
¼ cup raisins
¼ cup chopped walnuts, lightly toasted (see page 179)
Grated zest of ½ lemon
⅜ teaspoon ground cinnamon
1½ tablespoons unsalted butter, cut into small pieces
⅔ cup water or fresh sweet cider, if you can
1 to 2 tablespoons rum (optional)

Preheat the oven to 350°F. Core the apples through the bottom and enlarge the holes slightly. Set the apples in a pan just large enough to hold them without touching. Combine the sugar, raisins, walnuts, lemon zest, and cinnamon, and stuff the mixture into the holes. Scatter any that is left in the pan. Dot the butter on top of each apple, and pour the water into the pan. Cover tightly with a lid or aluminum foil.

Bake the apples for about 30 minutes. Uncover, baste with the syrup in the bottom of the pan, and bake until they are tender but not mushy, about 10 minutes more, depending on the variety. Put the apples on serving plates. If you like, add the rum to the syrup and reduce slightly over high heat; spoon the syrup over the apples and serve warm or at room temperature, perhaps with cream or ice cream.

MAKES 4 TO 6 SERVINGS

APRICOTS

Just as the ancient Greeks supposed the peach to have originated in Persia, the apricot—*Prunus armeniaca*—was thought to have come from Armenia, so well established was it in that hospitable climate. The fruit's English name apricot comes from the Latin *praecox*, meaning precocious, for its habit of ripening early.

A member of the large rose family, the apricot is a drupe, like its cousins the peach, plum, cherry, and almond. Its cleft pit protects a kernel that tastes remarkably like the almond and is often used in brandies, preserves, marzipan, amaretti, and other confections. In bitter varieties, however, this kernel contains a strong compound which can be poisonous if eaten raw in large quantities over a period of time—an unlikely possibility.

The apricot has a velvet skin, fuzzier than that of the peach (whose down has often been removed before reaching market), and a color ranging from yellow-orange blush to deep golden amber, depending on its ripeness and variety. When allowed to mature fully on the tree, the apricot has an intensely tangy flavor to match its glowing color. In this country its season is from May to August, peaking in late May and June.

At market, try to choose fresh apricots that are deep in color, plump, and firm yet yielding slightly to the touch, and store them in the refrigerator. Slightly immature apricots will ripen somewhat at room temperature (faster in a bag), but then use them right away. Avoid pale yellow or green apricots that are too hard or too soft. Unfortunately, apricots shipped from afar are often pallid, rock-hard, mushy, or otherwise disappointing. Better to eat them canned or, better still, dried, when their characteristic sweet tang is concentrated. Apricot nectar is also available in cans.

Apricots have been sun-dried in the Far and Middle East since ancient times. In today's domestic market, California is the biggest producer. The drying process is often speeded up with sulfur dioxide, which can impart a nasty taste, so try to find high quality, naturally dried apricots. Middle Eastern markets carry apricot leather, strips of skinless paste, which are useful in the kitchen. It also makes a wholesome and novel snack for children.

In cooking, the skins and pits of fresh apricots, as with peaches, are removed after poaching. Apricot preserves are essential in baking and confectionary, especially as pastry fillings and glazes. Dried apricots, because they travel well and keep through the seasons, are used extensively in savory as well as sweet dishes. In the Middle East in particular, many savory recipes include dried apricots, where their sharp sweetness complements lamb, pork, and poultry. Even more than peaches, apricots retain some of their eastern exoticism in gastronomy.

Fresh ripe apricots are very nutritious, high in vitamin A, potassium, and fiber, with some vitamin C and iron. An average-size fresh apricot contains about fourteen calories. Dried apricots come from tree-ripened fruit, requiring six pounds of fresh fruit for one pound of dried, losing nothing but water and concentrating their nutritional benefits. One large dried apricot half contains about thirteen calories, and two ounces about 135 calories, providing a large amount of potassium and vitamin A, with a good deal of iron and some riboflavin, niacin, phosphorus, and magnesium, as well as other minerals. Dried apricots are convenient and healthful snacks for children, picnickers, and hikers. As with all dried fruit, they can be plumped in liquid before cooking, and the liquid with its nutrients should be used again.

Pork Pâté Studded with Apricots

Pork and apricot enhance each other in this simple but exotic pâté, fragrant with the suggestion of spices. It makes excellent picnic fare. Dried prunes can replace the apricots for an equally delicious version.

½ pound sliced bacon
2 pounds pork, not too lean, such as boneless country-style ribs, coarsely ground
4 ounces dried apricots, cubed
2 ounces shelled pistachios (undyed and unsalted)
2 cloves garlic, minced
1 small white onion, chopped
½ teaspoon ground coriander
¼ teaspoon ground allspice
¼ teaspoon freshly grated nutmeg
2 tablespoons brandy
1 teaspoon salt, or to taste
½ teaspoon freshly ground black pepper, or to taste

Preheat the oven to 325°F. Dice half the bacon, reserving 3 or 4 strips. In a large bowl, mix together the diced bacon and the rest of the ingredients. Pack the mixture into a 6-cup loaf pan, and lay the reserved strips of bacon lengthwise across the top. Cover the pâté tightly with aluminum foil and bake for 1½ hours. Let the pâté cool, then chill it, weighted if you like for a denser texture. Allow the flavors to ripen for a few days before serving.

To serve, remove the pâté from the pan, scrape off the congealed juices and fat, leave the bacon on or not as you like, and slice it across. Refrigerated, it will keep for a week.

MAKES 8 SERVINGS

Apricot Pilaf

This colorful and aromatic rice dish makes an excellent side dish for lamb or other meat. Or turn it into a stuffing for roast chicken scented with cloves.

2 tablespoons butter
1 small onion, chopped
¾ cup long grain white rice
1½ cups stock or water
¼ cup diced dried apricots
3 tablespoons chopped pistachios (undyed and unsalted) or pine nuts, lightly toasted
    (see page 179)
¼ teaspoon coriander seeds
Salt and freshly ground black pepper to taste

Melt the butter in saucepan over low heat. When it begins to foam, add the onion and cook, stirring, until softened, about 3 minutes. Add the rice, stir until the grains are coated with butter, and cook about 2 minutes. Pour in the stock and bring to a boil. Stir in the apricots, lower the heat, and cover; simmer over low heat until all the water is absorbed and the rice tender, about 17 minutes. Just before serving, stir in the pistachios and coriander, and season with salt and pepper to taste.

MAKES 4 SERVINGS

Fruit Raita

An Indian raita, a mixture of vegetables or fruit with yogurt, can make a cooling accompaniment to hot curries and other spicy dishes. This raita includes dried apricots and sultanas with fresh apple, balanced by chopped scallions, fresh coriander or mint, and the intriguing flavor of whole cumin.

½ teaspoon cumin seeds
1½ cups plain yogurt
1 scallion (green and white parts), chopped
2 tablespoons diced dried apricots
2 tablespoons golden raisins (sultanas)
2 tablespoons diced tart apple
1 tablespoon chopped pistachios (unsalted and undyed) or other nuts, lightly toasted (see
    page 179)
2 tablespoons chopped fresh coriander (cilantro) or mint

Heat a small pan over medium heat. Add the cumin seed and shake the pan to toss it for a minute or two, until the cumin is toasted. Turn it out.

Mix together all the ingredients except the fresh coriander. Cover and refrigerate for at least 30 minutes before serving for the flavors to develop. Serve topped with the coriander.

MAKES ABOUT 2 CUPS; 4 TO 6 SERVINGS

Gingered Apricot Butter

Tangy and intense, this butter is wonderful spread on toast, muffins, and scones. Use up the last bits to moisten baked chicken or pork chops. Or add diced stem ginger and sliced almonds to the butter, dot the hollows of peach halves with it, and bake.

¼ cup fresh orange juice
½ cup (2 ounces) dried apricots, chopped
½ cup (1 stick; ¼ pound) unsalted butter, softened
3 to 4 tablespoons honey
1 teaspoon ground ginger, or to taste

Heat the orange juice to boiling in a small nonreactive saucepan, then stir in the chopped apricots. Take off the heat and leave them to soften for 30 minutes (or soak them overnight at room temperature). Drain them, reserving the juice.

Put the softened butter in a food processor and add the drained apricots. Process until well blended, scraping down the sides once or twice with a rubber spatula. In a steady stream through the feed tube, slowly add the reserved orange juice. Finally add the honey and ginger to taste. When the mixture is well combined, scrape it into a crock, cover tightly, and chill in the refrigerator for several days to a week; soften slightly before serving. Or roll it into a log on a sheet of plastic wrap and slice off rounds for serving. Keeps for a month or more in the freezer.

MAKES ABOUT 1 CUP

Apricot Preserves

These preserves are less stiff than commercial jam, but full of flavor. The almondlike kernel found in the pit of the apricot makes the flavor even more pronounced—almonds and apricots are cousins in the drupe family—omit it if you like.

2 pounds fresh apricots, preferably slightly underripe
2 cups sugar
¼ cup fresh lemon juice
1 cup water

If you want to remove the apricot skins (this is not necessary), drop the apricots into boiling water, drain them, and slip off the skins. Cut the apricots in half, remove the pits, and cut each half in two. Crack four of the pits, remove the kernels, and reserve (this too is unnecessary, but it gives a more pronounced almond flavor).

Combine the sugar, lemon juice, and water in a nonreactive saucepan. Bring the liquid to a boil and let boil until the sugar is dissolved, about 5 minutes. Add the apricots, return to a boil, and simmer over low heat until they are soft and transparent, about 20 minutes. With a slotted spoon, put the apricots in clean warm jars. Boil the syrup down until it reaches the jelling point, 220°F on a candy thermometer. Put a little preserve on a cold saucer to test it: after a few seconds push your finger through the preserve. If it wrinkles, then it is ready. Pour the syrup over the apricots to cover and, if you wish, bury 1 apricot kernel in each jar. Wipe the threads clean, put on the tops and bands, and sterilize the jars in a hot water bath (see page 321). Store the preserves in a cool dark cupboard.

MAKES ABOUT 4 HALF-PINT JARS

Muesli

Muesli is a healthful breakfast cereal mixed with nuts and fruits, both dried and fresh, devised by Dr. Bircher-Benner, the Swiss counterpart of Sylvester Graham of graham cracker fame. You can easily make your own muesli to suit your particular taste and may find it far superior, as well as cheaper, than commercial brands. The recipe here, for two servings, is merely a suggestion. Choose your favorite dried fruits, seeds, and nuts, include bran instead of wheat germ, or sweeten with honey (added with the milk) instead of brown sugar. A little grated orange or lemon zest gives zing, dried coconut gives crunch. Try toasting the oatmeal in a dry pan first for a nuttier flavor.

You can make a larger quantity, balancing proportions to suit yourself, and add the fresh fruit and milk, yogurt, buttermilk, or cream at the last minute. Fresh fruit is essential—apples, bananas, peaches, and berries are perhaps best—changed according to preference and season.

1 cup rolled ("old-fashioned") oats
3 tablespoons chopped dried apricots
2 tablespoons raisins
3 tablespoons wheat germ
3 tablespoons chopped hazelnuts, lightly toasted (see page 179)
1 tablespoon brown sugar, or to taste
½ tart apple, peeled, cored, and chopped
Milk

Mix together all the ingredients, except the apple and milk, ahead of time. Just before serving, stir in the chopped apple or other fresh fruit, and pour on the milk.

MAKES 2 SERVINGS

Fresh Apricot Berry Compote

This simple summer compote captures evanescent fruits that ripen together. The formula is infinitely variable: be imaginative. You can serve it with a slice of pound cake or dab of cream but it truly needs nothing more.

½ cup sugar
1 cup water
One 2-inch strip lemon zest
2 pounds fresh apricots
3 tablespoons rum, brandy, or other liquor
1 cup raspberries
½ cup currants

Put the sugar in a saucepan with the water and lemon zest. Bring to a boil and let boil until the sugar is dissolved, about 5 minutes. Add the apricots and rum, cover, and poach over low heat until the apricots are barely tender, 5 to 8 minutes, depending on their ripeness. Turn the apricots once to cook them evenly, but take care not to break them up. Let them cool in the liquid (or if very tender, remove them with a slotted spoon). When the apricots are cool, cut each in half along the natural line. Discard the pits and the lemon zest and return the apricots to the syrup. Just before serving, stir in the fresh raspberries and currants.

MAKES ABOUT 6 SERVINGS

Dried Apricot and Fresh Fruit Compote

Serve this in late winter when you crave the full tangy flavors of fresh fruit.

12 ounces dried apricots
2 cups fresh orange juice
¼ cup orange-flavored liqueur (optional)
2 tablespoons sugar, or to taste
4 whole cloves
One 2-inch stick cinnamon
1 large banana, peeled and thinly sliced
¼ pineapple, peeled, cored, and cut into chunks
1 lime
¼ cup pistachios (unsalted and undyed), chopped

Soak the apricots in orange juice for several hours or overnight to soften them. Drain the juice into a large nonreactive saucepan and heat it with the liqueur to boiling. Add the apricots, sugar, and spices. Simmer over low heat, uncovered, until the apricots are soft but not mushy, about 10 minutes. Set aside off the heat and allow the apricots to cool in the liquid.

Just before serving, remove the cloves and cinnamon and stir in the banana and pineapple. Cut the lime zest into julienne and squeeze the juice; add both to the compote. Divide the fruit among six glass bowls and garnish each with the pistachios.

MAKES 6 SERVINGS

Apricot Almond Meringue Cookies

These light, tender meringue cookies are a good way to use up extra egg whites.

4 large egg whites, at room temperature
Pinch of salt or cream of tartar
¾ cup sugar, preferably superfine
1 teaspoon pure vanilla extract
4 ounces dried apricots, finely diced
¼ cup slivered almonds, lightly toasted (see page 179)

Preheat the oven to 225°F. Lightly grease two cookie sheets or, if you prefer, grease parchment or waxed paper spread on cookie sheets.

In a large bowl, beat the egg whites with the salt or cream of tartar until the whites make soft peaks. To make a tender meringue, gradually add all but 2 tablespoons of the sugar as you continue to beat. Check to see if the sugar has dissolved by pinching the meringue. When you can no longer feel the crystals, fold in the remaining sugar, then the vanilla extract, and finally the apricots and almonds.

Drop neat spoonfuls of the meringue batter onto the cookie sheets: give them attractive peaks, as they will not spread or change their shape. Bake for 1 hour without opening the door. Turn off the oven and keep them in the unopened oven for at least another hour or as long as overnight. Remove the cookies with a spatula. Store them in airtight tins or, closed tightly in a plastic bag, in the freezer, where they will keep indefinitely.

MAKES ABOUT 4 DOZEN

Apricot Phyllo Packages

These charming little bundles make unusual and delicate additions to the buffet table or picnic basket. Use whatever preserves you wish. Once you start making them, it's easy to multiply the ingredients to serve more people.

> *8 sheets frozen phyllo dough (18 x 14 inches), thawed and at room temperature*
> *½ cup (1 stick; ¼ pound) unsalted butter, melted (or use half butter and half*
>   *vegetable oil; choose a light, bland, pleasant-tasting oil)*
> *⅓ cup apricot preserves, homemade (see page 31) or storebought*
> *Confectioners' sugar for dusting*

Preheat the oven to 350°F. To prevent the phyllo sheets from drying out and cracking, work with only two at a time, keeping the others wrapped and covered with a damp towel. Have everything organized and laid out before you begin.

Spread two sheets of pastry on a counter and cut each lengthwise into three long strips. Quickly brush the surface of each with melted butter and stack the strips in pairs. Place 1 generous teaspoon of preserves near the bottom center of each. Fold over the whole right and left lengths of phyllo to meet in the middle, then wrap up the pillow of apricot in a rectangle. Place the package seam-side down on a greased cookie sheet and brush the top with more butter. Repeat with the remaining apricot preserves and phyllo.

Bake the phyllo packages in the preheated oven until the tops are golden, about 15 minutes. You can also freeze them filled but unbaked, putting them directly into the oven from the freezer. Increase the baking time slightly if frozen. Just before serving, dust them with confectioners' sugar.

MAKES 12 RECTANGLES; 4 TO 6 SERVINGS

Caramelized Apricot Tart

This gorgeous tart celebrates fresh apricots when you can find them. Caramelizing brings out the flavor, and the fruit doesn't have to be perfectly ripe.

1¼ cups sugar
2 cups water
2 tablespoons fresh lemon juice
1 pound fresh apricots
One 9-inch pâte sucrée (recipe follows) or almond pastry shell (see page 14), baked

Preheat the oven to 400°F. Put 1 cup of the sugar in a saucepan with the water and bring to a boil. Let boil until the sugar dissolves, about 5 minutes. Add the lemon juice and apricots and poach them over low heat for 5 minutes, covered. The apricots should be barely tender; do not let them get mushy. Drain them, saving the syrup for another recipe. Cut them in half along the natural segmentation, and remove the pits. Place the apricot halves in the tart shell hollow-side up, and strew them evenly with the remaining sugar. Bake until the sugar is lightly caramelized, about 20 minutes. If necessary, run the tart under the broiler briefly, watching closely to avoid burning. Cool the tart and serve it with caramel cream (see page 213) or crème fraîche (page 155).

MAKES ONE 9-INCH TART; 6 SERVINGS

Pâte Sucrée

1 cup all-purpose flour
2 tablespoons sugar
Pinch of salt
6 tablespoons (¾ stick) unsalted butter, very cold or even frozen, cut into pieces
1 tablespoon fresh lemon juice (optional)
1 large egg

Put all the ingredients in a food processor and process just until a ball forms on the blades. You may need to moisten the dough with a little water so that it clings together. Enclose the ball in plastic wrap and chill for an hour or more.

Roll the dough out thinly on a lightly floured board and fit it into a 9-inch tart pan. Trim the edges so that the dough extends slightly above the rim. Cover and chill again thoroughly.

Preheat the oven to 400°F. Prick the dough all over with the tines of a fork and line it with aluminum foil, shiny-side down. Fill the tart with dried beans or pastry weights and bake it for 10 minutes to set the dough. Remove the pan from the oven and lift out the foil and weights. If the pastry has puffed up, prick those areas with a fork and press down with a spatula to deflate it. For a partially baked tart shell, put it back in the oven until the pastry loses its raw, translucent look and turns the palest beige, about 5 minutes more. Remember to press it down if it puffs up again. Cool the partially baked tart shell on a rack. If you are continuing directly with the recipe, lower the oven to 350°F.

For a completely baked tart shell, return the shell to the slightly cooler (350°F) oven and bake another 10 to 15 minutes, until the pastry is golden brown. Cool the finished shell on a rack.

Pie and tart pastry can be frozen at each stage: mixed in a ball, raw and fitted in a tart shell, partially baked, and fully baked. Be sure it is tightly wrapped and clearly labeled.

MAKES ONE 9-INCH PASTRY SHELL

NOTE: If the partially baked pastry shell is to hold a moist or juicy filling, before it has cooled you can brush the bottom with an egg wash of 1 whole egg beaten with 1 tablespoon water and bake an additional 5 minutes or so, to seal the crust and prevent it from becoming soggy.

Tarte Amandine

This shimmery tart has a stunning harlequin design made from tangy apricot and currant glazes. Unlike for most tarts, you can make the basic amandine far ahead, wrap and freeze it, and decorate it later. Or finish the tart a day or two before serving and keep it in a tightly covered tin. To achieve a fine almond powder that is not oily or pasty, freeze the almonds, then grind them in a blender rather than a food processor. This recipe comes from my friend Sarah Boardman.

One 9-inch pâte sucrée (see page 35) in a false-bottom pan, unbaked

FOR THE AMANDINE (FRANGIPANE) FILLING
6 tablespoons (¾ stick) unsalted butter, softened
¼ cup plus 2 tablespoons sugar
1 large egg yolk
3 ounces almonds, finely ground (about ¾ cup ground)
3 tablespoons all-purpose flour
Grated zest of 1 large lemon
2 large egg whites, at room temperature

FOR THE HARLEQUIN TOPPING
¾ cup strained apricot preserves, homemade (see page 31) or storebought
1 tablespoon egg white (about ½ egg white)

¾ *cup confectioners' sugar*

2 *tablespoons red currant jelly, homemade (see page 85) or storebought*

Preheat the oven to 375°F. Prick the pâte sucrée shell with a fork and chill well. For the filling, cream together the butter and sugar until light, then stir in the egg yolk. In a small bowl, mix the almonds, flour, and lemon zest together. Beat the egg whites until stiff peaks form; fold most of the egg whites into the butter-and-sugar mixture alternating with the almond mixture. Add the remaining egg white at the last moment for lightness. Spread the amandine in the tart shell and bake for 20 to 25 minutes. The top should not brown (if it starts to color or puff up, lower the heat to 325°F). Cool the tart on a rack and remove it from the tin.

In a small saucepan, melt the apricot preserves, stirring. Brush thickly over the top of the tart and thinly over the outside of the crust to make it shimmer; chill to set the glaze.

Make royal icing by beating together the egg white and confectioners' sugar with a wooden spoon until icing held up on the spoon forms a point that just falls over. (As royal icing can dry out quickly, either proceed quickly, cover it with a damp towel, or cover tightly in plastic wrap until ready to use.) Using a number 2 tip or a small plastic bag with the corner snipped off, pipe crisscross lines into a diamond lattice, with the angled lines 1 inch apart, on top of the tart. Chill to set it.

In a small saucepan, melt the currant jelly, stirring. With a small teaspoon, carefully put a thin layer of jelly in every other diamond of the lattice, remelting the jelly as needed. Let it cool to set the decoration.

MAKES ONE 9-INCH TART; 8 SERVINGS

Apricot Orange Pavé

Pavé, the French word for paving stone, gives this sensational rectangular cake its name. With apricots, it looks like orange cobblestones on yellow pavement with crushed green pistachios. All the parts can be made ahead.

FOR THE SPONGE CAKE

4 *whole large eggs, separated, plus 1 egg white, at room temperature*

⅔ *cup sugar*

2 *tablespoons fresh orange juice*

2 *tablespoons grated orange zest*

½ *cup all-purpose flour*

½ *teaspoon baking powder*

Pinch of cream of tartar

FOR THE POACHED APRICOTS

2 cups sugar

2 cups water

3 tablespoons peeled and coarsely chopped fresh ginger

Two 2-inch strips orange zest

9 fresh apricots

FOR THE BUTTERCREAM

4 large egg yolks

1¼ cups (2½ sticks; 10 ounces) unsalted butter, cut into tablespoons and softened

3 tablespoons orange-flavored liqueur

TO COMPLETE

½ cup apricot preserves, homemade (see page 31) or storebought, melted and strained

¾ cup chopped pistachios (undyed and unsalted), lightly toasted (see page 179)

First make the sponge cake base. Preheat the oven to 375°F. Grease and flour a jelly-roll pan (16 x 11 x 1 inches), shaking off the excess flour; set it aside.

In a large bowl beat together the egg yolks and sugar until the mixture forms ribbons. Stir in the orange juice and zest. Sift together the flour and baking powder and stir into the yolk mixture.

In another large bowl, with dry clean beaters, beat the egg whites with the cream of tartar until stiff but not dry. Fold a quarter of the whites into the batter to loosen it. Gently fold in the remaining whites. Spread the batter in the prepared pan. Bake until golden brown and springy to the touch, about 15 minutes. Cool on a rack.

To prepare the apricots, put the sugar and water in a medium-size saucepan, bring to a boil, and let boil until the sugar is dissolved, about 5 minutes. Add the ginger and orange zest and boil 5 minutes, covered. Add the apricots and poach over low heat until tender, depending on their firmness, about 5 minutes. Let them cool in the syrup. Drain the apricots, reserving and straining the syrup through a fine sieve. Slip off the apricot skins, cut the fruit in half along the natural segmentation, and remove the pits. Saving ½ cup of syrup for the buttercream, pour the rest over the apricot halves.

To make the buttercream, boil the reserved ½ cup syrup until a candy thermometer registers 238°F (soft-ball stage). Place the yolks in a large bowl. With an electric mixer at low speed, slowly dribble the syrup into the yolks to make a mayonnaiselike emulsion, a few drops at a time to start, then in a slow, steady stream. Continue beating until light, fluffy, and cool, about 5 minutes. On medium speed, beat in the butter 1 tablespoon at a time. Beat in the liqueur in a slow, steady stream.

To assemble the pavé, cut the sponge cake across into three equal strips. Cut a piece of cardboard the same size as one cake strip and cover with aluminum foil. Set a cake piece on the cardboard. Brush the cake with some of the syrup, covering the apricots. Cover with a thin layer of preserves and let it stand until firm. Spread it with a thin layer of buttercream. With the two remaining pieces of cake, repeat the layers of syrup, preserves, and buttercream, then stack them on the first piece of cake. Frost the sides of the cake with buttercream and press the crushed pistachios onto the sides. Spoon the remaining buttercream into a pastry bag fitted with the star tip and pipe rosettes along the edge of the cake. Chill until firm.

Just before serving, drain the apricot halves. Arrange them rounded-side up in three neat rows on top of the cake. Serve the pavé at room temperature.

MAKES 8 TO 10 SERVINGS

Chocolate Apricot Roulade

This roulade is simple, quick, and pretty, appropriate for all ages, and can be dressed up or down as you wish. It's also delicious with raspberry jam and fresh raspberry garnish.

5 large eggs, separated, at room temperature
¾ cup sugar
⅓ cup all-purpose flour
¼ cup unsweetened cocoa powder
½ teaspoon baking powder
½ cup apricot preserves, homemade (see page 31) or storebought
1 cup chilled heavy cream
3 to 4 tablespoons confectioners' sugar, or to taste

Preheat the oven to 375°F. Line a jelly-roll pan with waxed paper, aluminum foil, or parchment paper. Butter and flour it, then shake out the excess.

In a medium-large bowl, beat together the egg yolks and sugar. In a small bowl sift together the flour, cocoa, and baking powder. Gradually stir them into the egg yolk mixture. In a large clean bowl, beat the egg whites until they form stiff peaks. Stir a spoonful of whites into the batter, then quickly fold in the remaining whites. Spread the batter into the prepared pan and smooth it out into the corners. Bake it in the preheated oven until the top is golden, about 15 minutes.

When you take the sponge cake out, loosen the edges. Let it cool 5 minutes, then spread a tea towel over the cake, invert and remove the pan, and peel off the paper. While the cake is still warm, turn it so a long edge is before you, and roll up the cake in the towel, keeping the long edges uncurled. This may be done a day ahead. Keep the cake covered to stay moist, and let it cool completely.

A few hours before serving (not at the last minute), unroll the cake, trim the long edges with a serrated knife, and spread the apricot preserves over the sponge. Whip the cream until firm peaks form, sweeten it to taste with confectioners' sugar, and spread the cream over the preserves not quite to the edges. Roll up the cake again and set it seam-side down on a serving plate. With a serrated knife trim the two ends. Chill well.

To serve the roulade, dust the top with confectioners' sugar and slice it across into spiral rounds.

MAKES 8 OR MORE SERVINGS

Chocolate Hazelnut Soufflé Crêpes with Apricot Rum Sauce

This combination of crunchy hazelnuts and melting chocolate puffed in a souffléed crêpe, all bound together with apricot rum sauce, is sublime. It is another dazzler that is really quite simple once all the parts are prepared.

> 5 large egg whites, at room temperature
> ½ cup sugar
> ¼ cup plus 2 tablespoons crushed hazelnuts, lightly toasted (see page 179)
> 2 ounces bittersweet chocolate, coarsely grated
> 12 crêpes (see page 23)
> 3 tablespoons confectioners' sugar
> Apricot Rum Sauce (recipe follows)

Preheat oven to 350°F. Butter a cookie sheet and set aside. In a large bowl, whip the egg whites until they hold stiff peaks. Fold in the sugar and beat a few seconds more. With a rubber spatula, fold in the hazelnuts and chocolate just enough to distribute them evenly but no more.

One at a time, lay a crêpe flat on the cookie sheet, good-side down. Put a large spoonful of the meringue mixture on one half of the crêpe and fold the other half over to enclose it. Quickly repeat with the other crêpes. They should not overlap on the sheet. Sprinkle their tops with half of the confectioners' sugar.

Bake the filled crêpes until puffed and lightly browned, about 13 minutes. Quickly sprinkle with the remaining confectioners' sugar. With a spatula, put two crêpes back to back on each warmed serving plate, drizzle some of the warm apricot rum sauce between, and serve immediately.

MAKES 6 SERVINGS

Apricot Rum Sauce

In winter when fresh fruit is scarce, this sauce is luscious with pineapple or other fruit or folded into whipped egg whites and baked in little soufflé dishes.

1 cup (4 ounces) dried apricots
1½ cups fresh orange juice
¼ cup dark rum

Put the apricots and orange juice in a small nonreactive saucepan. Bring the liquid to a boil, cover tightly, and simmer over low heat until the apricots are soft, about 10 minutes. Let them cool, still covered. Purée the apricots with the rum in a food processor. Thin, if desired, with water. Store in a covered container in the refrigerator for a week or more.

MAKES ABOUT 2 CUPS

BANANAS AND
PLANTAINS

The forbidden fruit of paradise, it is written in the Koran, was the banana. According to Islamic legend, when Adam and Eve were sent out of the garden of Eden, its leaves were used to cover their nakedness. Even today in India, one kind of banana is called paradise, another Adam's fig tree. Indeed, the size of the banana leaf makes it more suitable—shall we say fitting?—to cover their shame, rather than the diminutive fig leaf.

The western world first discovered the fruit on Alexander the Great's travels to the east. Pliny, the Roman naturalist, had read Alexander's description of the banana. "The leaf is like birds' wings," Pliny wrote in the first century A.D., unfamiliar with its relative, the bird-of-paradise plant. "The fruit grows straight from the bark, and is delightful for the sweetness of its juice."

The banana tree, genus *Musa*, is actually an herb, albeit an oversized one, and the fruit its berry. The bottom of the large, overlapping leaves forms a false trunk, a sheathlike support through which the true stem grows when the plant reaches maturity. Blossoms held in spirals on the tip grow into upturned "fingers," as many as twenty in a "hand," as many as fifteen hands in a bunch. The weight of the bananas, especially when heavy with rain and dependent plants, can uproot the whole stalk. Because the hybrid banana cannot reproduce from seed, the tree is cut down at harvest, and new plants grow from shoots on its extensive underground rhizome.

Native to Asia, the banana has been known for many thousands of years, since before the cultivation of rice. It is the only staple food that is not a grain, and was spread westward first by Arab traders and then by Spanish and Portuguese explorers. Originally its fruit had tasteless flesh with bitter black seeds, but man has refined it into many varieties that thrive in the tropics around the world.

Small fragrant lady's finger bananas, Canary bananas from the island of the same name, round lemon bananas from Banana Island in the Nile, and the perfumed Lakatan from the Philippines are a few of three or four hundred tantalizing varieties. Unfortunately, few of the more exotic cultivars appear in North American supermarkets, but the influx of Asians and Latin Americans—those populations that knew the banana before its nineteenth-century introduction here—has made a difference. Sometimes we can find tobacco-colored red bananas, odoriferous, pink-fleshed, and sweet, or green plantains—ripening to yellow and then black—which are cooked as a starchy vegetable.

The truth is, although we may consider the banana a bland and even boring fruit best relegated to bag lunches, we are timid about trying different approaches to its preparation. Dried banana chips, available at health food and specialty stores, can be treated as a starchy flour and baked into puddings. The smooth pulp of sweet fresh bananas can be blended into milkshakes, sherbets, and soufflés, substituting for less slimming fats and flours and yet providing valuable nutrients.

The vegetable banana, plantain, needs to be cooked before eating, but otherwise it is extremely versatile. It can be baked, grilled, sautéed, deep-fried, braised, boiled, and even mashed like a potato, as it often is in Caribbean, South American, and eastern countries, to be eaten with savory or sweet foods. At every stage of development, when the peel is green, yellow, or brown-black, the firm starchy pulp of the plantain can be prepared. Gradually the interior flesh softens with ripening, becoming more fragrant with the banana's characteristic smell, and gains sweetness as it loses starch. But even black-ripe, the plantain remains firm without breaking up, a quality that can be very useful in cooking.

To ripen plantain, keep it at room temperature. Except for the occasional woody plantain, it will eventually mature through the various stages, but the process is much slower than that of a regular banana. When the plantain has reached the stage you wish, the peel is less pliable and more firmly attached than one on a sweet banana. First nip off the ends of the plantain. Unless it is very ripe, you will probably need to cut three or four shallow slits lengthwise in the peel down to the pulp, perhaps also slicing it across into sections. You can keep peeled plantain in acidulated or salted water before cooking to prevent the flesh from darkening. You can also boil plantain in thick or thin cross-sections with the peel still on, to be removed later.

The banana has an affinity for many different flavors and foods, both savory and sweet, assertive and mild. Among fruits, the acidic citrus family, as well as strawberries and raspberries, marry well with it, as do all the exotic fruits such as pineapples, kiwi, papaya, and mangoes. As for drinks, coffee, rum, and a wide assortment of spirits and liqueurs combine with it into glamorous desserts. Hot and spicy main course dishes, like the *nasi goreng* of Indonesia, a highly seasoned fried rice, would be incomplete without the banana. Certainly Indian curry dishes are more intriguing with the inclusion of its contrasting flavor and texture. In its native habitat, banana leaves are used for wrapping and cooking food—like oven bags—as well as for thatching and matting, like the leaves of the coconut and date.

The Cavendish is the variety familiar to most of us, shipped from Central American "banana republics." The fruit is picked mature but green, ripening about three weeks later. The ethylene gas given up by bananas as they mature ripens those nearby. For that reason, you can hasten the ripening of many other fruits if you enclose them in a bag with a ripe banana. Store regular bananas at room temperature; refrigeration, though harmless, will blacken the skin. People have individual preferences, but firm yellow ones are better for cooking, softer yellow ones speckled black are ready for immediate consumption. Fully ripened fruit if not eaten or cooked right away can be peeled, covered in plastic wrap, and frozen: eat it as a banana "popsicle" or mash and cook it as it begins to thaw.

No wonder the banana is often recommended for diets. One average banana contains eighty-eight calories, the plantain somewhat more. The banana provides large quantities of vitamins B and C, nearly as much as the orange and tomato, and a generous dose of vitamin A. Although low in sodium, it is a good source of minerals, especially potassium, iron, phosphorus, and calcium, and very high in easily assimilable sugars. The fruit has the added virtue of being filling but not heavy or bulky in the stomach, where it stimulates digestion.

Deep-Fried Banana Puffs

Made with dried banana chips, these banana fritters puff up like choux pastry. Serve these dessert puffs with apricot rum sauce.

4 ounces sweetened banana chips (dried bananas, available in health food stores)
2½ tablespoons unsalted butter, cut into small pieces
¾ cup cold water
2 large eggs
Vegetable oil for deep-frying
Apricot Rum Sauce (see page 40)

Put the banana chips in a food processor with the metal blade and process until fine, about 30 seconds.

Heat the butter and water in a small saucepan over low heat until the butter just melts. Pour the hot liquid through the feed tube with the motor running and process until the banana mixture thickens, about 15 seconds. Cool 5 minutes, then add the eggs one at a time, processing about 5 seconds after each. The batter will be quite loose.

Pour the oil in a deep-fryer to a depth of 3 inches, and heat to 360°F. As neatly as possible, drop spoonfuls of the batter into the oil and fry until the puffs turn golden brown, turning to color them evenly. Do not crowd them, or the temperature of the oil will drop and the puffs will be soggy. Continue until all the batter is used, keeping the finished puffs warm in a low oven.

Serve the banana puffs on warm plates with a little of the apricot rum sauce dribbled over.
MAKES 6 SERVINGS

Banana Nut Bread

This makes a moist, flavorful, textured bread, neither too sweet nor too heavy. Toast it in slices or not, as you choose.

¼ cup (½ stick) unsalted butter, softened
⅔ cup sugar
2 medium-large very ripe bananas, mashed (1 cup)

2 large eggs, lightly beaten
Grated zest of 1 lemon
1¾ cups all-purpose flour
1 teaspoon baking soda
½ teaspoon salt
½ cup chopped nuts, lightly toasted (see page 179)

Preheat the oven to 350°F. Butter and flour a loaf pan measuring 8½ x 4½ inches, shake out the excess flour, and set aside.

In a large bowl cream together the butter and sugar until light. Put the bananas in another bowl and stir in the eggs and lemon zest. Mix together in a third bowl the flour, baking soda, and salt. Alternately stir the banana and flour mixtures into the butter and sugar. Finally fold in the nuts. Spoon the batter into the prepared loaf pan and bake until the bread tests done, about 1 hour. Cool the bread on a rack before turning it out and slicing.

MAKES 1 LOAF

Banana Cream Pie with Chocolate

One associates banana cream pie with stodgy cafeteria fare, but made fresh it can be first-rate. If you prefer, omit the chocolate; or bake the pastry ahead, make your custard or pastry cream (see page 300) on the stove, chill it, and spoon into the shell to be covered with the bananas and whipped cream.

One 9-inch pâte sucrée shell (see page 35), unbaked
3 ounces bittersweet chocolate, fine grated or chopped

FOR THE CUSTARD
2 large eggs, lightly beaten
½ cup sugar
2 cups light cream or half-and-half
1 teaspoon pure vanilla extract

FOR THE TOPPING
2 large, ripe bananas
1 tablespoon orange juice
1 tablespoon coffee-flavored liqueur or rum (optional)
1 cup heavy cream
2 tablespoons confectioners' sugar, or to taste
½ teaspoon pure vanilla extract
Freshly grated nutmeg

Preheat the oven to 350°F. Put the pie shell on a cookie sheet and scatter the chocolate in the shell. To make the custard, mix together the eggs, sugar, cream, and vanilla. Pour into the pastry shell and carefully put it in the oven. Bake until the custard is nearly set in the middle, about 40 minutes. Let the custard cool, then cover and chill.

Right before serving, peel and slice the bananas, and toss them with the orange juice and coffee liqueur. Spread the slices on the custard. Whip the heavy cream, sweeten it with confectioners' sugar, and flavor with vanilla. Spread the cream over the bananas, dust with nutmeg, and chill until serving time. Don't let the completed pie wait long.

MAKES ONE 9-INCH PIE; 8 SERVINGS

Caramelized Banana and Pineapple Strips with Coffee Custard Sauce

The Caribbean flavors of banana, pineapple, and coffee blend together perfectly, while the textures of caramelized sugar and creamy custard contrast.

2 medium-large ripe bananas
¼ large pineapple, cut into quarters lengthwise
¾ cup brown sugar, broken up into fine lumps and granules
Coffee Custard Sauce (recipe follows)

Peel the bananas and remove the strings. Press your finger into the center of the tips to separate each banana into three longitudinal sections, pulling them apart lengthwise without breaking them in the middle. Place in a baking dish.

Cut out and discard the central pineapple core; slice the pineapple quarter in three pieces lengthwise through to the skin and cut off the skin. Cut each of the three slices in half lengthwise, so that you have 6 long strips of pineapple similar in size to the banana strips. This sounds more complicated than it is. Place in the dish with the bananas.

Arrange the broiler rack 4 inches from the heating unit and preheat. Just before serving, sprinkle a generous ⅛-inch layer of sugar on the outer side of the banana strips and the wide side of the pineapple strips. Carefully set them under the broiler. Watch closely as the sugar caramelizes, turning the pan if necessary so that it browns evenly but does not burn. Immediately, with a large spatula, put one strip each of banana and pineapple on six serving plates and serve with the coffee custard sauce.

MAKES 6 SERVINGS

Coffee Custard Sauce

This sauce goes with other fruit such as apricots and raspberries and of course with chocolate in any form.

1 cup milk
3 large egg yolks
⅓ cup sugar
2 tablespoons coffee-flavored liqueur
¾ cup chilled heavy cream

Scald the milk in a saucepan over medium-high heat: heat it until little bubbles appear around the edges. In another saucepan beat together the egg yolks and sugar until the mixture turns pale and forms ribbons. In a slow steady stream, pour the milk into the egg mixture, stirring continuously. Cook the custard over low heat, still stirring, until it thickens and coats the back of the spoon; be careful not let it curdle. Strain the custard through a fine sieve into a bowl. Stir in the liqueur and continue stirring to release the steam. Allow the custard to cool, then cover and refrigerate.

Shortly before serving, when the custard is well chilled, beat the cream until stiff and fold it into the custard. Keep chilled until serving time.

MAKES 2 GENEROUS CUPS

Bananas Foster

This famous dessert, from Brennan's Restaurant in New Orleans, is equally delicious with peaches or pineapple. Simply multiply for the number of servings you need. The original calls for banana liqueur and white rum, which you can use if you like. I think the orange gives a spark. You can serve the dessert with vanilla cream and pour the warm sauce over to melt it.

1 tablespoon unsalted butter
2 tablespoons firmly packed dark brown sugar
1 medium-large ripe banana, peeled and halved lengthwise
2 tablespoons dark rum
1 tablespoon fresh orange juice
1 teaspoon grated orange zest
Dash of ground cinnamon

Over low heat, melt the butter and brown sugar in a wide pan or chafing dish and let the sugar dissolve, stirring. Add the banana and cook until it is heated through, turning it over several times. Add the rum, orange juice, zest, and cinnamon, and baste the banana with the sauce. Ignite it, if you like, and serve the banana as soon as the flame has burned out with the sauce spooned over it.

MAKES 1 SERVING

Banana Chocolate Soufflés

These light little soufflés, depending on very ripe banana pulp, cocoa powder, and a single egg yolk, eliminate the need for butter, flour, and a cream base. The crystallized ginger gives a little burst of pungency.

1 medium-large very ripe banana, peeled and sliced
1 large egg yolk plus 2 egg whites, at room temperature
2 tablespoons unsweetened cocoa powder, plus extra for dusting
2 tablespoons sugar
1 tablespoon chocolate-flavored liqueur
1 tablespoon chopped crystallized ginger (available in Oriental and specialty food stores)

Smear a thin coating of vegetable oil on the insides of four 6-ounce soufflé cups, and dust the inside walls with a little cocoa powder. Set the cups slightly apart in a shallow pan. Preheat the oven to 350°F.

Purée the banana in a food processor. Add the egg yolk, cocoa powder, sugar, and liqueur, and combine until completely smooth.

In a medium-size bowl whip the egg whites until stiff but not brittle. Quickly fold the banana mixture into the whites until no streaks of white remain. Pour the soufflé batter into the prepared cups, and run your finger around inside the rim of each to help the soufflés rise evenly. Sprinkle the chopped ginger on top, and immediately set the pan in the oven. Bake them until they have risen and turned brown on top, 20 to 25 minutes. Serve the soufflés immediately.

MAKES 4 SERVINGS

Banana, Pineapple, and Lime Sherbet

The puréed banana gives the illusion of creaminess, even though this sherbet contains no cream or milk whatsoever. Add a little rum or gin if you wish.

2 medium-large ripe bananas, peeled and sliced
½ pineapple, peeled, cored, and cut into chunks (about 2 cups)
½ cup fresh lime juice

Grated zest of 1 lime
4 to 6 tablespoons honey, or to taste

Purée the bananas thoroughly in a food processor and put them in a nonreactive bowl. Purée the pineapple until it is completely smooth and add it to the banana. Stir in the lime juice, zest, and honey and blend well. Taste to see if the mixture needs more honey. Chill thoroughly, covered, in the refrigerator.

To freeze the fruit sherbet, see page 307.

MAKES 4 TO 6 SERVINGS

Tostones

Tostones are simple and fun to make, and children love to help. They are delicious on their own with a wedge of lime, as an appetizer with spicy salsa or guacamole, or as a vegetable accompaniment to meat. You can also deep-fry thin coins of green plantains as a variation on the potato chip.

2 unripened or partially ripe plantains (green or yellow)
Vegetable oil for deep-frying
Salt and freshly ground black pepper to taste

Peel the plantains (see page 43) and cut them across into ¾-inch-thick rounds, more or less.

Pour the oil into a wide skillet to a depth of one inch, and over medium flame heat to about 325°F. Fry the plantain rounds for a few minutes until they turn pale golden on both sides, then remove them with a slotted spoon to drain on paper towels. You may need to cook them in batches so as not to crowd them in the skillet, thus lowering the temperature of the oil.

With a mallet, rolling pin, or similar heavy tool, smack the plantains on a heavy board to flatten them (aim first for the center, then the edges).

Meanwhile, raise the heat of the oil slightly (to about 375°F) and return several plantain rounds to the pan at a time to fry them until golden brown, quicker this time (about 2 minutes). Drain the rounds again on fresh paper towels and salt and pepper them lightly. Serve the tostones hot, warm, or at room temperature.

MAKES 4 TO 6 SERVINGS

Baked Spicy Plantains and Bacon

Here is an interesting side dish for chicken, pork, or fish. Regular bananas can be cooked the same way, but need quicker broiling. Use whichever spice complements the rest of the meal.

2 medium to fully ripe plantains (yellow to black)
1 lemon heel
½ teaspoon ground coriander or cumin or chili or curry powder, or to taste
4 thick strips bacon

Preheat the oven to 400°F. (If at the same time you are baking something else at a slightly higher or lower temperature, you can cook this dish for a little shorter or longer time.)

Peel the plantains (see page 43), then cut them in half lengthwise so that they lie flat and lay them in a shallow nonreactive baking pan. Squeeze the lemon heel over the cut flesh, then sprinkle with the spice. Lay the bacon strips over the plantain halves, the leaner side facing the inside of each curve. Place a toothpick at each end with slack allowed for the bacon to shrink, to hold the strips on as they crisp and curl in cooking. Bake until the bacon is crisp and golden, about 30 minutes. Use a large spatula to set the plantains on warm serving plates and remove the toothpicks.

MAKES 4 SERVINGS

Baked Plantains in Gingered Lemon Syrup

Bake the plantains ahead at your convenience, perhaps while cooking another dish in the oven, and quickly finish them in their golden sauce before serving. The gingery lemony syrup is a lovely contrast to the creamy, smooth plantains.

2 ripe plantains (deep brown or black)
¼ cup sugar
4½ teaspoons fresh lemon juice
¼ cup water
1 tablespoon unsalted butter
3 knobs preserved stem ginger, diced (available in Oriental and specialty food stores)

Preheat the oven to 375°F. Snip off the ends of the plantains and bake them on a rack until softened and fragrant, 40 to 45 minutes. Let them cool in their peels. Protected from the air, they can wait several hours if need be.

Put the sugar in a nonreactive saucepan with the lemon juice and water, bring to a boil and let boil, covered, until the sugar has dissolved into a syrup, about 5 minutes. Stir in the butter and diced ginger; once the butter has melted, taste the sauce for balance.

Meanwhile, peel the plantains and thinly slice them on the diagonal into the syrup. Over low heat, warm the plantain slices through, stirring gently. Spoon them, still warm, onto serving plates and bathe them in the gingery lemon sauce.

MAKES 4 SERVINGS

BLUEBERRIES

When Governor John Winthrop arrived in Boston in 1630, his band of Puritans found the peninsula that is now the North End covered with blueberry bushes. For New Englanders, this berry remains the quintessential fruit of high summer.

A century ago Winslow Homer drew pictures of children in their pinafores and straw hats picking blueberries on the rocky shore. In his journal Henry David Thoreau described mountaintops carpeted in their blue. Robert Frost gathered his memories of blueberry picking, portraying in poetry the drumming of the first berries in an empty pail. If he could have, Charles Ives would have depicted the fruit in his music, along with the Fourth of July parades that punctuate his symphonies. This native American fruit somehow captures the signs, sounds, and scents of a New England July.

The wild blueberry shares something with the Yankee character: unassuming outside and spirited inside. The pale bloom on its untouched skin—Frost's "mist from the breath of the wind"—hides an intensely deep purple juice within. Its velvety sweetness is balanced by a refreshing edge of tartness. Small and modest, the berry's plain appearance is transformed by cooking into splendid pies, jams, cobblers, cakes, muffins, syrups, and scores of other pastries and confections. The blueberry has a way of working itself into your memory.

This hardy shrub thrives in the acid soil, year-round rainfall, and cold climate of New England, often on rocky land good for little else. It belongs to the genus *Vaccinium* that includes the bilberry of northern Europe and the seedier huckleberry—also known as the whortleberry or hurtleberry—as well as the cranberry that also favors the poor acid soil along the coastline.

The blueberry comes in two basic varieties, highbush and lowbush. Crossbreeding has produced the cultivated hybrids we mostly see in markets, with berries much larger in size, paler in color, and blander in flavor. New Jersey, North Carolina, and Michigan grow a lot of these, increasing the geographical range of the popular fruit. To compensate in cooking for the difference between wild and cultivated, add a little sugar on the one hand or a lemon accent on the other. Wild berries from the blueberry barrens of northeastern Maine ship fresh poorly; fortunately they are increasingly available in supermarkets throughout the year in their frozen state. The latest trend in blueberry marketing is freeze-dried "blueberry raisins"—actually an age-old method adapted from the American Indians who dried them in the sun, like grapes.

Whether you pick or purchase your fresh berries, remove at once any squishy ones, and store the rest unwrapped in the refrigerator in an open basket. The cold will retard their ripening, and the flow of air will help keep them from rotting. Blueberries can last surprisingly well in the refrigerator, as long as a week. Shortly before cooking, pick over the basket to discard any stems or leaves. Only at the last minute rinse the blueberries under cold running water and let them drain thoroughly.

Frozen wild berries are excellent for cooking. Use them directly from the freezer without thawing to avoid leaks and streaks of purple (watch out for juice stains). If you want to freeze blueberries yourself, spread them unwashed in one layer to freeze them individually, then pack them in plastic containers from which you can take only as many as you need. Just remember that, compared to cultivated berries, wild ones are smaller in size—an asset for pancakes and muffins—and higher in acid, showing off their lively character.

Blueberries are high in vitamin C, with some potassium and vitamin A, and plenty of fiber. One cup has about eighty calories. Besides their excellence in all kinds of baked dishes both homespun and elegant, fresh blueberries are delicious combined with other fruit or simply tossed on top of cereal, pancakes, or ice cream.

Blueberry Cornmeal Muffins

Cornmeal gives crunch and texture, but if you prefer, use two cups of flour instead, perhaps with a little more sugar. You can also substitute ½ cup of dried cranberries for the blueberries.

> *1 cup all-purpose flour*
> *1 cup cornmeal*
> *⅓ cup sugar*
> *½ teaspoon salt*
> *1 tablespoon baking powder*
> *1 cup milk*
> *1 large egg, lightly beaten*
> *¼ cup (½ stick) butter, melted*
> *1 cup blueberries, preferably small wild ones (if frozen, use unthawed)*

Preheat the oven to 400°F. Butter a small 12-muffin tin and set aside.

Mix together in a medium-large bowl the flour, cornmeal, sugar, salt, and baking powder. Beat together the milk and egg, and quickly stir it into the dry ingredients along with the melted butter, mixing just enough to incorporate them but not to smooth out the batter entirely. Quickly fold in the blueberries. Spoon the batter into the muffin tins, filling them two-thirds full. Bake until the muffins are risen and golden, 20 to 25 minutes. Cool the muffins slightly before removing them from the tin.

MAKES 12 SMALL MUFFINS

Blueberry Pancakes

A handful of blueberries can transform a pedestrian breakfast into one quite special. The small wild berries rather than the large cultivated ones work better in these pancakes.

> 2 cups all-purpose flour
> 2 tablespoons sugar
> 4 teaspoons baking powder
> ½ teaspoon salt
> 2 large eggs, at room temperature, lightly beaten
> 2 cups milk, at room temperature
> 2 tablespoons butter, melted and cooled
> ¾ cup blueberries, preferably small wild ones (if frozen, use unthawed)

Sift together in a large bowl the flour, sugar, baking powder, and salt. Stir the eggs into the milk. Make a well in the center of the dry ingredients and pour in the milk and eggs, stirring to make a smooth batter. Stir in the butter and finally the blueberries.

Heat a griddle over medium-high heat and lightly grease it. Ladle the batter onto the griddle in rounds as usual for pancakes and cook them, turning once, until golden. Continue until all the batter is used, keeping the finished pancakes warm in a low oven. Serve with fresh butter and maple syrup.

MAKES ABOUT FIFTEEN 4-INCH PANCAKES; 6 SERVINGS

Blueberry Shortcake

In this variation on the strawberry classic, the blueberry filling, with half the berries cooked and half added later uncooked, is deliciously juicy, yet the fruit keeps its integrity. This filling also works well spooned into a prebaked tart shell.

> FOR THE SHORTCAKE
> 2 cups all-purpose flour
> 3 tablespoons sugar
> 1 level tablespoon baking powder
> ½ teaspoon salt
> 6 tablespoons butter (¾ stick), cut into pieces

1 large egg, lightly beaten
¾ cup milk

TO COMPLETE
4 cups blueberries
½ cup sugar
3 tablespoons fresh lemon juice
1 teaspoon grated lemon zest
¼ teaspoon ground ginger or allspice
3 tablespoons dark rum
1 tablespoon cornstarch
2 cups chilled heavy cream
Confectioners' sugar to taste

First make the shortcake. Mix together in a bowl the flour, sugar, baking powder, and salt. Add the butter cut into pieces and with a pastry blender, two knives, or your fingertips, quickly break up the butter into the flour until the texture resembles oatmeal. Beat the egg into the milk and stir them into the dry ingredients to make a smooth, soft dough. Quickly knead it on a lightly floured board, no more than 1 minute, and roll it out to ½ or ¾ inch thick. With the sharp edge of a glass or biscuit cutter, cut the dough into 2½-inch circles and place them well apart on an ungreased cookie sheet. (The shortcake can wait up to a few hours if necessary; it is important to serve it still warm from the oven.)

Combine half the blueberries (2 cups) in a pot with the sugar, lemon juice, zest, ginger, and half the rum. Cover and bring to a gentle boil. Make a paste with the remaining rum and cornstarch and stir it into hot berry mixture. Return it again to the boil, remove the pan from the heat, and stir until the liquid has thickened. Cool the mixture, then stir in the remaining berries. Taste carefully to see if it needs more seasoning. Set aside.

Whip the cream until stiff and sweeten to taste with confectioners' sugar. Unless you are serving it right away, cover and chill.

Preheat the oven to 450°F. Bake the shortcake for 12 to 15 minutes, until they are just done. Let them cool somewhat, but be sure to serve them still warm. To serve, split the shortcake, spoon some of the berries and juice over the bottom, top with a generous dollop of whipped cream, and set the cap on top. If you like, dust the top with more confectioners' sugar and pass extra cream on the side.

MAKES 6 OR MORE SERVINGS

Fresh Blueberry Tart with Mascarpone

This tart, combining a nutty shell with a sweet mascarpone lining and acid berries, is as suave as the grunt is homely. You can substitute cream cheese for the mascarpone or, for fewer calories, try a combination of ricotta and yogurt. If you like, use a plain tart without nuts or individual tartlets.

One 9-inch walnut pâte sucrée (see page 35), partially baked.

FOR THE FILLING
3½ ounces mascarpone cheese
2 tablespoons heavy cream
2 tablespoons sugar or to taste
1 tablespoon Grand Marnier or other orange-flavored liqueur
1 teaspoon grated orange zest
2 cups fresh blueberries

Preheat the oven to 400°F. Line the tart shell with aluminum foil and fill it with dried beans or other weights. Bake the crust for 12 minutes. Remove the liner and bake it until crisp and golden, about 12 minutes more. Cool the shell and put it on a serving plate.

Mix the mascarpone with the cream, sugar (add more or less sugar, depending on whether your berries are wild or cultivated), Grand Marnier, and orange zest. Shortly before serving, spread the cream mixture over the bottom of the tart shell and scatter the blueberries on top. Garnish if you like with a sprig of fresh mint or curl of orange zest.

MAKES ONE 9-INCH TART; 6 SERVINGS

Deep-Dish Blueberry Pie

A deep-dish pie can be made with a double crust or top crust only, the latter sometimes made from biscuit dough. This crust is fashioned from regular pie dough, enough for three 9-inch crusts or one double crusted deep-dish pie. This recipe pays homage to Esther Grimes.

FOR THE DOUGH
3 cups all-purpose flour
1 teaspoon salt
1 cup (2 sticks; ½ pound) unsalted butter, chilled and cut into pieces
½ cup ice water

FOR THE FILLING
1¼ cups sugar, or to taste
1 teaspoon ground cinnamon
½ teaspoon ground cloves

8 cups blueberries
1 lemon
3 tablespoons cornstarch
1 tablespoon unsalted butter

First make the dough. This amount is enough for a very large deep-dish pie made in a 2-quart casserole or extra-large pie dish. Mix the flour and salt in a large bowl. Add the butter, cutting it into the flour with a pastry cutter, two knives, or your fingertips, quickly rubbing the butter into the flour to form flakes. (Have your hands very cold and handle the dough as little as possible.) Add the ice water gradually, stirring around the sides of the bowl, using just enough water to form a mass. If you prefer, mix the dough in a food processor, running the motor until the dough begins to form a ball on the blades. Gather the dough into a ball, enclose in plastic wrap, and refrigerate for at least an hour.

Preheat the oven to 425°F and prepare the blueberry filling. For blander cultivated berries, more lemon juice accents their flavor; wild berries may need extra sugar: adjust accordingly. Mix the sugar and spices and stir into the berries. Grate the lemon zest and squeeze the juice, about ¼ cup. Make a paste with the lemon juice and cornstarch and stir into the blueberries along with the zest.

Cut the dough into two pieces, one twice as large as the other. On a well-floured board, roll the larger ball of dough out evenly to form a thin round crust. Fit it into the bottom of the dish with the extra hanging over the rim. Spoon in the blueberry filling and dot the top with the butter. Roll out the smaller crust and fit it over the top. Trim the excess dough around the rim, wet the edge, and press the two crusts together into a rolled or fluted pattern. Cut air holes in the middle of the top crust in a pretty design. If you like, brush the surface with an egg wash (1 egg beaten with 1 tablespoon of water) or with water and then sprinkle with sugar; this is not necessary.

Bake the deep-dish pie for 15 minutes, then lower the heat to 350°F and bake until the crust is golden, about 35 to 40 minutes more. Cool somewhat and serve with heavy cream, vanilla ice cream, or hard sauce (recipe follows).

MAKES ONE DEEP-DISH PIE; 10 TO 12 SERVINGS

Hard Sauce

You can use white sugar and various flavorings, but this hard sauce is my favorite.

½ cup (1 stick; ¼ pound) unsalted butter, softened
1½ cups firmly packed dark brown sugar
3 to 4 tablespoons dark rum, or to taste
1 tablespoon grated orange zest

Combine all the ingredients in a bowl, stirring well, or use a food processor, scraping down the sides of the bowl once or twice with a rubber spatula. Taste the seasoning carefully. You can make the hard sauce ahead and keep it covered and chilled. Let it soften slightly before serving. Hard sauce will keep for a week in the refrigerator or for several months in the freezer.

MAKES ABOUT 2 CUPS

Blueberry-Orange Roulade

This festive roulade is pretty, light, and easy to make. Furthermore, it can accommodate extra servings for unexpected guests by rolling it the shorter or longer way. Flavor the roulade with lemon rather than orange if you prefer, or use other berry fillings.

FOR THE ROULADE
5 large eggs, separated, at room temperature
¾ cup sugar
3 tablespoons fresh orange juice
1 tablespoon grated orange zest
½ cup all-purpose flour
½ teaspoon baking powder

FOR THE FILLING
4 cups blueberries
½ cup sugar
2 tablespoons fresh orange juice
1 tablespoon orange zest
½ teaspoon freshly grated nutmeg
2 tablespoons water
1½ tablespoons cornstarch

TO COMPLETE
Confectioners' sugar
1 cup chilled heavy cream, whipped until firm peaks form
Nutmeg

First make the sponge cake. Line a 16 x 11 x 1-inch jelly-roll pan with aluminum foil or parchment paper. Butter and flour it, then shake out the excess. Preheat the oven to 375°F.

In a medium-large bowl, beat together the egg yolks and sugar. Stir in the orange juice and zest. In a small bowl sift together the flour and baking powder. Gradually stir the dry ingredients into the wet. In a large clean bowl, beat the egg whites until stiff peaks form. Stir one spoonful of whites into the batter, then fold the batter back into the rest of the whites just until no more white streaks remain. Spread the batter into the prepared pan and smooth it out into the corners. Bake it until the top is golden, about 15 minutes.

As soon as you take the sponge cake out, loosen the edges. After it has cooled somewhat, put a tea towel over the cake, invert the pan, and peel off the foil or paper. While the cake is still warm, roll it up in the towel. Keep the cake covered so it stays moist, and let it cool completely.

To make the blueberry filling, put half the blueberries in a medium-large saucepan with the remaining sugar, orange juice, zest, nutmeg, and water. Cover and bring to a boil. Make a paste with the cornstarch and a little water (1 to 2 tablespoons), and stir it into the hot berry mixture. Return to a boil, take the pan off the heat, and stir until the liquid thickens. Let it cool, then stir in the remaining blueberries, and check the seasoning.

Shortly before serving, unroll the cake. With a serrated knife, trim the two unrolled edges. Spread the blueberry mixture over the cake and roll it up again. With a knife, neatly trim the two rolled ends, and set the roulade seam-side down on a serving dish. Dust the top liberally with confectioners' sugar. To serve, slice the roulade across into individual rounds. Pass on the side a bowl of whipped cream lightly sweetened with confectioners' sugar and sprinkled with nutmeg.

MAKES 6 TO 10 SERVINGS

Blueberry Grunt

This homespun dessert from early New England is not for the boss's visit, but for sharing with close friends and family. Whether the name grunt comes from the sound of dumplings falling into the berries or from the satisfaction of the diners around the table is for you to determine.

FOR THE DROP-BISCUIT DOUGH
1 cup all-purpose flour
2 tablespoons white sugar
1 teaspoon baking powder
Dash of salt
½ cup milk

TO COMPLETE
½ cup firmly packed brown sugar
1 cup water
2 cups blueberries
2 tablespoons fresh lemon juice
1 teaspoon grated lemon zest
¼ teaspoon ground nutmeg or cinnamon

Sift together all the dry ingredients for the dough in a bowl. Make a well in the center and stir in the milk to make a soft dough; you may need slightly more milk. Set aside.

Put the brown sugar and water in a medium-size saucepan (to allow enough room it should be about 7 inches wide and 3 inches deep). Bring to a boil, add the blueberries, lemon juice, zest, and nutmeg, and let boil just until the berries burst, about 3 minutes. Off the heat, drop spoonfuls of the dough onto the hot blueberries, allowing plenty of room for the dumplings to expand. Cover and simmer over low heat about 12 minutes. To serve, dish the grunt into bowls and serve with a pitcher of heavy cream.

MAKES 4 OR MORE SERVINGS

Maple Walnut Cups with Vanilla Ice Cream and Blueberry Rum Sauce

This dessert is at once traditional and contemporary, down-home and sophisticated. The parts can all be made ahead. The blueberry sauce, both spiced and spiked, tastes delicious on all kinds of other desserts. Try it, for example, on Lemon Buttermilk Sherbet (see page 150).

8 Maple Walnut Cups (recipe follows)
8 scoops vanilla ice cream, homemade (see page 61) or good quality storebought
Blueberry Rum Sauce (see page 62), preferably warm

Set the walnut cups on serving plates. Put a generous scoop of vanilla ice cream in the middle of each, and spoon some warm blueberry rum sauce on top. Serve right away.

MAKES 8 SERVINGS

Maple Walnut Cups

1 cup walnut halves
½ cup sugar
½ cup all-purpose flour
¼ cup pure maple syrup
4 large egg whites

Preheat the oven to 425°F. Combine the walnuts and sugar in a food processor, and process until the nuts are coarsely—not finely—ground, about 10 seconds. Put them in a bowl and mix in the flour, maple syrup, and egg whites. The batter should be quite runny.

Generously grease two cookie sheets. Put two spoonfuls of batter on each sheet with plenty of space between them. Let the batter spread into two rounds 5 to 6 inches across. Bake until the edges begin to brown, about 7 minutes. Remove from the oven and, one at a time, carefully lift each round with a spatula and place in a small bowl. With your fingertips, quickly ruffle the edges like a flower to form a cup. If the pastry cools and stiffens, soften it again in the warm oven. Repeat until 8 cups are made.

These fragile cups shatter easily, so handle with care. Store them in a cool dry place such as an airtight cookie tin. In humid weather, enclose them in plastic bags and store in the freezer; they need only very brief defrosting.

MAKES 8 CUPS

Vanilla Ice Cream

2 cups light cream
One-inch piece vanilla bean, split and seeds scraped out, or 1 teaspoon pure
    vanilla extract
4 large egg yolks
½ cup sugar
1 cup heavy cream

Put the cream in a saucepan with the vanilla bean and scald over medium-high heat: heat it until little bubbles appear around the edges, but do not let it boil. Once the cream is infused with vanilla, take out the bean, and rinse and dry it to use again in another recipe.

In another saucepan beat together the egg yolks and sugar until well combined. In a slow steady stream, stirring constantly, pour the hot scalded cream into the yolk mixture. Cook it over medium-low heat, still stirring, until the custard thickens enough to coat the spoon heavily. Watch closely so the yolks don't scramble. Cool the custard (add the vanilla extract here if you are using it), then cover and chill thoroughly.

Fold the heavy cream into the custard (you might want to whip it first for added lightness), and freeze in an ice cream machine according to the manufacturer's directions. You can also freeze it in a covered bowl, stirring at intervals to smooth the ice crystals. The texture of homemade ice cream is best when made about 2 hours before serving. If it is made ahead and frozen hard, soften it slightly in the refrigerator before serving.

MAKES 1 QUART

Blueberry Rum Sauce

1 teaspoon cornstarch
2 tablespoons water
¼ cup sugar
¼ cup dark rum
1 tablespoon grated lemon zest
3 tablespoons fresh lemon juice
2 cups blueberries
⅛ teaspoon ground cinnamon
⅛ teaspoon ground allspice

In a small saucepan mix the cornstarch into a paste with the water. Add the sugar, rum, lemon zest and juice, and 1½ cups of the blueberries. Cook the berries over high heat, stirring from time to time; when the liquid has thickened and the berries have just burst, remove the pan from the heat.

Purée the berries through a sieve lined with a triple layer of cheesecloth rinsed in water and squeezed dry. With the back of a spoon, press the juice through the lined sieve, filtering out and discarding the skins, stems, and seeds. Mix a spoonful of the sauce with the cinnamon and allspice, then stir it in with the rest; sharpen the seasoning to taste. Add the reserved whole berries and serve warm or cooled.

This blueberry sauce may be made a day or two ahead. For a smooth texture, cook all the blueberries together.

MAKES ABOUT 1⅓ CUPS

Blueberry Syrup

This syrup, a distillation of New England summer, has many excellent uses. Drizzle it over breakfast pancakes or waffles. Or spoon it over dessert crêpes garnished with fresh blueberries, toasted slivered almonds, and crème fraîche. Or serve it in a cooling cocktail: put a spoonful in a tall stemmed glass, pour in some chilled white wine, and top with a splash of soda water and a slice of lime.

2 cups blueberries
3 tablespoons fresh lime juice
1 teaspoon grated lime zest
¼ cup water
⅓ cup sugar, or to taste

Combine all the ingredients in a saucepan. Over low heat, gently cook the mixture until the berries have burst and suffused the water with their juice, about 15 minutes. Strain the mixture through a sieve, pressing the berries with the back of a spoon to extract their liquid. Discard the solids. Line a fine sieve with a triple layer of cheesecloth rinsed in cold water and squeezed dry and strain the blueberry syrup again to remove the seeds, discarding the cloth and seeds. Cool the syrup and store it in a tightly covered jar in the refrigerator, where it will keep for several months.

MAKES ¾ TO 1 CUP

Blueberry Sherbet

This is an elegant and intensely fruity sherbet to serve in small portions, not to wolf down in volume.

1 cup sugar
1 cup water
4 cups blueberries
3 tablespoons fresh lemon juice, or to taste
1 tablespoon grated lemon zest
3 to 4 tablespoons crème de cassis (black currant liqueur)

Put the sugar and water in a large saucepan, bring to a boil, and let boil until the sugar is dissolved, about 5 minutes. Add the berries to the syrup along with the lemon juice and zest; cover and return to a full boil. Turn off the heat and let the mixture cool, covered.

Strain the berries through a sieve into a bowl, pressing on them with the back of a spoon to extract all the juice; discard the solids. Line a clean sieve with a double layer of cheesecloth rinsed in cold water and squeezed dry and set it over a clean bowl. Strain the blueberry syrup once more through the cloth to remove most of the seeds. (This is tedious, but makes for a more finished result.) Cool the syrup, add the cassis to taste, and chill well.

To freeze the sherbet, see page 307.

MAKES 6 OR MORE SERVINGS

CHERRIES

Cherries are among the most attractive of all orchard fruits, as anyone with a cherry tree knows. Climbing in our neighbor's orchard to feast on the plump, sweet, irresistible cherries before the birds could get them was one of the gastronomical high points of my childhood. Even after we were caught *in flagrante delicto*, it was still worth it.

Cherries are of two types, the sweet cherry (*Prunus avium*), from western Asia, and the sour cherry (*P. cerasus*), probably from Asia Minor and the Caucasus. There are also hybrid crosses between the two. Among sweet varieties, which are usually eaten out of hand, the large, crimson, sweet, juicy Bing is a leading commercial variety in the United States. The Lambert (similar to the Bing but slightly smaller and ripening a little later), Rainier (creamy golden with pink blush, clear juice, and delicate flavor), and Royal Ann (called Napoleon in Europe; yellow, large, firm) are also common in America.

Sour varieties are hard to find fresh in the United States, since most of the large crop goes directly to canning and is generally preferred for pies and other pastries. Among these more acid varieties, the dark Morello and light Montmorency are best known and lend their name to both savory and sweet dishes where their tart, complex flavor is much welcomed. Hungary has its sour cherry soup, France its duckling Montmorency, Germany and Scandinavia venison and pork cooked with sour cherries. Creamy custards, pastries, and preserves go naturally with the fruit, as do all the other drupes, or stone fruits. The cherry pit kernel, called *noyau* in French, has an almond flavor than can be used to effect and explains why the fruit and nut are often paired in pastries.

Wine brings out the rich flavor of cherries, and many liqueurs are made from them, such as Heering's cherry brandy from Denmark. Alsatian kirschwasser (*kirsch* is the German word for cherry), colorless like all *eau-de-vie*, is distilled from the fruit and whole stones, while maraschino, originally from the Dalmatian coast of Yugoslavia and made from the bitter Marasca cherry, uses crushed stones and kernels. Our maraschino cocktail cherries, artificially colored and preserved in heavy syrup, are a distant and garish imitation.

Since cherry season is short and the right type often unobtainable, canned cherries can be substituted for fresh in cooking. A one-pound can of pitted cherries is the equivalent of one pound of fresh, each yielding about two cups of pitted fruit. If you are using sweet cherries for tart, lower the amount of sugar called for and add a little lemon juice.

As for pitting fresh cherries, find the method that suits you and watch out for the juice, which stains. Some people prefer a small sharp knife, a new hairpin, or simply pulling out the stem and pinching the cherry to push the pit out through the stem hole. Assorted cherrystoners are on the market at every price from ninety-nine cents on up. Europeans often leave the pits in pastries as part of the sport, a practice Americans find unappealing. If you are serving whole cherries with the pits still in, it is advisable to leave the stem attached to indicate to your friends that they should chew gently to avoid breaking a tooth.

In the market look for shiny, plump, firm fruit with good color, whether deep mahogany, bright red, or pale gold. The stems should be fresh and light in color, not dry and shriveled. Avoid immature cherries that are hard or comparatively light-colored or small for their variety; likewise avoid sticky, soft, or dull cherries that have passed their prime. Chill the cherries when you get them home, but use them as soon as possible, since they quickly deteriorate. Besides, if you do not serve them promptly, others in the household, particularly children, will find other ways to dispose of them.

Dried cherries with the pits still in them are available in Greek and Middle Eastern stores. Dried and pitted Morello cherries from Michigan can be found in upmarket food shops (American Spoon Foods of Petoskey is a widely distributed brand). The latter are far more expensive, but for convenience and flavor well worth the cost. Just don't get into the habit of popping them into your mouth like raisins.

Cherries are in season May through August. A three-and-one-half-ounce serving (one hundred grams) offers a good amount of potassium, some vitamin A, and about seventy calories (four in each cherry).

Hungarian Sour Cherry Soup

This soup makes a beautiful and refreshing first course on a hot summer night.

1 pound fresh tart cherries or one 16-ounce can sour cherries with their juice
1 bottle dry white wine (or half a bottle of wine and 1½ cups water)
¼ cup sugar, or to taste
One 2-inch stick cinnamon
3 allspice berries
3 whole cloves
Dash of salt
1 lemon
1 cup heavy cream
Whipped cream or sour cream loosened with a little heavy cream for garnish
Ground cinnamon for garnish

Pit the cherries, saving any juices and the pits (omit the pits if using canned cherries or if you don't want to bother). Crack the pits with a mallet or rolling pin, and put them in a nonreactive pot with the wine, sugar, spices, and salt. Peel a 2-inch strip of zest from the lemon, squeeze the juice (about 4 tablespoons), and add them to the pot. Bring the liquid to a boil, cover, and let boil until the sugar is dissolved, about 5 minutes. Strain the liquid through a fine sieve into a clean pot and discard the solids. Add the cherries with their juice and cook over low heat until the cherries are tender, 5 to 7 minutes. Do not let them break up. Allow the soup to cool.

Slowly stir the cream into the soup. Although not authentically Hungarian, you may purée some or all of the cherries to thicken it. Chill the soup well. Shortly before serving, taste for the balance of seasonings, and add a little lemon juice if it needs sharpening. Serve the chilled cherry soup in bowls or cups, each garnished with a spoonful of unsweetened lightly whipped cream and a dash of cinnamon.

MAKES 6 TO 8 SERVINGS

Cherry Wine Sauce

This tangy sauce is made with sour Morello cherries, pitted and dried, from Michigan, far superior to the unpitted dried cherries found in Middle Eastern markets. The Michigan cherries are expensive, but their burst of flavor goes a long way toward making this dish irresistible. Serve this cherry sauce with roast pork, lamb, venison, pheasant, duck, or other game.

  3 ounces dried sour cherries
  ½ cup dry red wine
  1 tablespoon butter
  1 shallot, chopped

Marinate the cherries in the red wine for at least 30 minutes or overnight, so that they begin to plump up.

Over low heat melt the butter in a saucepan. When it begins to foam, add the shallot and cook, stirring, until the shallot is softened, about 2 minutes. Add the cherries and wine to the pan, and simmer over low heat until the liquid is reduced by half. This may be done well ahead.

Stir the sauce into the defatted pan juices of a roast, or use the sauce to deglaze a pan in which meat was sautéed. Stir up the combined liquids, spoon them over or around the meat, and serve at once on hot plates handsomely garnished.

MAKES ABOUT 6 SERVINGS

Montmorency Sauce for Roast Duckling

Montmorency cherries are a sour French variety, whose tartness balances the richness of duck. Use any sour, not sweet, cherry for this recipe.

2 tablespoons sherry wine vinegar
2 tablespoons sugar
1 cup rich duck or chicken stock
1 duck, roasted until crisp but not quite finished, cooled, and cut into 4 serving pieces
¼ cup dry red wine
1 cup pitted tart cherries (½ can or ½ pound fresh cherries)
Salt and freshly ground black pepper to taste

In a large pan cook the vinegar and sugar over high heat until it caramelizes into a rich, deep color. Add the stock (if possible, deglaze the pan you roasted the duck in with the stock first) and wine to the pan, and cook until reduced to 1 cup. Place the duck pieces in the pan along with the cherries, and simmer, partly covered, for 10 minutes. Uncover and simmer over low heat 10 minutes more, basting, until the duck is done and the flavors have mingled. With a slotted spoon, place the duck and cherries on warm serving plates. Skim any remaining fat from the sauce and reduce it slightly to concentrate it. Add salt and pepper, taste carefully for seasoning, and spoon the sauce over the duck.

   MAKES 2 TO 4 SERVINGS

Cherry Port Compote

This compote makes a fine accompaniment to meat and game dishes as well as a dessert in its own right, served with ice cream or pound cake. The kernels in the cracked pits impart an almond flavor, a method found in old recipe books. You can make the compote in quantity to put up in jars for autumn (see page 321).

1 cup port
1 to 4 tablespoons sugar, according to type of cherry and your taste
One 2-inch strip orange zest
1 pound fresh sweet or sour cherries

Put the port and sugar in a pot with the orange zest. Bring the liquid to a boil and let boil until the sugar is dissolved, about 5 minutes. Meanwhile, pit the cherries and save the pits. Crack them open with a heavy mallet or rolling pin and tie the pits in a piece of cheesecloth. Put the pits into the port syrup and boil for 5 minutes. Add the cherries, reduce the heat to low, and cook gently until the cherries are tender but not falling apart, about 5 minutes.

With a slotted spoon, remove the cherries to another container. Boil down the syrup to thicken it. Discard the cherry pits and orange zest. Cool the syrup somewhat and pour it over the cherries.

MAKES ABOUT 2½ CUPS

Cherries in Currant and Kirsch Glaze

This recipe is based on Lindsey Remolif Shere's Cherry Compote in her *Chez Panisse Desserts* (Random House). Its utter simplicity brings out the rich, luscious flavor of the cherries.

 1 pound fresh Bing cherries, pitted
 2 tablespoons sugar
 1 tablespoon red currant jelly, homemade (see page 85) or storebought
 1 tablespoon kirsch or cherry brandy

Put the cherries in a wide pan with the sugar and currant jelly. Over fairly high heat cook them until the sugar and jelly are melted and mixed and the cherries begin to give off their juices. Shake the pan and cook about 5 minutes, taking care not to break up the cherries or let them soften too much. Remove the pan from the heat and stir in the kirsch to mix the juices. When cool, spoon the cherries with the accumulated juices into a container and chill.

These cherries are beautiful served in saucer champagne glasses with their juices spooned over and perhaps yogurt or crème fraîche passed on the side. Or dissolve a little softened gelatin in the juices to glaze the cherries, spread them in a sweet tart shell or puff pastry base, and chill before serving.

MAKES 4 SERVINGS

Cherries Jubilee

Named for Queen Victoria's Diamond Jubilee, cherries jubilee made with fresh cherries is a revelation, but out of season canned Bing cherries in syrup are still festive. A 16-ounce can substitutes for 1 pound of whole fresh cherries. Heat the canned cherries in their syrup with the arrowroot and lemon zest but no additional sugar.

 1 pound fresh Bing cherries
 1 cup water
 ¼ cup sugar
 One 1-inch strip lemon zest
 1 teaspoon arrowroot or 2 teaspoons cornstarch

¼ *cup kirsch or cherry brandy*
Vanilla ice cream, homemade (see page 61) or storebought

First pit the cherries. While you are pitting them, make a syrup with the water and sugar. Add the cherries and lemon zest, bring to a boil, and let boil until the sugar is dissolved, about 5 minutes. Mix the arrowroot with a little cold water to make a paste. Stir it into the boiling syrup and cook until thickened (for cornstarch, cook 2 minutes to remove the starchy taste). Add the pitted cherries and poach over low heat until tender, 5 to 7 minutes; do not let the cherries break apart and get mushy. Discard the lemon zest. Heat the kirsch in a separate pan, pour it into the cherry mixture, and ignite. Spoon the cherries and their syrup over vanilla ice cream scooped into glass bowls. Serve at once.

MAKES 6 SERVINGS

Cherry Almond Crumble

This old-fashioned crumble is deep red and delicious, the almonds adding a complementary texture and flavor.

1 *tablespoon white or brown sugar, more for tart cherries*
1 *teaspoon cornstarch*
1½ *pounds fresh sweet or tart cherries, pitted*

FOR THE TOPPING
¾ *cup all-purpose flour*
⅓ *cup firmly packed brown sugar*
¼ *teaspoon ground cinnamon*
¼ *teaspoon ground coriander*
6 *tablespoons (¾ stick) unsalted butter, cut into pieces*
¼ *cup chopped slivered almonds, lightly toasted (see page 179)*

Preheat the oven to 375°F. Mix together the sugar and cornstarch and toss the cherries in it to coat them evenly. Turn the cherries into a 9-inch pie plate or similar small dish or casserole.

In a medium-size bowl, mix together the flour, sugar, and spices (use other spices such as clove and nutmeg if you prefer). With your fingertips or a pastry cutter, rub or cut in the butter to make a fine crumble. Mix in the almonds, then spread the crumb topping over the cherries. Bake until the topping is golden brown and the juices thick and bubbly, about 45 minutes. Serve warm with whipped cream or vanilla ice cream.

MAKES 4 SERVINGS

Lattice Cherry Pie

The ruddy color of tart cherries peeking through the lattice makes this pie as inviting as ever.

FOR THE PASTRY DOUGH
(halve the ingredients if making a single bottom crust only)
2 cups all-purpose flour
½ teaspoon salt
⅔ cup (1⅓ sticks) unsalted butter, chilled and cut into pieces
5 to 6 tablespoons cold water

FOR THE FILLING
2 pounds tart cherries, pitted, with any juice, or two 16-ounce cans pitted tart cherries
    with ¼ cup of their juice
⅔ to 1 cup sugar, according to taste
3 tablespoons quick-cooking tapioca
1 tablespoon kirsch (optional)
1 teaspoon grated lemon zest
1 tablespoon unsalted butter, cut into bits

FOR THE EGG WASH
1 large egg
1 tablespoon water

First make the dough. Put the flour, salt, and butter in a food processor and process to cut up the butter finely in the flour. Add the water and run the machine just until the dough forms a ball on the blades. Divide the dough in two (if making a single crust, do not divide), enclose each slightly flattened ball in plastic wrap, and chill for an hour or more. On a lightly floured board, roll out one ball of dough to about 10 inches in diameter, and cut it into ½-inch-thick strips. This will be the lattice top. Put them in the refrigerator or even the freezer for a few minutes for easier handling. Roll out the other ball of dough, and fit it into a 9-inch pie plate, leaving a generous overhang. Trim the rough edge to ½ inch.

Preheat the oven to 400°F. Put the pitted cherries and juice in a bowl with the sugar, tapioca, kirsch, and zest. Mix well and let the filling sit for 15 minutes.

Pour the cherry filling into the lined pie plate and dot with the bits of butter. Make the lattice top, woven and twisted or not, as you prefer, and moisten the pie lip with water to fasten the strips. Fold the lower layer of dough over the strips and crimp to make an attractive edge. Beat together the egg and water, and brush a thin layer on the lattice. Bake the pie until the lattice is golden brown and the cherry juice makes thick bubbles, about

1 hour. You may need to cover the edges with aluminum foil about halfway through to keep them from overbrowning. Serve the pie warm or at room temperature with scoops of vanilla ice cream.

MAKES ONE 9-INCH PIE; 8 SERVINGS

Clafoutis de Limousin

This peasant pudding from Limousin in central France, spelled either clafouti or clafoutis, uses a pancakelike batter. It was traditionally made with unpitted black cherries for grape harvesters. You can also make the pudding with tart cherries or dried pitted cherries that are plumped and drained, or with another fruit such as grapes or plums.

1 pound fresh sweet cherries, pitted, or one 16-ounce can, drained
½ cup plus 2 tablespoons all-purpose flour
Dash of salt
3 large eggs
2 cups milk
¼ cup plus 2 tablespoons sugar (more if using tart cherries)
Confectioners' sugar to garnish

Preheat the oven to 350°F. Generously butter a deep pie or au gratin dish of at least 6-cup capacity. Scatter the cherries in the dish.

Put the flour and salt in a bowl and break the eggs on top. Slowly beat the eggs together with a fork, then gradually incorporate a little flour at a time to make a smooth batter. Slowly stir in the milk, then the sugar. Pour the batter over the cherries and bake the pudding until puffed and golden around the edges, about 45 minutes. The pudding will settle as it cools. Just before serving, dust it with confectioners' sugar. It is best eaten warm, but also tastes delicious cold.

MAKES 6 SERVINGS

Black Forest Cake

This lusciously rich cake, from the Schwarzwald of southwest Germany, makes an extravagantly beautiful presentation. It may look complicated, but the separate steps are simple: the finished cake is easier than the sum of its parts.

FOR THE KIRSCH SYRUP
¼ cup kirsch
3 tablespoons sugar

FOR THE CAKE
Two 8-inch chocolate sponge cake rounds (recipe follows)

FOR THE CHERRY CREAM FILLING
1 cup chilled heavy cream
3 tablespoons confectioners' sugar, or to taste
2 tablespoons kirsch
½ pound canned pitted sour cherries, well drained (½ can)

FOR THE CHOCOLATE GANACHE
4 ounces bittersweet chocolate, broken into pieces
½ cup heavy cream
2 tablespoons kirsch

TO DECORATE
4 ounces bittersweet chocolate
16 perfect fresh cherries, stems on, or canned cherries, well drained

Make the kirsch syrup. Combine the kirsch and sugar in a small saucepan and bring to a boil; let boil until the sugar is dissolved, about 5 minutes. Spoon the kirsch syrup over each round of chocolate sponge cake.

Make the cherry cream filling. In a chilled medium-size bowl, whip the cream until stiff peaks form. Fold in the confectioners' sugar and then the kirsch. Spread half the cream on one round of sponge cake. Put the well-drained cherries on the cream, spread a little more cream over, then carefully place the second cake on top. Cover and refrigerate the cake. Also cover and refrigerate the remaining cherry cream.

Make the chocolate ganache. In a double boiler over gently simmering water, combine the the chocolate and cream. Stir until melted, mixed, and glossy, then add the kirsch. While still warm, quickly spread the chocolate ganache smooth over the top of the cake, allowing some to drip down over the sides, and chill to firm it. With a spatula spread the rest of the reserved cherry cream around the sides of the cake and chill.

To decorate, gently melt the bittersweet chocolate, and with a spatula spread it thin on a baking sheet. Let the chocolate cool somewhat, then push it with the spatula into curls. Correct temperature is crucial—rewarm the chocolate if necessary. Carefully press the curls around the sides of the cake and chill. (For a quicker alternative, grate bittersweet chocolate and press it into the sides of the cake.) Just before serving, garnish the cake with the fresh cherries.

MAKES ONE 8-INCH CAKE: 8 SERVINGS

Chocolate Sponge Cake

This basic sponge becomes the basis for many fancy decorated cakes.

5 large eggs, separated
¾ cup sugar
1 teaspoon pure vanilla extract
½ cup all-purpose flour
3 tablespoons sifted unsweetened cocoa powder
½ teaspoon baking powder
1 to 2 tablespoons milk (optional)
Pinch of salt

Lightly butter and flour two 8-inch cake pans; shake out the excess flour and set aside. Preheat the oven to 375°F.

In a large bowl, beat together the egg yolks and sugar until the yolks turn paler and the sugar starts to dissolve; stir in the vanilla. In another bowl, sift together the flour, cocoa, and baking powder, and gradually stir them into the egg yolk mixture until smooth. If the mixture seems too stiff, stir in the milk. In another large bowl, beat the egg whites with the salt until stiff peaks form. Fold a spoonful into the batter, then quickly and deftly fold in the rest of the whites until no more white streaks appear. Pour the batter into the prepared pans and bake until cakes have risen high and turned golden brown, the edges shrink away from the pans, and the centers test done, 22 to 25 minutes. Run a knife around the inside of the pans and let cool somewhat. When the cakes have slightly deflated but are still warm, turn the cakes in the pans upside down, to keep their volume, until completely cooled. Turn the cakes out of the pans. If you are not using them right away, enclose the cakes in plastic wrap and refrigerate (or freeze).

MAKES TWO 8-INCH ROUNDS

CRANBERRIES

The cranberry that grows in coastal bogs and swampy marshes of New England greeted the Pilgrims when they first came to America. They recognized the brilliant crimson fruit, *Vaccinium macrocarpon*, from a much smaller variety native to northern Britain. Like its cousin the blueberry and the beach plum, the cranberry grew wild in sandy acid soil they could not cultivate. They also knew it for its healthful properties, particularly in preventing scurvy. Among other virtues, the cranberry's protective skin and high acidity kept it fresh, harvested or not.

The Pilgrims called the fruit fogberry, fenberry, or bogberry. The word cranberry came from the flower stamen's resemblance to a crane's beak. The American Indians, who paid homage to the cranberry in their legends, taught the settlers to make pemmican—the dried buffalo, venison, or bear meat preserve, pounded with animal fat and berries, that they took on hunting trips as a high-energy convenience food. The benzoic acid in the berry acted as a preservative.

Cranberries still grow behind the sand dunes of the Massachusetts coast in large cooperative bogs, but the creeping evergreen vine is tricky to cultivate. Acid peat soil, sand, and fresh water are needed, as well as five years for a new planting to bear fruit. In spring frosts threaten the pink blossoms and in fall the vines must be pruned. By the nineteenth century, advanced methods were used, to the chagrin of Henry David Thoreau. "[I] admired, though I did not gather, the cranberries," he wrote, "small waxen gems, pendants of the meadow grass, pearly and red, which the farmer plucks with an ugly rake, leaving the smooth meadow in a snarl, needlessly measuring them by the bushel and the dollar only." Today their cultivation is a major industry in Massachusetts.

The cranberry's tartness, suiting both savory and sweet dishes, makes its cooking range far wider than we usually allow. The berry is delicious with poultry, game, and pork, as well as in sauces, puddings, and pies. It pairs well with nuts, wild rice, and wholemeal grains. Compatible with other fall fruits such as apples and pears, its red color can magically enhance an otherwise mundane dish. Instead of sugar, maple syrup can make an interesting and appropriate sweetener. In the cold weather of fall and winter, the berry's crimson hue brightens festive celebrations such as Thanksgiving dinner.

The berry is similar enough to raspberries and currants that you can substitute it in recipes, adjusting the sweetness accordingly. Dried cranberries can be used like raisins. Cranberry juice, which unlike most fruit juices must be sweetened and diluted with water to be palatable, makes a refreshing drink for all generations. It also makes an excellent deglazing liquid, nonalcoholic and attractively colored, in place of wine. As with all red berry juices, watch out for stains.

Cranberry season comes in early autumn, and fresh berries are available from September through December. Since they freeze well in their 12-ounce plastic bags and keep indefinitely in the freezer, it is wise to buy extras to keep on hand frozen. The berries should be used without thawing. The states of Massachusetts, Wisconsin, and Washington are the major suppliers of cranberries.

Cranberries are high in vitamin C and also in fiber and pectin. Low in sodium, one cup contains only fifty calories.

Cranberry Kir Royale

To set a brilliant mood for the winter holidays, greet your guests with this festive version of Kir, made with a light cranberry syrup rather than *crème de cassis* (black currant liqueur).

2 cups cranberries, picked over
1 cup sugar, or to taste
1 cup water
One 2-inch strip orange zest
Champagne, well chilled
Orange zest for garnish (optional)

Put the cranberries, sugar, water, and orange zest in a pot. Cover, bring to a boil, and simmer over low heat until the skins have burst and the sugar is dissolved, about 5 minutes. Strain through a fine sieve, pressing the berries with the back of a spoon to extract the juice. For perfect clarity, strain again through a double piece of cheesecloth rinsed in water and squeezed dry. Cool the syrup, pour it into a jar, and chill well. The syrup will keep in the refrigerator for several months.

For each drink, pour 1 ounce (2 tablespoons) of cranberry syrup into a wineglass and add about 3 ounces of champagne, depending on the size of your glass. Add more or less cranberry syrup if you prefer. To make a pretty garnish, score the orange zest into a thin 1½-inch strip and tie it into a simple knot to float in the glass.

MAKES ABOUT 2 CUPS SYRUP

Acorn Squash with Cranberry Apple Stuffing

Serve this as a vegetable side dish to roast poultry, pork, or lamb. For more servings, multiply the ingredients and taste carefully to adjust the seasonings. If you have too much filling, do not overstuff the squash.

1 acorn squash
2 tablespoons butter, melted
¼ cup chopped scallions (green and white parts)
½ cup peeled, cored, and cubed apple (about ½ apple)
½ cup cranberries, picked over
2 tablespoons chopped walnuts, lightly toasted (see page 179)
2 tablespoons pure maple syrup
⅛ teaspoon ground cinnamon
Salt and freshly ground black pepper to taste

Preheat the oven to 350°F. Cut the squash in half lengthwise and scoop out the seeds and strings. Cut a slice off the bottom to make the halves stand stably. Brush a little of the butter over the cut surfaces of the squash. Put the halves cut-side down in a pan, add a little water to cover the bottom of the pan, and bake until tender, 30 to 35 minutes.

Meanwhile, reheat the remaining butter in a small saucepan over low heat and cook the scallions, stirring, until softened, about 3 minutes. Add the apples and cook about 3 minutes more, stirring. Add the cranberries, walnuts, and maple syrup, cover, and cook until the berries pop, about 5 minutes. Uncover the pan and let some of the moisture evaporate. Season the mixture to taste with cinnamon, salt, and pepper. Spoon the stuffing into the squash cavities and bake 15 to 20 minutes more.

MAKES 2 SERVINGS

Wild Rice Pilaf with Dried Cranberries and Mushrooms

This pilaf makes an excellent side dish or stuffing for roast poultry, game, and meat. The concentrated sweet-tart taste of the vermilion berries sparks the dish. Use wild mushrooms if you can.

3 tablespoons butter
3 ounces mushrooms, thinly sliced
2 shallots, minced
1 cup uncooked wild rice, well rinsed and drained

2½ cups chicken stock or water
½ cup dried cranberries
¼ cup hazelnuts or other nuts, lightly toasted (see page 179)
3 tablespoons chopped fresh watercress
Salt and freshly ground black pepper to taste
Watercress for garnish

Melt half the butter in a saucepan over medium-low heat. When it begins to foam, add the mushrooms and cook, stirring, until their juice is mostly evaporated, about 5 minutes. Toss in the shallots and cook a few minutes more to soften. With a slotted spoon remove the mushroom mixture to a bowl and reserve. Add the remaining butter to the pan and stir the wild rice in it for about 2 minutes. Add the chicken stock, bring to a boil, and simmer over low heat until the grains of rice are plump and tender but not splayed, about 30 minutes. You may need to drain a little of the liquid at the end. Stir in the cranberries, cover, and let the rice steam in its own heat for a few minutes. Mix in the mushrooms and shallots, hazelnuts, and watercress. Season with salt and pepper, and serve with sprigs of fresh watercress.

MAKES 6 TO 8 SERVINGS

Sautéed Pork Medallions with Shallots in Cranberry Madeira Sauce

Lean pork medallions in an elegant crimson sauce make a perfect holiday starter. Or serve double the amount as a main course.

1 tablespoon vegetable oil
3 tablespoons butter
8 shallots, peeled and a shallow X cut in the root end
2 whole pork tenderloins, cut into ¾-inch-thick rounds, making 16 pieces
⅓ cup Madeira
1 cup cranberry juice
½ cup chicken stock
½ bay leaf
1 sprig fresh parsley
Whole fresh cranberries and watercress for garnish

Put the oil and 1 tablespoon of the butter in a large frying pan and melt over low heat. When the butter begins to foam, cook the shallots for about 5 minutes, turning to color them on all sides. Remove them from the pan. Raise the heat to medium and add the pork medallions, browning them well on both sides; lower the heat and cook until they are just done in the middle but still springy to the touch, about 15 minutes in all. Remove them to serving plates and keep warm. Spoon off any fat from pan.

Over high heat, deglaze the pan with the Madeira, stirring briskly to dissolve the dark crust. Add the cranberry juice, stock, and herbs, and return the shallots to the pan. Boil to reduce the liquid to ½ cup. Remove the shallots and place them around the pork medallions; discard the herbs. Reduce the liquid a bit more, until syrupy and concentrated in flavor. Cool slightly, then swirl in the remaining butter. Spoon the sauce over the pork medallions, garnish with the whole cranberries and watercress, and serve.

MAKES 8 FIRST-COURSE SERVINGS

Cranberry Orange Relish

This simple fresh relish is as delicious now as it was on my mother's Thanksgiving table. Don't tell children how good it is for them!

One 12-ounce package cranberries (3½ to 4 cups), picked over
1 large seedless or seeded orange, coarsely chopped (peel included)
¾ cup plus 2 tablespoons sugar, or to taste

Put the cranberries and orange in the food processor and process until chopped and combined; be sure to keep a fairly coarse texture. Stir in the sugar to taste. Let the relish sit for several minutes until the sugar dissolves on its own by the action of the citric acid. No further doctoring necessary. The relish can be served right away or allowed to mellow for several days. Covered tightly and well chilled, the relish will keep for a week or more.

MAKES ABOUT 2 CUPS

Molded Cranberry Jelly

Cranberries are high in pectin, so they jell easily. Embed pineapple, orange sections, or other fruit in the jelly if you want to make it fancier. Or pour the jelly into a shallow pan and cut out fanciful shapes. You can spice the syrup with a cinnamon stick, cloves, or allspice berries, discarding the whole spices before molding.

One 12-ounce package cranberries (3½ to 4 cups), picked over
1¼ cups water
1 cup sugar

Put the cranberries in a nonreactive pot with the water and bring to a boil. Boil over medium-low heat for 20 minutes, take the pan off the heat, and strain the cranberries through a fine sieve into a bowl, pressing on the solids with the back of a spoon to extract the juices. Discard the solids. Stir the sugar into the pot and boil over medium heat for a minute or two to dissolve the sugar, stirring. Skim off any foam, then pour the sauce into a wet 2 to 2½-cup mold, cool, cover, and chill until set. To serve, unmold the jelly onto a serving dish.

MAKES ABOUT 2 CUPS

Fresh Cranberry Maple Mustard Chutney

This chutney presents traditional autumn flavorings in a new way. Serve it with grilled or roasted chicken and turkey, ham, pork, or game.

4½ teaspoons whole mustard seed, or to taste
1¼ cups cranberries, picked over and chopped
½ cup diced unpeeled apple, preferably Granny Smith (about ½ apple)
3 scallions (green and white parts), chopped
¼ cup chopped walnuts, lightly toasted (see page 179)
2 tablespoons fresh lemon juice
¼ cup pure maple syrup, or to taste

Soak the mustard seed in water to cover for at least 15 minutes to bring out its heat; drain well. Mix together all the ingredients, adding the mustard and maple syrup last and a little at a time to avoid overdoing it. Let the chutney ripen a half hour or more before serving. Covered tightly and well chilled, this chutney lasts several days.

MAKES ABOUT 2 CUPS

Winter Pudding

This twist on the English classic Summer Pudding (see page 277), usually made with currants and raspberries or other juicy summer fruits, is stunning, inexpensive, and luscious. It is also bursting with vitamin C, low in calories, and conveniently made a day or two ahead. You can even freeze it, thawing it thoroughly in the refrigerator before your party.

2 seeded oranges
One 12-ounce package cranberries (3½ to 4 cups), picked over
¾ cup sugar, or to taste
1 juicy pear, cored, peeled, and cubed
½ cup orange juice
Stale white bread, firm-textured, thin-sliced, with crusts trimmed
Lightly sweetened whipped cream for garnish

Squeeze the juice from the oranges, saving the rinds. Place the juice in a nonreactive pot with the cranberries and sugar. Cover, bring to a boil, and cook until the berries have popped, about 5 minutes. While the cranberries are cooking, coarsely chop the orange skins, then mince them in a food processor. Add the pear and process just until no large chunks remain. When the cranberries have popped, pour the contents of the pan through a sieve set over a bowl. Put the cranberry solids in the food processor with the orange peel and pear, and process just enough to combine the fruits. Add the extra half cup of orange juice to the cranberry-orange juice in the bowl.

Cut the bread to fit a 5- to 6-cup bowl or pudding mold with steep sides: one bread round on the bottom with fan-shaped pieces around the sides works best. Dip both sides of the bread in the reserved cranberry-orange juice, then fit each piece in place. Fill any holes with leftover pieces of bread to completely line the bowl. Taste the cranberry-pear-orange mixture to see if it needs more sugar (oranges can vary considerably in sweetness; stir in a little more sugar if needed), then spoon the mixture into the bread-lined bowl. Trim off the pieces of bread extending beyond the fruit and cover the top of the fruit with leftover bread. Cover the pudding with plastic wrap and set a saucer on top that just fits inside the bowl. Place a heavy object on top to weight the pudding down. Refrigerate the pudding at least overnight, weighted. Save the remaining juice in a jar and chill it too.

When you are ready to serve the pudding, run a knife around the inside edge of the bowl, invert it onto a platter, and jerk it down once or twice to unmold the pudding. Spoon the reserved juice over the pudding to cover any pale spots. Decorate the top with fresh mint leaves, candied angelica, or other festive nontoxic greenery (holly berries are toxic), and pass lightly sweetened whipped cream on the side.

MAKES 6 OR MORE SERVINGS

Cranberry Sherbet

For a variation on this vibrant sherbet, use orange juice instead of water (omit the lemon juice) and serve in orange cups.

2 cups sugar
3 cups water

One 12-ounce package cranberries (3½ to 4 cups), picked over
2 tablespoons fresh lemon juice
¼ cup Curaçao or other orange-flavored liqueur

Put the sugar and water in a pot, bring to a boil, and let boil for 5 minutes, covered. Add the cranberries, return to a boil, and cook until the berries burst. Pour the mixture through a fine sieve into a bowl, pressing the berries with the back of a spoon to extract as much liquid as possible. Discard the skins and seeds. To strain out the rest of the seeds (this may seem a nuisance but will make for a more finished sherbet in the end), pour the liquid through a sieve lined with a triple layer of cheesecloth moistened in cold water and squeezed dry. Add the lemon juice. Cover and chill the liquid thoroughly.

Freeze the cranberry syrup in an ice cream machine or sorbetière according to the manufacturer's directions. Or freeze it according to the directions on page 307. This sherbet holds its smooth texture well.

MAKES ABOUT 1 QUART

CURRANTS

The currant is a small vermilion berry, translucent with pale veins showing through, strung in clusters along green stems like glass beads on a necklace. The first part of the botanical name of the leafy shrub, *Ribes rubrum*, refers to its fruit's pleasantly tart flavor. The red berry actually comes in black and white too, the opaque black being a muskier, larger species, while the luminous white is a colorless and milder variety of red. Although no relation, the currant acquired its name from the raisin whose name is a corruption of the Greek city of Corinth, on whose surrounding hills the small grapes were grown and dried, to be shipped all over the known world.

The currant berry is popular in northern European countries, especially Great Britain, Germany, Scandinavia, and Russia, but it has never caught on in southerly regions. One reason may be that the currant and its cousin the gooseberry are host to a disease called white pine blister rust, so that the cultivation and sale of the host plants are curtailed in some states where the eastern white pine grows. Perhaps another reason the currant has not gained popularity in cooking is its healthful properties; ironically, people associate it with medicine.

In France, the village of Bar-le-Duc gives its name to the preserve made there, combining red and white berries, and red currant jelly glazes pastry desserts with an appealing shimmer. The summer aperitif called Kir, popularized by the Resistance hero and mayor of Dijon named Kir, tinges white wine with *crème de cassis*, the black currant liqueur. In Finland, peasants make a currant-strawberry drink to carry them through the long, dark winter. In northern Europe and Russia, a variation of the fruit dessert called kissel is made from the currant. In England, the berry is essential to summer pudding, usually made with raspberries that also ripen in midsummer. In the English tradition, Amelia Simmons included recipes for currant pie, preserves, and jelly in *American Cookery*, the first cookbook published here (1796), to encourage their cultivation.

Currants can be frozen spread on flat pans, then combined in containers from which you need take only as many as you wish; use them in cooking without thawing. Like other tart berries, currants go well with poultry, pork, venison, and lamb, as well as in puddings, compotes, sherbets, and pastries. Try substituting them in recipes for raspberries and cranberries, tasting to see if more sugar is needed. Fully ripened, brilliant red berries are better for desserts; for jellies and preserves, include some paler berries not yet fully ripe to take advantage of their high pectin content.

The best place to find red currants, aside from your friends', or your own, backyards, is in local farm markets, depending on what state you live in. Their season is July. Black and white currants are especially hard to come by in the United States. Keep currants in the refrigerator and use them within a few days, washing them just beforehand, or stem and freeze them as described above. Currants still on the stem make an exquisite garnish that is simplicity itself.

Currants are high in vitamin C, potassium, and fiber; they are low in sodium and calories. Although hard to find in this country, black currants are spectacularly high in vitamin C.

Lamb and Currant Salad

This elegant salad for a special occasion uses currant juice instead of vinegar. The whole berries, besides looking pretty, give pleasing little bursts of acidity. Rock Cornish hen, roasted or grilled and cut in half, sliced breast of duck, or other meat would be delicious in place of the lamb.

½ cup currants plus 2 tablespoons whole currants, off the stem, for garnish
4½ teaspoons extra virgin olive oil, or to taste
Salt and freshly ground black pepper to taste
2 handfuls arugula or other bitter lettuce
6 ounces sliced cooked lamb or other meat
2 tablespoons chopped walnuts, lightly toasted (see page 179)
2 tablespoons snipped fresh chives

Press the ½ cup currants through a fine sieve to yield about 1½ tablespoons of currant juice. Mix it with the olive oil and salt and pepper. Arrange the arugula on two serving plates and spread the lamb slices on top. Scatter the walnuts, chives, and whole currants on top. Mix the dressing together again and drizzle it over the salads. Serve at once.

MAKES 2 SERVINGS

Cumberland Sauce

This traditional English game sauce—sweet, tart, and spicy all at once—can also be made with cranberry jelly in place of currant. It is delicious with poultry, pork, and lamb as well as game. Colman's mustard, powdered and potent, is the authentic mustard to use here.

1 orange
½ lemon
2 shallots, finely minced
¼ cup plus 2 tablespoons red currant jelly, homemade (see page 85) or storebought
¼ cup plus 2 tablespoons port
½ teaspoon prepared Colman's mustard or 1 teaspoon Dijon
Dash of ground cayenne pepper
Dash of ground ginger

Cut the orange and lemon zest into fine julienne. Drop the julienne into a pan of boiling water and cook 3 minutes to remove the bitterness; drain and reserve. Squeeze the orange juice (about 6 tablespoons) and lemon juice (about 2 tablespoons). To blanch them, drop the shallots into boiling water just until it returns to a boil, then drain the shallots and squeeze dry.

Melt the currant jelly in a nonreactive saucepan over low heat. Stir in the citrus juices, zest, shallots, and port. Remove a spoonful of the sauce to make a paste with the mustard, then stir it back into the pan—go slowly at first so as not to overseason. Season with the cayenne and ginger, stir well, and taste the seasoning carefully for balance. Briefly simmer the sauce over low heat to combine the flavors. Cool and chill in a tightly covered jar; it keeps indefinitely. Serve the sauce at room temperature with game and other meats.

MAKES ABOUT 1 CUP

Currant Beurre Rouge

This unusual savory sauce is made by the same principle as beurre blanc or lemon butter sauce, with a subtle balance of sweetness and acid. For a special occasion, it is excellent with lamb and game, also pork and poultry.

6 ounces currants (about 2 cups; you need not remove the stems)
2 shallots, coarsely chopped
1 sprig fresh parsley
½ cup dry red wine
½ cup (1 stick; ¼ pound) unsalted butter, softened
Salt and freshly ground black pepper to taste
Fresh currants on the stem for garnish

Combine the currants, shallots, and parsley in a small nonreactive pan with the wine. Cover, bring to a boil, and simmer over medium-low heat until the currants are soft. Strain the contents of the pan through a fine sieve into a small saucepan. Press lightly on the solids with the back of a spoon to extract most of the juice; do not press hard. Over very low heat, slowly cook the liquid to reduce it to about ¼ cup, skimming any scum from the surface. Let it cool slightly, then 1 tablespoon at a time whisk in the softened butter until all of it is absorbed into the warm liquid. Taste carefully for seasoning and add salt and pepper. The sauce should be deep red, with a glossy sheen.

You can hold the finished sauce, which should be served warm, over warm—not boiling—water. If at all possible, garnish the dish with stems of fresh currants.

MAKES ABOUT ¾ CUP

Currant Jelly

My mother's currant jelly has a tang and intensity that I have never tasted in any other. As a child I can remember her jelly bags dripping, dripping in the pantry, a ritual that followed our annual picking of currants under the hot summer sun—a chore we tried to avoid. Now that fresh currants are so hard to find, we have come to appreciate those bushes. Here is my mother's recipe.

3 pounds currants on the stem, including some unripe ones
2¼ cups sugar

Put enough water in a large, thick-bottomed pan to cover the bottom. Add the currants; do not bother to remove the stems. Bring to a boil, stirring occasionally to keep them from sticking, and cook over low heat until the berries are soft and pulpy, 15 to 20 minutes. Put the currants and liquid into a jelly bag or fine-holed colander, and let the currants drain into a bowl for 12 hours or more. To avoid clouding the jelly, do not press or squeeze the fruit. Discard the solids.

Measure the currant juices and put them back in the clean pan. You will have approximately 3 cups. For every cup of juice, add ¾ cup (or slightly more) of sugar. Heat the mixture over low heat, stirring to dissolve the sugar. Bring to a boil, skimming off any scum with a slotted spoon, and boil hard for about 15 minutes, until the temperature reaches the jelling point of 220°F on a candy thermometer. Test to see if a little jelly spooned on a cold saucer wrinkles when you touch it. Or give it the sheet test by watching drips of jelly fall from a spoon: when two drops become one before falling, it is ready. Spoon the jelly into warm clean jars and sterilize them in a hot water bath (see page 321).

MAKES ABOUT 4 HALF-PINT JARS

Molded Currant Port Ring

Overuse of gelatin in the 1950s banned it from American tables for decades, but molded desserts can make elegant, handsome, and healthful fruit finales, as in this easy ring. You can use raspberries with (or in place of) the currants.

1½ pounds currants
1 cup ruby port or dry red wine
¾ cup sugar
1¾ cup water
2 tablespoons strained fresh lemon juice
2 envelopes unflavored gelatin
Frosted currants (see page 124) on the stem for garnish and a few currant leaves (optional)
Lightly sweetened whipped cream

Put the currants in a pot with just enough water to cover the bottom. You needn't stem them. Bring to a boil, reduce the heat to low, and cook until the berries are soft. Pour everything into a fine sieve set over a bowl and press the pulp with the back of a spoon to extract the juice or, for a crystal-clear jelly, do not press on the fruit at all. You should have about 1½ cups of purée. Discard the skins and stems. Add the port, sugar, ¾ cup water, and lemon juice, and return the mixture to the pot. Cover, bring to a boil, and simmer over low heat until the sugar is dissolved, about 5 minutes. Taste carefully to see if it needs more sweetening.

Put the remaining 1 cup water in a small pan, sprinkle the gelatin over it, and stir to soften for 5 minutes. Dissolve the gelatin over low heat, then stir into the currants. Pour the mixture into a wet 5-cup mold. Cover and chill for several hours, until set. You can make the gelatin a few days ahead, but it will gradually grow firmer, so plan to use the ring in a day or so.

To serve, dip the mold into hot water for a few seconds, place a platter upside down on top, and invert the jelly onto it, giving a few firm shakes to unmold it. If possible, garnish it with stems of frosted fresh currants and fresh currant leaves for greenery. Pass lightly sweetened whipped cream on the side.

MAKES 6 SERVINGS

DATES

In parts of the tropical world, the date palm, *Phoenix dactylifera*, is considered essential to life. The tree grows to a hundred feet in height over as many years, offering welcome shade. After maturity, it produces bunches of berries one to two hundred pounds in weight each year and reaches its greatest productivity at about eighty years of age. Indeed, the tree rarely dies on its own, but topples over from its own weight after a century or so. Besides its fruit, the date is also valuable for its sap, from which alcoholic drinks are made. The leaves are used for woven mats and baskets as well as roof thatching, the trunk for building or firewood, the seeds roasted for coffee or pressed for oil, the residue fed to livestock. The huge leaves are meteorological instruments, changing position according to heat and humidity.

But the most important part of the date is its fruit. Since prehistory it has been a staple in its native northern Africa and Arabia, cultivated between the Tigris and Euphrates since the time of the Mesopotamians. The name date comes from the Greek *dactyl*, meaning finger or toe, which the amber or brown fruit resembles. The Romans liked them stuffed and as a sweetening. For desert nomads, it remains an ideal convenience food either dried or ground into flour. With a very high sugar content—70 percent of the weight of the dried fruit—the date supplies most of the nourishment needed to sustain life in that climate.

Major foreign producers are Iran, Iraq, and Saudi Arabia, with imports depending on the current political situation. Domestic dates are grown mostly in the desert areas of California and Arizona. Dates are available from September through May, with fresh dates obtainable from October through December. There are many varieties of dates, generally dividing into soft fruit with high moisture content, relatively less sugar, and mild flavor (Khadrawy and Halawy); semisoft, with low moisture, higher sugar content, but aromatic flavor (Deglet Noor and Medjool, and the Zahidi to a lesser extent in the West); and dry varieties, hard and with high sugar content, rarely imported into the United States. Here semisoft dates are most popular.

When selecting dates, look for plump, shiny, glossy fruit. Most varieties have smooth skins, but the large dark Medjool are wrinkled, sometimes with a thin white film of invert sugar on the surface that is quite normal. Soft dates should be refrigerated or frozen; dried dates store indefinitely at room temperature. The skins of fresh dates can be peeled or slipped off. Usually the best dates still have their pits; you may wish to cut open the flesh and remove them.

Fresh dates are eaten as a fruit, while semisoft dates are often plumped or steamed in liquid and cooked in sundry ways. As an hors d'oeuvre or end-of-meal sweetmeat, dates are delicious pitted and stuffed with cheese, nuts, or spices. Many of the recipes for figs, apricots, and other dried fruits are also suitable for dates.

Dates are a rich source of potassium, with a fair amount of iron, protein, and fiber, and vitamins A, B, C, and D. With a high sugar content, they are generous in calories, about 230 in three ounces (ten or eleven medium-size dates).

Marsala, Date, and Olive Marinade

This marinade for chicken, pork, or lamb balances sweet dates and Marsala with briny olives and capers. The unusual combination was suggested by my sister, Emily Klarberg, who entertains with great style and ease. She braises the meat in this marinade, cooking it ahead and rewarming it later when her guests arrive. Sometimes she uses dried figs instead of dates.

¼ cup olive oil
8 whole shallots, peeled, roots trimmed, and a shallow x cut in the root ends
1 large clove garlic, minced
1 cup Marsala
1 cup (4 ounces) pitted dates, preferably peeled
8 green Mediterranean olives in brine, pitted and drained
2 tablespoons capers, drained
Two 2-inch strips lemon zest
Juice of ½ lemon (about 2 tablespoons)
½ bay leaf
½ teaspoon dried rosemary, crumbled
Salt and freshly ground black pepper to taste
Lemon slices for garnish

Heat the olive oil in a saucepan and cook the shallots over low heat for about 5 minutes, turning to cook them evenly without letting them brown. Add the rest of the ingredients and simmer over low heat to let the flavors meld, about 10 minutes. Taste carefully for seasoning and balance. Marinate poultry, pork, or lamb in the marinade for several hours or, better still, overnight before cooking. Before serving, discard the lemon zest and bay leaf and reduce the marinade over high heat until syrupy. Spoon some of it over the meat and garnish with lemon slices.

MAKES ABOUT 2½ CUPS

Date Pudding

This old-fashioned pudding was a holiday favorite in Lyn Sleigh Sellers's family, where its sticky consistency endeared itself to all generations. Replace the dates with dried figs, if you like, for a Christmas figgy pudding. Be sure to coat the dates and walnuts in the flour mixture to keep them from sinking to the bottom of the batter.

> 3 large eggs
> 1¼ cups sugar
> 3 tablespoons milk or heavy cream
> ¾ teaspoon pure vanilla extract
> ⅓ cup all-purpose flour
> 1½ teaspoons baking powder
> 1½ cups chopped walnuts, lightly toasted (see page 179)
> 1½ cups dates, cut into fine pieces

Preheat the oven to 325°F. Generously butter an 8 x 8-inch square pan.

Lightly beat the eggs together in a bowl. Gradually add the sugar, milk, and vanilla. Combine the flour and baking powder in another bowl, and toss the walnuts and dates in it to coat each piece. Stir the walnuts, dates, and flour into the egg mixture. Turn the batter into the prepared pan and bake until the pudding is set but still sticky, 40 to 45 minutes. Cool the pudding, cut it across into 9 or 12 pieces, and serve with hard sauce, vanilla ice cream, or whipped cream.

MAKES 9 TO 12 SERVINGS

Date Nut Cinnamon Coffee Cake

Dates give this rich, sweet, aromatic coffee cake a slightly chewy texture.

> ¾ cup (1½ sticks) unsalted butter, softened
> 1 cup white sugar
> 2 large eggs
> 1 cup sour cream
> 1 teaspoon pure vanilla extract
> 2 cups all-purpose flour
> 2 teaspoons baking powder
> 1 teaspoon baking soda
> ½ teaspoon salt
> 1 cup firmly packed dark brown sugar
> 1 tablespoon ground cinnamon
> ⅔ cup chopped dates
> ½ cup chopped pecans, lightly toasted (see page 179)

Preheat the oven to 350°F. Butter a springform 8-inch pan and set aside.

In a large bowl, cream the butter and sugar together until light and fluffy. Stir in the eggs one at a time, then the sour cream and vanilla. In another bowl, sift together the flour, baking powder, baking soda, and salt, and fold them into the moist ingredients until well blended.

Spoon half the batter into the baking pan, spreading it to the edges. In a small bowl, mix together the brown sugar, cinnamon, dates, and pecans. Scatter half the mixture on top of the batter. Repeat with the remaining batter, then the rest of the date mixture. With a round-tipped or palette knife inserted down into the batter, marbleize the layers by swirling the knife around. Bake the cake until it tests done: the cake should shrink from the sides of the pan and a skewer inserted into the center should come out clean, about 1 hour. Serve warm or at room temperature.

MAKES ONE 8-INCH CAKE; 12 SERVINGS

Stuffed Spiced Sugar Dates

These after-dinner sweetmeats, like visions of sugarplums, make excellent holiday offerings. Vary the flavorings to suit your taste.

30 pitted dates
¼ cup brandy
2 tablespoons fresh orange juice
30 blanched whole almonds
¼ cup sugar
1 teaspoon ground cinnamon
Grated zest of 1 orange

Put the dates in the top of a double boiler with the brandy and orange juice. Cover and steam over simmering water, turning once, until the dates are plump and softened and their skins are curling off, 15 to 20 minutes. Let the dates cool somewhat and peel off the skins while they are still warm. Stuff each date with an almond. Mix together the sugar, cinnamon, and orange zest in a small bowl. Roll the stuffed dates in the spiced sugar and let them dry on a plate for a few hours. Pack them layered in waxed paper or aluminum foil in an airtight tin. Let them dry for several days before eating. Kept in an airtight tin, these dates will keep indefinitely.

MAKES 30 STUFFED DATES

FIGS

"The trees were heavy with fruit, beguiling all the senses—the lustrous cherry, the tender apricot, the fig, white or green, sweeter than sugar, the lemons gold lamps against the green." So goes one of Scheherazade's tales in the *Arabian Nights*. Among Persia's luxurious orchard fruits, the fig's high sugar content (12 percent), voluptuous shape, and inverted form—the interior seeds are actually multiple fruits inside a closed receptacle— bring suggestions of sensuality that can truly beguile all the senses.

One of the oldest cultivated plants, the fig (*Ficus carica*), a member of the mulberry family, comes from western Asia and the eastern end of the Mediterranean. Drawings of figs were found in the Giza pyramid of ancient Egypt, and figs are mentioned in Homer as well as the Old Testament, starting with the Garden of Eden. Because they were used for sweetening before sugar refining was understood, figs quickly traveled east to India and China and west all around the Mediterranean.

From the inedible fruit of the small wild fig tree, or caprifig, come the many hundreds of varieties available today. The earliest cultivated fig is what we now call the Smyrna fig, originally from Turkey. Most figs today are self-pollinating common figs, which enjoy a far wider geographical range. The Romans took the common fig north as far as Britain and, although it lapsed into obscurity after their departure, the monasteries revived it during the sixteenth century. At about the same time it was taken to the New World, where it thrived in California. The Spanish missions were instrumental in establishing it there, and the Mission fig, a black common fig, is one such variety.

The fig enjoys long warm summers that are not too wet and moderate winters. It adapts well to various soils. The common fig produces two crops, in early and late summer. Much of the harvest is preserved in syrup, relishes, and jams, or else dried. Since the fresh fruit is a luxury outside its areas of cultivation, dried figs are important commercially. Fig trees often grow in a climate suitable to olives, almonds, citrus, and grapes and, not surprisingly, figs go uncommonly well with all of them.

The Smyrna fig, called Calimyrna in California, is pale golden amber and large. Eaten both dried and fresh, it is considered an excellent fig. The Mission fig, also known as Black Mission and Franciscana, is dark purple with a red interior and fine fresh taste. Dried, it becomes small and black, with an intense, dark, almost burnt flavor. The light green Kadota fig is usually canned in syrup. Adriatic and Genoa are other good varieties, but unlike other fruit, we don't often bother to recognize figs by their varietal names.

When choosing fresh figs, look for soft, dry fruit. Those that have begun to shrivel will be especially sweet. Avoid any that smell sour. Unripe figs, which exude a milky liquid from the stem, should be left at room temperature to mature. Ripe figs can be held briefly in the refrigerator, to be used soon after purchase. To prepare them, simply snip off the stems.

Figs are delicious with creamy bland cheeses, honey, citrus, nuts, and spices, all recalling the fruit's Mediterranean and Asian heredity. Fine ham makes an excellent accompaniment to figs, whether draped with paper-thin prosciutto or grilled with good-quality bacon. Braise figs along with lamb, pork, and duck for a richly complementary sauce. Dry or fortified wine is a good cooking medium. Dried figs, of course, can be cooked with all these foods, either mixed into stuffings or hollowed and stuffed themselves. When plumping dried figs, you may prefer to steep them in tepid liquid rather than poach them in order to retain their flavor. Be sure to use the rich steeping liquid again in another recipe. Dried figs can be used in many recipes instead of other dried fruits, especially apricots, prunes, and dates.

Very nutritious, dried figs are high in potassium, calcium, magnesium, copper, and iron, and are a rich source of fiber. One half cup of dried figs contains 220 calories. One fresh fig contains about thirty-seven calories.

Fig Tapénade

Tapénade, a thick Provençal paste whose name derives from the dialect word for capers, comes in many piquant variations. Here dried figs add a mellow depth of flavor. Serve it as an hors d'oeuvre with pita or other thin crisp bread, if possible on a brightly colored plate. Cream cheese or fresh chèvre goes very well.

4 ounces dried figs, stemmed and coarsely chopped
¼ cup dry white wine or vermouth
2 tablespoons brandy
2 tablespoons fresh lemon juice
Half a 2-ounce can flat anchovy fillets, drained
1 clove garlic, minced
½ cup black Mediterranean olives, stoned
2 tablespoons capers, drained
⅓ cup extra virgin olive oil, or to taste
Freshly ground black pepper to taste

Cover the figs with boiling water and let stand about 30 minutes to plump them; drain well, discarding the water. Or steep them overnight in the white wine, brandy, and lemon juice, saving the liquid for the tapénade.

Put all the ingredients except the pepper in a food processor and combine until fairly smooth. Keep some texture. Give a good twist or two with the pepper mill and taste carefully for balance, adjusting as needed. If the texture is too thick, thin with additional oil. Cover tightly and chill. (This may be done up to a week ahead; it keeps even longer.) Serve the tapénade at room temperature with pita or other thin crisp bread, or spread it on split rounds of pita, crumble a little chèvre on top, and toast under a broiler until melted.

MAKES ABOUT 1½ CUPS

Grilled Figs and Pancetta

Serve as an elegant first course or accompaniment to grilled meat or poultry, or serve in half portions as an hors d'oeuvre. For more servings, simply multiply the ingredients.

4 large fresh figs
2 slices pancetta or strips of good bacon
A little Marsala or sherry

Adjust the rack to about 6 inches from the flame and preheat the grill.

Snip off the stems and cut the figs in half lengthwise through the skin. Thread them on skewers with the pancetta, wrapping the strips back and forth on either side of the figs like a ribbon. Brush the figs with the Marsala. Grill the figs and pancetta, turning the skewers to cook the pancetta evenly and baste the figs with their melting fat. Timing varies—watch very closely to avoid burning. Serve as soon as the pancetta is golden and crisp.

MAKES 4 APPETIZER SERVINGS

Figs Poached in Madeira

Dried figs, alone or mixed with other fruit, take well to poaching in wine, either red, white, or fortified, as here. Add the sugar at the end, to avoid toughening the dried figs; use less sugar for a savory side dish for meat.

12 ounces dried figs, stemmed
½ cup Madeira
One 1-inch stick cinnamon
3 whole cloves
One 2-inch strip orange zest
1 to 2 tablespoons sugar, or to taste
2 tablespoons pine nuts or other nuts, lightly toasted (see page 179)
Plain yogurt, labneh (see page 187), sour cream, or heavy cream
Sprig fresh mint for garnish

Pour water over the figs in a small saucepan to cover. Soak the fruit for several hours or overnight; if time is short, pour boiling water over the figs and let steep until cool. Add the Madeira, cinnamon stick, cloves, and orange zest, and poach over low heat until the figs are tender, about 30 minutes. Remove the figs with a slotted spoon and put them in a serving bowl or dishes; discard the spices. Add the sugar to the poaching liquid and boil down until syrupy and concentrated in flavor. Pour the hot syrup over the figs. (This can be done up to a week ahead, the dish covered and chilled.)

Serve the figs warm or chilled with the toasted pine nuts scattered on top. Pass plain yogurt, sour cream, or heavy cream on the side. A sprig of mint adds color and fragrance.

MAKES 4 TO 6 SERVINGS

Figs with Marsala and Mascarpone

This simple dessert is equally good with Madeira and chèvre. You can scatter a few toasted hazelnuts on top to gild the lily.

3 tablespoons sugar
¼ cup water
¼ cup Marsala
1 teaspoon grated fresh lemon zest
4 fresh figs
1 ounce mascarpone (about 3 tablespoons)
3 tablespoons cream or milk

Preheat the oven to 350°F. Combine the sugar and water in a small saucepan, bring to a boil, covered, and let boil until the sugar is dissolved, about 5 minutes. You should have approximately ¼ cup of syrup. Stir in the Marsala and lemon zest.

Snip the stems off the figs and cut an X from the top down almost to the bottoms. Press up from the bottom to spread the figs open. Spoon the Marsala syrup over the figs. Bake the figs until tender, about 20 minutes. While they are cooking, mash together the mascarpone and cream. When the figs are done, place them in serving dishes, dab some of the cheese mixture into the center of each fig flower, and spoon the syrup around. Serve warm or at room temperature.

MAKES 4 SERVINGS

Baked Figs in Brandy

Figs are so beautiful on their own that the simplest preparations, such as this, are quite enough.

12 fresh figs
1 teaspoon grated orange zest
¼ cup fresh orange juice
¼ cup brandy or port
2 tablespoons honey

Preheat the oven to 350°F. Cut the stem ends off the figs to form a base to stand on, and cut the figs across in half. Set them rounded-side down in a shallow ovenproof dish just wide enough to hold them in one layer. Mix together the remaining ingredients and pour over the figs. Bake until tender, about 20 minutes. The fig juice will mingle with the liquids to form a red syrup. Shortly before serving, divide the figs among the serving plates and spoon the syrup over and around. Serve warm or at room temperature.

MAKES 4 TO 6 SERVINGS

Mina's Turkish Fig and Walnut Dessert

This simple but exotic dessert, *incir tatlisi*, comes from my friend Mina Artuner Gürpinar. Labneh, or yogurt cheese (see page 187), goes very well with it.

12 dried figs (about 6 ounces)
½ cup crushed walnuts
1 tablespoon sugar
½ teaspoon ground cinnamon
12 whole cloves

Cut off the stems of the figs well below the tip. Insert a finger into the stem hole and push out the sides of the fig until you have formed a little bowl. Mix together the walnuts, sugar, and cinnamon and stuff the fig cavities with the mixture, tamping it down as if stuffing a pipe. Stick 1 clove into the outside of each fig. Pack the figs together tightly in a pan or casserole just large enough to hold them upright in one layer. Add enough water to come one third of the way up the sides of the figs and cover tightly with a lid or aluminum foil. Make sure the figs do not tip over. Simmer over low heat for 30 minutes or more, replenishing the water every ten minutes or so as the figs absorb it. Let them steep for 15 minutes more off the heat. Serve the figs, two or three for each serving, at room temperature.

MAKES 4 TO 6 SERVINGS

Cake Pique-nique
(DRIED FRUIT CAKE)

This picnic cake, from my Swiss friend Anne-Dominique Spertini, is based on a recipe of Betty Bossi, the Swiss counterpart of Betty Crocker. It is typical of the traditional Swiss-German fare her name implies, with no leavening or fat but chockful of dried rather than candied fruit. Wrapped and chilled, it keeps for a month or more. Substitute other dried fruit, Anne-Dominique suggests, firmly packed brown sugar for the white, or whole-wheat flour for half the white. Serve it sliced and toasted for breakfast or tea.

> 1 cup sugar
> Pinch of salt
> 4 large eggs, lightly beaten
> 1¼ cups plus 2 tablespoons all-purpose flour
> 2 cups milk
> ¼ cup whiskey or kirsch
> 1½ cups (6 ounces) chopped nuts, lightly toasted (see page 179)
> 1 generous cup (6 ounces) golden raisins (sultanas)
> 6 ounces dried apricots, cut into strips
> 6 ounces dried figs, stemmed and cut into strips
> Grated zest of 1 lemon
> Dried fruit for decoration (optional)

Preheat the oven to 350°F. Line a 9 x 5 x 3-inch loaf pan with parchment paper and butter it well.

Put the sugar and salt in a large bowl and mix in the eggs. Gradually stir in the flour, then the milk and whiskey, blending the ingredients to make a smooth batter. Finally stir in the nuts, dried fruit, and lemon zest. Turn the mixture into the prepared pan and bake for 30 minutes; lower the heat to 325°F and bake until it tests done, 60 to 75 minutes more. If you like, decorate the cake halfway through baking by lightly pressing dried fruit into the top in a row, then return to the oven to finish baking. Cool it on a rack and store tightly wrapped in aluminum foil in the refrigerator.

MAKES 1 LARGE LOAF

Fig Frangipane Tart

Frangipane, a rich almond custard, can be baked over or under many fruits in addition to figs.

One 9-inch pâte sucrée tart shell (see page 35), baked
8 ounces fresh figs, stemmed and cut in half across

FOR THE FRANGIPANE
¼ cup (½ stick) unsalted butter, softened
¼ cup sugar
1 large egg, separated, at room temperature
2 ounces almonds, finely ground (⅓ to ½ cup ground)
1½ tablespoons all-purpose flour
¼ teaspoon freshly grated nutmeg

Preheat the oven to 375°F.

In a medium-large bowl, cream together the butter and sugar until light, then stir in the egg yolk. Combine the almonds, flour, and nutmeg in a small bowl, and stir into the butter mixture. In another small bowl whisk the egg white until stiff peaks form, then fold it into the custard. Spread the frangipane into the shell. Place the figs on top of the frangipane layer in the tart shell, cut-side up. Bake until the frangipane is pale golden and set, 15 to 20 minutes. Serve the tart warm or chilled.

MAKES ONE 9-INCH TART; 6 TO 8 SERVINGS

GOOSEBERRIES

The whiskery stubble on the gooseberry, *Ribes grossularia*, has given it a bad name. Whatever the derivation of the word gooseberry, and there are many explanations, it has become a term of disparagement. It means either the devil, "Old Scratch" himself, or someone who won't get lost when two lovers wish to be alone together. But the gooseberry is beloved by English country people. In an old wives' tale, for instance, a wart will vanish if pricked by a gooseberry spine that has passed through a wedding ring.

The gooseberry is among the first fruits of spring and summer to be picked, especially in the north, where it thrives in a cool, moist climate. It is best eaten early, green and unripe, when its tartness provides much of its flavor. Of the many varieties—large or small, smooth or spiny, transparent or opaque—some ripen into white, yellow, pink, or red berries suitable for eating raw or in desserts during midsummer, but the earlier acid ones are still considered tops for taste.

Like its close cousin the currant (and also host to the white pine rust disease), the gooseberry has found little favor in southern regions. In France, almost the only gooseberry dish is a sauce for mackerel in which its puckery tartness balances the fish's oiliness. In fact, in French the gooseberry is designated by the name of that dish, *groseille à maquereau*, meaning mackerel currant.

When buying fresh gooseberries in the market, select those that are firm and shiny; those found in supermarkets, where they are increasingly available from New Zealand, are usually smooth, like large glass marbles. They keep well in the refrigerator, gradually ripening further. The berries freeze well spread in one layer on trays, then packed in containers; use them directly from the freezer without thawing. You can also keep gooseberries in syrup. Unless they are going to be puréed, top and tail them—that is, remove the spiny axis from top and bottom with scissors or knife—so as not to spike your guests.

In England, gooseberry fool is a classic dish and cream is a natural and complementary companion. Loaded with pectin, the berries are excellent in jellies and preserves of all kinds. Puréed gooseberries in a velouté sauce accompany chicken and fish, with a hint of fennel, and whole berries make a contrasting stuffing for rich goose, pork, and fish. Gooseberries are delicious in pies and pastries, perhaps combined with apples. The English enjoy the subtle muscat scent of elderflowers with gooseberries.

Gooseberries, like currants, are high in vitamin C, also in potassium and fiber. One cup contains about seventy calories.

Savory Gooseberry Sauce

This tart, refreshing sauce makes an unusual accompaniment to oily fish such as mackerel and salmon. Like applesauce, it is also good with rich pork.

6 ounces green gooseberries (about 1¼ cups)
4½ teaspoons sugar, or to taste
1 teaspoon butter
1 teaspoon flour
Salt and freshly ground black pepper to taste
2 teaspoons chopped fresh fennel leaves

In a small pan, stew the gooseberries over low heat with 1 tablespoon water until the berries soften and the skins burst, about 10 minutes. Pass the fruit and juice through a nonreactive sieve to remove the skins and seeds. Stir the sugar into the purée.

Melt the butter in another small saucepan, add the flour, and cook over low heat, stirring, for 2 minutes. Add ½ cup water, bring to a boil, still stirring, then simmer over low heat until smooth and somewhat thickened. Add the gooseberry purée, salt, and pepper, and simmer together to form a smooth sauce. Stir in the fennel just before serving.

MAKES ABOUT ¾ CUP

Gooseberry Jam

Whether you use green or red gooseberries, this jam is rich and flavorful. If you have a ready source for the berries, you may want to make it in larger quantity. Just continue to use similar proportions of berries and sugar.

1 pound gooseberries (about 3½ cups)
2 cups sugar

Put the berries in a heavy pot with about ½ cup water, enough to cover the bottom. Cover and cook slowly to soften the berries, then gradually add the sugar and cook until it is dissolved. Return the liquid to a boil and continue boiling, stirring toward the end to prevent burning, until it reaches the setting point of 220°F. Spoon the jam into clean, warm half-pint jars, cover, and cool. Process it in a hot water bath (see page 321) for long keeping.

MAKES 2 OR MORE HALF-PINT JARS

Gooseberries in Light Lemon Syrup

This is a good way to keep gooseberries, especially the ripe red ones, without freezing them. You can process them in jars in a hot water bath (see page 321), if you wish, to store on the shelf. Combine these gooseberries with other fruits in sweet compotes or toppings for ice cream and pound cake. Like sour cherries or cranberries in a sweet-and-sour sauce, add the gooseberries with some of their syrup to the pan juices of sautéed or roast meat; or purée the berries, adding a little syrup, for a pleasing alternative to applesauce; or stir them into a savory bread stuffing for meat roasts.

½ pound red gooseberries (about 1½ cups)
½ cup sugar
1 cup water
1 strip lemon zest
1 tablespoon fresh lemon juice

Carefully top and tail the gooseberries; this should make a small hole or two in each berry, which will keep them from losing their shape in the hot syrup.

Meanwhile, combine the sugar, water, lemon zest, and juice in a small nonreactive saucepan. Bring to a boil, and boil for 5 minutes to dissolve the sugar. Pour the syrup while still hot over the berries, then let them cool to room temperature. Discard the lemon zest. Cover and chill.

MAKES 2 CUPS

Gooseberry Fool

This English dessert, a beautiful celadon color, makes a refreshing finish to a simple country meal. Traditionally, the gooseberry skins were left in the fool to impart their flavor, but contemporary tastes prefer them removed.

1 pound gooseberries (about 3½ cups)
About ½ cup sugar
1 cup heavy cream
Freshly grated nutmeg

Put the gooseberries in a small nonreactive saucepan with just enough water to cover the bottom. Bring to a gentle boil over medium heat, reduce the heat to low, and cook, stirring once in a while, until the berries have turned opaque and pale whitish. Purée the berries in a food processor and strain the purée through a nonreactive sieve, pressing on the fruit with the back of a spoon. Gradually sweeten the purée to taste with sugar, cover, and chill. At serving time, swirl the cream into the gooseberry purée, as much or as little as you like, dust with a little nutmeg, and serve.

MAKES 4 SERVINGS

GRAPEFRUIT

The grapefruit is a relatively new citrus fruit, first observed in Jamaica in the early nineteenth century. It may have come about as an accidental cross between the pomelo (or pummelo, also called shaddock) and the citron or orange. The grapefruit, *Citrus paradisi*, was classified as a separate species in 1830, soon after it was introduced to Florida. It is large and juicy, relatively bitter and thin-skinned compared to its pomelo parent. The grapefruit's name, from the French *grappe*, meaning cluster, describes its habit of growing on the tree in bunches, like giant grapes.

The Duncan grapefruit, seedy but flavorful, and the Marsh, seedless but less flavorful, are the two main varieties. There are now pink cultivars of each, and growers are developing deeper red pigmentation. In this country, Florida and Texas lead grapefruit production, followed by California and Arizona. Grapefruit is available year-round, but reaches its peak from January through April, when its bracing flavor provides a spring tonic.

Grapefruit's nutritional benefits help to inspire our sense of well-being. Low in sodium and calories—with fifty calories in a half you hardly need to count them—grapefruit is high in vitamin C, calcium, potassium, and fiber. Spokesmen for the industry say that, despite the public's perception to the contrary, there is no difference in sweetness between white and pink varieties, but that the rind of pink grapefruit contains more beta carotene, which is converted into vitamin A in the body. Beta-carotene research has shown that it may help to prevent cancer. In addition, researchers recently observed that grapefruit juice, either fresh or frozen, somehow helps the absorption of medicine taken with it, which orange juice or water does not.

When buying grapefruit, look for heavy, thin-skinned specimens with smooth rinds and a round shape. Dark specks or green tinges have no effect on quality. Unless you plan to use them right away, store them loose in the refrigerator, removed from plastic wrapping, where they should keep well for as long as a few weeks.

Half a grapefruit for breakfast is hard to improve upon, especially with the juicy sweet seedless varieties recently developed. To the delight of the cook, a good citrus spoon eliminates the need to separate the flesh from the membrane. Fresh sections and juice are luscious in fruit compotes, salads, seviches, and sherbets. After you have consumed the inside, the tangy zest and rind are delicious in conserves and confections.

The pomelo looks very much like a large grapefruit, its more common descendant. The largest of the citrus family, the round pomelo may protrude somewhat at the stem end. The skin is yellow, perhaps with a cast of green or pink, very thick and spongy, and easily removed. The flesh is drier than that of grapefruit, and the large juice sacs within are more separate from each other. The flesh is usually sweeter and drier than grapefruit's, without any bitterness. Pomelo, which is available in late winter, can be used like grapefruit. The skin is particularly valuable for preserves of one sort or another.

Broiled Spiced Grapefruit

This is refreshing any time of day, to begin or end a meal. You can also spread a little maple syrup over the cut surface and caramelize it under the broiler. To let the maple flavor come through, omit the spices.

1 grapefruit, cut across in half
1 tablespoon dark brown sugar
¼ teaspooon ground allspice or other spice, or to taste

Preheat the broiler. Set the grapefruit halves in an ovenproof dish. (If the grapefruit half won't stand level, cut a thin slice off the bottom to help it do so.) Mix together the brown sugar and allspice, and spread the mixture over the surface of the fruit. Run the grapefruit under the broiler for 3 to 5 minutes, until the sugar is bubbly and caramelized—watch closely.

MAKES 2 SERVINGS

Shrimp and Grapefruit Salad

Place the pink crescent shrimp and grapefruit sections to accent each other.

1 large pink grapefruit
½ pound large shrimp (about 12)
¼ cup olive oil
Salt and freshly ground black pepper to taste
2 Belgian endives
1 bunch watercress
2 scallions (green and white parts), thinly sliced

With a sharp serrated knife, cut the rind off the grapefruit in a spiral, removing all the white membrane and pith but as little flesh as possible. Cut out the individual sections and set them aside (there should be about 12). Squeeze as much juice as you can from the interior membrane and the inside of the peeled rind; discard the solids and reserve the juice (about ¼ cup).

Put the shrimp in a small pot, add water to cover them, and bring to a boil. Cover and poach until they turn pink, about 3 minutes. Drain and shell the shrimp, deveining them if necessary. Mix together in a nonreactive bowl the reserved grapefruit juice, olive oil, salt, and pepper; taste to correct the seasoning and balance. Steep the shrimp in the marinade, turning them a couple of times, for an hour or two, covered in the refrigerator.

Remove any ragged outer leaves from the Belgian endives and wipe the heads with a damp cloth; do not wash them. Cut off a thin slice from the bottom and remove the leaves whole, slicing off more of the bottom as the leaves work up the core. Lay several of the leaves on each serving plate and place sprigs of watercress between. Drain the shrimp, saving the marinade, and arrange them and the grapefruit sections on the endive. Scatter the scallions on top, drizzle the remaining marinade over all, and serve.

MAKES 4 TO 6 SERVINGS

Grapefruit and Mango Salad

The exotic lushness of mangoes, like peaches, pineapple, and melon all in one, perfectly complements the taste of grapefruit. Sweeten with a little ruby grenadine.

2 grapefruit, preferably ruby
1 fully ripe mango or papaya
¼ cup grenadine (see page 254)

With a sharp serrated knife, peel the grapefruit in a spiral pattern, removing the skin and membrane. Cut out and reserve the individual sections. Squeeze and reserve any juice from the membrane.

Stand the mango upright on end and cut two parallel slices lengthwise on either side of the flat central seed. Peel or pull off the skin from the two outer sections and cut the flesh into slices. Peel the central seed section and slice off the flesh around the seed. Arrange the mango and grapefruit slices on individual serving plates, showing off their colors to best effect. Pour over the reserved grapefruit juice. Just before serving, drizzle about a tablespoon of grenadine over each plate.

MAKES 4 SERVINGS

Salmon Grapefruit Seviche with Avocado

This makes a perfect starter for an early spring party because it literally cooks itself, freeing you for other tasks.

One ½-pound salmon fillet
2 pink grapefruit
1 bunch arugula or other sharp greens
1 medium-size ripe avocado, halved lengthwise, pitted, peeled, and sliced
3 scallions (green and white parts), sliced across at an angle
¼ cup olive oil, or to taste
Salt and freshly ground black pepper to taste

Remove the skin of the salmon and pull out the row of pin bones with tweezers, or have the fishmonger do this for you. You should have about 6 ounces of skinless, boneless fillet. With a sharp knife, at an angle almost parallel to the cutting board, cut the salmon into very thin slices. Lay them in a shallow nonreactive dish. Squeeze the juice from half a grapefruit and pour over the salmon to cover. If it doesn't cover, squeeze the other half. Marinate for an hour or more (if more, cover and refrigerate). The acid will "cook" the salmon flesh; in about an hour, when the flesh is opaque, it is ready.

With a sharp serrated knife, remove the peel from the second grapefruit, taking all the pith and membrane and as little flesh as possible. Carefully cut out the sections and set aside.

To serve, drain the sliced salmon and pat dry. Divide the arugula between the serving dishes and lay the salmon slices on top. Alternate grapefruit and avocado crescents around the salmon, and scatter the scallions on top. Drizzle with olive oil, season with salt and a couple of twists of grated pepper, and serve.

MAKES 4 SERVINGS AS A FIRST COURSE OR LIGHT SALAD

Sautéed Shrimp with Grapefruit and Avocado

This combination of curved shapes plays off colors and flavors.

1 grapefruit
1 medium-size ripe avocado
3 tablespoons olive oil
3 scallions (green and white parts), sliced
1 clove garlic, minced
1¼ pounds medium-size raw shrimp, shelled and deveined
3 tablespoons chopped fresh coriander (cilantro)
Salt and freshly ground black pepper to taste

With a serrated knife, peel the grapefruit so that no white pith remains. Cut out the individual sections and set aside. Shortly before serving, peel, pit, and slice the avocado.

In a large skillet over low heat, heat the olive oil and cook the scallions and garlic, stirring, until wilted, about 3 minutes. Raise the heat to medium and stir-fry the shrimp about 3 minutes more, just until they turn pink. Stir in the coriander, salt, and pepper. Divide the shrimp among four warm serving plates, and surround them with the avocado and grapefruit crescents. Serve at once.

MAKES 4 SERVINGS

Grapefruit Orange Lime Marmalade

Since the bitter Seville oranges traditionally used in marmalade are hard to find even in their brief late-winter season, this citrus combination offers another tangy fruit conserve. The citrus should weigh about two pounds total, and you can vary the types, using tangerines in place of oranges, for example, or lemons for limes.

    1 large grapefruit
    2 oranges
    2 limes
    3½ cups sugar

Cut up the grapefruit, oranges, and limes, saving the seeds. Slice the peels into thick or thin pieces, as you prefer, and chop up the pith and flesh. Tie the seeds in a cheesecloth bag (the pectin in the seeds will help the marmalade to jell). Put everything—peels, seeds, flesh, and juice—into a large heavy-bottomed nonreactive pot and add water to cover. Cover, bring slowly to a boil over medium heat, and cook, uncovered, until the volume is reduced by about a third, 30 to 40 minutes. The citrus peels should have turned translucent.

Fish out the cheesecloth bag, let the liquid drip from it back into the pot without pressing, and discard the bag. Slowly add the sugar, stirring over low heat to dissolve it. Raise the heat, bring the syrup to a hard boil, and let it boil until it reaches the jelling point of 220°F on a candy thermometer. Test it on a cold saucer—once cold it should wrinkle when you push your finger through it. Skim any scum from the surface, and let the marmalade sit for 10 minutes (to keep the peels from rising). Sterilize the marmalade in half-pint jars to store on a cupboard shelf (see page 321). Let the marmalade mellow for at least a week before opening.

MAKES ABOUT 5 HALF-PINT JARS

Winter Fruit Compote

Ordinary fruits enlivened with crystallized ginger combine in this dish, suitable for every meal.

    1 grapefruit
    1 orange

1 apple, cored, quartered, and thinly sliced
1 banana, peeled and sliced
1 small bunch seedless red grapes, halved
2 tablespoons chopped crystallized ginger (available in Oriental and specialty food stores)

Peel and section the grapefruit and orange, squeezing any juice from inside the rind. Put the juice and sections in a nonreactive bowl and chill. Not long before serving, add the sliced apple and banana, stirring to coat the cut flesh with the citrus juice to prevent it from discoloring. Stir in the halved grapes. Spoon the fruit salad into serving dishes and top with the crystallized ginger.

MAKES 3 TO 4 SERVINGS

Grapefruit Champagne Sherbet

This sherbet makes an elegant, light, and refreshing ending to any dinner. Make it ahead when you happen to have a leftover glass of champagne or find grapefruit on sale, then store the fruit-wine syrup in ice cubes, smoothing them into the finished sherbet when an occasion presents itself. Grapefruit with deep red flesh will give a beautiful rose color, pink flesh a pale blush.

3 large pink or ruby grapefruit (about 3 pounds)
Grated zest of 1 grapefruit
¾ cup plus 2 tablespoons sugar, or to taste, depending on the sweetness of the grapefruit
1 cup champagne (it can be flat)

Squeeze the juice from the 3 grapefruit, scraping the inside with a spoon to remove as much pulp (but not membrane) as possible. Strain the juice through a fine sieve, pressing on the pulp with the back of a spoon. Mix the sugar with the grapefruit juice, stirring every once in a while. The acid will dissolve the sugar in 20 minutes or so. Stir in the champagne.

Freeze the mixture in a sorbetière or ice cream machine according to the manufacturer's directions. Or freeze the sherbet according to the directions on page 307. Serve the sherbet with more champagne in glasses, if you like, but this is unnecessary.

MAKES ABOUT 1 QUART

Candied Grapefruit Peel

This makes an excellent after-dinner confection or holiday present, especially if you combine various kinds of citrus candied in the same way. Save the thick peels as you use the flesh for other purposes, and store them in a plastic bag, refrigerated, until you have enough.

To remove some of the bitterness from the grapefruit, you can initially blanch the peels once or twice in fresh water, but I think the tingle is much of the pleasure.

3 large grapefruit, preferably pink-fleshed
3 cups sugar plus more for dusting
2 cups water

Completely remove the inner flesh and membrane of the grapefruit. If the skin is very thick, cut some of the inner white pith away. Quarter the grapefruit peel and cut each quarter into quarters (or into any shape you wish), to measure about 5 cups.

Put the peels in a pot and cover generously with cold water. Bring to a boil and cook until the peel is tender, about 20 minutes. Drain the peels.

In a heavy-bottomed pot, combine the sugar and water, bring to a boil, and let boil until the sugar is dissolved, about 5 minutes. Add the grapefruit peels and boil slowly over medium low heat, until the peel is nearly translucent and the syrup mostly absorbed. This may take as long as an hour. Toward the end, watch to see that the sugar does not scorch; if necessary, lower the heat. When the peels are translucent, lift them out with a slotted spoon and put them on a pan spread with sugar. When cool, roll the peels in the sugar to coat them and let dry overnight in the sugar. Store the candied citrus peels in tightly closed tins where they will keep indefinitely. Use the leftover sand sugar in citrus desserts.

GRAPES

   Grapes have grown on earth for so long that they were probably well established before the advent of man. The fruit of the vine originated somewhere near Mount Ararat by the Caspian Sea in western Asia and gradually spread over much of the temperate world. Beyond Asia Minor and the Mediterranean, grapes reached the Neolithic Swiss lake villages, and an ocean away the American Indians also enjoyed them two millennia B.C.

Man has cultivated the fruit long enough for it to have played a part in many ancient religions. In Genesis, after the ark landed on Mount Ararat, Noah planted a vineyard, drank the wine, and became drunk. The Egyptians, who by 2440 B.C. depicted grapes in mosaics and tomb paintings, later buried King Tutankhamen with grape juice. The hanging gardens of Babylon on the shores of the Euphrates included grapevines.

To the ancient Greeks, Dionysus was the god of wine. He was associated not only with wine, fertility, and drunkenness, but also with the fine arts. Ever since, the "luscious clusters of the vine," as Andrew Marvell described it, have continued to inspire music, dance, and drama, indeed, all the arts.

During the Roman Empire, Bacchus took over many of the characteristics of Dionysus. Like the Greeks, the Romans particularly favored grapes. Pliny, the natural historian, described ninety-one distinct varieties of grapes and fifty different wines. Along with honey, raisins were one of the few sources of sugar available until the sugarcane industry was developed many centuries later. As their empire spread, Romans introduced viticulture to northern Europe.

In the New World, Leif Eriksson and his Norsemen found wild grapes so abundant that they named the land they discovered in the eleventh century Vinland. Much later, American colonists were strongly encouraged to plant grapes. Lord Delaware and Thomas Jefferson, among others, tried to grow European grapes unsuited to the climate's humid summers and severe winters. In time, native species were found that could resist insects and disease. At missions west of the Rocky Mountains, Spanish padres planted European grapes for making sacramental wines, and they fared well in the dry climate. By the late eighteenth century, California vineyards were established from San Diego to the Sonoma Valley.

Grapes grow best in a warm climate with long, dry, sunny summers and cool winters.

The best soil is not too rich. Old-World grapes, *Vitis vinifera*, cannot tolerate much moisture, but New-World grapes, *V. labrusca*, can bear greater humidity and colder winters. The vine climbs walls and guidewires by its curling tendrils, which are themselves edible. The handsome green leaves can be eaten wrapped around food. Even the woody prunings can be burned to flavor grilled food. The hanging clusters of flowers develop into grapes that are pale green, red, or blue-black. Beneath the skin, the flesh is usually light green, so the color of the juice depends mainly on whether the skins are included during pressing.

Table grapes are available year-round, but most of the supply is from June through January. California is by far the leading domestic producer. Chile exports substantial quantities from January through May. Of the thousands of grape varieties, only about ten are significant as table grapes. The more complex flavor of wine grapes is excellent for cooking, but they are usually hard to obtain.

Of the green varieties of table grapes, Thompson Seedless (called sultana in Britain) are available from June through November. They are medium in size, pale green to gold, firm yet tender, with a sweet, uncomplicated taste. They are the most popular table grape, but can be made into dessert wine and are the usual California grape for raisins. Calmeria grapes are large, pale green, with a firm pulp and thick rough skin (October to April). Other green grapes are the small, juicy, seedless, waxy-looking Perlette (May through July); Italia Muscat, with its huge grapes, thick skins, and aromatic, rich, sweet flavor (August through November); Almeria, with fairly large, pale green seeded fruit with tough skins (October through April); and the Niagara, a pale native grape, large, seeded, and sweet (September).

Of red table grapes, the Flame Seedless is fairly new and fast growing in popularity (June to September). These small grapes are favored for their appealing color, rich sweet flavor, juicy, crisp texture, thin skins, and lack of seeds. They also offer an alternative to the sometimes ubiquitous and bland Thompson Seedless. Tokay grapes (also called Flame Tokay) are large and deep red, with a subtle flavor, fairly tough skins, seeds, and firm flesh (September into later fall). Emperor grapes are large, firm, light red to purple, with seeds and thick skins (September through February).

Other red varieties include Ruby Seedless (August through January), Red Globe, with very large berries (fall), Christmas Rose (August into fall), Red Malaga (August and September), and Catawba, with red-purple skin and the distinctly sweet flavor typical of native varieties (October). Delaware (September through November), a small pink thin-skinned grape, is one of the native American varieties used both for eating and wine. A newcomer is the tiny sweet champagne variety whose bunches make very attractive desserts and still-life displays (mid July through August).

Of the blue varieties, Concord grapes are large, round, and purple, with a pronounced bloom on the skin and skins that slip off when squeezed (September and October). They have a "foxy" aroma, big seeds, and more acidity than most varieties. Their fragility in shipping sends most of the crop, best found at local farmstands, into juice, jellies, and wine not preferred by connoisseurs. Concord grapes come from a cross of the wild native eastern *labrusca* grape first cultivated in Concord, Massachusetts, and they are grown mostly in the Northeast.

Among other blue table grapes, Ribier are deep purple, fat, firm grapes with large seeds and thick skins, lower in acid (August into February). Exotic are very similar (available in the summer months). Beauty Seedless are black, sweet, and medium-size (May through July).

Whatever the variety, look for plump, firm berries well attached to pliable green stems. Grapes of uniform size on full bunches are best. Any remaining bloom shows minimal handling. For green grapes, a touch of yellow or amber indicates sweetness. For red, choose bunches that are mostly red with no greenish tinge. For blue, look for deep rich color. Bunches packed in tissue are usually the finest; plastic indicates medium quality, no packaging shows less care.

Store grapes loosely wrapped for ventilation and well chilled to keep them fresh for a week or two. Wash them gently in cold water and drain before serving. Grapes that have fallen off their stems are sweetest, so use them right away unless they are overripe.

Bunches make a beautiful addition to the fruit bowl and a handsome centerpiece for any table, casual or formal. Grape scissors make it easy to remove a stem without ruining the look of the whole bunch. Make grapes available to children—the fruit is a handy, healthy snack far preferable to junk food. In hot weather, grapes are thirst-quenching as well as tasty. They make a sophisticated finale to dinner when paired with interesting cheeses, perhaps also nuts, other fruit, and dessert wine. Remember this the next time you are pressed for time when entertaining.

As for cooking, although peeling grapes is tedious, it can refine an otherwise simple dish and elevate it far above the everyday. Add some to any fruit salad, or fold a few into creamed chicken. Americans are not in the habit of cooking with grapes, but their juice, accented with wine, can give subtlety and depth to sauces without cloying sweetness. On desserts, frosted grapes can look magical.

Dried grapes in the form of raisins demand to be treated as altogether another foodstuff. In the Middle East fruit has been preserved by drying in the sun for untold centuries. Europeans encountering it on the Crusades recognized its keeping qualities as well as the intensely sweet, tangy richness lacking in its fresh counterpart. Returning home, they incorporated dried fruit and spices into their cooking, giving the sweet and savory taste of the eastern Mediterranean from which many European dishes today descend.

California's San Joaquin Valley produces virtually all domestic raisins as well as 40 percent of the world's. Nearly all the American crop comes from Thompson Seedless, mostly dried in the sun for two to three weeks without preservatives. When dried in ovens and cured with sulfur dioxide to retain the amber color, they become "golden seedless" raisins. Dried currants (zante currants) are small dark tart raisins from the Black Corinth grape that grew around the Greek port of Corinth, which gave them their name. Sultana raisins came originally from Smyrna and were grown for the Turkish sultans.

Whichever type, four pounds of fresh grapes yield one pound of raisins, reducing the moisture to about 15 percent. Raisins are usually plumped in liquid before cooking; the drained liquid is rich in nutrients and flavor. Raisins in baked goods help to inhibit mold and staleness.

Grapes provide vitamin C and some of the B vitamins, with potassium and fiber, but little sodium. One cup of fresh grapes has approximately sixty calories. Raisins, with many more calories—five hundred per cup—are very nourishing. They are a very good source of iron and potassium, as well as phosphorus, calcium, magnesium, copper, and some of the B complex vitamins, and their high sugar content in the form of easily assimilable fructose (70 percent) makes them an excellent snack for athletes and hikers.

Malaguenan Grape Gazpacho

This soup, startling to Americans but celebrated in Malaga, Spain, where it is called *ajo blanco con uvas* (white garlic and grapes), combines grapes, garlic, almonds, vinegar, and olive oil with bread. On a sultry night its contrast of sweet and savory thoroughly refreshes. Make it early in the day you plan to serve it, and serve very cold.

> *3 slices white bread, preferably Italian or "country" bread, crusts trimmed*
> *1 cup (4 ounces) blanched almonds*
> *2 cloves garlic, minced*
> *1 scallion (green and white parts), finely sliced (optional)*
> *⅓ cup extra virgin olive oil*
> *1¼ pounds seedless green grapes, stemmed*
> *2 cups water*
> *3 tablespoons white wine vinegar*
> *Salt and freshly ground black pepper to taste*

Moisten the bread in some water, then squeeze it dry. Put the bread in a food processor with the almonds, garlic, scallion, and olive oil and process until the almonds are well chopped. Add 1 pound of the grapes and process until well combined and smooth. Put the mixture in a bowl, add the water, cover, and chill well. Peel the remaining ¼ pound of grapes for a garnish; cover and chill them.

Shortly before serving, stir the vinegar into the soup, tasting carefully for balance. Season with salt and pepper. If the soup seems too thick, thin it with more water. Ladle the soup into serving cups or bowls and top each with the peeled grapes.

MAKES 4 OR MORE SERVINGS

Grape and Pecan Salad

Use any grape variety except Concord for this salad, but don't bother to use dark and light together: when peeled, the difference is barely noticeable. This salad goes well with chicken, duck, and pork for a special occasion or by itself for an elegant light lunch.

¼ cup extra virgin olive oil
2 tablespoons fresh lemon juice
Salt and freshly ground black pepper to taste
2 cups grapes (about ¾ pound)
1 tablespoon snipped fresh chives
1 tablespoon chopped fresh parsley
⅓ cup chopped pecans, lightly toasted (see page 179)
4 handfuls Boston or other whole loose lettuce leaves

To make the vinaigrette, mix together the olive oil, lemon juice, salt, and pepper.

Peel the grapes, cut them in half, and seed them unless the seeds are very small. Toss the grapes with the herbs and pecans.

Make beds of lettuce on four serving plates and put a mound of the grapes in the center of each. Drizzle with the vinaigrette and serve at once.

MAKES 4 SERVINGS

Rice Pilaf with Grapes and Citrus

Here is an interesting pilaf to serve with poultry, pork, or seafood. Or stir in a little meat or fish at the end for a main course.

1 orange
½ lemon
3 scallions (green and white parts)
1½ tablespoons butter
1 cup uncooked rice
1½ cups chicken or vegetable stock or water
1 cup seedless white grapes (about 6 ounces), peeled
1 tablespoon ground coriander
Salt and freshly ground black pepper to taste

Grate 1 tablespoon of zest each from the orange and lemon. Squeeze the juice from both to measure ½ cup of orange juice and 2 tablespoons lemon juice. Set the zest and juice aside.

Chop the scallions, keeping the green and white parts separate. Melt the butter in a nonreactive saucepan and cook the white scallions over low heat for a few minutes, stirring, until softened. Add the rice, stir to coat the grains with butter, and cook 1 minute more. Add the citrus juice and chicken stock, cover, and bring to a boil. Stir with a fork, reduce the heat to very low, and cook until the liquid is absorbed and the rice tender, about 18 minutes. Stir in the reserved zest, green scallions, grapes, coriander, and salt and pepper.

MAKES 6 SERVINGS

Sole Véronique

In this classic dish, simple to prepare, the sweetness and acidity of white grapes complement the delicacy of sole. With skinned boned chicken breasts, it becomes *poulet à la vigneronne*— in the style of the winegrower's wife.

¼ cup chopped shallots
8 small sole or flounder fillets
½ cup dry white wine
2 tablespoons fresh lemon juice
Fish stock or water to cover
½ cup heavy cream
Salt and ground white pepper to taste
1 cup seedless white grapes (about 6 ounces), peeled

Butter a large, shallow pan and scatter the shallots in it. Lay the fillets over in one layer, whiter side up. Add the wine, lemon juice, and enough stock to cover the fish. Cover the pan tightly, bring to a simmer on the burner, and poach gently over low heat until the fish is just cooked through and flakes easily, about 8 minutes. Do not overcook it.

With a large spatula, transfer the fillets to warm serving plates. Strain the liquid left in the pan through a fine sieve into a saucepan and boil to reduce it by half. Add the cream and reduce further, until the sauce is thick and concentrated. Taste carefully for balance and season with salt and pepper.

Meanwhile, place the peeled grapes around the sole. (It is not absolutely necessary to peel the grapes, but it makes for a more refined dish. If you do not peel them, heat the grapes gently in the sauce to warm them through without letting them boil.) Spoon the sauce over the sole fillets and serve immediately.

MAKES 8 FIRST-COURSE SERVINGS

Grape and Wine Conserve

This intense and deeply flavored conserve makes a beautiful garnet accompaniment to roast poultry or meat or an unusual dessert sauce. Make it slowly, without rushing, while you are tending something else in the kitchen. If you reduce it further still, it will become a fruit butter, far indeed from the grape jelly often paired with peanut butter.

2½ cups dark red, blue, or black grapes (about 1 pound), stemmed
¼ cup water
½ cup red wine or port
2 tablespoons fresh lemon juice
1 tablespoon julienned lemon zest
2 whole cloves
1 to 2 tablespoons sugar, or to taste

Put the grapes in a large pot with the water, and cook over low heat, stirring occasionally, until the grapes burst and turn soft, 10 to 15 minutes. Press the grapes through a sieve set over a bowl, pressing on the solids with the back of a spoon. Return the liquid to the pan with the wine, lemon juice, zest, and cloves, and continue cooking over very low heat until reduced to a sauce, stirring occasionally, about 30 minutes. As it thickens, it will need more attentive stirring. Be careful not to cook it too fast and scorch the bottom.

You can serve the purée as a fairly loose sauce or reduce it further to a thick "ketchup" or fruit butter. Discard the cloves and stir in the sugar, the amount depending on the sweetness of the grapes. The conserve will last several months, covered, in the refrigerator. If you like, put the sauce up in hot jars and sterilize for the cupboard shelf (see page 321).

MAKES 1 TO 1¼ CUPS

Oatmeal Raisin Bread

This recipe makes a moist and satisfying breakfast bread with a good crumb. For more texture you can substitute half a cup of chopped walnuts for a third of the raisins and scatter some oatmeal flakes on top of the loaf.

2 cups rolled ("old-fashioned") oats
3 cups boiling water
1¼ cups raisins
2 packages dry yeast
⅓ cup honey
2 tablespoons unsalted butter, melted and cooled
1 teaspoon salt
6 cups all-purpose flour
1 teaspoon ground cinnamon

Put the rolled oats in a large bowl with the boiling water, stir, and let cool. Put the raisins in another small bowl and pour boiling water over to cover; set aside to let the raisins plump as the water cools. Take ¼ cup warm (not hot) water from the raisin bowl and sprinkle the yeast over it to dissolve and let it proof.

In about 5 minutes, when the yeast should be bubbly, stir the mixture into the oatmeal along with the honey, butter, salt, and enough flour to make a stiff but pliable dough. Turn the dough out onto a well-floured board and knead 10 minutes, taking in more flour as needed, until the dough is smooth, elastic, and not so sticky. Form it into a ball and put it in a large bowl smeared with butter; turn the dough in the bowl to coat it with butter. Cover with a clean cloth and set in a warm draft-free place to rise and double in bulk.

Drain the raisins and pat them dry. When the dough has risen, punch it down and divide it in two. One half at a time, flatten and stretch the dough out on a lightly floured board to about 14 x 9 inches. Scatter the raisins and cinnamon over the dough, leaving an inch-wide border on all but one long side where the raisins can go to the edge. Starting on that side, roll the dough up tightly, pinch the seams closed, and tuck the ends underneath the seamed side to form an even loaf. Put the dough in a buttered 9 x 5 x 3-inch loaf pan seam-side down. Repeat with the other half of the dough, and let both loaves rise again in the pans, covered with cloths, until doubled in bulk.

Preheat the oven to 375°F. Bake the loaves until they sound hollow when tapped, about 45 minutes. At the end you may want to take the loaves out of the pans and bake them slightly longer on the oven rack to make a firm crust. Cool the bread on racks and slice them only after they have cooled.

MAKES 2 LARGE LOAVES

Fromageon

Make this simple country dessert from Gascony, where local cows' and goats' milk cheeses are as plentiful as Armagnac. The method is like that for *coeur à la crème* (see page 298) without the heart shape. With an attractive assortment of fresh grapes, perhaps also pears, apples, nuts, and other fall fruit, it makes a relaxed end to a cozy autumn evening of good company and conversation.

> *6 ounces fresh, mild chèvre*
> *3 to 4 tablespoons heavy cream*
> *2 tablespoons brandy*
> *1½ tablespoons sugar, or to taste*
> *Bunches of grapes*

Put the chèvre in a bowl and mash it with a fork or spoon. Add the cream, brandy, and sugar, and blend thoroughly. Taste carefully for balance.

Line a crock or ramekin with a double layer of cheesecloth, rinsed in cool water and squeezed dry, the cloth generously overlapping the sides. Spoon the chèvre mixture into the mold, then pull up the sides of the cloth to enclose the cheese, and twist the ends together on top. Refrigerate the fromageon overnight or for as long as a few days.

At serving time, lift the fromageon out of the mold, draining off any whey. Unwrap the cheesecloth, taking care not to smear the pattern of lines on the cheese. Set the fromageon on a plate, and serve it with good crusty bread, the grapes, and brandy.

MAKES ABOUT 6 SERVINGS

Sultana Cake

This cake, based on a recipe given me by Lydia Barrett, is so easy and good that I usually make two, with a spare to give away or keep in the freezer. For tea or dessert it is pretty with a dusting of confectioners' sugar on top. Chopped dried apricots instead of sultanas are just as delicious.

> 1 pound seedless golden raisins (sultanas)
> 2 cups (4 sticks; 1 pound) unsalted butter, softened
> 2 cups sugar
> 8 large eggs, separated, at room temperature
> 2 tablespoons grated lemon zest
> 2 tablespoons fresh lemon juice
> ¼ cup whiskey
> 4 cups all-purpose flour
> 4 teaspoons baking powder
> Confectioners' sugar for dusting (optional)

Preheat the oven to 350°F. Butter and flour two loaf pans, each about 5 x 9 x 2½ inches, tapping out any excess flour. Pour boiling water over the raisins to plump them; let them sit about 30 minutes, then drain well.

In a large bowl cream together the butter and sugar until light and fluffy. Add the egg yolks one at a time and stir to combine them. Add the lemon zest, juice, and whiskey. Mix the flour with the baking powder and stir into the mixture. In a clean, dry, very large bowl, whip the egg whites until stiff peaks form. Fold them into the batter by thirds, stirring only enough to combine them. Finally fold in the drained sultanas. Spoon the batter into the prepared cake pans and bake for 30 minutes. Turn the heat down to 300°F and bake until the cakes test done, about 45 minutes more. Cool on racks and turn out. If you like, dust the top with confectioners' sugar before slicing.

MAKES 2 CAKES; ABOUT 10 SERVINGS EACH

Grape Tart

Made with any variety of red, blue, or black grapes, this makes an attractive informal tart, especially for eating alfresco. With seedless grapes, the preparation is quick.

One 9-inch pâte sucrée (see page 35) or walnut (page 14), unbaked
4 cups red, blue, or black grapes (about 1½ pounds)
4 teaspoons cornstarch
2 tablespoons fresh lemon juice
½ cup sugar, or to taste
1 tablespoon grated lemon zest
¼ teaspoon ground cinnamon
¼ teaspoon ground allspice
Vanilla ice cream or whipped cream

Preheat the oven to 450°F. Have the pie shell well pricked and chilled.

To prepare the filling, stem the grapes, cut them in half, and if the seeds are large remove them with your fingertip or the point of a knife. (If you are using Concord grapes, slip the pulp from the skin into a pot, reserving the skins; cook the pulp over low heat until it softens, then press it through a coarse sieve to separate the seeds; add the pulp to the skins and discard the seeds.) Mix the cornstarch to a paste with the lemon juice, then stir in the sugar, zest, and spices. Mix thoroughly with the grapes.

Place the tart shell on a cookie sheet and bake it for 10 minutes; if it puffs up, prick to deflate it. Remove from the oven, fill it with the grape mixture, turning most of the halves cut-side down, and bake 10 minutes more. Lower the heat to 350°F and bake an additional 15 minutes, when the filling should be set. Cool the tart on a rack. Serve with vanilla ice cream or whipped cream.

MAKES ONE 9-INCH TART; 6 TO 8 SERVINGS

Mincemeat

This old-fashioned mincemeat includes meat and suet to flavor and moisten the filling as well as a generous amount of alcohol to preserve it while ripening. Although untraditional, the food processor makes preparation infinitely easier than chopping by hand. Making mincemeat in small quantities is impractical, so this recipe provides enough for both one large mincemeat pie (about 4 cups) and 12 tartlets (about ¼ cup filling each). Since mincemeat is not to everyone's taste, individual tartlets allow the cook to serve—and the guest to take—only as much as desired.

½ pound lean beef such as round, cut into 1-inch cubes
3 ounces suet, broken up

2 firm, tart cooking apples, peeled, cored, and coarsely chopped
1 seedless orange, quartered and coarsely chopped
4 ounces pitted prunes, halved
4 ounces dried figs, halved
4 ounces candied citron
4 ounces golden raisins (sultanas)
4 ounces dried currants
½ cup broken walnut meats or other nuts, lightly toasted (see page 179)
3 tablespoons peeled and chopped fresh ginger
1 teaspoon ground cinnamon
½ teaspoon ground allspice
½ teaspoon freshly ground nutmeg
½ cup firmly packed dark brown sugar
¾ cup sherry
¾ cup brandy

Put the beef in a saucepan and cover with boiling water. Simmer over low heat for 10 minutes, then let it cool in the water; drain. Chop the beef in a food processor, using the pulse button, until coarsely shredded. Put it in a large bowl. Chop the suet in the food processor until it is fine in texture and add it to the beef.

With the metal blade still in place, continue chopping all the fruit, fresh and dried, adding each batch of mince to the bowl. Be careful not to reduce anything to a gummy purée. Chop the apples just long enough to dice them finely. Chop the orange, skin included (if the skin is thick, you may want to peel off the outer zest with a vegetable peeler, discard the white interior pith, and chop only the zest and pulp for the mincemeat), along with the prunes and figs. Chop the citron and raisins together; the currants are probably too small to need chopping. Add the walnuts, spices, and sugar, stirring to combine all the ingredients. Finally add the sherry and brandy, and stir the mincemeat well. Refrigerate, covered, or put it up into covered jars or crocks for storage on a cool cupboard shelf. Let the mincemeat mature for at least two weeks or as long as six.

MAKES ABOUT 6 CUPS

Yorkshire Mousies

Another use for mincemeat is Yorkshire mousies, traditional but imaginative, as suggested by my friend Chandler Steiner. Morsels of mincemeat are wrapped in flaky pastry, with pointed noses, almond ears, and currant eyes fashioned at one end, pastry or orange zest tails at the other. At Christmastime, Yorkshire mousies are excellent for large parties or holiday presents. You can freeze them filled but uncooked and thaw just before baking. In this case, use tails scored from orange zest with a citrus groover rather than from fragile pastry. This quantity makes enough for a crowd, but you can easily scale it down. Or simply wrap the mincemeat in purchased puff pastry.

FOR THE FLAKY PASTRY
 6 cups all-purpose flour
 1¼ cups plus 2 tablespoons (3¾ sticks; 15 ounces) unsalted butter, cut into pieces and frozen
 1 tablespoon salt
 1 cup ice water
 6 tablespoons (¾ stick) unsalted butter, softened

TO COMPLETE
 1 recipe mincemeat (see previous recipe)
 Sliced almonds for ears
 Currants for eyes

Make flaky pastry (mock puff pastry) in two or three batches, depending on the size of your food-processor workbowl: put the flour in the workbowl with the frozen butter and salt and pulse three times. Add the ice water, starting with a small amount and increasing as needed; process just until the dough forms a ball on the blades. Flatten each ball into an oblong, enclose it in plastic wrap, and chill in the refrigerator for 2 hours or more.

On a lightly floured workboard and with a floured rolling pin, roll each piece of dough out into a rectangle. Spread the softened butter over two thirds of the sheet and fold the unbuttered part back on top as if folding a business letter, then fold over the remaining third. Roll out again and fold into thirds a couple of times more. If the dough becomes too elastic, enclose in plastic wrap and chill.

One at a time, on a lightly floured board, roll the prepared dough out thinly to about ¼-inch thickness. With the point of a sharp knife, cut out 3-inch-long ovals and put 1 tablespoon of mincemeat in the center of each. Wrap the filling in the dough, sealing it on the bottom and making a point at one end for the mouse's nose. Set the filled dough spaced well apart on a greased cookie sheet and continue until all are done. With the leftover dough cut long strips; roll each strip between the palms of your hands to make long tails. Attach them to the back of each mouse with a little water and curl the tails. Poke the points of slivered almonds into the heads for ears and make currant eyes. Do not brush with egg wash.

Preheat the oven to 425°F. Two at a time put the cookie sheets in the oven, immediately turn the heat down to 350°F, and bake until the dough is golden brown and puffed, about 15 minutes. Let the pastries cool slightly, then with a spatula carefully move them to a serving tray. Serve the Yorkshire mousies warm or at room temperature.

MAKES ABOUT 8 DOZEN

Autumn Pudding

Here is a fall variation on the classic Summer Pudding (see page 277) that is welcome in every season. You can use half the berries and add a red apple or two.

1 pound red or black grapes, stemmed and halved
1 pound red or purple plums, pitted and coarsely chopped
1 pound blackberries or raspberries
½ cup sugar, or to taste
White bread, preferably a tight-textured, extra-thin-sliced loaf, crusts trimmed (stale
*   bread is fine)*

Put the grapes in a pan with just enough water to cover the bottom, and simmer until the fruit begins to soften. Add the plums and simmer until their juices too become runny. Finally add the berries, but do not allow them to get mushy. Stir only enough to mix them.

Line a pudding bowl or other deep bowl, 8-cup capacity or larger, with slices of bread, trimming them to fit together and filling any gaps with trimmings. Saving 1 cup of strained fruit juices, spoon the fruit into the lined mold with a slotted spoon. Trim the bread that extends above the fruit and cover the top with bread, to enclose the fruit completely. Cover the pudding with plastic wrap. Fit a saucer inside the top of the bowl and weight it, to press the fruit juices into the bread. Chill the pudding, still weighted, overnight, and chill the extra juice too in a covered jar.

To serve, unwrap the pudding, run a knife around the inside edge of the bowl, put a serving plate on top, and carefully invert the pudding onto the plate. Spoon the reserved juice over the bread to paint out any pale patches. Serve the pudding garnished if possible with a few grape leaves, and pass cream on the side.

MAKES 8 SERVINGS

Plum Pudding

On "Stir-up Sunday" in England, the Sunday before the beginning of Advent, the collect begins, "Stir up, we beseech thee, O Lord, the wills of thy faithful people; that they, plenteously bringing forth the fruit of good works, may by thee be plenteously rewarded." This reminds faithful housewives to stir up their Christmas puddings so that they may be plenteously rewarded on December 25th.

Traditional plum pudding recipes call for suet to moisten the dried fruit and raw flour. This one is lighter, containing neither suet nor flour, and requires less time to steam—a mere seven hours. This recipe comes from my friend Rosemary Milner Cock, based upon one by the English food writer Francis Bissell.

3 cups (½ pound) fresh white or whole-wheat bread crumbs
2 cups (½ pound) coarsely chopped muscat raisins
2 cups (½ pound) coarsely chopped golden raisins (sultanas)
½ pound coarsely chopped dried apricots
¾ cup (2 ounces) crumbled macaroons or amaretti
¾ cup (3 ounces) chopped almonds, lightly toasted (see page 179)
1 apple, peeled, cored, and grated or finely chopped
Juice and grated zest of ½ orange
1 teaspoon ground cinnamon
1 teaspoon freshly grated nutmeg
½ teaspoon ground allspice
½ teaspoon ground coriander
½ teaspoon ground cloves
2 tablespoons orange marmalade
3 large eggs, lightly beaten
½ cup port, Madeira, or sherry
¼ cup brandy

In a large bowl, combine all the ingredients down through the apple and mix them well with your hands. In another large bowl, mix the orange juice and zest with the spices, then the remaining wet ingredients. Blend them well. Pour the wet ingredients over the dry and mix again with your hands. Cover and let sit in a cool place, if possible overnight, for the flavors to develop.

Generously butter a 6- or 7-cup pudding mold or steep-sided ovenproof bowl and spoon in the pudding mixture, allowing a half inch of space at the top (it will not expand). Cover with a piece of buttered aluminum foil and tie it in place with string, buttered side down. Set the pudding on a rack in a large, deep saucepan; you can improvise this if necessary with aluminum foil. Pour boiling water to reach halfway up the sides of the pudding, cover the saucepan tightly, and return to a boil over high heat. Turn down the heat to low and simmer the pudding for 5 hours, replenishing the water as it evaporates. Be careful not to let the pan boil dry. Let the pudding cool completely. This much can be done ahead, the pudding turned out of the mold, wrapped in fresh cloth or greaseproof paper, and stored in a cool, dark, dry place. Give it a month or more to allow the flavors to ripen and mellow.

To serve, unwrap the pudding, return it to the pudding mold, cover the top with buttered aluminum foil as before, and steam it in boiling water as described above for 2 more hours. Lift it out of the saucepan carefully, run a knife around the inside of the lid, and turn the pudding out onto a serving platter. You can flame the pudding with warmed brandy if you wish. Garnish the pudding with festive nontoxic greenery (keep in mind that holly berries are toxic) and serve with hard sauce (see page 57) or crème anglaise (see page 17).

MAKES 10 TO 12 SERVINGS

Rum Raisin Ice Cream

This rich ice cream, wonderful on its own, goes supremely well with many traditional desserts, such as persimmon ice cream (see page 233) and apple pie (see page 11).

½ cup dark rum
1 cup (5 ounces) seedless raisins
2 cups milk
5 large egg yolks
⅔ cup sugar
Pinch of salt
3 cups heavy cream

First plump the raisins. In a small saucepan, heat the rum nearly to boiling, then remove from the heat. Place the raisins in the rum to steep until cool, stirring occasionally. If convenient, you can do this well ahead of time. Cover and set aside. Refrigerate once the raisins cool to room temperature.

Pour the milk in a saucepan and scald over medium heat: heat until little bubbles appear around the edges, but do not let it boil. In a medium-size bowl, beat together the egg yolks, sugar, and salt until the yolks turn pale and thick. In a slow, steady stream, stirring constantly, pour the hot milk into the yolk mixture. Pour the mixture back into the saucepan and cook it over low heat, still stirring, until the custard thickens enough to coat the spoon heavily. Watch closely to see that the yolks don't scramble. (On a thermometer the temperature should reach 170°F, so that the eggs are sufficiently cooked to avoid the risk of salmonella.) Take the custard off the heat. Cover it, let it return to room temperature, and chill thoroughly.

Fold the heavy cream into the custard (you might want to whip it first for added lightness), and freeze in an ice cream machine according to the manufacturer's directions. You can also freeze it in a covered bowl, stirring at intervals to smooth the ice crystals. When the ice cream is nearly set, fold in the raisins and any unabsorbed rum. Let the ice cream mellow for about 2 hours before serving. If you make it ahead, let it soften somewhat before serving.

MAKES ABOUT 1½ QUARTS

Grape Sherbet

You can make this sherbet with any kind of grape, perhaps contrasting the flavors and colors of two. The most aromatic grapes are best, even those very ripe ones that fall off the bunch just before they turn overripe. For depth, add a little wine; for velvety richness, fortified wine.

3 pounds grapes, stemmed
2 tablespoons fresh lemon juice
⅓ cup sugar, or to taste

Purée the grapes in a food processor, in batches if necessary. Strain the juice through a sieve fitted over a bowl, pressing on the pulp with the back of a spoon to extract the juice. Discard the solids. Add the lemon juice and sugar to the grape juice, stirring to dissolve the sugar in the acid. Depending on the variety and ripeness of the grapes, you may need to add more sugar. Cover and chill the grape syrup thoroughly.

Freeze the grape syrup in a sorbetière or ice cream machine according to the manufacturer's directions. Or freeze it according to the directions on page 307.

MAKES ABOUT 1 QUART

Frosted Grapes

These frosted grapes make a very pretty garnish for other desserts or for a table decoration. Champagne grapes, the tiny ones in large bunches, work especially well here. Other berry and stem fruits, particularly those in clusters, look beautiful frosted, such as currants and blueberries on the stem, stemmed strawberries, raspberries, and cherries, as well as edible blossoms and leaves. Your own garden or a pick-your-own establishment are the best sources. Try combining several fruits in little baskets at place settings or one large basket as a centerpiece.

1 large egg white
Grapes in small bunches
Sugar, either large or fine crystals

Lightly beat the egg white in a bowl, just enough to make it loosen and foam a little, not fluff up. Dry the grapes and put the sugar on a plate. Dip the grapes in the egg white, shake off the excess, then turn them in the sugar crystals to coat the grapes all over. Set the grapes on a rack to dry for an hour or so. The egg white will dry out and form a sparkling crust. Frosted grapes keep well for a day.

KIWI

There are fashions in food as well as in everything else. The kiwi is a perfect exemplar of the theory that for every action there is an equal and opposite reaction. When kiwi came in about fifteen years ago and was used to excess in nouvelle cuisine, the fad crashed so suddenly that no one would dare serve it. Now we may eat kiwi for reasons beyond fashion.

Kiwi, a.k.a. *Actinidia chinensis* or Chinese gooseberry, is native to China, where it has largely been ignored. Early in this century seeds were taken to New Zealand by way of Europe. A horticulturist named Hayward Wright developed the one variety we know, which bears his first name. In the early 1950s, with an eye to the American market, it was dubbed the kiwifruit to distance it from its Communist past and to allude to the curious fuzzy New Zealand bird. The marketing ploy succeeded wildly, and today New Zealand supplies the American market from June to October, California from November through May.

The translation of the French term for kiwi is vegetable mouse, which is more descriptive than any of its other names. The small oblong is covered in brown fuzz, making it look like a cowering mouse. Inside the thin skin is jade green flesh, with small black seeds radiating from a central white core. Cut either across in sections or lengthwise in wedges, the kiwi is strikingly beautiful, unique in appearance. The juicy flesh balances a smooth sweetness with a refreshing acidity.

Kiwi has two great assets not to be overlooked. Fruit purchased firm keeps very well in the refrigerator for several weeks and even longer, so that you can buy it when you see it on sale to have on hand. To ripen it up, leave the kiwi at room temperature for a few days until slightly softened. Like many fruits, ethylene gas (captured in a bag, especially if you wrap a banana or apple in with it) hastens the process. Once soft, kiwi should be used before the texture gets mushy. Kiwi's other asset is that the cut flesh does not darken with exposure to air: you can cut or purée fruit several hours before serving without fear of discoloration.

Kiwi is delicious in all kinds of fruit salads and compotes, where its bright color and flavor enliven blander fruits. Slices make a pretty topping for pastries, such as the fresh strawberry tart on page 299, paired with the red berries or alone. Kiwi purée is silky smooth with custards, pastries, and other fruits, or frozen into a refreshing sherbet with some of

125

the black seeds left in. Kiwi has an affinity for chocolate, cutting the richness and highlighting the bittersweet darkness. Kiwi also goes well with fish, chicken, and ham—but beware the excesses of nouvelle cuisine.

Kiwi, like pineapple and papaya, contains an enzyme that tenderizes meat. It also curdles milk (but not heavy cream) and interferes with the action of gelatin unless the kiwi is first cooked. Since cooked kiwi loses its flavor and color, enjoy it fresh.

Buy kiwi firm and ripen as described above. To use it, simply remove the thin skin with a vegetable peeler and cut out the shallow tough stem at one end. Cut the kiwi across into thin slices or lengthwise into wedges. You can also cut the kiwi in half and scoop out the flesh with a citrus spoon or melon baller. Fuzz on or off, the skin is edible but unpalatable. Kiwi size varies, but six or seven of average size comprise a pound. One pound of the fruit yields about one and a half cups of purée.

Kiwi is extremely high in vitamin C, with a healthy amount of fiber and potassium, approximately the same as in a banana. One kiwi contains about fifty-five calories.

Shrimp and Kiwi Salad

This salad takes advantage of kiwi's refreshing acidity. Its unusual coloring and crescent shape when cut lengthwise in wedges look striking with shrimp.

> 1 pound medium-large raw shrimp in the shell
> 3 tablespoons chopped red onion
> 1 small jalapeño pepper, seeded and cut into rings
> 1 tablespoon peeled and minced fresh ginger
> 3 tablespoons vegetable oil
> 2 tablespoons fresh lime juice
> Salt to taste
> Pinch of sugar
> 2 kiwi
> Loose leaf lettuce

Put the shrimp in a pot, cover with cold water, and bring to a boil. Cover with a lid and poach over low heat until they turn pink, about 3 minutes. Drain the shrimp and shell and devein them, if necessary, when they are cool.

In a small bowl, mix together the onion, jalapeño pepper, ginger, oil, lime juice, salt, and sugar; taste carefully for balance. Toss the shrimp in the dressing and let marinate for a few minutes or hours, covered and chilled, even overnight if convenient.

Peel the kiwi, slice them in half lengthwise, then lay each half flat and cut into thin lengthwise wedges as if it were an orange or apple. Unlike most cut fruit, you needn't worry about its turning dark with exposure to air.

Shortly before serving, lay a bed of lettuce leaves on serving plates. Put the shrimp on the lettuce with the vinaigrette, surround attractively with the kiwi wedges, and serve.

MAKES 4 OR MORE SERVINGS

Banana Kiwi Raita

My friend Laxmi Rao, who comes from Andhra Pradesh in southeastern India, tops her banana raita untraditionally with sliced kiwi, sparking the dish with its color and acidity. As a savory side dish for meat, she serves it in a glass bowl to reveal the contrasting colors and shapes. This raita shows her gift for combining old and new with perfect logic.

1 teaspoon Dijon mustard
Salt to taste
2 cups plain yogurt
2 large bananas
1 teaspoon fresh lemon juice
1 tablespoon vegetable oil
¼ teaspoon black mustard seed
¼ teaspoon cumin seed
2 or 3 kiwi

Stir the Dijon mustard and salt into the yogurt. Peel the bananas, slice them fairly thin, and toss them with the lemon juice to keep them from turning dark. Stir the banana slices into the yogurt mixture.

In a small pan over medium heat, heat the vegetable oil. Add the mustard seed, then the cumin, and continue to heat for a minute or two until the mustard seeds sputter and pop. Pour the spice mixture over the yogurt and stir it in.

Peel the kiwi and slice them into thin rounds. Lay them over the surface of the raita. The dish can be prepared ahead, covered, and chilled for a few hours, or served right away.

MAKES 4 TO 6 SERVINGS

Bittersweet Chocolate Cake with Kiwi Sauce

The brightness of kiwi, like orange, complements bittersweet chocolate, so surround a slice of this cake with kiwi sauce. The deep, dense, dark cake is based on a recipe of Nela Rubinstein's, wife of the pianist Arthur Rubinstein, published in *Nela's Cookbook* (Knopf, 1983). Tightly wrapped, the cake keeps and freezes well.

4 ounces bittersweet chocolate
1 ounce bitter chocolate
¾ cup (1½ sticks) unsalted butter, softened
¾ cup sugar
3 large eggs, separated, at room temperature
3 tablespoons coffee-flavored liqueur or double-strength coffee
¾ cup all-purpose flour
Unsweetened cocoa powder (optional)
Kiwi Sauce (recipe follows)

Preheat the oven to 350°F. Butter and flour a 4- to 6-cup loaf pan or ring mold. Gently melt the chocolates together in the top of a double boiler over simmering water, then let cool somewhat. In a medium-size bowl cream the butter and sugar until light and fluffy, then stir in the chocolate. Beat in the egg yolks one at a time until well combined, then the coffee liqueur. Finally stir in the flour until smooth.

In a large clean bowl, beat the egg whites until stiff and glossy. Stir in a spoonful of the whites to loosen the batter, then quickly fold in the rest until no streaks of white remain. Spoon the batter into the prepared pan. Bake the cake until it tests done, about 45 minutes; the cake should shrink from the sides of the pan and a skewer inserted into the center should come out clean. Since the batter is heavy, the top may crack slightly— no matter. Cool the cake on a rack before unmolding. If you like, dust the top with cocoa powder before cutting the cake into thin slices. Put a slice of cake on an individual serving plate and spoon some of the kiwi sauce around it.

MAKES 1 SMALL LOAF; ABOUT 8 SERVINGS

Kiwi Sauce

Kiwi sauce also goes well with custards, pound cake, and fruit combinations. Or blend it with ripe bananas for a low-calorie "creamy" sherbet (see page 129).

1 cup kiwi purée (made from about ⅔ pound peeled and stemmed fruit)
3 tablespoons sugar, or to taste

Peel the kiwi and cut out the hard stem at one end. Coarsely chop the flesh and purée it in a food processor. Put the purée in a bowl, straining out some of the seeds if you wish fewer speckles. Stir in the sugar; it will dissolve on its own in a few minutes. You can add a couple of tablespoons of kirsch, rum, or other spirit, but this is not necessary. The sauce can be made well ahead, covered, and chilled.

MAKES ABOUT 1 CUP

Kiwi Sherbet

The speckled green color and tart taste make this sherbet unusually refreshing, almost a frozen kiwi daiquiri. For a spectacular combination of exotic fruits, pair it with mango ice cream (see page 164).

¾ cup sugar
¾ cup water
1 pound kiwi
½ cup fresh lime juice (from about 4 limes)
¼ cup white rum

Combine the sugar and water in a small pan, bring to a boil, and let boil until the sugar is dissolved, about 5 minutes. Let the syrup cool. You should have about 1 cup.

Peel the kiwi and cut out the hard stem at one end. Coarsely chop the kiwi and purée them in a food processor. You should have about 1½ cups. If you wish to remove some or all of the seeds (I think they identify the fruit and add appeal), press the purée through a fine sieve. Stir in the lime juice, cooled syrup, and rum and taste carefully for balance. Since the color fades slightly in freezing, you might want to add a drop or two—no more—of green food coloring. Cover and chill the fruit syrup, then freeze it in an ice cream machine or sorbetière according to the manufacturer's directions or according to the directions on page 307.

MAKES ABOUT 1 QUART

KUMQUATS

Kumquat in Cantonese means "golden orange," and indeed this fruit is a beautiful miniature orange globe. It grows widely in the Orient, both as a full-sized tree and as an ornamental dwarf. Despite its endearing appearance, the kumquat is not a true citrus. Its botanical classification, *Fortunella*, honors the Englishman, Robert Fortune, who introduced it to the Royal Horticultural Society in London in 1846.

The kumquat has an aromatic, sweet skin and a sour interior flecked with little green seeds. Its shape can be oval or round, depending on variety. The small size is just right for popping in the mouth, making it perfect for garnishes, either left whole or cut into rounds or quarters. In addition, the kumquat's sweet-and-sour flavor makes it a decorative and delicious addition to savory salads, meats such as duck and pork traditionally cooked with bitter orange, and preserves, either pickled or candied, alone or with other fruit. For dark chocolate desserts it makes a stunning garnish. Its shape makes it irresistible for skewering, but its relative expense makes it impractical for cooking in ways that disguise its appearance.

Most of the kumquats we see in American markets are grown in Florida or California, and their season is fall to spring. Choose firm, unshriveled specimens with good color, if possible with fresh leaves attached, and store them in the refrigerator. Because of their thin skins, they keep less well than oranges and other citrus, so use kumquats fairly soon after purchase. Wash them well and, if cut open, pick out the tiny seeds. Following Elizabeth Schneider's suggestion, plump them by blanching them briefly in boiling water, especially if using them whole.

Golden Glow Cocktail

A poor man's champagne cocktail.

Ice
1 tablespoon Grand Marnier
6 ounces dry white wine

Splash of soda water
Slice of kumquat for garnish

Put a few cubes of ice in a large wineglass. Add the Grand Marnier, wine, and a splash of soda, and garnish with the sliced kumquat.

MAKES 1 COCKTAIL

Rice Salad with Kumquats and Snow Peas

This salad with its Oriental flavorings makes an excellent accompaniment to roast or grilled meat or an attractive addition to the buffet table. As a main dish in itself, stir in a little cubed cooked pork or chicken or a few baby shrimp.

½ cup uncooked white rice
¾ cup plus 2 tablespoons water
4 kumquats
1 ounce snow peas, trimmed
2 tablespoons slivered blanched almonds
¼ cup peanut oil
2 scallions (green and white parts), sliced
1 tablespoon peeled and minced fresh ginger
2 tablespoons rice wine or white wine vinegar
½ teaspoon hot chile oil, or to taste (optional; available in Oriental or specialty food stores)
Salt and freshly ground black pepper to taste
3 tablespoons chopped fresh coriander (cilantro)
Fresh coriander sprigs for garnish

Put the rice in a small saucepan with the water. Bring to a boil, stir with a fork, cover, and simmer over low heat until the rice is just cooked through but still firm, about 15 minutes. It should not be mushy. Leave it with the top on to steam and stir with a fork to fluff up.

While the rice is cooking, drop the kumquats in a pot of boiling water and cook for about 30 seconds to blanch them. Remove them with a slotted spoon, refresh in cold water, and drain. Drop the snow peas into the same water, cook for about 30 seconds, drain, refresh in cold water, and drain again. Slice the kumquats into thin rounds, removing any seeds, and set aside. Slice the snow peas on the diagonal at half-inch intervals and set aside on the same plate with the kumquats.

Put the almonds in a small sauté pan without any oil in it and heat it over medium flame, watching closely, to brown the nuts (or toast them in the oven; see page 179). Stir occasionally to color them evenly. When golden brown, turn them out and reserve on the same plate with, but separate from, the kumquats and snow peas. Put 1 tablespoon of the peanut oil in the pan and cook the sliced scallions over low heat, stirring, just until they begin to soften, about 2 minutes. Add the ginger and cook 30 seconds more, stirring. Set the scallions and ginger aside near the almonds.

Mix together the remaining peanut oil, the vinegar, chile oil, salt, and pepper, and mix into the warm rice. Let the rice cool completely to room temperature. Just before serving, stir in the snow peas, kumquats, almonds, scallions, ginger, and coriander. Taste to correct the seasonings, and serve garnished with fresh coriander sprigs.

MAKES 4 SERVINGS

Pork and Kumquat Kebabs in Hoisin Marinade

The hoisin marinade makes a wonderfully rich and spicy sauce. To avoid bursting or burning the kumquats, they must be broiled separately for a shorter time than the pork.

2 tablespoons hoisin sauce (available in Oriental and specialty food stores)
2 tablespoons soy sauce
2 tablespoons sugar
4½ teaspoons orange juice
4½ teaspoons whiskey
1 tablespoon peeled and minced fresh ginger
1 tablespoon minced garlic
2 pounds pork such as boneless country-style ribs, cut into 1-inch cubes
2 cups kumquats

Mix the hoisin and soy sauces, sugar, orange juice, whiskey, ginger, and garlic together well in a shallow dish. Put the pork cubes in the marinade, turn to coat them on all sides, and marinate for an hour or two in the refrigerator, covered.

Arrange the broiler or grill rack 6 inches from the heat source and preheat. Thread the pork and kumquats on separate skewers. Broil or grill the pork, turning to brown it on all sides and brushing with additional marinade, about 12 minutes altogether. Brush the kumquats with the marinade and broil about 5 minutes total, turning them to cook evenly. Take the pork and kumquats off the skewers and serve immediately.

MAKES 8 OR MORE APPETIZER SERVINGS

Brandied Kumquats with Star Anise

Playing on their Oriental origin, these beautiful kumquats are tantalizingly spiced with star anise. If you can't find this Chinese spice (available at Oriental and specialty markets), substitute one 2-inch stick of cinnamon or four whole cloves. Give the brandied kumquats away at holiday time, put up in attractive jars (see page 321), or serve them with roast poultry or pork.

1 pound kumquats (about 3½ cups)
1 cup sugar
2 cups water
2 star anise
¼ cup brandy

Prick each kumquat with a needle clear through to the center to keep it from bursting. Bring a pot of water to a boil and drop the kumquats in to blanch them; return the water to a boil, then drain.

Combine the sugar and water in a pot, bring to a boil, and let boil until the sugar is dissolved, about 5 minutes. Add the kumquats and star anise, return the water to a boil, and simmer over low heat for 5 minutes. Remove the kumquats with a slotted spoon to a jar or bowl. Add the brandy to the pot, boil to reduce the syrup slightly, and pour it over the kumquats. Cool, cover, and chill the kumquats; they will keep in the refrigerator for several weeks or more. Or put them up in sterilized jars (see page 321) to keep in the cupboard or give away.

MAKES ABOUT 1 QUART

Glazed Kumquat Custard Tartlets

In these creamy-crackly little tartlets a rich Grand Marnier custard is topped with kumquats under a caramelized glaze. You can skip the tartlet shells and spoon the custard into individual soufflé ramekins, making something more like a crème brûlée.

1 cup heavy cream
1 cup light cream or half-and-half
2 large eggs plus 2 egg yolks, at room temperature
⅓ cup sugar
Pinch of salt
¼ cup Grand Marnier or other orange-flavored liqueur
2 tablespoons grated orange zest
6 tartlet shells (recipe follows), baked
6 kumquats
Sugar for glaze

Pour both creams into a saucepan and scald over medium flame: heat until little bubbles appear around the edges, but do not let it boil. In a medium-size bowl beat all the eggs, sugar, and salt together well. Stir in the Grand Marnier and orange zest. In a thin, steady stream, slowly pour the scalded cream into the egg mixture, beating steadily. Return to the pan and cook over low heat, stirring constantly, until the custard thickens and coats the back of a spoon. Strain the custard through a fine sieve into a bowl, then spoon the custard into the tartlet shells, and chill thoroughly. (Since the surface will be covered with the kumquats and glaze, you needn't cover the custard to prevent a skin from forming.) The custard will stiffen as it chills, but will remain tender under the surface.

Shortly before serving, arrange the broiler rack 3 to 4 inches from the heat source and preheat. Remove the tartlets from the refrigerator; chill them again if there is any delay. Slice the kumquats across into thin rounds, removing any seeds, and place them on the custard in a pretty flower pattern. Sprinkle granulated sugar on each tartlet, about 2 teaspoons each, wipe the rims of any stray custard or sugar, and set the tartlets in a shallow ovenproof pan. Run the tartlets under the preheated broiler for about 2 to 3 minutes, just long enough to caramelize the sugar—watch closely to avoid burning. You may need to turn the pan or cover the crusts with aluminum foil. Once caramelized, let the glaze cool for a few minutes, but serve the tartlets soon.

MAKES 6 TARTLETS

Pâte Sucrée Tartlet Shells

1 cup all-purpose flour
3 tablespoons sugar
Pinch of salt
6 tablespoons (¾ stick) unsalted butter, cold, cut into small pieces
1 large egg yolk
1 tablespoon fresh lemon juice
1 tablespoon grated lemon zest
1 tablespoon or more ice water, if needed

Process all the ingredients in a food processor just until the mixture begins to form a ball on the blades. (To make the dough by hand, mix the flour, sugar, and salt in a bowl. Add the remaining ingredients, cutting them into the flour with a pastry cutter, two knives, or your fingertips, quickly rubbing the butter into the flour to form flakes. Keep your hands very cold and handle the dough as little as possible. If needed, add the ice water gradually, stirring around the sides of the bowl, using just enough water to form a mass.) Gather the dough together, enclose in plastic wrap, and flatten into a disk. Refrigerate at least 1 hour.

Roll the dough out to a thickness of ¼ inch on a well-floured board. Arrange six 3-inch tartlet pans on the work surface, sides touching. Place the dough over the pans, letting it settle into each. Run the rolling pin over the dough to cut it. Fit the dough into the pans and prick well with a fork. Chill thoroughly.

Preheat the oven to 400°F. Line the pastry shells with aluminum foil and fill with dried beans or pie weights. Arrange the tartlets on a cookie sheet and bake 8 minutes. Remove the foil and beans, and bake 4 minutes more. Cool the tartlet shells completely on a rack.

MAKES SIX 3-INCH TARTLET SHELLS

LEMONS

The lemon's image has suffered from poor press. We associate the fruit with duds, amusement park rides, and shifty used-car dealers. But through the ages this citrus has proved itself invaluable. Arab traders brought it from India to the Middle East and spread it throughout the Mediterranean. In 1493 Columbus introduced it to the New World.

The *Citrus limon* grows on a tall and beautiful evergreen tree that thrives in warm, dry climates, where it can be trained into hedges and espaliers. It blooms several times a year in clusters of fragrant white flowers tinged with purple and bears fruit continuously. Its seasonal peak in spring meets our desire for the fresh seafood, vegetables, and fruit that a few drops of lemon juice set off so well.

The lemon's superb self-packaging helps it withstand shipping and storing over time and distance. The outer yellow zest of the skin contains essential oil, concentrating its lemony flavor and adding the element of scent. Inside, the white pith is bitter in taste, but rich in the pectin that makes jams jell. The juice has more vitamin C than any other citrus fruit, warding off scurvy and other diseases. Not to mention its medicinal, pharmaceutical, cosmetic, and household uses, the lemon's sourness is a basic and versatile flavoring for countless sweet and savory dishes.

For the health-conscious, the little lemon offers a powerful package. It is high in fiber, with no fat or sodium and so low in calories you needn't count them (eighteen per medium-size lemon). Better yet, lemon juice seems to inhibit the absorption of fats. For those of us who limit our salt intake, a gentle squeeze heightens the flavor of other foods so that we don't miss the salt. In addition to its wallop of vitamin C, one medium-size lemon provides vitamins A and B and the mineral potassium.

Lemon juice slows the discoloration of cut fruits and vegetables such as apples, avocados, and artichokes. It lightens the color of mushrooms in cooking and turns royal icing bright white. In seafood marinades, the acid "cooks" the flesh without heat, a boon for sultry summer days. When we forget to buy buttermilk, a few drops of lemon juice in regular milk sour it within minutes. When our hands are stained from slicing fruit or smelly from preparing fish, a cut lemon rubbed over them shows the juice's potency for bleaching and deodorizing. The seeds and pith work wonders in low-pectin fruit jellies. A leftover heel can flavor syrup, and a strip of zest buried in a jar of sugar can impart its subtle perfume to desserts made with the sugar.

The main varieties of lemon sold in the United States are Eureka and Lisbon, with California and Arizona by far the largest producers not only for this country but for a third of those consumed worldwide. The small, sweet, thin-skinned Meyer that Californians cherish in their backyards is rarely, alas, to be found elsewhere. The best lemons are heavy for their size, indicating juiciness, with finely textured, thin skins. Lemons with coarse, thick rinds and large pores should be left behind along with those that are shriveled, soft, spongy, or hard-skinned. A few dark splotches or a greenish tinge are fine.

Refrigerated, the lemon will keep a month or more. Since the aromatic zest intensifies lemon flavor in cooking, add it whenever you can. Remove only the outer colored layer, avoiding the white pith, with a zester, vegetable peeler, or fine grater before squeezing the juice. To get the most juice out of a lemon (almost 4 tablespoons for a medium-size lemon), drop the whole fruit into hot water for a few minutes before cutting and squeezing, or, far simpler, roll it back and forth on the counter a few times while pressing on the lemon, to help the juices flow.

Old-Fashioned Lemonade

Homemade lemonade is far superior to the frozen or cartoned variety. The yellow zest gives a deeper lemony flavor, but zest boiled or used with the white pith imparts a bitter taste, so take care. Start the night or morning before you plan to serve it, or make the lemon syrup to keep on hand in the refrigerator. If you are serving this without lemon slices or diluted with lots of ice, add less water.

1 cup sugar
4 cups cold fresh water
4 lemons plus 1 additional lemon, cut across into very thin slices for serving

First make a syrup: combine the sugar and 1 cup of the water in a pot, bring to a boil, and let boil gently until the sugar is dissolved, about 5 minutes. Meanwhile, with a vegetable peeler, remove the outer yellow zest from 1 lemon, taking as little of the bitter white pith as possible. When the sugar is dissolved, take the pot off the heat and add the lemon zest to steep in the syrup. Squeeze the juice from 4 lemons, about ⅞ cup, and reserve. When the syrup is cool, strain out and discard the lemon zest; stir in the lemon juice. Stir in the remaining cold fresh water and chill thoroughly.

Serve the lemonade in a pitcher with thin slices of lemon floating on top. Pour the lemonade over ice cubes into tall glasses and garnish with a slice of lemon and, if possible, fresh sprigs of mint, borage, or sweet woodruff.

MAKES ABOUT 1¼ QUARTS

Taramosalata

This Greek spread can be made with any of various fish roes, canned or smoked. I have even used fresh raw flounder roe "cooked" by the lemon juice with success. As for quantities, taste carefully for balance and your own palate. To fill out the appetizer for a summer meal—ideal for a hot summer night—add shrimp and Greek olives with sliced tomatoes, onions, and cucumbers.

    5 slices white bread, crusts trimmed
    5 ounces carp, gray mullet, smoked cod, or other roe, rinsed and drained
    1 cup olive oil
    1 small white onion, chopped
    1 clove garlic, minced
    3 tablespoons chopped fresh parsley, preferably Italian flatleaf
    Juice of 1 lemon
    Salt and freshly ground black pepper to taste
    1 lemon, quartered
    Fresh parsley sprigs for garnish
    Pita or crusty bread

Moisten the bread with a little water, then squeeze it dry. Put it in a food processor or blender (or use a mortar and pestle) with the roe. Try to have an approximately equal volume of bread and roe. Combine them briefly, then, with the machine on, add the olive oil in a slow, steady stream to make a mayonnaiselike emulsion. Add the onion, garlic, parsley, lemon juice, salt, and pepper, and taste carefully for balance. Cover and chill the taramosalata before serving. (It will keep well for a week or even longer.) Serve it garnished with the lemon wedges, parsley, and crisp pita or other bread.

MAKES 6 TO 10 APPETIZER SERVINGS

Fennel Avgolemono Soup

This light and restorative soup recalls the high esteem in which the ancient Greeks held fennel.

    1½ tablespoons unsalted butter
    One ½-pound fennel bulb, trimmed and cut lengthwise into julienne strips (about 1½ cups)
    2 shallots, minced
    6 cups chicken broth
    ¼ cup fresh lemon juice

2 large egg yolks
3 tablespoons minced fennel leaves
Salt and freshly ground black pepper to taste

In a large heavy saucepan over medium-low heat, melt the butter. When it begins to foam, add the fennel strips and shallots and cook, stirring occasionally, for about 5 minutes without letting them color. Add the broth, bring it to a boil, and simmer over low heat, covered, until the fennel is just tender but not soft, about 15 minutes.

Whisk together the lemon juice and yolks in a bowl. Stirring constantly, whisk a cup of the hot liquid into the egg yolk mixture, a little at a time, then pour it back into the soup, whisking. Do not allow it to boil again. Simmer the soup over low heat, stirring constantly, remove the pan from the heat, and stir in the fennel leaves. Season with salt and pepper. Ladle the soup into six heated bowls and serve.

MAKES 6 SERVINGS

Artichokes in Olive Oil and Lemon Broth

Lemon juice keeps the cut flesh of artichokes (as well as other vegetables and fruits) from turning dark with exposure to air. Its acidity also complements the taste of this Mediterranean vegetable. The broth of olive oil, stock, lemon juice, and seasonings is full of savor, and far more healthful than the hollandaise and mayonnaise sauces usually served with artichokes. This recipe comes from my brother, Rob Gawthrop.

4 large artichokes
Juice of 2 lemons
¼ cup olive oil
2 cups chicken, meat, or vegetable stock
1 stalk celery, chopped
1 medium-size onion, sliced
1 clove garlic
3 sprigs fresh parsley
½ teaspoon dried rosemary
½ bay leaf
8 black peppercorns

Wash the artichokes under cold running water. One at a time, trim the base flat with a sharp knife. Immediately rub the cut flesh with a cut lemon to keep it from darkening; continue to rub the cut flesh with lemon as you trim the artichokes. Pull off the tough outer leaves and trim all around the base with the knife. Cut across to remove the top inch of the crown. With scissors, snip off the spiky tops of the large outer leaves. Continue until all the artichokes are prepared, dropping them as you finish into a bowl of water mixed with 2 tablespoons of the lemon juice.

Mix together the olive oil, remaining lemon juice, and chicken stock in a nonreactive pot large enough to hold the artichokes. Add the celery, onion, garlic, herbs, and peppercorns. Put the artichokes in the liquid, bottoms down, and add fresh water to cover. Put the lid on and over medium heat bring the liquid to a boil. Reduce the heat to low and cook at a gentle bubble until a leaf pulls out easily, about 30 minutes. Cool the artichokes somewhat in the liquid. (This much may be done a day or two ahead, the artichokes covered and chilled; return them to room temperature before continuing.)

With a slotted spoon, remove the artichokes to a deep plate or soup bowl. Strain the broth through a sieve, pressing on the vegetables with the back of a spoon to extract any liquid. Reduce the broth over high heat until it is concentrated in flavor. Serve the artichokes warm or at room temperature with some of the reduced broth and good crusty bread to soak it up. Supply a plate for the leaves and choke and plenty of fresh napkins.

MAKES 4 SERVINGS

Lemon Allspice Pepper Seasoning

Homemade lemon pepper spiked with fresh zest, garlic, allspice, and black and white peppercorns has much more subtlety and zing than the commercially prepared mixture. The flavor of this dry marinade pressed into skinless chicken breasts, lamb chops, or other meat for a few hours before cooking permeates the flesh with its aroma. It also cuts down on the need for salt. Make it in larger quantity, adjusting the seasoning to your taste, if it suits your purpose.

24 black peppercorns
18 white peppercorns
12 allspice berries
Grated zest of 1 large lemon
1 clove garlic, finely minced
1 teaspoon kosher salt

Put the peppercorns and allspice berries in a piece of cloth and twist to enclose them. Pound the spices several times with a heavy mallet or rolling pin to crack and crush them. Mix them well with the zest, garlic, and salt.

This marinade should be used fresh. Spread it on a pan and press the meat into it so that it adheres; cover with plastic wrap and chill for several hours or overnight. Before broiling or grilling, slowly drizzle the meat with a little oil, perhaps mixed with lemon juice, to avoid washing off the dry marinade. Try not to cook the meat too close to the heating unit.

MAKES ABOUT 2 TABLESPOONS

Maître d'Hôtel Butter

This classic compound butter, otherwise known as lemon parsley butter, can also be made in a flash in the food processor. Use it to flavor vegetables or grilled fish, poultry, and meat. Try the butter with other herbs too, for instance fennel with fish, tarragon with lamb. Since it enlivens the taste of almost anything savory, keep it on hand.

½ cup (1 stick; ¼ pound) unsalted butter, softened
3 to 4 tablespoons chopped fresh parsley
1 tablespoon minced shallot
2 tablespoons fresh lemon juice
¼ teaspoon salt
Freshly ground white pepper to taste

In a bowl cream together the butter, parsley, and shallot; add the lemon juice gradually, beating until it is incorporated. Stir in the salt and pepper. (You can also mix the butter in a food processor, scraping down the sides of the bowl with a rubber spatula.) Pack the compound butter in a crock, or roll it up in plastic wrap in a log and chill until firm, cutting off slices as needed. Wrapped tightly and chilled, it keeps for a week; frozen, for several months.

MAKES ½ CUP

Lemon Butter Sauce

Rich but sublime, especially with poached or baked seafood.

¼ cup juices from cooked seafood or chicken, or fish or chicken stock
2 tablespoons fresh lemon juice
½ cup (1 stick) unsalted butter, softened and cut into tablespoons
2 tablespoons chopped fresh parsley or other herb (optional)
Salt and freshly black ground pepper to taste

In a small nonreactive saucepan, combine the fish or chicken juices and lemon juice; over high heat reduce the liquid to a glaze; be careful not to let it burn. Over the lowest possible heat, whisk in the butter a tablespoon at a time, letting each be absorbed before adding the next. Do not let the sauce overheat. Stir in the herbs and season with salt and pepper. Spoon the sauce over the fish or chicken and serve.

MAKES ½ CUP

Hollandaise Sauce

The classic method takes more time, but produces a finer, thicker, "well-mounted" sauce. The machine method is quicker, but produces a thinner sauce. Since the blade of a food processor sits above the bottom of the workbowl, a blender can work better.

Leftover hollandaise keeps well for a few days, covered and chilled. Spoon a little onto hot vegetables, eggs, fish, or chicken, or quickly glaze under the broiler. For sauce mousseline, gently warm it in a double boiler and fold in some whipped cream. Sauce maltaise is hollandaise flavored with a little juice and grated zest of a blood orange.

If the sauce should curdle, start again in a fresh clean bowl, beating 1 to 2 tablespoons of cream or milk into a little of the sauce and slowly, gradually, after it is smooth, adding the rest. Another method is to start with a fresh egg yolk in a clean bowl and slowly begin beating the curdled sauce into it, proceeding little by little when the revived sauce is smooth. When it is properly emulsified and you are about halfway through, you can speed up.

CLASSIC HOLLANDAISE

½ to ¾ cup (1 to 1½ sticks; 4 to 6 ounces) unsalted butter
3 large egg yolks
1½ tablespoons fresh lemon juice, or to taste
Salt to taste
Paprika or ground cayenne pepper (optional)

Gently melt the butter, reserving 2 to 3 tablespoons at room temperature. Put the yolks in a double boiler and whisk them over gently simmering water; whisk in most of the lemon juice. Slowly add the melted butter in a steady stream, whisking constantly to incorporate it into the yolks. When they have thickened, remove the top of the double boiler from the heat and whisk in the reserved butter one tablespoon at a time; continue beating to cool the sauce and make sure it won't curdle. Add more lemon juice, and season with salt and paprika; check the seasoning carefully. Hold the sauce in a warm but not hot spot until ready to use.

MAKES ABOUT 1 CUP

BLENDER HOLLANDAISE

Put the egg yolks and lemon juice in a blender or food processor, and turn the machine on for a moment to combine them. Gently melt all the butter in a small pan until hot and bubbly. With the motor running, pour the hot butter into the yolk mixture in a slow, steady, thin stream and continue whizzing until the yolks thicken. Season with paprika.

Lemon Horseradish Sauce

This simple sauce, much lighter than sour cream with horseradish, makes a fine accompaniment for smoked fish, chicken, or turkey, and an authoritative dip for the hors d'oeuvre table. Garnish the plate, if you like, with thin lemon slices or twists.

½ cup plain yogurt or labneh (see page 187)
½ lemon
1 tablespoon prepared horseradish, or to taste

First drain the yogurt, unless you are using labneh. You can do this by spooning the yogurt into a small coffee cone lined with a paper filter and setting it over a cup. Leave it there for 30 minutes or more to drain off some of the whey. Grate the zest from the lemon and squeeze the juice, about 2 tablespoons. In a small nonreactive bowl, stir them into the drained yogurt with the horseradish. Covered and chilled, the sauce will keep for several days or longer.

MAKES ABOUT ½ CUP

Moroccan Preserved Lemons

The peel and pulp of these lemons are used whole or chopped in Moroccan and Middle Eastern dishes of rice, fish, or meat. Reduce the spices if you prefer. The brine can flavor salads. Preserved in winter, the lemons will be ready to serve with summer grills and barbecues. To avoid the need for sterilizing, keep the jar in your refrigerator.

6 lemons, preferably thin-skinned lemons, about 1¾ pounds
½ cup coarse salt
One 1-inch stick cinnamon
½ teaspoon allspice berries
½ teaspoon black peppercorns
2 whole cloves
1 bay leaf

Bring a pot of water to a boil. Add the lemons, return the water to a boil, and cook 3 minutes. Drain, drop the lemons into cold water, changing it once or twice to cool the lemons; drain again and dry.

Stand the lemons on end and cut them lengthwise nearly into quarters so that they open out but remain attached at one end. Spread each open and sprinkle the inside liberally with the salt; close it up and pack it into a wide-mouthed 2-quart preserving jar, or two 1-quart jars, pressing down to squeeze out some of the juice. Continue with the remaining lemons. Add the spices to the jar (or divide them between two jars) along with the remaining salt, and pour in fresh boiling water up to the top. Wait a bit until all the bubbles have risen, then seal and sterilize (see page 321). Store at least 1 month in a cool, dry place. To use, rinse the lemons and quarter, slice, or chop them with or without the pulp. After opening, store in the refrigerator.

MAKES 2 QUARTS

Lemon Chess Pie

The name of this old favorite is a corruption of the word cheese, from its custardy "cheese" filling. Like much Southern food, it is rich and delicious.

One 9-inch pastry shell (see page 35), not too deep, partially baked
½ cup (1 stick; ¼ pound) unsalted butter, at room temperature
1 cup sugar
3 large eggs
Grated zest of 1 lemon
¼ cup fresh lemon juice
¼ cup buttermilk
½ teaspoon pure vanilla extract
1 tablespoon cornmeal
¼ teaspoon freshly grated nutmeg

Preheat the oven to 400°F. In a medium-size bowl, cream together the butter and sugar. Beat in the eggs one by one, until they are well combined. Stir in the lemon zest and juice, buttermilk, vanilla, and cornmeal. The mixture should be smooth and light.

Set the partially cooked pastry shell on a cookie sheet and pour in the filling. Sprinkle a little grated nutmeg over the surface. Very carefully, with a steady hand, place the baking sheet in the middle of the oven. Bake for 10 minutes, then lower the heat to 325°F and bake until the filling has risen, turned golden brown, and is nearly set in the middle, about 20 minutes more. Allow the pie to cool on a rack and the filling to settle before serving.

MAKES ONE 9-INCH PIE; 6 TO 8 SERVINGS

Lemon Meringue Pie

This is the old American favorite without any gussying up.

FOR THE FILLING
1¼ cups sugar
¼ cup cornstarch
¼ teaspoon salt
1 cup water
½ cup fresh lemon juice
3 large egg yolks
2 tablespoons unsalted butter
Grated zest of 1 lemon

FOR THE PIE SHELL
One 8-inch pie shell (see page 35), baked

FOR THE MERINGUE TOPPING
3 large egg whites, at room temperature
¼ teaspoon cream of tartar
¼ cup plus 2 tablespoons sugar

For the filling, combine the sugar, cornstarch, and salt in a nonreactive saucepan. Gradually add the water and lemon juice, stirring to make a smooth mixture. Over medium-high heat, bring the mixture to a boil, stirring constantly. Boil 1 minute, still stirring, as it turns thick and clear, then remove from the heat. Pour half the hot mixture into the yolks, stirring constantly, then pour the mixture back into the pan, stirring to keep the eggs from scrambling. Cook over low heat, stirring, a few minutes more. Stir in the butter and lemon zest. Pour the lemon mixture into the baked pie shell and smooth with a spatula.

Preheat the oven to 350°F. To make the meringue, beat the egg whites in a large clean bowl with the cream of tartar. When they make soft peaks, gradually add the sugar and continue until the meringue becomes stiff and glossy and the sugar crystals are dissolved (rub a little between your fingers to feel). Spoon the meringue over the lemon filling, making sure the edges are covered and sealed (otherwise the filling will bubble out). Smooth the meringue, then make peaks (or whatever design you wish) with the back of a spoon. Bake until the surface is lightly browned, about 12 minutes. Cool before serving; refrigerate if not serving right away.

MAKES ONE 8-INCH PIE; 8 SERVINGS

Tarte au Citron

This simple but elegant tart in the French style is intensely lemony. If you want yours a little sweeter, mix the lemon juice and sugar, taste, and add more sugar before mixing in the eggs. You can also make it with limes, oranges, or tangerines, adjusting the amount of sugar accordingly.

Grated zest of 2 lemons
⅔ cup fresh lemon juice, strained
1 cup sugar, or to taste
3 large eggs, lightly beaten
⅔ cup heavy cream
One 9-inch Almond Pâte Sucrée (see page 14), partially baked
Whipped cream, crème fraîche (see page 155), confectioners' sugar, berries, or sprigs of
*   fresh herbs for garnish*

Preheat the oven to 350°F. Mix together in a small bowl the lemon zest, juice, and sugar. Taste for sweetness, then stir in the eggs and cream, mixing thoroughly. Set the partially baked tart shell on a cookie sheet near the oven and pour in the filling; do not overfill the shell. With a very steady hand, put the tart in the oven. Bake until the tart is set, about 30 minutes. It should not color or rise as it bakes. Cool the tart thoroughly. Dust the top if you like with sifted confectioners' sugar and serve it with whipped cream or crème fraîche. Fresh berries and sprigs of mint or lemon balm make a pretty garnish for a special occasion.

MAKES ONE 9-INCH TART; 6 TO 8 SERVINGS

Lemon Hazelnut Cheesecake

The lemony freshness and incorporated air keep this cheesecake, though rich, from being heavy. Hazelnuts add texture and depth. For a lighter version, substitute low-fat cottage cheese and ricotta for the cream cheese. Make the cheesecake a day ahead and chill it thoroughly before serving in thin wedges.

½ cup hazelnuts, lightly toasted (see page 179)
¾ cup sugar
1 cup graham cracker crumbs (made from 8 whole graham crackers)
¼ cup (½ stick) unsalted butter, melted and cooled
1 pound cream cheese, preferably fresh
2 lemons
3 tablespoons all-purpose flour
1½ teaspoons pure vanilla extract

5 large eggs, separated, at room temperature
1 cup chilled heavy cream

First make the crust. Put the hazelnuts and ¼ cup of the sugar in a food processor and pulse until the nuts are coarsely chopped. Add the graham cracker crumbs and pulse to combine them. Turn the mixture into an 8- or 9-inch springform pan and mix in the butter, just enough to hold the crumbs together. Press them three quarters of the way up the sides of the pan and pat them over the bottom. Chill the pan to firm the crust.

Preheat the oven to 300°F. To make the filling, chill one very large mixing bowl. Wipe the food processor and blade with a cloth. Put the remaining sugar in the food processor with the cream cheese and process until light and fluffy, scraping down the sides once or twice with a rubber spatula. Grate the zest of the lemons and squeeze the juice to measure a scant ½ cup. Add the lemon zest, juice, flour, vanilla, and egg yolks to the cream cheese; process until well combined.

In the very large chilled bowl, beat the heavy cream until stiff peaks form. In another large bowl with a clean beater or whisk, beat the egg whites until they form stiff peaks. Fold the cream cheese mixture into the whipped cream (do not mix in the food processor). Then fold the egg whites into the cream mixture.

Pour the batter into the prepared crust. Bake for 30 minutes. Lower the heat to 275°F and bake until the cheesecake is risen and lightly gilded on top, about 1 hour more. Open the oven door to allow the cake to cool. Cool completely on a rack at room temperature, then chill thoroughly in the refrigerator, preferably overnight. Run a knife around the edge and remove the springform collar before serving the cheesecake cut into thin wedges. If you like, garnish the top with candied lemon slices (see page 158), spiral strips of blanched lemon zest, or a few hazelnuts toasted and halved.

MAKES ONE 8- OR 9-INCH CAKE; 12 SERVINGS

Lemon Sponge Pudding

This favorite childhood pudding, easily made from kitchen staples, separates during baking into a light cake topping and loose custard bottom. Dress it up if you like with whipped cream, berry purée, or confectioners' sugar, but it's not necessary.

1½ tablespoons unsalted butter, softened
¾ cup sugar
2 large eggs, separated, at room temperature
2 tablespoons all-purpose flour
Grated zest of 1 lemon
¼ cup fresh lemon juice (1 large lemon may be enough)
1 cup milk

Butter four 7-ounce custard cups and set them in a larger pan or bain marie. Preheat the oven to 350°F.

Cream the butter in a large bowl until light, then thoroughly blend in the sugar. Beat in the egg yolks one at a time until incorporated, then stir in the flour, lemon zest and juice, and finally the milk.

In medium-size bowl, beat the egg whites until they make soft peaks, then fold them into the custard batter until no more white streaks show. Spoon the pudding into the prepared custard cups, and pour boiling water into the pan to reach halfway up the sides of the cups. Bake the pudding until golden, about 45 minutes. Serve warm or chilled.

MAKES 4 STANDARD CUSTARD CUP SERVINGS (7 OUNCES EACH) OR
6 INDIVIDUAL SOUFFLÉ RAMEKIN SERVINGS (5 OUNCES EACH)

Lemon Snow Pudding

This old-fashioned American dessert comes from my friends Liz Tate and Steve Parks. Their version is intentionally tart: add more sugar if you wish. Custard sauce made with the leftover egg yolks is traditional (see page 300), but a rich fruit purée such as Brandied Plum Sauce (page 248)—deep rose, light, and lustrous—is less caloric. You could garnish the pudding with plum slices arranged like flower petals.

> 1 envelope unflavored gelatin
> ¼ cup water
> ¾ cup boiling water
> ½ cup fresh lemon juice, strained
> Grated zèst of 1 lemon
> ⅓ cup sugar, or to taste
> 3 large egg whites, at room temperature
> Pinch of salt or cream of tartar

In a small saucepan soften the gelatin in the cold water. Pour in the boiling water and stir until the gelatin is dissolved. Add the lemon juice, zest, and sugar, and stir until the sugar is dissolved. Cover and chill the mixture until it gets thick and globby but is not quite yet set (about 3 hours).

Chill a 5- or 6-cup bowl or mold. In a large bowl, beat the egg whites with the salt until they make soft peaks. Gradually beat the lemon jelly into them to make a froth. Pour the pudding into the chilled mold, cover, and refrigerate for several hours until set. (This can be done a day or two ahead.)

To serve, briefly dip the bowl into hot water, put a serving plate on top, and invert the pudding onto the plate to unmold it. Surround the pudding with sauce.

MAKES 6 SERVINGS

Lemon Curd

Lemon curd, an English favorite, is very handy: serve it on toast for breakfast; layer it on sponge cakes and roulades; spoon it into tarts; bake it under meringue for a quick lemon meringue pie; fold whipped egg whites into it and bake as a souffléed dessert topping; or mix it into an equal volume of whipped cream for an airy mousse for fresh fruit.

> *3 lemons*
> *½ cup (1 stick; ¼ pound) unsalted butter, cut into pieces*
> *1 cup sugar*
> *3 large eggs, beaten*

Grate the lemon zest; squeeze and strain the juice to measure ½ cup or more. Put the lemon zest and juice in the top of a double boiler with the butter and sugar. Heat the mixture over gently simmering water until the butter is melted and the sugar dissolved. Taste to see if you have enough sugar to balance the lemon juice. In a slow, steady stream, beating all the while, pour in the eggs. Continue stirring the mixture until it thickens and the lemon curd lightly coats the back of a spoon, 15 to 20 minutes. Be careful not to go too far and scramble the eggs.

Take the pan off the heat and continue stirring a little longer until the curd has cooled a bit. Strain it through a sieve into a container with a tight lid. Cool, cover tightly, and keep in the refrigerator for two weeks or more.

MAKES ABOUT 1¾ CUPS, ENOUGH TO FILL A 9-INCH TART OR 8 TARTLETS

Light Lemon Soufflés

These little soufflés are festive and elegant, yet easily prepared from staples. Since they contain no butter-flour-cream base, they are lower in calories and cholesterol than the classic soufflé. Individual cups sprinkled with sugar crystals allow the light batter to rise high and require no serving at table. This recipe is also excellent with half Grand Marnier and half orange juice in place of the lemon juice, accented by the zest of an orange.

> *¼ cup sugar, including sugar for soufflé cups*
> *3 large eggs, separated, plus 1 white, at room temperature*
> *¼ cup fresh lemon juice, strained*
> *Grated zest of 1 lemon*

Preheat the oven to 350°F. Smear the insides of six 5-ounce soufflé cups with butter or vegetable oil. Over a medium-size bowl to catch any excess crystals, sprinkle the sides of the soufflé cups with about 1 tablespoon of the sugar. Set the soufflé cups in an ovenproof pan large enough to hold them without touching.

In the same bowl, lightly beat together the egg yolks and remaining sugar. Stir in the lemon juice and zest. In a larger bowl, whip the egg whites until they hold a springy but not brittle peak. Fold a spoonful of whites into the yolk mixture, then quickly but gently fold the yolks back into the remaining egg whites until no streaks remain. Spoon the batter into the soufflé cups. Set them in their pan and bake until the soufflés have risen and are golden brown on top, about 18 minutes. Serve them immediately as they are or dusted with confectioners' sugar. For a very special occasion you may want to pass Fresh Strawberry Sauce (see page 295) or hot Apricot Rum Sauce (see page 40) separately.

MAKES 6 SERVINGS

Lemon Butter Cookies

Made with the best ingredients, these simple cookies accompany any fresh fruit to perfection.

> ½ cup (1 stick; ¼ pound) unsalted butter, softened
> ½ cup sugar
> 1 large egg yolk
> ¼ cup fresh lemon juice
> Grated zest of 1 lemon
> ¾ cup plus 2 tablespoons all-purpose flour
> Pinch of salt
> Confectioners' sugar for dusting

Preheat the oven to 375°F. Grease the cookie sheets.

Cream together the butter and sugar in a medium-size bowl until light, then mix in the egg yolk. Stir in the lemon juice and zest, then fold in the flour and salt.

Drop the batter by the teaspoonful onto the cookie sheets, allowing plenty of room for the cookies to spread. Bake until the edges of the cookies begin to brown, 8 to 10 minutes. Cool the cookies slightly, then loosen them from the sheet with a spatula to prevent sticking. Sift confectioners' sugar on top and cool completely before serving. Store the cookies in airtight tins.

MAKES ABOUT 3 DOZEN COOKIES

Lemon Honey Buttermilk Sherbet

This lovely lemon sherbet is subtle, fresh, light, and aromatic. Serve it if possible with flowering sprigs of thyme.

1 quart buttermilk
1 cup fresh lemon juice, strained
Four 2-inch strips lemon zest
¾ cup honey
2 sprigs fresh thyme (optional)

Mix together all the ingredients in a large bowl, and let the flavors infuse overnight or at least for several hours. Discard the lemon zest and thyme sprigs. Taste carefully for balance.

Freeze the sherbet in a sorbetière or ice cream machine according to the manufacturer's directions, or in a bowl, stirring at intervals to smooth the ice crystals as they freeze. Or freeze according to the directions on page 307. If made ahead, this sherbet should be softened slightly in the refrigerator before serving.

MAKES ABOUT 1½ QUARTS

LIMES

British sailors acquired their nickname, limeys, from their daily ration of lime juice issued to ward off scurvy, caused by lack of vitamin C. Sir James Lind, the Scottish naval surgeon, observed the dramatic effect eating oranges and lemons had on sailors during long voyages and revived a practice begun as early as 1593. But not until 1795 were limes made regulation issue, their juice drunk with the daily ration of rum while officers watched. Limes could be imported cheaply and without risk from the English colony Jamaica, while lemons had to be bought from Mediterranean countries with whom Britain was often at war.

Limes are classified as *Citrus aurantifolia*, separate from lemons, despite their similarity. Limes need year-round warmth and grow in this country only in southernmost Florida and California. There are two types of lime, sweet and sour, but only the sour has caught on in the United States. The Key lime, also called West Indian or Mexican lime, was brought by Columbus to Hispaniola (now Haiti), and Spanish settlers soon established it in Florida. There it acquired its modern name from the southerly chain of islands. The Key lime is smaller, yellower, sourer, and seedier than the Persian or Tahiti lime commonly available. As for other varieties of limes, the yellowish Bearss is mainly sold in California. The bitter Kaffir lime, whose leaves often flavor Southeast Asian cooking, is not a lime at all, and the very acidic Calamansi popular in the Philippines is a cross between a lime and a kumquat.

The season for limes peaks in late spring and summer, ideal for use in refreshing drinks, seviches, marinades, sherbets, and, of course, Key lime pie. The influx of new ethnic groups from the Caribbean, Mexico, and Asia has brought new interest in many dishes which use the cooling lime with chiles, ginger, cumin, coriander, and other spicy seasonings. In hot weather especially, the fragrance of a squeeze of fresh juice and grating of zest perfectly sets off tropical fruits such as melon, papaya, and mango. Often a small amount of the aromatic citrus will add a whole dimension, so many recipes containing lime are given under other fruits. Of course, recipes for lemon and lime, with virtually identical cooking properties, are often interchangeable (quantity and sweetness may have to be adjusted), although the flavor is not the same. Lime's fragrance is unmistakable yet elusive.

Limes are best stored at 55°F. In the colder temperatures of the refrigerator, where they will keep for a week or ten days, the skin will soon become pitted with brown. If you are setting up a bar, avoid putting limes directly on the ice. Limes yellow and age quickly in bright sunlight.

A medium-size lime contains twenty calories, half as much vitamin C as a lemon, and about three scant tablespoons of fresh juice. Four to five limes will yield about ½ cup of juice, but yields can vary widely. To get as much juice as possible from a lime, roll it back and forth on a flat surface under the fingers and palm of your hand before squeezing.

Shrimp Grilled with Ginger, Lime, and Coriander Butter

This hors d'oeuvre is very simple—just watch the shrimp closely to avoid overcooking. Leftover butter is deliciously useful, turning prosaic vegetables such as sautéed parsnips and carrots into something exotic.

½ cup (1 stick; ¼ pound) unsalted butter, softened
3 thin slices fresh ginger, peeled and minced
1 clove garlic, minced
1 scallion (green and white parts), chopped
2 tablespoons chopped fresh coriander (cilantro)
2 tablespoons grated lime zest
2 tablespoons fresh lime juice
Salt and freshly ground black pepper to taste
1 pound medium-large raw shrimp, shelled and deveined
Lime slices or wedges for garnish

Put all the ingredients except the shrimp and garnish in a food processor. Combine well, scraping down the sides once or twice with a rubber spatula. Taste carefully and sharpen the seasonings to taste. (This may be done several days ahead, packed in a crock or rolled in plastic wrap in a log, and chilled or frozen. It will keep a week or more in the refrigerator, a month or more in the freezer. Before proceeding, soften the butter.)

Soak 8 bamboo skewers in water for half an hour. Preheat the broiler. Thread the shrimp onto the bamboo skewers, dividing them evenly, and brush liberally with the seasoned butter. Broil, uncovered, for 2 minutes; turn, brush again, and cook about 2 minutes more, until the shrimp are barely opaque but still juicy. Serve a skewer of shrimp on each plate garnished with a slice or wedge of lime.

MAKES 8 FIRST-COURSE SERVINGS; ABOUT ¾ CUP FLAVORED BUTTER

Scallop Seviche

Serve this first course in hot weather: lime juice "cooks" the scallops with its acid, so that no heat is needed. Season it as spicy hot as you like, in contrast to the pearly scallops.

1 pound scallops (if using large sea scallops, cut them across in half)
¼ cup plus 2 tablespoons fresh lime juice
3 tablespoons extra virgin olive oil
¼ cup chopped red onion
1 clove garlic, minced
1 fresh hot chile pepper or ¼ medium-size red bell pepper, seeded and chopped
2 tablespoons chopped fresh coriander (cilantro) or parsley
1 tablespoon julienned lime zest
Salt and freshly ground black pepper to taste
Lime slices for garnish

Put the scallops in a nonreactive bowl and add the lime juice. Stir well and make sure all the scallops are immersed in the liquid. Cover and chill for one or two hours, stirring occasionally. The scallops will turn opaque all the way through when they are "cooked" by the action of the lime juice.

To serve, drain the lime juice from the scallops, discarding the juice, and mix them with the rest of the ingredients. Divide the scallops among individual serving plates (scallop shells are ideal), and garnish with slices of lime.

MAKES 4 TO 6 FIRST-COURSE SERVINGS

Shrimp Seviche with Crème Fraîche

This makes an excellent first course when your attention must be elsewhere. Don't substitute large shrimp: the small size allows the acid to penetrate.

¾ cup fresh lime juice
3 tablespoons sliced scallions (green and white parts)
Salt and freshly ground black pepper to taste
2 pounds small to medium-size very fresh raw shrimp, shelled and deveined (4 cups shelled, about 1½ pounds)
3 tablespoons capers, drained and rinsed
⅔ cup crème fraîche (recipe follows)
Lettuce leaves for serving
1 tablespoon minced green scallion tops for garnish
Lime slices for garnish

Combine the lime juice, chopped scallions, salt, and pepper in a medium-size nonreactive bowl. Add the shrimp and stir well. Cover and refrigerate for at least 2 to 4 hours (8 hours maximum), stirring occasionally to mix the shrimp in the marinade. The acid of the lime juice will "cook" the shrimp without heat, turning them pale pink and white in color and leaving them quite delicate in texture.

To serve, drain the shrimp thoroughly, discarding the marinade. Fold in the capers and crème fraîche so that every shrimp is coated. Lay a bed of lettuce on individual plates or scallop shells and nestle the shrimp on top. Sprinkle with the minced scallion tops and garnish with very thin slices of lime. Serve at once.

MAKES 8 SERVINGS

Crème Fraîche

The culture in crème fraîche helps it to keep much longer than fresh cream.

1 cup heavy cream
4½ teaspoons buttermilk

In a small jar mix together the cream and buttermilk. Screw on the top of the jar and shake well for at least 1 minute. Leave the jar, still covered, at room temperature for 8 hours, then chill. Crème fraîche will keep for several weeks.

MAKES ABOUT 1 CUP

Chicken and Lime Salad

This salad combines zesty, crunchy, sweet, and spicy flavors. To complete the light main course, serve with a loaf of crusty whole-grain bread.

2 limes
¼ cup vegetable oil
½ teaspoon cumin seeds or ¼ teaspoon ground, or to taste
Salt and freshly ground black pepper to taste
2 cups cubed cooked chicken
½ cup diced jícama or cucumber
¼ large red bell pepper, seeded and cut into 2-inch strips
3 scallions (green and white parts), chopped
2 tablespoons chopped fresh parsley
1 head redleaf or other loose leaf lettuce

Grate the zest from one of the limes and squeeze the juice, saving 2 tablespoons of juice and the zest (use the remaining juice for another recipe). With a sharp knife remove the peel from the second lime, cut out the individual sections, and set aside. Mix together the oil, lime juice, zest, cumin, salt, and pepper in a nonreactive bowl. Stir the chicken into the vinaigrette and let it marinate for an hour or two for the flavors to develop.

Shortly before serving, stir the lime sections into the chicken along with the jícama, pepper, scallions, and parsley. Lay a bed of lettuce on serving plates, and mound the chicken salad on top.

MAKES 3 TO 4 SERVINGS

Jellied Herbed Cucumber and Lime Soup

This lightly jellied soup makes a delicate and refreshing first course for an elegant summer party. It contains almost no calories and can be made entirely ahead of time. Use zucchini instead of cucumber, if you like, or mint for the dill. If you have chive flowers in your garden, they make a beautiful garnish.

1 envelope unflavored gelatin
¼ cup water
2 cups chicken stock
1 large cucumber, peeled, seeded, and coarsely chopped
3 scallions (green and white parts), chopped
⅓ cup fresh lime juice, or to taste
3 tablespoons chopped fresh dill
2 tablespoons snipped fresh chives
Salt and freshly ground black pepper to taste
Lime slices for garnish

Soften the gelatin in the water for 5 minutes. Pour it and the stock into a small saucepan over low heat and dissolve the gelatin, stirring. Put the mixture in a food processor along with the cucumber, scallions, and lime juice. Combine the ingredients without reducing them to a fine purée: be sure to leave a little texture. Season the soup with the dill, chives, salt, and pepper, and taste carefully to see if it needs sharpening with more lime juice. Pour the mixture into a bowl, cover, and refrigerate for at least 3 hours, until the gelatin is set.

To serve, stir to mix the solids throughout the jellied soup, scoop it into cups, and garnish with thin slices of lime. If the weather is very hot, serve the soup quickly, before it begins to melt, since it contains a minimal amount of gelatin.

MAKES 6 SERVINGS

Lime Soy Marinade

This marinade with Oriental overtones is terrific with seafood and chicken. For a simple but stylish barbecue for a crowd when you haven't time to fuss over the main course, marinate an unskinned side of salmon in it for 2 hours, chilled, or 30 minutes at room temperature, before grilling.

⅓ cup soy sauce
⅓ cup peanut oil
⅓ cup dry white vermouth
⅓ cup fresh lime juice
Grated zest of 2 limes
2 scallions (green and white parts), chopped
3 slices fresh ginger, peeled and minced
1 large clove garlic, minced
2 tablespoons snipped fresh chives
2 tablespoons chopped fresh coriander (cilantro)

Mix together in a large pan or bowl all the seasonings. Covered and chilled, it should keep for a few days, during which the flavor will strengthen. Add the herbs shortly before marinating your seafood or meat.

MAKES ABOUT 1½ CUPS

Key Lime Pie

The Key lime, a small yellow-green variety from Mexico with a characteristically tart flavor, is the traditional lime to use, but it is hard to find even in the Florida Keys that give them their name. The Persian lime commonly available still makes a delicious pie, sharpened with a touch of lemon juice. This pie uses sweetened condensed milk, introduced by Borden in 1858, because dairy cows were scarce on the Keys. Some versions are unbaked, chilled or frozen, but cooking eliminates the danger of egg yolks contaminated with salmonella.

4 large egg yolks
One 14-ounce can sweetened condensed milk
½ cup fresh lime juice
1 tablespoon fresh lemon juice
1 or 2 drops green food coloring (optional)
One 9-inch graham cracker or regular pastry crust (see page 35)

Preheat the oven to 350°F.

With an electric mixer, hand beater, or whisk, mix the egg yolks together well in a bowl. Continue beating as you gradually add the condensed milk in a slow, steady stream, then the lime and lemon juice. The mixture should be thick and creamy. For green color—it will otherwise be yellow—add a drop or two of green food coloring. Add one drop and stir to see if you need another: garish green is not your aim. Pour the custard into the prepared shell and bake until set, about 13 minutes. Cool the pie; cover and chill it if you are not serving it right away. Serve it at room temperature with a meringue topping made from the 4 egg whites (see Lemon Meringue Pie, page 145) or with lightly sweetened whipped cream. Lime zest julienne makes a pretty garnish.

MAKES ONE 9-INCH PIE; 6 TO 8 SERVINGS

Candied Lime Slices

This method of candying works for any citrus fruit. You can candy limes, lemons, and small oranges or tight-skinned tangerines all at once, to contrast their colorful peels. It is important to slice them ³⁄₁₆ of an inch thick—less and the pulp will disintegrate, more and the rinds will be tough. Keep the liquid at a slow simmer so the pulp doesn't fall apart.

  2 cups sugar
  4 cups water
  1 pound limes or other citrus fruit, seedless and thin-skinned if possible

Put the sugar and water in a wide shallow pan, bring to a boil, and let boil until the sugar is dissolved, about 5 minutes. Meanwhile, cut the limes across into rounds ³⁄₁₆-inch thick; pick out any seeds and save the heels for another purpose. Drop the citrus slices into the syrup one after another, avoiding crowding or double-layering in the pan. Simmer over low heat (do not let the syrup boil) until the pulp is translucent and the rind tender, 45 minutes to 1 hour or even longer (if you are cooking different citrus fruits, cooking times will vary; it's better not to mix batches). Halfway through you can turn the rounds over with tongs or a slotted spoon; if the slices are submerged this is not necessary. If you like, let the rounds cool in the syrup.

With tongs or a slotted spoon, transfer the slices as they are done to a rack to drain. Leave them to dry for at least 1 hour, when they will be soft and pliable, suitable for garnishing cakes and other pastries; you may want to boil the syrup down to a glaze to brush on the slices. To dry them further, leave them out to dry several hours to several days, depending on the weather and your purpose. They will eventually dry out completely and become firm, suitable for serving as a sweetmeat. Before they are completely dry, you can coat them with sand sugar spread on a plate. Dry or sugared, layer the citrus slices in waxed paper in an airtight tin, where they will keep for several days or as long as several months, depending on moisture content.

Lime Granita

This granita is supposed to have granular ice crystals—the better to refresh you on a hot summer afternoon. You can dress this ice up in many ways, but here is the essential recipe.

1 cup fresh lime juice, strained
Grated zest of 2 limes
1 cup sugar
2½ cups water

Combine the lime juice, zest, and sugar in a large nonreactive bowl. Stir until the sugar is dissolved by the acid, then add the water. Cover the bowl and put it in the freezer. After an hour or so, stir every once in a while to break up the crystals. In a few hours, when it has achieved a pleasantly granular texture, serve it in cups or bowls.

MAKES ABOUT 1 QUART

MANGOES

The mango's prehistoric origins are perfumed in the luxurious exoticism of India. In a Hindu legend, the beautiful daughter of the sun escaped from a wicked sorceress by hiding in a mango tree. When the tree flowered and the fruit ripened, the king fell in love with it, only to see the ripe mango fall from the tree and split open, revealing his beloved wife, as resplendent as the golden sun.

Like the pomegranate, the Asian mango made its way east to the Far East and west, via Portuguese rather than Arab traders, to Africa and then the New World. But India still grows more mangoes than anyplace else, 60 percent of the world's crop, and perhaps its most luscious specimens. Throughout the tropics it is a staple food of importance comparable to the temperate zone's apple, prepared in many ways both savory and sweet: unripe and cooked, ripe and fresh, preserved in chutneys and pickles, or dried and powdered.

As my friend Laxmi Rao puts it, summers in India are woven around mangoes, and baskets of them nestled in straw are left to ripen for two weeks or so, with great anticipation by the household. A gift of these is a warm gesture of friendship. How many mangoes did you eat today? is a frequent question during their short season. In the United States Laxmi's family rarely buys mangoes, but she sometimes purchases canned purée at Indian shops. On visits home to India she tries to find the Alphonso, the "king" of mangoes, a variety unavailable in North America but shipped to Europe and said to be a regular consignment to the English royal family—a holdover from the days of the Raj.

Mangifera indica is a tall evergreen tree with many long, pointed, glossy leaves and a yellow or red flower. There are many hundreds of varieties. The fruit can weigh from a quarter of a pound to nearly five pounds. Its widely variable shape can be oval, long, or teardrop, with a curved tip—this last a form on which many Indian decorative patterns are based. The thin leathery skin may be colored either green, yellow, orange, purple, or red, with the interior in similar mix-and-match shades. Some mangoes have coarse, fibrous flesh and a turpentine taste, but these unpleasant characteristics are less apparent in fruit that has been carefully grafted rather than grown from seed. At its best the mango is considered by many to be supreme of all fruit—exotic, rich, and fragrant.

Mango season is spring and summer, with most fruit in American markets imported from Mexico and Haiti. In the continental United States, only southern Florida has a climate reliably warm enough for it. A recent change in regulations has meant more mangoes being imported from Central and South America and the West Indies. Markets will gradually be carrying more mangoes year-round.

Of the varieties available in American markets, the oblong Tommy Atkins is most common. It weighs about a pound, with colorful yellow, orange, and reddish splotched skin, and smooth, firm, yellow flesh with little fiber. The oval Van Dyke is smaller, with skin color ripening to similar multicolors and orange flesh with a more pronounced flavor. The Keitt is large, about two pounds or more, remaining greenish when ripe, with golden flesh. The Francisque, Haden, Kent, and Oro are other varieties.

To choose a ripe mango, go by scent and feel rather than look (although refrigeration can temporarily dull the scent). The stem end should give off a pleasing fragrance and the skin yield to gentle pressure. Avoid fruit that smells sour or has no smell, or fruit with skin that feels baggy or has soft or black spots. Color varies widely according to variety and is not necessarily an indication of maturity. Ripen the fruit at room temperature, in an enclosed bag if you wish to hasten the process. Once ripe, refrigerate it only briefly: this tropical creature does not like the cold.

Mango is notoriously messy to eat, part of the sensual pleasure of eating this exotic fruit. To get to the juicy flesh, first remove the flat oblong pit which clings to it stubbornly. If you want slices, peel off the skin with a vegetable peeler, then cut the flesh in long parallel slices down to the pit, freeing the slices from it.

If you want to cube or purée the flesh, the best method is to stand the mango upright with the thin side toward you and slice down in two parallel strokes on either side of the pit, making two flat boats. Cut crisscrosses into the flesh of each boat down to the skin (but not through), and turn the skin inside out to splay the flesh. Cut close to the skin to free the flesh. Then remove the skin around the pit and cut off any flesh clinging to the pit. This flesh tends to be the most fibrous, so you may prefer to suck the pit in private, cook's prerogative.

Mangoes vary greatly in size, but as a rule of thumb, a three-quarter-pound mango will yield about one and a quarter cups of cubed flesh and about one cup of purée. Since mangoes are rarely cheap in North America, we usually eat them fully ripe without exploiting their diversity, as is done in the tropics. They are delicious in a wide variety of dishes, spicy or delicate, complex or simple. They go with all tropical fruits and flavorings, taking well to ginger, chiles, and coconut, as well as to creamy custards and smooth sherbets. Prepare them much as you would papayas, peaches, and melons, but bear in mind mango's more assertive fragrance and rich sweetness. Lime or other citrus sets off mango well. So does rum, gin, Grand Marnier, or other spirits, either drizzled on sliced or cubed mango or mixed into mango purées and cocktails.

Mangoes are a rich source of vitamins A and C and to a lesser extent vitamin B_6, as well as the minerals potassium and copper, with little sodium but lots of fiber. Half a pound of mango pulp contains about 130 calories. Be careful of getting the juice on clothing, as it stains. The fruit is a member of the cashew family, which also includes poison ivy and poison oak. Mango skins and juice can cause a similar allergic reaction in the skin of some sensitive people, although eating the ripe flesh may result in no problem.

Frozen Mango Daiquiri

Frozen strawberry daiquiris have been a favorite summer cocktail in recent years. Here is a mango variation, and on a warm summer day this sun-colored cocktail tastes as luscious as it looks. The concoction does not work in a food processor; you really do need a blender. For a strawberry daiquiri, substitute 4 large (not huge) frozen strawberries for the mango. Frozen pineapple chunks are another variation.

¼ ripe mango
2 jiggers light rum (3 ounces)
1 jigger fresh lime juice (1½ ounces) or juice of 1 large lime
3 tablespoons sugar, or to taste
2 cups crushed ice (about 10 large cubes)

Ahead of time, peel a quarter of the mango and slice the flesh off the pit. Cut the slices into chunks, wrap them in plastic, and freeze them solid. Use the rest of the mango for another recipe (or for additional cocktails).

In the blender combine the frozen mango chunks with the rum, lime juice, sugar, and crushed ice. Blend the mixture on low for a few minutes until it is homogenized and chopped fine. Quickly check for sweetness, then increase the speed to high for a few seconds more, until the mixture is snowy and firm. Pour the cocktails into pretty stemmed glasses such as a saucer champagne glasses and serve at once.

MAKES 2 DRINKS

Curried Chicken and Mango Salad

Serve this salad with a little chutney (not mango) passed separately.

½ cup sour cream or plain yogurt
2 tablespoons fresh lemon juice
1 tablespoon curry powder, or to taste
2½ cups cubed cooked chicken meat
⅔ cup peeled, cored, and diced apple
3 scallions (green and white parts), thinly sliced
2 tablespoons chopped fresh coriander (cilantro)
Salt and freshly ground black pepper to taste

Redleaf lettuce
1 medium-size ripe mango (about 1 pound), pitted, peeled, and sliced
3 tablespoons sliced blanched almonds, lightly toasted (see page 179)

Mix together in a bowl the sour cream, lemon juice, and curry powder, adding the curry gradually to avoid overseasoning. Taste carefully, as palates and brands differ, and add more if desired. Stir in the chicken, apple, scallions, coriander, salt, and pepper to taste. There should be just enough sour cream to hold it together.

Lay a bed of lettuce on individual plates and mound the chicken mixture in the middle. Place the mango slices around it attractively and top with the toasted almonds.

MAKES 6 APPETIZER SERVINGS

Fresh Mango Chutney

In the west we are familiar with bottled mango chutney preserved in a thick spicy vinegar syrup. In India, *chatni*, a Hindi word meaning "mashed," comes in an infinite variety extending beyond the Anglo-Indian understanding of the term. Not surprisingly, fresh mango chutney served the same day it is made is at least as appealing as the commercial version. Make the chutney as hot or cool, spicy or mild as you like, but be sure the flavors are balanced. Serve with cold meats and other savory dishes.

1 medium-size mango, firm and fragrant but not yet fully ripe (about 1 pound)
1 fresh hot chile pepper, seeded and chopped (include the seeds for more heat)
1 scallion (green and white parts), chopped
2 tablespoons chopped fresh coriander (cilantro)
2 tablespoons unsweetened shredded coconut (optional)
1 tablespoon peeled and minced fresh ginger
2 tablespoons fresh lime or lemon juice
Pinch of salt

Pit and peel the mango, and cut the flesh into small dice. Stir in a bowl with the remaining ingredients until they are well mixed. Let the chutney flavors develop in the refrigerator, covered, for 30 minutes to a few hours. Serve the chutney the same day it is made.

MAKES 1 GENEROUS CUP

Sliced Mango Dessert with Gin

This luscious dessert is simplicity itself and needs nothing more. The juices thicken slightly as the mango macerates.

1 medium-size ripe mango (about 1 pound)
2 tablespoons fresh lime juice
1 tablespoon gin
2 dabs sour cream, plain yogurt, or crème fraîche (see page 155)
Brown sugar for sprinkling

Stand the mango upright and cut two lengthwise slices on either side of the pit. Pull or peel off the skin and cut the fruit into thin slices. Keeping the slices together, lay them in a shallow nonreactive dish, and splash them with the lime juice and gin. Let the mango macerate for 30 minutes or more. To serve, place the slices on serving plates, arranging them attractively, and spoon the juices over them. Garnish each plate with a dab or stripe of sour cream and sprinkle a little brown sugar on top.

MAKES 2 SERVINGS

Mango Ice Cream

This ice cream is actually made with buttermilk: the texture is thick and smooth but without ice cream's fat, calories, and cholesterol. Buttermilk's natural acidity blends perfectly with the orange juice and mango.

2 ripe mangoes (¾ to 1 pound each), peeled, pitted, and cubed
⅓ cup sugar, or to taste
¼ cup fresh orange juice
2 cups buttermilk
Sprigs of fresh mint for garnish

Purée the cubed mangoes in a food processor, then pass it through a nonreactive sieve to remove any fibers. It should measure about 2 cups. Stir in the sugar and orange juice; the sugar will dissolve on its own in a few minutes. Mix in the buttermilk. Cover and chill.

Freeze the mixture in a sorbetière or an ice cream maker according to the manufacturer's directions. Or freeze it according to the directions on page 307. To serve, scoop the ice cream into pretty glass dishes or saucer champagne glasses and garnish with sprigs of mint.

MAKES ABOUT 5 CUPS

NOTE: For mango sherbet, follow the recipe for persimmon sherbet (see page 233), substituting mango purée for persimmon.

Mango Purée

Contrast the mango's beautiful color and flavor with other tropical fruits such as banana, citrus, coconut, and pineapple. In India, mango purée is often spread on a dish, with various other fruits, whole or sliced, set around it. Sometimes bread is served with it for scooping up the luscious purée.

1 medium-size ripe mango (about 1 pound)
2 tablespoons fresh lime juice
2 to 3 tablespoons light or dark rum, or to taste

Purée the mango in a food processor, then pass it through a nonreactive sieve to remove any fibers. Stir in the lime juice and rum and chill. Spoon the purée over ice cream, cake, or other fruits. Covered tightly and chilled, the purée will keep for several days in the refrigerator and several months in the freezer.

MAKES ABOUT 1¼ CUPS

MELONS

In one of the stories in the *Arabian Nights* a child buys a melon to quench his thirst. On cutting it open he sees a tiny city, so he enters this microcosm filled with buildings, people, and animals. This tale, a variation on the house of Peter Pumpkin Eater's wife, shows the melon's Near Eastern origin and its importance to the people there. Via Arabs and Moors the fruit found its way to Spain and from there, on Columbus's second voyage in 1493, to the New World. There are countless varieties of melon, *Cucumis melo*, so many in fact that it is impossible to keep up with them all. These members of the squash, or gourd, family cross-pollinate so promiscuously that farmers know they must plant them well separated from each other.

Of the basic types, the musk melon, sometimes called netted melon or nutmeg melon, includes what Americans call the cantaloupe. The musky scent and netted skin, looking rather like a large nutmeg, accounts for the name of this group. The flesh is usually orange, occasionally green. The skin can be ridged in segments, but always has the characteristic raised netted pattern on the skin, whether golden beige or green. The Persian melon is another larger musk melon, with finer netting on its darker green rind and pinker flesh.

The true cantaloupe, named for the town of Cantalupo near Tivoli outside Rome, is widely grown in Europe. It is smaller, rounder, and exceptionally aromatic. The skin is hard, sometimes rough, scaly, or segmented, but never netted like the American cantaloupe. The French Charentais is a delectable example, but American growers do not like its small size and fragility, so it is hard to find in the United States. The lovely Israeli Ogen, with green flesh and green stripes that segment the skin, is another true cantaloupe.

All musk melons and cantaloupes need to ripen on the vine for the natural fruit sugar to reach its peak, what we call ripeness. At this point, a separation layer in the stem pulls away from the fruit, and a ripe melon can be picked easily, leaving a scar. One whose stem has been torn or cut has been picked prematurely and, once picked, cannot grow sweeter. Other ways to help determine ripeness are a heady fragrance and a smooth softness around the blossom as well as stem end. On American cantaloupes, the background color behind the netting should turn from green to golden tan.

Winter melons ripen slowly and are harvested later, even after frost. Lacking the separation layer in the stem, they can withstand cold. When ripe they still have no aroma.

Their skins are harder, so they travel well, with a texture varying from smooth to furrowed, and in many colors. Their flesh can be white, pale green, or orange. The Cavaillon is a celebrated French winter melon not grown commercially in the United States.

Honeydew, with creamy white skin and green flesh, is a popular winter melon in America, but supermarket specimens are too often underripe and flavorless. To choose a good one, don't sniff for smell. Instead, look for a creamy rind with a touch of yellow (not dead white or greenish white). Feel for some softness and a matte finish, avoiding hard, shiny skins; a little roughness to the rind, even veins or freckles, is a sign of sweetness. A flavorful honeydew should be heavy for its size, weighing at least five pounds.

Of the many new hybrid melons on the American market, the oval Casaba weighs four to seven pounds, with lengthwise wrinkles meeting at the pointed end, and pale yellow skin and creamy, mild flesh. As it is a winter melon, it has no scent. The Crenshaw (sometimes Cranshaw) has golden yellow skin, somewhat wrinkled, with very sweet salmon-colored flesh. It has a strong, almost spicy aroma and weighs four to six pounds or even more. The Galia, from Israel, looks like a cantaloupe with a yellower color behind the netting and greenish flesh. The Juan Canary has canary yellow skin, an oblong shape, and white flesh tinged with pink. The large late-season Santa Claus melon, sometimes called Christmas melon, has a speckled green-and-yellow rind that turns greener with ripeness, and pale green flesh tasting like honeydew. The luscious Sharlyn looks much like a cantaloupe, with rough streaks in the rind tinged with apricot, but creamy white flesh with a sweet cinnamony flavor.

The watermelon, from Africa rather than Persia, is in a different botanical family from these melons and has its own chapter.

Since the sweet, cool nectar of a ripe melon is the perfect refreshment in hot weather, the fruit benefits from simple treatment, perhaps nothing more than a wedge of lemon or lime. As an appetizer, Italians like to serve it with paper-thin slices of prosciutto, the fine ham from Parma. The French serve cantaloupe halves filled with port as an hors d'oeuvre. The English like a sprinkling of ground ginger. Indeed, ginger in any form seems to go uncommonly well with the fruit. Melons large or small can be scooped out and mixed with other fruit and put back in the shell, with liqueur added or not. Cooked chutney preserve can be made from melon, especially a disappointing one.

We tend to overchill melons, robbing them of their flavor. For all melons, keep them at room temperature until ripe and chill only briefly before serving. Since the flesh next to the seeds has the most intense flavor, take care to remove only the seeds and leave the top layer of flesh. Melons are available year-round, but late summer offers the widest choice of varieties.

Cantaloupe is very high in vitamins A and C, with a considerable amount of folic acid. Honeydew is a rich source of vitamin C, with some potassium. All melons are high in fiber and low in sodium. Mostly water, they have few calories.

Cantaloupe, Chicken, and Ham Salad

This simple savory salad, gently redolent of the Middle East, makes a satisfying lunch.

½ medium-size cantaloupe, seeded
1 tablespoon fresh lemon juice
1 tablespoon honey, or to taste
¼ cup plain yogurt
1 cup cubed cooked chicken
¼ cup cubed ham
2 tablespoons sesame seeds, lightly toasted (see page 179)
Redleaf lettuce
1 tablespoon chopped fresh coriander (cilantro) or other herb

Cut off the rind from the cantaloupe, removing all the green, and cut the flesh lengthwise into thin slices. Mix together the lemon juice and honey, then stir it into the yogurt. Fold in the chicken, ham, and sesame seeds. Lay a bed of lettuce on two salad plates. Arrange the cantaloupe slices on top in a ring or on either side like parentheses. Mound the chicken mixture in the middle and top with the coriander.

MAKES 2 SERVINGS

Honeydew Chutney

This pale green and gold chutney, accented with cumin, can be made with any melon. It will assuage the disappointment of a hard and flavorless honeydew. If you multiply the recipe, reduce the amounts of spices.

¼ cup distilled white vinegar (at least 5% acidity)
½ cup sugar
¼ cup golden raisins (sultanas)
¼ cup chopped white onion
½ teaspoon cumin seeds, crushed, or ¼ teaspoon ground
¼ teaspoon red pepper flakes, or to taste
¼ teaspoon salt
2 generous cups cubed honeydew cut down to the rind (¾- to 1-inch cubes)
2 tablespoons fresh lime juice
2 tablespoons chopped fresh coriander (cilantro)

Combine the vinegar, sugar, raisins, onion, cumin seeds, red pepper, and salt in a pot. Bring the liquid to a boil and let boil until the sugar is dissolved, about 5 minutes. Reduce the heat to medium-low, add the melon, and cook until the syrup thickens. Raise the heat and, stirring, boil off the moisture given up by the melon. It will turn translucent. Cool slightly, then stir in the lime juice and coriander. Cooled completely, covered, and chilled, the chutney will keep for several weeks or longer. Or put up the chutney in a sterilized jar (see page 321).

MAKES 1 GENEROUS CUP

Melon Balls in Gingered Lime Syrup

This makes a colorful and cooling light dessert for high summer.

> 2 limes
> ½ cup sugar
> 1 tablespoon peeled and minced fresh ginger
> 1 small cantaloupe, seeded
> ¾ honeydew, seeded
> One 4-pound piece watermelon

With a vegetable peeler, cut two 2-inch strips of green zest from one lime, leaving the white pith beneath. From the other lime cut 1 tablespoon of zest into julienne; reserve. Squeeze the lime juice, about ⅜ cup, and add enough water to bring the liquid to ½ cup. Put it in a small nonreactive saucepan with the sugar and ginger, bring to a boil, and let boil until the sugar is dissolved, about 5 minutes. Add the strips of lime zest to steep in the syrup as it cools. When cool, strain the lime syrup into a bowl and discard the solids. Add the reserved julienne to the syrup.

Cut melon balls from the three melons, about 3 cups of each. To make round balls, press the melon baller deep into the flesh until juice comes out the hole in the bottom of the melon baller. Twist to cut a whole ball and remove. Use the smaller scoop in shallow flesh to avoid getting the rind. Carefully remove or avoid any watermelon seeds. (Use the leftover craters and peaks for pickles, sherbets, or granita.) Put the melon balls into the syrup and toss gently. Cover and chill for a few hours. Just before serving, gently toss again and spoon the melon balls into glass bowls or saucer champagne glasses.

MAKES 6 TO 8 SERVINGS

Cantaloupe Summer Fruit Cup

Serve this fragrant fruit cup in the melon shell or in a glass bowl if you prefer.

1 small fragrant cantaloupe
½ cup fresh sweet cherries, pitted
1 tablespoon orange juice
1 tablespoon cassis or orange-flavored liqueur
½ cup fresh raspberries, blackberries, or blueberries
Fresh mint sprigs for garnish

Cut the cantaloupe across in half, scoop out the seeds, and remove the ripe flesh with the small end of a melon baller. To make round balls, press the baller deep into the flesh until juice comes out the hole in the bottom of the baller; twist to cut a whole ball and remove. Put the melon balls in a bowl with the cherries and let them macerate with the orange juice and liqueur. Scoop out the remaining craters of flesh to make a smooth container (use the flesh for another recipe, such as sherbet). Just before serving, gently toss the melon and cherries with the berries and divide the fruit between the two melon shells. Garnish them with sprigs of mint.

MAKES 2 SERVINGS

Cantaloupe with Ginger Ice Cream

Melon and ginger, savory or sweet, have a great affinity for each other.

2 cups light cream
1 vanilla bean or 1 teaspoon pure vanilla extract
3 large egg yolks
⅓ cup sugar
1 cup heavy cream
½ cup preserved stem ginger, chopped (available in Oriental and specialty food stores)
¼ cup ginger syrup from the preserved ginger
1 large cantaloupe, seeded and cut into wedges

Scald the cream with the vanilla bean in a small pan; cook it over medium heat until little bubbles appear around the edges. Do not let it boil. Remove the vanilla bean, rinse it, and reuse it in another recipe. Beat together in a bowl the egg yolks and sugar. In a thin, steady stream, pour the scalded cream into the egg yolk mixture, stirring constantly. Pour it back into the pan and cook it over simmering water, still stirring, until the custard coats the spoon heavily. Cool the custard thoroughly and add the heavy cream. If using vanilla extract, add it here. Stir in the preserved ginger and syrup. Cover and chill thoroughly.

Freeze the ice cream in an ice cream machine according to the manufacturer's instructions, or in a bowl, stirring to smooth the ice crystals as it freezes. Let it mellow in the freezer, covered, for about 2 hours before serving.

To serve, put cantaloupe wedges on serving plates and put a scoop of ginger ice cream on top of each.

MAKES 6 TO 8 SERVINGS, ABOUT 1¼ QUARTS ICE CREAM

Gingered Honeydew Parfait

This dessert can be frozen in tall parfait glasses, small individual dishes, or a soufflé dish or dishes fitted with a paper collar tied around tightly. In the last case, pour the mousse mixture above the rim so that when frozen it looks like a risen hot soufflé. This dessert is also delicious with peaches, apricots, persimmons, papaya, mangoes, or another melon, so long as the fruit is very ripe, flavorful, and aromatic.

2 tablespoons fresh lime juice
3 cups seedless honeydew purée (made from about ¾ of a large melon)
3 large egg whites, at room temperature
Pinch of salt
2 cups chilled heavy cream
¾ cup sugar
¾ cup water
⅓ cup preserved stem ginger, cut into small dice, with syrup (available in Oriental and specialty food stores)

Stir the lime juice into the honeydew purée and chill well. In a large bowl, beat the egg whites with the salt until stiff peaks form. In another bowl with a clean whisk, beat the cream until it makes firm peaks; keep chilled.

In a small saucepan, bring the sugar and water to a boil, cover, and let boil until the sugar has dissolved, about 5 minutes. Uncover and continue boiling until the syrup reaches the spun-thread stage, 232°F on a candy thermometer. In a slow stream, pour the hot syrup directly into the egg whites, beating steadily until the meringue cools to room temperature.

Fold the melon purée into the meringue, then fold in the whipped cream. Quickly fold in the ginger with its syrup. Pour the mixture into parfait glasses or soufflé dishes and freeze. Whichever container you use, be sure to take it out of the freezer ahead of time to soften slightly before serving.

MAKES ABOUT 9 CUPS, 8 TO 12 SERVINGS, DEPENDING ON SIZE OF CONTAINER

Honeydew Lime Mint Sherbet

This makes a subtle, light, and refreshing dessert for spring or summer.

¾ cup sugar
¾ cup water
½ cup tightly packed fresh mint leaves
3 cups seedless honeydew purée (made from about ¾ of a large melon)
¼ cup fresh lime juice
Grated zest of 2 limes
Fresh mint sprigs for garnish

Make a syrup by combining the sugar and water in a saucepan. Bring to a boil, cover, and let it boil over low heat until the sugar is dissolved, about 5 minutes. Add the mint leaves to steep in the syrup as it cools. Since different kinds of mint have different strengths, taste to see that the mint does not overwhelm the syrup. Strain it, discarding the mint.

Stir the honeydew purée into the cooled mint syrup (hold a little back: if your melon is very ripe, you might not need so much sweetening) along with the lime juice and zest. Chill the mixture, covered, in the refrigerator.

Freeze the sherbet in a sorbetière or an ice cream machine according to the manufacturer's directions. Or freeze it according to the directions on page 307. To serve, scoop sherbet into saucer champagne glasses and garnish with sprigs of fresh mint. A tablespoon of crème de menthe spooned over will not go amiss.

MAKES ABOUT 1 QUART

Cantaloupe Sherbet

This sherbet can be made with any type of melon or, for special effect, with a combination of several. It is a fine way to catch the evanescent perfume of an absolutely ripe melon.

1 medium-size cantaloupe, seeded
⅔ cup sugar, or to taste, depending on the sweetness of the melon
⅓ cup water
2 tablespoons fresh lemon juice
Fresh berries for garnish

Cut the ripe cantaloupe flesh into chunks and purée them in a food processor to measure about 3 cups. Put the sugar and water in a small saucepan, bring to a boil, and let boil, covered, until the sugar is dissolved, about 5 minutes. Cool the syrup, then stir it into the melon purée with the lemon juice and chill thoroughly.

Freeze the sherbet in a sorbetière or an ice cream machine according to the manufacturer's directions. Or freeze it according to the directions on page 307. Serve scoops of the sherbet garnished with colorful berries.

MAKES ABOUT 1 QUART

ORANGES AND TANGERINES

If you have ever visited an orange grove, you may remember the exquisite fragrance of delicate blossoms and the brilliant color of ripe fruit against shadowy deep green leaves. The trees bear flowers and fruit together, so that standing beneath the laden branches you can experience, all within reach, both promise and fulfillment.

The orange is some twenty million years old, a native of China. Arabs traders brought the bitter orange, *Citrus aurantium*, from the east and spread it around the Mediterranean. The Moors introduced it to Spain, where it established itself and became known as the Seville orange. Eventually, returning Crusaders took it to northern Europe. Although the climate proved too cold for the tropical and semitropical tree to flourish, royalty and aristocrats could show off the fruit of their orangeries as a status symbol. The sour orange, appreciated in Europe for the scent of its flowers and skin and for the sourness of its juice in cooking, was followed in the fifteenth century by the introduction of the sweet orange, *Citrus sinensis*, also from China.

Columbus brought both sweet and sour oranges to the New World on his second voyage in 1493. Spanish missionaries planted groves in Florida in 1565, where the climate was perfect, and again in Arizona and California in the early eighteenth century. The fruit has brought enormous prosperity to those regions. Growers have cultivated so many varieties and combinations of these and other citrus fruits that their myriad names confuse us, so it is helpful to learn some distinctions for the cold months that are their peak season, December to May.

The sweet orange has always been favored in this country. We have two main varieties: the Valencia, grown in Florida and California as both an eating and a juice orange, and the West Coast Navel, aptly named for the characteristic bulge, which is a new orange trying to form. The Navel, large, seedless, and with distinct segments, is ideal for desserts, but its juice turns bitter with exposure to air. The sweet blood orange, common in the Mediterranean, has skin that may be ruddy and pulp that can be speckled red to varying degrees. The luscious Moro variety, named for the Moors, has flesh that turns raspberry in color and flavor. Available from California intermittently from December through July, blood oranges can be found in specialty markets and increasingly in supermarkets.

The tangerine, which acquired its name in Tangiers on its westward migration, arrived about 150 years ago and is known as the mandarin orange everywhere but in the United States. The tangerine is a loose grouping of several types of smaller oranges, often possessing a "zipper" skin and tangy flavor. The early-ripening Dancy is fairly sweet but bland in flavor, small, seedy, with a bright shiny rind that slips off. The Kinnow is slightly larger and zestier, the Satsuma especially wrinkly and seedy. The pungent Clementine is a small, sweet, juicy, tight-skinned, seedless hybrid that came about by accident and is grown mostly in the Mediterranean.

Crossbreeding has produced several other delicious citrus fruits loosely grouped with oranges. Tangelos are a cross between the mandarin and grapefruit. Yet the Minneola tangelo—with protuberant stem end, deep orange peel, and delectable flavor—shares little likeness with the coarse-skinned but juicy and pungent ugli fruit tangelo (pronounced "óogly" in its native Jamaica) that looks more like its grapefruit parent than its mandarin one. Tangors are a cross between the mandarin and sweet orange. The two tangors we see available are the Murcott (or honey tangerine) and the Temple, seedy and thin-skinned, with sweet, tangy juice.

The influx of Hispanic immigrants has brought a new demand for bitter oranges which used to be all but impossible to find in the United States. With the popularity of Mexican, Caribbean, and Latin American cooking, perhaps they will be soon be more widely available. Look for the nubbly, rough-skinned sour orange in a Hispanic grocery store if your city or town has a population big enough to support one. Another possibility is to freeze the bitter orange juice when you are able to find the oranges. A more practical solution is to combine orange with grapefruit and lime juice and zest to achieve the same approximate level of bitterness. For half a cup of mock Seville orange juice, Diana Kennedy, the authority on Mexican cooking, suggests combining three tablespoons each of orange and grapefruit juice with two tablespoons of lemon juice and one teaspoon of grated grapefruit zest.

When shopping for citrus, choose fruit that are heavy for their size, indicating sweet, juicy specimens, with firm, taut skins. The peel's thickness is irrelevant to quality: California Valencia oranges have thicker skins, which were developed to protect them from the dry climate, than do those from Florida. Avoid skins with soft or puffy spots, but ignore mottling and blotching. Green coloration has nothing to do with ripeness, only showing that the fruit has been through cold nights before picking. Bright color does not mean better flavor. Store oranges and tangerines, like all citrus, in the refrigerator removed from any plastic wrapping, where they keep well for a month or more.

In cooking, take advantage of the sweet and sour ambiguity of oranges and tangerines, a balance exploited in European cuisines that became acquainted with the sour orange first. The outer colored zest contains essential oils which can contribute depth and subtlety to a dish. Blanching the zest briefly in boiling water will remove its bitterness, if that is appropriate to a recipe. Orange zest also flavors many liqueurs, and a small amount of liqueur can add a great deal of nuance. In addition, orange zest or sections can make an attractive garnish that raises a dish above the ordinary. A blood orange garnish can raise a dish to the extraordinary.

Oranges of all types are very high in vitamin C, although only about a quarter of it is in the flesh, the rest in the zest and white pith, and heat destroys it. Even so, oranges are full of fiber, but low in calories (about fifty in a medium orange, thirty-five in a tangerine). One orange will give about half a cup of juice, about one generous tablespoon of grated zest, and about eleven sections. In cooking you can substitute oranges and tangerines for each other in many recipes.

Nantucket Fog Cocktail

Guaranteed to make you glow through the fog.

1 jigger vodka
1 ounce orange-flavored liqueur
2 ounces orange juice
2 ounces cranberry juice
Splash of soda water
Slice of orange

Pour the vodka and liqueur into a highball glass filled with ice. Fill nearly to the top with the orange and cranberry juices, top with a splash of soda, and garnish with a slice of fresh orange.

MAKES 1 COCKTAIL

Orange Brandy Liqueur

This mock Grand Marnier, though not fine enough for drinking neat, is an excellent substitute in cooking, especially as Grand Marnier is so expensive. For a distilled orange liqueur such as Cointreau, Curaçao, or triple sec, use vodka instead of brandy. This recipe comes from Maude Slagle, my early mentor and inspiration in the kitchen.

6 or more oranges
3 cups brandy
½ cup sugar
¼ cup water

With a vegetable peeler, remove all the zest from the oranges; try not to take the bitter white pith. (Use the rest of the oranges for another recipe.) Pack the zest in a jar, and cover with the brandy. Screw the top on tightly and let the brandy steep for 1 month or more in a cool, dark cupboard or the refrigerator. Strain the liqueur and discard the zest.

To make a heavy syrup, combine the sugar and water in a small saucepan and bring to a boil. Lower the heat and let it boil, covered, until the sugar is dissolved, about 5 minutes. Let the syrup cool. Pour the syrup into the orange brandy, sweetening it to taste. (If you prefer, stir about ¼ cup sugar into the brandy, which eventually will dissolve it.) This liqueur keeps indefinitely, tightly covered, in the refrigerator.

MAKES 3½ CUPS

Scallops in Orange Butter Sauce

The pearly white scallops in this orangy sauce make a great dinner party starter. If you can persuade your fishmonger to give you the scallop roes, by all means include them for their delicate flavor as well as coral color.

1 orange
1½ pounds bay scallops
½ cup dry white wine
2 scallions (green and white parts), thinly sliced
3 tablespoons chopped fresh parsley
Fish stock or clam juice to cover (about 1 cup)
¼ cup (½ stick) unsalted butter, softened

Remove the zest from the orange, about 3 tablespoons chopped zest, and drop it into a small pan of boiling water. Cook 3 minutes to remove the bitterness, drain, and reserve. Squeeze the juice from the orange, about ¼ cup.

Place the scallops in a nonreactive pan with the orange juice, wine, scallions, parsley, and enough fish stock to cover. Cover and bring to a boil, then immediately pour the contents of the pan through a sieve set over a bowl. Return the liquid to the pan, keep the solids warm in the bowl, and boil the liquid down to a thick syrupy glaze, about ¼ cup. Cool slightly, then whisk in the butter 1 tablespoon at a time, letting each be absorbed before adding the next. Divide the scallops among eight warm serving plates (scallop shells, if possible), top with the reserved zest, and top with the sauce.

MAKES 8 FIRST-COURSE SERVINGS

Chilled Tomato-Orange Soup

The pairing of tomatoes and oranges at first teases you because, though both are familiar summer refreshers, they are so rarely combined as to be exotic. Their fragrance, boosted with basil or mint, will lift you from your hot-weather doldrums. The idea for this no-cook soup comes from my friend Cecie Clement.

4 pounds ripe summer tomatoes or 5 cups canned Italian plum tomatoes with their juices
3 large oranges
1½ lemons
1 fairly small onion, chopped
¼ cup packed fresh basil or mint, chopped
Salt and freshly ground black pepper to taste
Sprigs fresh basil or mint for garnish
Sour cream or plain yogurt for garnish

Drop the fresh tomatoes into a pot of boiling water for half a minute or so. Cut them across in half and gently squeeze each half over a bowl fitted with a sieve to catch the seeds, reserving the juice below. Use your little finger to poke out any recalcitrant seeds from the tomato cavities. Slip off the skins and discard them with the seeds. (If using canned, just press them through a sieve to remove the seeds.) Coarsely chop the flesh and put it in a food processor or blender with the juice.

Grate the zest from the oranges and lemons and squeeze the juices. Put the citrus zest and juice in the food processor or blender and add the onion and basil. Combine the ingredients, but be sure to leave a little texture. Season with salt and pepper. Cover and chill thoroughly in the refrigerator until serving time. To serve, ladle the soup in bowls, add a sprig of fresh basil, and pass sour cream or yogurt on the side.

MAKES ABOUT 6 SERVINGS

Munkaczina

This exotic salad, named for a town in eastern Europe, doubtless has Arab origins still farther east. With a loaf of interesting bread, perhaps some grilled meat, it makes a striking meal.

4 oranges
1 red onion, chopped
12 Mediterranean olives, halved and pitted
3 tablespoons extra virgin olive oil, or to taste
Ground cayenne pepper to taste
Salt to taste

With a serrated knife, cut a spiral to remove the orange peel and membrane. Remove any white pith. Cut the oranges across into thin slices, pick out any seeds, and spread the slices on a platter. Scatter the onion over the slices. Place the pitted olives on top of the onions in an attractive design. Sprinkle the olive oil over all, then dust with cayenne pepper and a judicious sprinkling of salt.

MAKES 4 SERVINGS

Curried Orange-Avocado Salad with Almonds

Make sure the avocados have ripened into fruity fullness to balance the tangy oranges and seasonings. This salad makes an excellent lunch or light supper.

¼ cup toasted slivered blanched almonds (see note below)
3 medium-size oranges, preferably seedless
2 ripe avocados
4 handfuls redleaf lettuce
¼ cup extra virgin olive oil
1 tablespoon sherry vinegar or good red wine vinegar
¼ teaspoon curry powder, or to taste
Salt and freshly ground black pepper to taste

Toast the almonds as below. With a serrated knife, cut off in a spiral the peel and white pith from the oranges. Remove the individual sections from the membrane, discarding seeds, and reserve.

Just before serving, cut the avocados in half lengthwise and remove the pits and peel. Put each half hollow-side up on a bed of lettuce on individual plates. Combine the orange sections and toasted almonds and fill the avocado hollows with them. Mix together the oil, vinegar, curry powder, salt and pepper, and drizzle some over each salad. Serve at once.

MAKES 4 SERVINGS

NOTE: To toast nuts: Preheat the oven to 350°F. Lay the nuts in a shallow pan and toast them, stirring once or twice, until lightly browned, about 5 to 7 minutes; set them aside off the pan to cool.

Beet, Orange, and Walnut Salad

Vibrant colors and bittersweet flavors make this salad a study in contrasts.

½ pound small to medium-size beets
¼ cup walnut or extra virgin olive oil
2 tablespoons fresh orange juice
1 tablespoon fresh lemon juice
1 tablespoon grated orange zest
Salt and freshly ground black pepper to taste
1 head chicory or other bitter green
1 orange, peeled, seeded, and sectioned
⅓ cup broken walnuts, lightly toasted (see note above)

Trim the beet tops to within an inch of the bulb and remove the taproot; do not peel. Drop the beets into a pot of boiling water. Return the water to a simmer, cover, and cook until just tender, 10 to 20 minutes, depending on their size.

Mix together the walnut oil, orange and lemon juice, orange zest, salt, and pepper. Pour two thirds of the vinaigrette into a small bowl. When the beets are done, drain them. One at a time, under cold running water, slip off their skins and while still warm cut them into fine julienne. Put the beets in the bowl and stir gently to coat them with the vinaigrette before they turn cold. (You may do this a couple of days ahead and keep them, covered, in the refrigerator; return them to room temperature before serving.)

To serve, line individual salad plates with the chicory, and divide the beets among them. Garnish each plate with the orange sections and toasted walnuts. Dribble on the remaining vinaigrette and serve.

MAKES 4 SERVINGS

Wild Rice Salad with Tangerines, Duck, and Snow Peas

The many strands of color, texture, and flavor in this unusual salad are woven together into a balanced whole.

½ cup uncooked wild rice
1¼ cups water
2 seedless tangerines (honey tangerines or clementines are best)
3 ounces sugar snap peas, strings trimmed
¼ cup chopped pecans, toasted (see page 179)
½ cup cubed cooked duck or pork, at room temperature
¼ red onion, thinly sliced
3 medium-size cultivated white mushrooms, thinly sliced
1 bunch watercress, stems trimmed
¼ cup olive oil
2 tablespoons sherry wine vinegar, or to taste
Salt and freshly ground black pepper to taste

Rinse the rice in a sieve under cold running water. Put the water in a small saucepan and bring to a boil. Add the rice, return to a boil, cover, and simmer for about 45 minutes; the grains of rice should plump up but not splay and curl. Drain off any unabsorbed water, remove the pot from the heat, and let the rice cool to room temperature, covered. (The rice can be cooked ahead, covered, and chilled; let it return to room temperature before continuing.)

On the top tier of the pie stand: Rhubarb Strawberry Tart (*page 289*), and clockwise from the bottom tier: Peach Blueberry Tart (*page 215*), Fig Frangipane Tart (*page 97*), Pumpkin Walnut Pie (*page 264*), and Pear Cranberry Tart (*page 227*).

Clockwise from top: Pears with Curried Crab Filling (*page 219*), Baked Spicy Plantains and Bacon (*page 50*),
Plum Salsa (*page 247*), Acorn Squash with Cranberry Apple Stuffing (*page 76*),
Kumquats with Star Anise (*page 132*), Sautéed Shrimp with Papaya and Peppers (*page 201*).

In the center: Three Citrus Marmalade (*page 106*), and clockwise from top right: Apple Cranberry Onion Marmalade (*page 8*), Fresh Mango Chutney (*page 163*), Bitter Orange Marmalade (*page 186*), Pumpkin Chutney (*page 261*), and Honeydew Chutney (*page 168*).

Clockwise from the top: Chilled Tomato-Orange Soup (*page 177*), Hungarian Sour Cherry Soup (*page 65*),
Malaguenan Grape Gazpacho (*page 112*), Cock-a-Leekie Soup (*page 246*),
Jellied Herbed Cucumber and Lime Soup (*page 156*).

Clockwise from the top: Persimmon Slices in Caramel Nut Sauce (*page 231*), Caramelized Banana and
Pineapple Strips with Coffee Custard Sauce (*page 46*), Orange Bavarian Cream (*page 189*),
Candied Grapefruit Peel (*page 107*), Gooseberry Fool (*page 100*),
Melon Balls in Gingered Lime Syrup (*page 169*).

On the shelf: Grapefruit and Mango Salad (*page 104*), on the drawer: Rice Salad with Kumquats and Snow Peas (*page 131*), and on the table, clockwise from the top: Pomegranate and Endive Salad (*page 255*), Shrimp and Kiwi Salad (*page 126*), Lamb and Currant Salad (*page 83*).

Clockwise from the top: Black Forest Cake (*page 71*), Strawberry Mousse Cake (*page 301*), Date Nut Cinnamon Coffee Cake (*page 89*), Bittersweet Chocolate Cake with Kiwi Sauce (*page 194*), Raspberry Charlotte Royale (*page 284*).

These exotic fruit include a Papaya at the top; immediately beneath it from the left are a green Cherimoya, bright orange Persimmon, and a green Fejoa; in the next row from the left are a few purple Passion Fruit, a Carambola (Star Fruit) with a slice, a yellow Asian Pear, and a thorny orange Kiwano; and at the bottom are a striped purple and yellow Pepino, a red Mango, and spotted green and red Prickly Pears.

While the rice is cooking, peel the tangerines, removing all the membrane and pith. Cut out the individual sections and reserve. Drop the sugar snap peas in a small pot of boiling water; return to a boil, drain, and refresh in cold water. Drain again and reserve.

Put the rice in a large serving bowl with the rest of the tangerines, peas, pecans, duck, onion, mushrooms, and watercress. Mix together the olive oil, vinegar, salt, and pepper. Dress the salad and toss it well. Serve at once.

MAKES 4 TO 6 SERVINGS

Sautéed Duck Breast Salad with Orange

This warm first-course salad (or main course for two) makes a special occasion all on its own. Searing the duck breasts melts off much of the fat but keeps the meat rare. You can buy duck breasts already boned, but by doing it yourself you get a whole bird for the same cost with the rest to enjoy later.

1 whole duck breast, boned and trimmed
1 orange (a blood orange is sensational, but not necessary)
¼ cup walnut or extra virgin olive oil
2 tablespoons red wine vinegar
1 shallot, minced
Salt and freshly ground black pepper to taste
1 head frizzy endive or other bitter lettuce
2 tablespoons chopped walnuts, lightly toasted (see page 179)

Unless you buy your duck breast already boned and trimmed, remove the duck breast from a whole carcass. Cut down the the breastbone and with your fingers lift the meat from both sides of the breastbone and ribs. Cut behind the wing bones to free the two portions. Trim the meat well, cutting off fat from the edges, but leaving the skin on. Score the skin at half-inch intervals, cutting into the fat but not the meat. Use the duck legs for another recipe and the carcass for stock.

With a zester or vegetable peeler, cut 1 tablespoon of orange zest into julienne and reserve. With a serrated knife, cut off the rest of the orange peel in a spiral. Cut out and reserve the individual sections and squeeze the juice from the membrane and rind. Mix together 2 tablespoons of the orange juice, the oil, vinegar, shallot, salt and pepper. Put two thirds of the vinaigrette in a nonreactive shallow dish just large enough to hold the breasts in one layer; reserve the rest. Marinate the duck in the dish for 2 hours, refrigerated, turning occasionally.

Drain the duck breasts on a paper towel. Heat a large skillet over high heat and sear the duck breasts, skin-side down, for about 4 minutes. Do not move them for the first few minutes. The fat will get smoky and much of it will melt away. Lower the heat, pour off the fat, and carefully turn the breasts with a spatula. Cook the meat side for about 3 minutes. Turn the breasts again, and cook until the skin browns and crisps but the meat inside remains rare, or according to your taste. Take the duck off the heat to rest for 5 minutes.

Arrange the frizzy endive on four warm salad plates. Carve the duck breasts into thin diagonal slices and divide them among the plates. Place the orange sections around and scatter the walnuts and reserved orange julienne on top. Drizzle with the reserved vinaigrette and serve.

MAKES 4 FIRST-COURSE SERVINGS

Orange, Avocado, and Prosciutto Salad

Creamy avocados balance the acidity of the oranges, and both are offset by the cured ham. If you can find them, blood oranges and imported prosciutto make this salad three-star.

4 medium-large oranges
5 tablespoons extra virgin olive oil, or to taste
Freshly ground black pepper to taste
2 medium-large ripe avocados
6 thin slices prosciutto
3 tablespoons slivered blanched almonds, lightly toasted (see page 179)

Peel the oranges with a serrated knife, and cut out the sections whole, removing any white pith and seeds. Squeeze and save any juice from the membrane and rind. Mix 2 tablespoons of the orange juice (use the remainder elsewhere) with the olive oil and pepper.

Shortly before serving, peel and pit the avocados. Cut the flesh lengthwise into even slices and place them alternately with the orange sections around six serving plates, like a pinwheel. Fold and furl the slices of prosciutto into flowers and place each in the center of a plate. Scatter the almonds over the avocados and oranges. Drizzle the orange juice-oil mixture lightly over the avocados and oranges, and serve at once.

MAKES 6 SERVINGS

Bulgur Pilaf with Fresh and Dried Fruits

This Persian pilaf, combining many sweet and savory elements, also makes a fine stuffing for roast poultry or lamb. Or braise browned chicken or chops with the bulgur as it cooks to make an easy and festive one-dish meal.

Good pinch of saffron threads
½ cup water
2 clementines, honey tangerines, or Minneola tangelos

2 tablespoons olive oil
1 large onion, chopped
1 clove garlic, minced
1 cup uncooked bulgur
2 cups chicken stock
3 tablespoons golden raisins (sultanas)
¼ cup chopped dried apricots
½ teaspoon coriander seeds
3 tablespoons pine nuts, lightly toasted (see page 179)
3 tablespoons chopped fresh coriander (cilantro)
Salt and freshly ground black pepper to taste

Steep the saffron in the water. With a zester or vegetable peeler, remove the zest from one clementine and cut it into julienne. Remove the peel and pith from the clementines with a serrated knife and cut out the sections. Reserve the clementine julienne and sections.

Heat the olive oil in a medium-size saucepan over low heat. Add the onion and garlic and cook, stirring, until softened. Stir in the bulgur, coating the grains with oil. Add the stock, the saffron and its soaking water, the clementine zest, dried fruit, and coriander. Cover, bring to a boil, and stir. Cook over low heat, covered, until the liquid is absorbed, about 20 minutes. Stir in the pine nuts, reserved clementine sections, and fresh coriander, and season with salt and pepper.

MAKES 4 TO 6 SERVINGS

Trout Stuffed with Fennel and Curried Orange Rice

This makes a festive dish for entertaining. It is full-flavored but light, and everything can be done ahead up to the final baking.

¼ cup vegetable oil
1 stalk fennel, chopped
3 scallions (green and white parts), chopped
¼ cup slivered blanched almonds, lightly toasted (see page 179)
¼ cup chopped fresh fennel leaves
Grated zest of 1 orange
¼ cup fresh orange juice
2 tablespoons sour cream
1 teaspoon curry powder, or to taste
2 cups cooked rice
Salt and freshly ground black pepper to taste
Six 1-pound trout (or mackerel), gutted, scaled, and boned, but with head and tail left on
3 seedless oranges for garnish

Heat 2 tablespoons of the oil in a small pan over low heat and cook the fennel and scallions, stirring occasionally, until softened, about 5 minutes. Stir in the almonds, fennel leaves, orange zest and juice, sour cream, and curry powder, then mix in the rice. Season with salt and pepper and add more curry if desired.

Preheat the oven to 400°F. One at a time, spread open the cavity of each trout and fill lightly with some of the rice mixture without overstuffing. Close the cavity with skewers or toothpicks. Place the trout in one layer in a large oiled baking pan and brush the tops of the fish lightly with oil.

With a sharp, serrated knife, cut the peel off the oranges and slice them across into thin rounds. Lay the rounds in a row along the top of each fish. Bake the stuffed trout in the preheated oven until the fish flesh turns opaque and is cooked through, about 18 minutes. With a spatula, carefully transfer the trout onto warm serving plates and remove the skewers or toothpicks. Serve hot, warm, or at room temperature.

MAKES 6 SERVINGS

Orange Sauce for Roast Duck

This bigarade sauce, named for a bitter orange, is delicious with roast chicken and other poultry and gamebirds as well as duckling.

> 2 tablespoons sherry wine vinegar
> 2 tablespoons sugar
> 1 cup duck or chicken stock
> 2 teaspoons cornstarch
> 2 tablespoons fresh lemon juice
> 1 cup orange juice
> Zest of 1 orange, cut into thin julienne (optional)
> Orange sections or slices (optional)

Place the sherry and sugar in a nonreactive saucepan and heat it over high heat to dissolve and then caramelize the sugar. You do not need to stir. As the syrup starts to brown around the edges in a few minutes, lower the heat. Swirl the pan to color the caramel evenly to a rich amber, but take care not to let it burn. If the caramel hardens, do not worry: it will dissolve later when liquid is added.

Pour off the fat from the duck roasting pan and deglaze it with the stock, stirring vigorously over high heat to dissolve the crusty brown sediment on the bottom. Pour the deglazing juices through a fine sieve into the saucepan with the caramelized sugar, and simmer over medium-low heat to reduce the juices and concentrate the flavor.

Mix the cornstarch to a paste in the lemon juice, and stir it into the saucepan along with the orange juice. Cook, stirring, until the sauce thickens slightly. If you can, simmer the duck pieces with the sauce for a few minutes before serving. To intensify the orange flavor at serving time, garnish the duck with blanched orange zest (blanched in boiling water for 3 minutes and drained) and orange sections or slices.

MAKES ENOUGH FOR 6 SERVINGS

Orange Curry Butter

This spicy butter turns grilled or barbecued chicken, pork, and lamb into something special. By omitting the onion and garlic and adding a spoonful of brown sugar, it can be used to baste grilled peaches, bananas, pineapple, and other fruit. It will keep in the refrigerator for a week, or freeze it for longer.

½ cup (1 stick; ¼ pound) unsalted butter, cut into pieces and softened
1 shallot, minced
1 small clove garlic, minced
Grated zest of 1 orange
Grated zest of ½ lemon
3 tablespoons orange juice concentrate, thawed
2 tablespoons fresh lemon juice
4½ teaspoons curry powder, or to taste
Salt and freshly ground black pepper to taste

Put the butter, shallot, garlic, and orange and lemon zest in a food processor and combine them. With the motor running, gradually add the orange and lemon juices. Add the curry powder, starting with a small amount to avoid overseasoning, as brands and palates differ. Season with salt and pepper. Process the ingredients thoroughly, scraping down the sides of the bowl with a rubber spatula. Pack the compound butter in a crock, or roll it in a log in plastic wrap, wrap tightly, and chill until firm. Slice off rounds as needed.

MAKES ABOUT ¾ CUP

Orange Honey Mustard

This condiment is spicy sweet, hot yet mellow. The citrus tang and aroma shine through. Serve it with ham and other cold cooked meats, or use it as a marinade for pork and chicken or other poultry to be roasted or grilled.

1 large orange
2 shallots, minced
2 tablespoons whole-grain Dijon mustard
2 tablespoons honey
⅛ teaspoon salt, or to taste

Grate the zest from the orange, about 2 tablespoons, and reserve; squeeze the juice to measure ½ cup. Put the chopped shallots in a small pan with the orange juice and cook slowly over low heat to avoid burning. Reduce the volume to 3 tablespoons or less, when it should be thick and jammy. Stir in the zest while still hot. Let the marinade cool, then mix in the mustard, honey, and salt. Taste carefully for balance. The seasoned mustard keeps well in a tightly covered jar in the refrigerator.

MAKES ABOUT ½ CUP

Bitter Orange Marmalade

Traditional marmalade is made with the Seville orange, with its thick rough skin and bitter juice. During its brief midwinter season the British madly make their supply for the year, but in the United States the sour orange can be very elusive. The best place to look is in Latin American markets.

2 pounds Seville or sour Jamaican oranges (about 9 oranges), well scrubbed
2 lemons
8 cups water
4¾ to 5 cups sugar

Cut up the oranges and lemons, saving the seeds. Slice the peels into thick or thin pieces, as you prefer, and chop up the pith and flesh. Tie the seeds in a cheesecloth bag (the pectin in the seeds will help the marmalade to jell). Put everything—peels, seeds, flesh, and juice—into a large, heavy-bottomed, nonreactive pot and add the water. Cover, bring slowly to a boil, and cook over medium heat, uncovered, until the volume is reduced by about a third, about 30 minutes. The citrus peels should have turned translucent.

Fish out the cheesecloth bag and let the liquid drip from it back into the pot; discard the bag. Slowly add the sugar, stirring over low heat to dissolve it. Raise the heat, bring the syrup to a boil, and boil until it reaches the jelling point of 220°F on a candy thermometer. Dribble some of the syrup on a cold saucer; if when you push your finger through the syrup it wrinkles, then it is ready. Skim any scum from the surface of the marmalade and let it sit for 10 minutes to keep the peels from rising. Scoop it into clean warm half-pint jars, wipe the threads, screw on the tops, and sterilize in a hot water bath (see page 321).

MAKES ABOUT 9 HALF-PINT JARS

Thickened Yogurt "Cheese" with Orange and Mint

This drained yogurt, called *labneh* in Lebanon, is perfumed with orange and mint. At once simple, elegant, and healthful, serve it in place of whipped or sour cream with all kinds of desserts. It is beautiful with fresh berries, figs, melons, peaches, quince, and papaya, or with dried fruit such as stewed apricots and prunes. For an exotic touch, add a little orange flower water.

1 pound plain yogurt (2 scant cups)
2 to 3 tablespoons orange juice
Grated zest of ½ orange
1½ tablespoons honey, or to taste
1 teaspoon orange flower water (optional; see note below)
2 tablespoons chopped fresh mint

Spoon the yogurt into a coffee cone fitted with a filter, and drain the yogurt over a cup for 6 to 8 hours (discard the whey or use it for another purpose). The longer it drains, the thicker it gets. If you like, drain the labneh in the refrigerator overnight. Mix the thickened yogurt with the orange juice, zest, honey, and orange flower water. Cover and chill; it will keep for several days or more. Just before serving, stir in the fresh mint.

MAKES ABOUT 1 CUP

NOTE: Orange flower water is available in Middle Eastern and specialty food stores, but be sure to purchase orange flower water intended for cooking, not cosmetic, use.

Citrus Bowl

After holiday bingeing, a bowl of orange, tangelo, and grapefruit sections is a glorious dessert, one we all love but somehow overlook. It needs no embellishment but zest and perhaps orange-flavored liqueur such as Curaçao, Cointreau, or Grand Marnier to intensify the flavor. To turn it into ambrosia, an old-fashioned Southern dessert, omit the zest and liqueur and layer the citrus (usually just oranges) with shredded coconut and perhaps sliced bananas or pineapple.

4 navel oranges
2 tangelos or 3 honey tangerines
2 grapefruit, perhaps 1 ruby and 1 white
Sugar to taste
Orange-flavored liqueur to taste (optional)

With a zester or a vegetable peeler, cut julienne strips of zest from one of each type of citrus, making about 3 tablespoons of zest in all. Put the zest in a large bowl. With a sharp serrated knife, cut the skin in a spiral from each piece of citrus, working over the bowl to catch any juice. Leave as much flesh as you can on each piece of fruit, and remove any white pith you may have missed. Cut out the sections whole and add them to the bowl along with any juice you can squeeze from the remaining membrane and skin.

Depending on the sweetness of the fruit, add sugar to taste (you may not need any) and flavor with liqueur, if desired. Cover and refrigerate until serving time.

MAKES 6 SERVINGS

Middle Eastern Sliced Oranges

This simple yet exotic dish, ideal for dieters, is scented with orange flower water and spice.

6 navel oranges
1 tablespoon orange flower water (see note on page 187)
A little sugar to taste, if necessary
Dash of ground cinnamon or cloves

With a sharp knife, remove the skin from the oranges in a spiral, taking the pith and membrane. Slice the flesh across into thin even rounds and layer them in a bowl. Squeeze into the bowl any juice from the membrane and inside of the peel, which also gives some fragrant oil from the zest. Sweeten, if necessary, with a discreet sprinkling of sugar. Sprinkle the orange flower water over the slices and dust with a little cinnamon or spice. Cover and chill well before serving.

MAKES 4 OR MORE SERVINGS

Oranges in Red Wine Syrup

Here's a fine use for leftover red wine, which imparts its deep garnet color to the oranges. In another similar dish, the wine syrup is cooked separately and poured over fresh orange slices.

6 large navel oranges
2 cups dry red wine
1 cup sugar
One 1-inch stick cinnamon
2 whole cloves

Remove the zest from one of the oranges with a zester or vegetable peeler, and cut it into thin julienne strips with a sharp knife. Drop the julienne zest into a small pan of boiling water and cook for 3 minutes to remove the bitterness; drain and reserve.

Put the red wine and sugar in a pot just large enough to hold the oranges in one layer. Bring to a boil and let it boil over low heat, covered, until the sugar is dissolved, about 5 minutes. Meanwhile, remove the peel and pith from all the oranges, cutting them in a spiral with a sharp serrated knife. Drop the peeled oranges into the hot syrup, and poach them lightly for 5 minutes, turning to cook them evenly. Turn off the heat and let the oranges cool in the syrup. With a slotted spoon, place the oranges in a glass serving bowl or individual dishes. Add the cinnamon and cloves to the syrup, and over high heat reduce it by half. Cool the syrup, discard the spices, and pour the deep red syrup over the oranges. If you are not serving them immediately, turn the oranges to color them evenly. Garnish the oranges with the reserved julienne, and serve with both fork and spoon.

MAKES 6 SERVINGS

Orange Bavarian Cream

This Bavarian cream, a mousse stabilized with gelatin, can be made well ahead and frozen. For a beautiful way to stretch the dessert, mold it in a ring filled with fresh fruit. It is also captivating made with lemon, spooned into cups, and topped with a few berries.

1 orange
3 tablespoons orange-flavored liqueur
½ envelope unflavored gelatin
¼ cup plus 2 tablespoons sugar
2 large eggs, separated, at room temperature
1 cup chilled heavy cream

Grate the zest from the orange, squeeze the juice, and put both in a small nonreactive saucepan; if necessary add more juice to make ½ cup. Pour the liqueur in a cup, sprinkle the gelatin over it, and let it soften for 5 minutes. Add the sugar to the saucepan and dissolve it over low heat, stirring. Add the gelatin mixture and stir until the gelatin is also dissolved.

Put the egg yolks in a small bowl and pour the hot orange juice mixture into them in a stream, stirring constantly. Pour the mixture back into the pan and stir over low heat, watching closely, just until the yolks have thickened. Do not let them scramble. Set aside off the heat.

In a medium-size clean dry bowl, whip the cream into soft peaks. In a large deep bowl with a clean beater, whip the egg whites until stiff but not dry. Stir a spoonful of whites into the orange mixture, then gently fold the orange mixture back into the rest of the whites until no streaks of white remain. In quick, gentle strokes fold in the whipped cream until no streaks of orange show. Pour the Bavarian cream into a 3½- to 4-cup mold, cover with plastic wrap, and chill for several hours, until set. You may freeze the mold for several months and thaw it in the refrigerator for a few hours or overnight before serving.

To serve, run a knife around the edges of the mold, dip it into a bowl of hot water, place a serving platter on top and, holding tightly, invert with a jerk. Sometimes this takes more than one try, so be patient and mop up any melted cream before serving. If you like, garnish the platter with orange segments, candied orange peel (see page 197), chocolate shavings, or fresh strawberries or other fruit.

MAKES 6 OR MORE SERVINGS

Chilled Orange Soufflé

This dessert, essentially orange curd lightened with egg whites, comes in handy when the cupboard is bare. Also delicious with lemon, you can spoon it over fresh fruit and lightly brown it in the oven. The yolks are cooked enough to allay fears of salmonella.

> 1 medium-size orange
> 3 large eggs, at room temperature
> 2 tablespoons sugar
> 1 tablespoon orange-flavored liqueur

Grate the zest of the orange and set it aside. Separate the eggs, putting the yolks in the top of a double boiler and the whites in a bowl. Stir the sugar into the yolks. Squeeze the orange juice and add it with the liqueur to the yolks. Over gently simmering water, whisk the yolk mixture constantly until the yolks thicken. Watch closely to see that they don't scramble. Take the pan off the heat and stir in the grated zest. Beat the egg whites until stiff peaks form. Stir a spoonful of egg whites into the yolk mixture, then gently fold the orange-yolk mixture back into the rest of the whites. Spoon the soufflé into pretty glass cups or bowls and chill. A sprig of mint or a few berries make a pretty garnish.

MAKES 4 SERVINGS

Orange Grand Marnier Soufflé

Here is the classic orange soufflé, accented with Grand Marnier (if you prefer to omit the liqueur, use ½ cup orange juice). Although light flourless soufflés work well in some instances (see page 149), I find that this large soufflé holds better with a cream sauce base.

For the practical purpose of timing this dessert at a dinner party, plan carefully and have everything done up to the beating of the egg whites. When you break before the previous course, whip the whites, fold them in, and put the soufflé in the preheated oven as you sit down. If the guests have to wait for their dessert, let them know it's worth waiting for—the slight delay will heighten their anticipation.

½ cup sugar
2½ tablespoons unsalted butter
3 tablespoons all-purpose flour
¾ cup milk
4 large egg yolks, at room temperature
¼ cup plus 2 tablespoons fresh orange juice (from about 1½ oranges)
Grated zest of 2 oranges
3 tablespoons Grand Marnier
6 large egg whites, at room temperature
Pinch of salt
Confectioners' sugar for dusting (optional)

Preheat the oven to 400°F. Butter the inside of a 7-cup soufflé dish and sprinkle a tablespoon of the sugar over the bottom and all the way up the sides. Tie a waxed paper or foil collar, buttered on the inside, around the rim of the dish if you like; this is not necessary, but helps the soufflé to rise high.

Over low heat, melt the butter in a saucepan and stir the flour in it for about 2 minutes to make a roux. Gradually add the milk and cook, stirring, until it thickens and becomes smooth, about 5 minutes. Let it cool slightly and, off the heat, stir in the egg yolks one at a time, blending them in well. Stir in the remaining sugar, the orange juice, zest, and Grand Marnier.

In a large bowl, beat the egg whites with a pinch of salt until they make stiff peaks. Stir one spoonful into the orange mixture, then fold the orange mixture back into the rest of the whites until no streaks of egg white remain. Pour the soufflé batter into the prepared dish, put it into the preheated oven, and immediately lower the heat to 350°F. Bake the soufflé until it has risen high and the crown turns deep brown, about 35 minutes.

Take the soufflé out and remove the collar. You can dust the top with confectioners' sugar but you need not gild the lily. Serve the soufflé immediately, scooping some from the runnier middle and as well as the crustier outside for each serving.

MAKES 4 TO 6 SERVINGS

Crêpes Suzette

This classic dessert, though simplified here, is not for the abstemious. Although you can heat the liqueurs, pour them over the warmed crêpes, and ignite them to burn off the alcohol and impress your guests, I must admit that I often don't bother. Instead, I use half the amount of spirits and cook the sauce until it bubbles and thickens, and some of the potency burns off in the heat, thus omitting the conflagration. The taste is impressive enough on its own.

FOR THE ORANGE BUTTERCREAM
1 orange
½ lemon
½ cup sugar
½ cup (1 stick; ¼ pound) unsalted butter, softened
¼ cup Curaçao or other orange-flavored liqueur

TO COMPLETE
18 crêpes (see page 23)
¼ cup brandy

First make the orange buttercream. With a vegetable peeler, peel the outer zest from the orange, leaving the bitter white pith beneath; peel one strip of zest from the lemon half. Put them in a food processor with ¼ cup plus 2 tablespoons of the sugar and process until the zest is finely minced. Add the softened butter and process until creamy smooth and light. Squeeze the juice from the orange (about ½ cup) and lemon (about 2 tablespoons), and slowly add them to the butter mixture. Slowly add the Curaçao until it too is absorbed. (This may be done well ahead, covered in a container, and chilled or frozen.)

Put the orange butter in a large nonreactive saucepan and heat over low flame until it is melted, mixed, and thickened into a syrup; remove the pan from the heat. One at a time, take a crêpe in your fingertips and dip first one side and then the other in the sauce. Fold the crêpe in quarters and put it on a serving platter. Repeat with the remaining crêpes, overlapping them on the platter. Sprinkle the remaining 2 tablespoons sugar over the crêpes and keep hot.

Heat the brandy in a small saucepan. Ignite it with a match and pour it over the crêpes: both the brandy and the crêpes need to be hot. Or, if you prefer, pour the hot brandy over the crêpes first and then ignite it on the platter. Spoon the flaming sauce over the crêpes and serve with fanfare.

MAKES 6 TO 8 OR MORE SERVINGS

Chocolate Grand Marnier Cake

Since orange and chocolate are total opposites, theirs is a marriage made in heaven, as this sublimely rich cake shows. With all the parts except the chocolate ganache made ahead, the cake is easy to assemble on the day of your party, which should be made very special indeed.

1 vanilla génoise (see page 302) or sponge if you prefer (page 283)

FOR THE SYRUP
¼ cup Grand Marnier
¼ cup sugar

FOR THE FILLING
¼ cup orange buttercream made without spirits (see page 192)

FOR THE CANDIED ORANGE JULIENNE
1 orange
2 tablespoons sugar plus sand sugar to coat the strands
2 tablespoons water

FOR THE CHOCOLATE GANACHE
4 ounces bittersweet chocolate, broken up into pieces
½ cup heavy cream
2 tablespoons Grand Marnier

Put the génoise on a wire rack set over a plate. Split the cake across in half as evenly as possible.

To make the Grand Marnier syrup, put the liqueur in a small saucepan with the sugar and bring to a boil. Let it boil until the sugar is dissolved, about 5 minutes. Remove the top layer of the cake and sprinkle the syrup over each layer. Spread the orange buttercream in a thin layer over the bottom half, then replace the top.

To make the orange garnish, remove the orange peel with a vegetable peeler, leaving the bitter white pith behind. Cut out the individual orange sections, cover, and reserve them for the final garnish. Cut the orange zest into thin julienne. Put the sugar and water in a small saucepan, bring to a boil, and let boil until the sugar is dissolved, about 5 minutes. Add the julienne (if your pan is not so small, add more water to cover the julienne comfortably), and simmer over low heat until the orange peel is cooked through and transparent and the water nearly evaporated, about 10 minutes. Take out the julienne with a slotted spoon and toss it on a plate covered with sugar, coating each strand with crystals. (This is the most decorative, but another time you may wish merely to dry out the julienne on towels without using the added sugar. Candied julienne stored in an airtight tin keeps indefinitely.)

To make the chocolate ganache, combine the chocolate and cream in the top of a double boiler over gently simmering water. Stir until the chocolate melts and blends with the cream. When the mixture becomes glossy, stir in the Grand Marnier. While the chocolate ganache is still warm, spread it evenly over the génoise, catching any drips on the plate below. Spread the remaining ganache around the sides of the cake. When the chocolate ganache is nearly cool, carefully arrange the reserved orange sections on top in the center like a pinwheel. Press the candied julienne into the sides and chill. Leave the cake at room temperature for 10 to 15 minutes before serving.

MAKES ONE 8-INCH CAKE; 8 SERVINGS

Bittersweet Chocolate Orange Cheesecake

The food processor makes this cheesecake easy to prepare, and everything can be completed a day ahead.

FOR THE CRUST
¼ cup blanched almonds, lightly toasted (see page 179)
2 tablespoons sugar
3 tablespoons grated orange zest
¼ teaspoon ground allspice
¼ cup unsweetened cocoa powder
1¼ cups graham cracker crumbs
¼ cup (½ stick) unsalted butter, melted and cooled

FOR THE FILLING
1 pound cream cheese
⅔ cup sugar
½ cup unsweetened cocoa powder
2 large eggs
¼ cup orange juice
¼ cup orange-flavored liqueur

FOR THE TOPPING
3 tablespoons orange marmalade
1 tablespoon orange juice
1 cup sour cream

To make the crust, put the almonds and sugar in a food processor and coarsely grate the nuts. Add the orange zest, allspice, and cocoa, and process to combine them. Add the graham cracker crumbs and, with the machine still running, pour in the butter, just enough to moisten the ingredients and make them cling together. Turn them into a 9-inch spring-form pan and press a thin layer of crumbs first around the sides, then in the bottom. Refrigerate the crust to firm it.

Preheat the oven to 375°F. In a clean workbowl, process the cream cheese or beat with an electric mixer until smooth. With the motor or mixer running, gradually add the sugar and cocoa. Add the eggs one at a time, then the orange juice and liqueur. With a rubber spatula, scrape down the sides of the bowl. When the batter is smooth, pour it into the prepared crust. Bake the cheesecake for 25 minutes and put it on a wire rack to cool.

While the cheesecake is cooling, strain the marmalade through a sieve into a small saucepan and add the orange juice. Over low heat, melt the marmalade and stir to combine the mixture. Off the heat, stir in the sour cream. When well blended and smooth, spread the topping evenly over the cheesecake while it is still hot. Let the cheesecake cool to room temperature, then chill it in the refrigerator for at least 4 hours or preferably over-night.

To serve, run a knife around the outside of the crust and carefully remove the spring-form sides from the cheesecake. Garnish it with shavings or curls of bittersweet chocolate or candied orange peel (see page 197). This cheesecake is dense and rich, so slice it into thin wedges.

MAKES ONE 9-INCH CHEESECAKE; 12 SERVINGS

Aunt Lucy's Fruit Cake

In my husband's family, Great Aunt Lucy presided over making the fruit cake each Saturday after Thanksgiving, to ripen in time for Christmas. The secret of her fruit cakes was dark molasses—either sorghum or blackstrap—and dark Barbados rum. My father-in-law carried on the tradition, so here is Jim Riely's interpretation of Aunt Lucy's receipt.

2 pounds (combined) candied orange, lemon, and citron
1 pound seeded raisins
½ pound candied pineapple
4 ounces dried figs
½ pound candied cherries
2 cups (4 sticks; 1 pound) unsalted butter, softened
1¾ cups sugar (¾ pound)
10 large eggs, at room temperature
5 cups all-purpose flour (1½ pounds)
½ pound pecans, chopped and lightly toasted (see page 179)
1 cup dark molasses (unsulfured)
1½ cups dark rum
2 teaspoons ground cinnamon
2 teaspoons ground nutmeg
1 teaspoon ground cloves
1 teaspoon ground ginger

First prepare the baking pans. Decide how many and what size cakes you want. This recipe makes eight pounds of cake, about twenty cups in volume. You can bake it in one single huge cake or in several smaller ones. The pans should be at least 3 inches deep.

Cut pieces of paper, either parchment, aluminum foil, or waxed, to fit the bottom and sides of each pan. Butter the pieces and the exposed sides of the pans, then flour them lightly and knock out the excess.

Then cut your fruit into cubes. Since this step takes time, it is best to accomplish it early. Whatever Aunt Lucy might think, in this instance I admit to finding a food processor a great saver of time, labor, and humor. Just be sure not to chop the fruit too fine and end up with a gummy purée. It's important to cut the cherries by hand, though, since their ruby color stands out in the mosaic texture of the cake.

Preheat the oven to 275°F. Half fill a pan or two with water and put them on the bottom of the oven for steam.

In a huge bowl, cream the butter and sugar together until light. Then add the eggs, one at a time, blending well after each addition.

Put the flour in another bowl. Gradually flour the fruit and nuts in it, a small amount at a time, shaking off any extra back into the bowl. This step keeps the fruit and nuts from sinking to the bottom of the batter. Stir the remaining flour into the butter-sugar-egg mixture. When well blended, mix in the fruit and nuts. This is best done with your hands, so roll your sleeves up beyond your elbows ahead of time.

Combine the molasses and rum, and stir in the spices. Pour the mixture into the batter and mix thoroughly with your hands.

Fill the prepared cake pans about three quarters full with batter and put them in the oven. Bake for 2 to 2½ hours for 3- to 6-cup pans, or as long as needed, until each cake tests done with a toothpick inserted in the middle (it's done when the toothpick comes out clean). One single cake made from all the batter takes up to 4 hours to bake.

Remove the cakes from the oven, cool on a rack for 20 to 30 minutes, then carefully invert them on the rack, remove the pans, and slowly peel off the paper. Cool them completely. To store the fruit cakes, wrap them together with a quartered apple (to keep them moist) in linen or cheesecloth soaked in rum, and seal each cake in an airtight tin. Keep the tins in a cool place. The cakes can be stored thus for several months and will improve with age. Several weeks before serving, my father-in-law liked to anoint his chosen fruit cake with a generous dose of rum, sherry, or brandy, a tradition carried on in his family and highly recommended. To serve the fruit cake, unwrap it carefully and cut it into thin slices. Rewrapped and chilled, the remaining cake will last for several weeks.

MAKES 8 POUNDS OF FRUIT CAKE

Tangerine Sherbet

This easy sherbet is elegant and intense, the tangerine truly tangy. Make it with any citrus juice, adjusting the amount of sugar, perhaps omitting the liqueur. Citrus sherbet is especially appealing served in its own shell.

    1⅓ cups sugar
    1 cup water
    Grated zest of 2 tangerines
    3 cups tangerine juice, strained (from about 9 to 10 juicy honey tangerines)
    2 tablespoons fresh lemon juice
    3 tablespoons Mandarine Napoléon or other orange-flavored liqueur (optional)

Combine the sugar and water in a pot and bring to a boil. Let it boil over low heat, covered, until the sugar is dissolved, about 5 minutes. When it is cool, stir the tangerine zest, juice, and liqueur into the syrup. (If you prefer, simply stir the sugar into the citrus juices and let the acid dissolve the crystals, then add the water.) Chill well.

    Freeze the mixture in a sorbetière or an ice cream machine, following the manufacturer's directions. Or freeze the sherbet according to the directions on page 307.

    It's attractive to serve the sherbet packed in its own skin as a shell. Before you squeeze the juice, cut out a cap one third of the way from the tops of the tangerine rinds and scoop out all the flesh and membrane. Freeze the shells enclosed in plastic bags ahead of time, then fill them with the finished sherbet an hour or so before serving. Keep them in the freezer until serving, garnished with a leaf of fresh or candied mint.

    MAKES 1 GENEROUS QUART

Candied Orange Zests

These sweetmeats make an attractive and economical present for the holidays. Any citrus fruit works: remove the thin colored outer skin before you squeeze the juice or cut out individual sections for another recipe. Use a vegetable peeler to remove the zest, and try to take as little as possible of the bitter white pith just below the zest. Whatever citrus you use, choose specimens with vibrant color. If you candy several different types of citrus—the various colors combined have great appeal—cook them separately. Some citrus may take longer to turn transparent than others.

1 cup sugar plus 2 cups or more sand sugar
1 cup water
Zest of 5 or so oranges, peeled off in thin strips about 2 inches long

Make a syrup by putting 1 cup of the sugar and the water in a pot and bringing it to a boil. Let boil over low heat until the sugar is dissolved, about 5 minutes. Add the zests (if the syrup is too shallow, add more water) and simmer until the zests turn transparent and the syrup thickens, about 10 minutes. Remove the zests with a slotted spoon and spread them on a plate covered with the sand sugar. Turn the strips in the sugar to coat both sides well and leave them to dry in the sugar. (Use the leftover sand sugar for another dessert.) Store the candied zest in a plastic bag or tightly closed tin. Candied citrus zests keep indefinitely.

If you like, you can dip the candied zests into melted white or bittersweet chocolate, leaving half uncolored for contrast.

PAPAYA

In his diary, Columbus described West Indians eating a "tree melon" which they called the "fruit of the angels." Our name papaya comes from the Carib word *ababai*, sometimes called pawpaw (easily confused with a North American fruit also called pawpaw but unrelated). Twenty feet tall and straight, with clustered fruit hanging beneath the plumed crown of fronds, the papaya plant looks like a cross between an upright coconut palm and, as Jane Grigson put it, an exotic Brussels sprout. Sublime or ridiculous, it's a wonderful fruit.

The voluptuous fruit of *Carica papaya* is decidedly melonlike, each ranging in size from half a pound on up to twenty pounds. As the papaya has spread throughout the tropical world, its berry has assumed different appearances. It can be round, pearlike, or even banana shaped, and its skin color pink, orange, yellow, or green. Inside the smooth skin, the flesh can vary in color from yellow to coral. The small seeds that fill the cavity are glistening gray to nearly black when ripe, looking like the finest caviar.

Most papaya found in American markets come from Hawaii and to a lesser extent from Mexico, Florida, the Dominican Republic, the Bahamas, or the Philippines. The trees bear fruit continuously and prolifically, with peak supplies coming between April and June and again between October and December. Although papaya taste best when allowed to mature on the tree, few of us have that luxury.

Hawaiian fruit, usually the smaller Kapcho Solo or Sunrise Solo varieties, are shipped partially mature, when green with a tinge of yellow at the larger blossom end. They will ripen in a few days at room temperature to mostly yellow-orange, when they can be held briefly in the refrigerator without loss of flavor. Do not chill them before they are ripe. To hasten the process, place a ripe apple in a bag with the papaya. A flavorful papaya need not have perfectly sleek skin, but the flesh should yield slightly to the touch.

In the tropics papaya have become a staple food, cooked and eaten unripe as a vegetable, rather like squash, or eaten ripe and raw, like a melon. Papaya shipped north are too expensive to treat as anything but an exotic fruit. To prepare papaya, simply peel off the thin skin with a potato peeler, cut the fruit in half, and scoop out the seeds. The soft but cohesive flesh can be hollowed and stuffed, sliced lengthwise or in rings, cubed, chopped, or puréed. The seeds too are edible, with a peppery crunch that can punctuate savory dishes.

Papaya are versatile in the kitchen, adapting to simple or complex handling. A ripe papaya with a squeeze of lime makes an exquisite breakfast, just as papaya draped in paper-thin slices of prosciutto makes a superb hors d'oeuvre or first course. The fruit holds together well enough, both in texture and flavor, to be sautéed with seafood, chicken, pork, and other savory foods, even combined with spicy peppers and onions. You can bake stuffed papaya, or broil or grill it for a sweet or savory treat. Like mango, it marries with all the exotic seasonings, such as ginger, coconut, rum, and chiles, in fact, many of the mango and persimmon recipes in this book are interchangeable with papaya. The warm color and smooth texture go naturally with diverse fruit and dessert compotes and combinations, tropical or traditional.

Green papaya contains the enzyme papain, similar to digestive enzymes found in pineapple and kiwi, that dissolves meat tissue and counters the effect of gelatin. In the tropics, papaya leaves wrapped around savory mixtures are a low-tech meat tenderizer. Papain is an ingredient in commercial tenderizer. Even ripened papaya contains some papain; for that reason, it should be added to chicken, fish, or seafood only right before serving to avoid a mushy texture.

A whole small papaya (about eleven ounces) contains about 160 calories, with lots of vitamin C, a generous amount of potassium and fiber, and some folic acid.

Chicken and Papaya Salad

Peppery papaya seeds season this exotic chicken salad, but you can omit them if you prefer.

> 1 whole chicken breast, about ½ pound, halved, boned, and skinned
> 1½ cups chicken stock
> 1 lime
> 3 scallions (green and white parts), thinly sliced
> ¼ cup peanut or other light vegetable oil, or to taste
> 1 tablespoon peeled and minced fresh ginger
> Salt to taste
> 1 medium-large, fully ripe papaya
> 4 handfuls redleaf lettuce

Put the chicken breast in a small saucepan, pour in chicken stock to cover, and bring to a gentle simmer. Cover and poach over low heat until the chicken is just cooked, about 8 minutes. Let it cool in the stock. Drain and cube the chicken, about 1½ cups, reserving the stock for another use.

Grate the zest from the lime and squeeze 2 tablespoons of the juice. Put the zest and juice in a nonreactive bowl with the chicken, and add the scallions, oil, ginger, and salt. Mix well and taste to correct the seasoning and balance of acid and oil. Cover and let stand about 30 minutes to let the flavors develop (if longer, cover and chill; return to room temperature before continuing).

Cut the papaya in half lengthwise and scoop out the seeds, saving 1 tablespoon. Rinse them in a fine sieve under cold running water and drain well. Lay beds of lettuce on four salad plates. Stir the chicken mixture again, scoop a mound of it onto each plate, and top with some of the papaya seeds. Peel the papaya with a vegetable peeler, slice the flesh into long thin strips, and place them around the chicken. Serve at once.

MAKES 4 SERVINGS

Sautéed Shrimp with Papaya and Peppers

The brilliantly colored shrimp, papaya, and peppers combine to make a delicious sweet-and-sour dish with a minimum of effort.

3 tablespoons peanut or other light vegetable oil
1 clove garlic, minced
1 tablespoon peeled and minced fresh ginger
3 scallions (green and white parts), sliced
¼ cup red bell pepper strips
¼ cup green bell pepper strips
½ medium-size jalapeño, seeded and minced
1 pound medium-large raw shrimp, shelled and deveined
½ medium-large, ripe papaya, peeled, seeded, and cubed
Juice of 1 lime
3 tablespoons chopped fresh coriander (cilantro)

Heat the oil in a large nonreactive skillet over medium-high heat. Cook the garlic and ginger for a few seconds until fragrant, stirring. Add the scallions and continue stirring briskly for about a minute more. Add the peppers and cook until they begin to soften, about 2 minutes. Lower the heat slightly and push the vegetables to the side of the pan. Add the shrimp and stir to cook them evenly on both sides until they have turned orange and are nearly cooked through in the middle, 2 or 3 minutes. Stir in the papaya and cook just enough to heat it through. Add the lime juice; stir to combine all the ingredients and finish cooking the shrimp in the steam. When the pan juices have formed a light sauce, stir in the coriander. Spoon the mixture onto warm plates and serve with steamed rice.

MAKES 4 SERVINGS

Broiled Papaya

You can add a little powdered spice to the sugar, but it hardly seems necessary. This dish is luscious for breakfast, lunch, or dinner.

1 medium-large, fully ripe papaya
1 tablespoon dark brown sugar
Sour cream, plain yogurt, or crème fraîche (see page 155)

Preheat the broiler. Cut the papaya in half lengthwise, remove the skin with a vegetable peeler, and scoop out the seeds. Set the halves hollow-side up in an ovenproof dish and sprinkle with the brown sugar. Run under the broiler until the sugar is melted and bubbly and the fruit hot, about 5 minutes. Spoon a little sour cream into the cavity or pass on the side. Serve immediately.

MAKES 2 SERVINGS

Fresh Papaya with Lime and Preserved Ginger

Fresh and lovely.

1 medium-large, fully ripe papaya, peeled, seeded, and cubed
2 tablespoons fresh lime juice
1 large knob preserved stem ginger, with a little syrup, minced (available in Oriental
   and specialty food stores)
¼ cup plain yogurt, or to taste
Grated zest of 1 lime

Sprinkle the papaya cubes with the lime juice in a nonreactive bowl. Toss the preserved ginger with the papaya. Add a little of the ginger syrup to the yogurt to sweeten it to taste. Divide the papaya between two serving plates and dab a dollop of yogurt beside or in the middle and garnish with the zest.

MAKES 2 SERVINGS

Pickled Green Papaya

This colorful pickle made from unripe papaya comes from my friend Cora Gemil, who comes from Manila. It shows the Filipino preference for intense flavors—sour, salty, and sweet—balanced by rice. Start it at least two days ahead.

1 pound green papaya, peeled, seeded, and cut into ⅛-inch julienne
1 large red bell pepper, seeded and cut into ⅛-inch julienne
1 large green bell pepper, seeded and cut in to ⅛-inch julienne
1 cup kosher salt
¼ cup slivered shallots

3 medium-size cloves garlic, slivered
2 tablespoons peeled and slivered fresh ginger
1⅓ cups distilled white vinegar (at least 5% acidity)
1 cup sugar
Freshly ground black pepper to taste

Mix the papaya, bell peppers, salt, shallots, garlic, and ginger in a large bowl, distributing the salt well. Cover the mixture and let it sit overnight at room temperature.

Drain the papaya mixture, rinse with cold water, and drain again. Return it to a fresh bowl and mix in ⅔ cup of vinegar. Let it marinate overnight at room temperature again.

Drain the papaya mixture again, rinse with cold water, and drain well. In a small, heavy, nonreactive saucepan, combine the sugar, remaining vinegar, and pepper. Bring the liquid to a boil, and let it boil, covered, until the sugar is dissolved, about 5 minutes. Pour it over the papaya mixture; cool, cover, and refrigerate for at least 2 hours. Drain the pickled papaya before serving. The pickle can be stored in a tightly covered jar in the refrigerator for up to one month.

MAKES ABOUT 12 SERVINGS

PEACHES AND
NECTARINES

Ever since Confucius, the peach—*t'ao*—has inspired poets, artists, and philosophers. In its native China, where wild peach trees still grow in the north, the fruit's significance is less as a foodstuff than as an emblem. In other parts of China, ornamental peaches are widely cultivated for their blossoms, an ancient fertility symbol. At New Year they augur good luck, and eating a peach supposedly brings immortality.

The peach made its way westward to Persia, where it thrived in the warmer climate. The botanical name for the peach, *Prunus persica*, shows that it was thought to be a native of Persia. From there it migrated to all temperate regions of the world. In the United States, where the Spanish brought it in the sixteenth century, only the apple tree rivals the peach in importance.

The peach's association with sensuality may come from the pale fragility of its flowers and the fruit's creamy pink color and downy softness, like skin: "All pink and yellow and dimpled and juicily cleft as Renoir's dappled baigneuses," wrote William Fahey. Surely, a lush peach perfectly poised between sweetness and acidity is one of summer's great pleasures. Its ambrosial juices have given the name nectarine to one type of peach. Mistakenly believed by some to be a cross between a peach and plum, the nectarine is actually a fuzzless peach. The two can be used interchangeably in recipes and, early in the season before local peaches are ripe, nectarines may be a better bet at market.

Peaches are divided into cling and freestone varieties. The former, earlier ripening and firmer of flesh, are mostly processed for canning; the latter are marketed fresh for the table. Peaches further divide into yellow and white varieties. Most of the peaches we see at market are yellow, but later in the season white peaches, with their delicate perfume and exquisite juiciness, are worth seeking out. White peaches are more fragile and expensive, but peach perfectionists prize them.

When choosing peaches at market, look for a yellow or cream background color rather than a red blush. A green undertone shows that the peach was picked prematurely and will never fully develop its flavor. Leave peaches at room temperature to make them ready for eating. To hasten the process, put them in a paper bag with a ripe apple or banana, whose natural ethylene gas will encourage ripening. A soft touch and luscious scent tell you that it is ready—as if you didn't know. Underripe fruit can work well, even better, for baking, sautéing, broiling, or preserving. Mealy peaches will never be good for anything.

Once peaches are cut, the air will darken their flesh, so toss them with a few drops of orange or lemon juice to protect them. To remove the skins quickly and easily, drop them in boiling water for ten to thirty seconds shortly before serving—the riper the fruit, the shorter the time. Remove them with a slotted spoon and drop them into cold water to stop the cooking. The skins should slip off easily. If you poach peaches in syrup, keep the skins on to retain their nutritional value and to transfer the blush onto the flesh; peel just before serving.

To halve a peach, cut around along the natural seam, then grasp the fruit with one hand on each half and twist in opposite directions. Once in a while you may need to remove the pit while keeping the peach whole. Cut an almond shape around the stem end through to the stone. At the blossom end, poke a potato nail or skewer into the peach and push the stone out through the cut you just made. Peach pits, particularly the kernels inside, add flavor to syrups, so you may want to save them for compotes, custards, and the brandy called *noyau* in French.

Peaches go beautifully with other fruit, especially raspberries and other drupes or stone fruits—apricots, cherries, plums, and almonds—that ripen at the same time. Peaches and cream are such natural companions that the words have become an idiom outside the kitchen. Wine, liqueurs, rum, and whiskey go exceedingly well with the fruit. Europeans like to slice a fully ripened peach right into a glass of the favorite local wine to savor at the end of the meal. A fine Sauternes or brandy is an ideal complement to a peach dessert.

The peach's acidity makes it surprisingly apt for savory dishes too, so that chicken, duck, pork, and ham work well with it. Exotic spices—ginger, saffron, cumin, cardamom, chiles, curry, and coriander, to name a few—do not overwhelm the peach, perhaps hinting at its Asian origin.

Peaches are in season from May to mid-October, with July and August the peak months. Most American peaches come from California, South Carolina, Georgia, and New Jersey. Two large or three medium-size peaches will weigh about a pound, yielding two cups of slices and one and a half cups of purée.

Among canned fruits, peaches are one of the most successful and can be substituted for poached fresh peaches in syrup. The flavor of dried peaches, unlike that of dried apricots, can be rather too elusive.

At about forty calories apiece, ripe peaches are so luscious on their own that you may prefer to eat them so. They are a good source of vitamin A, calcium, potassium, and fiber.

Bellini Cocktail

The secret of this celebrated cocktail, from Harry's Bar in Venice, is fragrant white peaches rather than yellow. Filtering the fresh juice, though tedious, is essential.

4 large, very ripe white peaches
1 tablespoon superfine sugar
1½ teaspoons fresh lemon juice, strained
12 ounces iced champagne

Peel, pit, and cube the peaches and purée the flesh in a food processor. Moisten a triple layer of cheesecloth in water and squeeze it out. Line a fine sieve with the cheesecloth and press the peach purée through. Spoon the purée a little at a time into a coffee filter set in a cone over a bowl. Stir gently once in a while, taking care not to break the filter. Replace it as it becomes clogged. Save the juice, covering and chilling it well; discard the solids in the filter. (This should be done early in the day you plan to serve them.)

Shortly before serving, stir the sugar into the lemon juice to dissolve it; then stir the mixture into the peach juice. To serve, pour 1 jigger (1½ ounces) of the peach juice into each champagne glass. Add 3 ounces of iced champagne and serve immediately.

MAKES 4 COCKTAILS

Chilled Peach Soup

Also luscious with nectarines, apricots, and melon or, out of season, with dried apricots thinned with water. If you prefer, use half white wine and half water. This makes a most elegant beginning or ending to a summer dinner party, and everything is made ahead.

4 large, ripe peaches, halved, pitted, and coarsely chopped
1½ cups dry white wine
2 to 3 tablespoons honey
2 tablespoons fresh lemon juice
⅛ teaspoon freshly grated nutmeg, or to taste
2 tablespoons sour cream, plain yogurt, or crème fraîche (see page 155)
2 tablespoons chopped pistachios (undyed and unsalted)

Place the chopped peaches in a large nonreactive saucepan with the wine, honey, and lemon juice. Bring the liquid barely to a boil, cover, and allow to cool. Purée the mixture in batches in a food processor. Strain the purée through a fine sieve into a bowl, pressing with the back of a spoon to extract all the juice. Delicately season the purée with a little nutmeg. Taste carefully for sweetening and balance. Cover and chill thoroughly.

To serve, ladle the soup into pretty glass cups. Swirl a spoonful of sour cream into each and sprinkle with some of the pistachios.

MAKES 3 TO 4 SERVINGS

Peach Salsa

This quick fresh salsa makes a lively accompaniment to poultry, pork, ham, or duck. Make the salsa about thirty minutes before serving.

1 large, ripe peach
2 tablespoons fresh lime juice
¼ cup diced red onion
¼ cup seeded and diced green bell pepper
2 teaspoons green peppercorns, rinsed and dried, or diced fresh,
  hot chile pepper, to taste
1 tablespoon vegetable oil
2 tablespoons chopped fresh coriander (cilantro)

Peel, pit, and cube the peach to measure about 1 cup. Toss it in a bowl with the lime juice right away to keep the flesh from turning dark. Add the onion, bell pepper, peppercorns, and oil, and stir. Taste carefully to adjust the seasonings. Just before serving, stir in the coriander.

MAKES ABOUT 1½ CUPS

Mostarda di Frutta di Cremona

(MUSTARD FRUIT CONSERVE)

This sweet and piquant relish, unusual for its inclusion of mustard, traces its roots to ancient Rome. There are many versions, but those from the city of Cremona are best known. In this rendering the whole fruit looks luminous in its amber syrup. You can use various types, but be sure to choose specimens that are underripe, and larger varieties should be small enough to fit into the jars.

2 cups sugar
8 or more cups water, enough to cover the fruit
½ cup fresh lemon juice
1 pound small, firm peaches, preferably pitted
1 pound small, firm quince, peeled and cored, or pears, peeled
½ pound firm, fresh apricots, preferably pitted
½ pound firm plums, preferably pitted
½ pound firm, fresh sweet or sour cherries, pitted
½ pound firm, fresh figs, stems snipped off
1 lemon, sliced into rounds
¼ cup yellow mustard seed
5 to 6 slices fresh ginger, peeled
6 whole cloves
1 cup dry white wine
⅔ cup honey

Combine the water, sugar, and lemon juice in a large heavy-bottomed nonreactive pot. Bring to a boil and and let it boil over low heat until the sugar is dissolved, about 5 minutes. Add the firmest fruit and let simmer about 10 to 15 minutes, then add the softer fruit and simmer a few minutes more. It is important not to let any of the fruit get mushy.

Carefully remove the fruit with a slotted spoon and place in a large ovenproof pan; leave the syrup in the pot. Traditional Italian recipes call for the fruit to be dried slowly in the sun over several days, but as this is impractical for many of us today, dry it slowly in a warm oven (120°F) for an hour or so. Let the fruit cool.

At least 10 minutes ahead of time, pour cold water over the mustard seed to cover. If you skip this step, the enzymes in the mustard will not be released and it will have no heat. Drain the mustard and add it to the syrup with the ginger and cloves tied securely in a cheesecloth bag. Add the wine and honey, bring the syrup to a boil, and reduce until it is very thick. Discard the cloves and ginger. Gently put the dried fruit in clean, warm large-mouthed canning jars with nonmetallic tops, and pour the syrup over to cover, saving any leftover syrup. Jiggle the fruit with a knife to release any air bubbles, and pour more syrup over the fruit to within a half inch of the top. Seal the tops and sterilize the jars (see page 321) to store in a cool dark cupboard. If you prefer not to sterilize it, simply refrigerate the jars. The *mostarda* does not need to mature. It will keep in the refrigerator for several months, in the cupboard for a year.

Serve the *mostarda* at room temperature with boiled and cold meats, in the traditional Italian style, or with anything as you would chutney.

MAKES ABOUT 2½ QUARTS

Peaches Preserved in Port

This is a fine way to catch the evanescent splendor of peaches, nectarines, or apricots. The fruit in its rich ruby syrup makes an excellent accompaniment to poultry and meat. Or serve it for dessert with ice cream, cake, cookies, or simply alone.

2½ cups sugar
1½ cups water
¾ cup port
½ cup fresh orange juice
3 tablespoons fresh lemon juice
Two 2-inch strips orange zest
One 2-inch strip lemon zest
3 whole cloves
One 1-inch stick cinnamon
¼ teaspoon freshly grated nutmeg
3 pounds small, perfect, ripe but firm peaches

Put the sugar and water in a large saucepan, bring to a boil, and let boil over low heat until the sugar is dissolved, about 5 minutes. Add the port, orange and lemon juices and zests, and spices. When the liquid returns to a boil, add the whole peaches. The liquid should just cover them; if not, add boiling water to cover. Poach the peaches over low heat for 5 minutes; do not let them get soft. Allow them to cool in the syrup.

With a slotted spoon carefully remove the peaches to a container. Boil the syrup down by about a third until it is thick and concentrated. Pour it over the peaches, cool, cover, and chill. The peaches will keep in the refrigerator for a month or longer. You can also put them up to store in a cupboard for several months (see page 321). Serve the peaches in the syrup.

MAKES ABOUT 1½ QUARTS

Whole Peaches Stuffed with Raspberries

Here is a simple yet sumptuous way to serve a perfectly ripe peach. Children like the surprise inside.

1 large, very ripe freestone peach
3 fresh raspberries
1 tablespoon orange-flavored liqueur or orange juice

Cut an almond shape around the stem end of the peach through to the stone. At the opposite blossom end, insert a potato nail or skewer into the peach and push the stone out through the cut you just made. Carefully poke the raspberries into the cavity. Gently rub the peach skin all over with the back of a knife to loosen the skin, then slip it off. Put the peach into a serving dish, spoon the liqueur or juice over, and serve, perhaps with a little cream, crème fraîche, mascarpone, or yogurt on the side. Serve with a spoon and fork.

MAKES 1 SERVING

Pesche Ripiene alla Piemontese

(STUFFED PEACHES IN THE STYLE OF PIEDMONT)

This dessert is to Piedmont what apple crisp is to New England.

6 large, ripe peaches
1 cup amaretti or other macaroon crumbs
¼ cup plus 2 tablespoons sugar
1 large egg yolk
¼ cup slivered blanched almonds
1½ tablespoons butter, cut into little pieces

Skin the peaches, cut them in half along the natural line, and stone them. Scoop out a little of the flesh to enlarge the hollows. Mash the scooped-out flesh in a bowl and mix it with the amaretti crumbs, ¼ cup of the sugar, the egg yolk, and almonds. The mixture should barely cling together.

Preheat the oven to 350°F. Put the peaches cut-side up in a buttered baking pan just large enough to hold them in one layer. Stuff the cavities with the amaretti filling, dot with butter, and sprinkle with the remaining sugar. Bake until the surface is golden, crisp, and caramelized, about 45 minutes. Serve hot with zabaglione (see page 278) or cold with cream.

MAKES 6 SERVINGS

Poached Nectarine Cups Filled with Red Wine Sherbet

Wine sherbet makes an exquisite counterpoint to many fruits, and nectarines and peaches are no exception. White wine or rosé works just as well.

FOR THE WINE SHERBET
3 cups dry red wine
1 cup sugar
1 cup water
3 tablespoons fresh lemon juice
One 2-inch strip lemon zest
2 whole cloves or one 2-inch stick cinnamon

FOR THE POACHED NECTARINES
1 cup sugar
2 cups water
2 tablespoons fresh lemon juice
One 2-inch strip lemon zest
2 large, ripe perfect nectarines or peaches

First make the wine sherbet. Combine in a medium-size nonreactive saucepan the wine, sugar, water, 2 tablespoons of the lemon juice, the zest, and cloves. Bring to a boil, then let boil over low heat until the sugar is dissolved, about 5 minutes. Strain through a fine sieve into a container and chill well. Freeze the wine syrup in a sorbetière or an ice cream machine according to the manufacturer's directions. Or freeze it according to the directions on page 307.

To poach the nectarines, place the sugar and water in a small nonreactive saucepan, bring to a boil, and let boil over low heat until the sugar is dissolved, about 5 minutes. Add the lemon juice, zest, and nectarines and poach over low heat until tender, about 5 minutes, depending on their ripeness. Let the nectarines cool in the syrup, then cover and chill. (This may be done a day or two ahead.)

To serve, remove the nectarines from the syrup, slip off their skins, cut them in half along the natural segmentation, and remove the pits. Put each nectarine half in a pretty dish or goblet, hollow-side up. Top with a scoop of the red wine sherbet.

MAKES 4 SERVINGS

Peach Melba

Escoffier created this famous dessert for the great soprano Dame Nellie Melba. A lusciously similar dish, pêche cardinale, named for its brilliant color, uses fresh unpoached peaches in the same sauce. In early autumn poached pears, standing whole, unstemmed, and enrobed in red, work nearly as well.

1 cup sugar
2 cups water
2 tablespoons fresh lemon juice
1 teaspoon pure vanilla extract
2 large, ripe perfect peaches
Vanilla ice cream, homemade (see page 61) or storebought
Fresh Raspberry Sauce (see page 279)

Put the sugar and water in a medium-size nonreactive saucepan, bring to a boil, and let boil until the sugar is dissolved, about 5 minutes. Add the lemon juice, vanilla, and peaches, and poach over low heat until tender, about 5 minutes, depending on their ripeness. Let the peaches cool in the syrup, then cover and chill. (This may be done a day or two ahead.)

To serve, remove the peaches from the syrup, slip off the skins, cut the peaches in half along the natural segmentation, and remove the pits. Put a scoop of vanilla ice cream in a pretty goblet or dish, top with half a peach, rounded-side up, and spoon some fresh raspberry sauce on top.

MAKES 4 SERVINGS

Peaches on Puff Pastry with Caramel Cream Sauce

With ready-made puff pastry, this elegant dessert can almost all be done ahead of time.

3½ cups water
1¼ cups sugar
1 lemon heel
3 large, ripe peaches or nectarines
1 sheet frozen puff pastry, thawed and chilled
⅓ cup apricot preserves, homemade (see page 31) or storebought
¼ cup bourbon
1 cup heavy cream

Combine the water and 1 cup of sugar in a large nonreactive saucepan. Bring the liquid to a boil and let boil over low heat until the sugar is dissolved, about 5 minutes. Add the lemon heel and the peaches and simmer over low heat until tender, 5 to 10 minutes, depending on their ripeness. Do not let them get mushy. Let the peaches cool in the pot; refrigerate, covered, if you are not serving them soon.

Unfold the puff pastry and roll it out with a rolling pin on a lightly floured board to enlarge it slightly. Cut out six rounds 4 inches in diameter. Working with one round at a time and keeping the rest well chilled, make a parallel cut with a small sharp knife just ⅜ inch inside the border of each round, nearly cutting through but leaving the dough attached at top and bottom. To make a raised rim, lift the right-side strip and and pull it to the left edge. Moisten the left lip and press down slightly. Lift the left-side strip and pull it to the right edge; moisten the right lip and press down slightly. Prick the inside of the round with a fork to keep it from puffing up. Repeat with the other five circles. Chill the pastry on an ungreased cookie sheet in the refrigerator for at least an hour.

Preheat the oven to 375°F. Bake the rounds until golden, about 20 minutes. If the centers have puffed up too much, press them down with a spoon. Set aside to cool. (Everything up to this point can be done ahead.)

To make the apricot glaze, push the apricot preserves through a sieve to remove chunks of fruit. Melt the preserves with 1 tablespoon of the bourbon over low heat in a small saucepan, stirring. Right before serving, brush a thin layer of apricot glaze inside each pastry round. Drain and skin the peaches and cut each in half along the natural segmentation; remove the pits and dry the peaches on paper towels. Place a half on each pastry round, hollow-side down, and brush the peach tops with the remaining glaze.

To make the caramel cream sauce, put the remaining sugar and bourbon in a saucepan and cook over medium-high heat until the sugar is dissolved, the liquid evaporates, and the syrup begins to color around the edges, about 5 minutes. Lower the heat and swirl the pan to color the caramel evenly to a rich amber. Watch closely and remove the pan from the heat before it gets too dark; it will continue to color off the heat. Put the pan in the sink in case the caramel spatters and slowly pour in the cream, stir well to dissolve the caramelized sugar into the sauce. Cook the cream sauce over low heat to thicken it slightly and spoon it around, not over, the pastry.

MAKES 6 SERVINGS

Peach Dacquoise

The dacquoise, a nutty meringue, can be made well ahead and stored in airtight tins or the freezer. Other juicy fruits, such as raspberries, strawberries, plums, and apricots, are delicious on the crunchy but tender dacquoise.

FOR THE DACQUOISE ROUNDS
3 large egg whites, at room temperature
Dash of salt
½ cup confectioners' sugar
⅛ teaspoon pure vanilla extract
2 ounces blanched almonds, lightly toasted (see page 179)
*   and ground to measure about ⅓ cup*

FOR THE PEACHES
1½ cups granulated sugar
2 cups water
2 large, ripe peaches
¼ teaspoon pure vanilla extract

TO COMPLETE
1 cup chilled heavy cream
1 tablespoon amaretto or kirsch
Confectioners' sugar to taste

Preheat the oven to 375°F. Butter and flour a cookie sheet; shake off the excess flour. Using a saucer, mark four separate circles 4 inches in diameter on the surface. Set aside.

In a medium-size bowl, whip the egg whites with the salt until soft peaks form. Gradually add the confectioners' sugar and continue whipping until the meringue forms glossy, stiff peaks. Fold in the vanilla and ground almonds.

Quickly fill an open or plain-tipped pastry tube with the meringue-nut mixture. Pipe 4-inch circles onto the prepared cookie sheet and fill in with spirals. Bake the meringue shells until light brown, about 20 minutes. Cool, then remove the dacquoise rounds from the sheet with a spatula, and allow them to cool completely in a dry place.

Combine the sugar and water in a small saucepan, bring to a boil, and let boil over low heat until the sugar is dissolved, about 5 minutes. Add the peaches and vanilla and poach over low heat, turning them once or twice, until tender, about 10 minutes, depending on their ripeness. Let them cool in the syrup.

Shortly before serving, whip the cream into soft peaks. Fold in the liqueur and sweeten with the confectioners' sugar. Cover and chill. To serve, place the dacquoise rounds on four dessert plates. Pipe or spread the whipped cream on top, allowing the dacquoise rims to show. Peel and halve the peaches, discard the pits, and set one peach half on top of each dacquoise cut-side down. Serve at once.

MAKES 4 SERVINGS

Glazed Peach and Blueberry Tart

This glorious tart shows off these two midsummer fruits that ripen at the same time. If you make it shortly before serving, you can omit the gelatin in the glaze.

One 9-inch pâte sucrée shell (see page 35), unbaked

FOR THE GLAZE
2 tablespoons orange-flavored liqueur
½ tablespoon unflavored gelatin
½ cup apricot preserves, homemade (see page 31) or storebought

FOR THE FILLING
3 large, ripe peaches
2 tablespoons fresh orange juice
¾ cup fresh or frozen (unthawed) blueberries, preferably small wild ones

Preheat the oven to 400°F. Prick the pastry shell with the tines of a fork; line with aluminum foil and weight it with dried beans, rice, or pie weights. Bake the shell for 15 minutes. Put the orange liqueur in a cup, stir in the gelatin, and let it soften for 5 minutes.

Meanwhile make the glaze. Press the apricot preserves through a coarse sieve into a small saucepan to remove chunks of fruit. Over low heat, gently melt the jam. Add the gelatin and liqueur, and heat to dissolve the gelatin, stirring. Bring the mixture to a boil, then set aside to let it partially cool. Take the pastry shell from the oven (if the pastry has puffed up, prick to deflate it) and let it cool somewhat, then spread a scant half of the glaze over the bottom. Bake it for 5 minutes more and let cool.

Peel, pit, and cut the peaches into thin slices. Put them in a bowl with the orange juice, stirring to coat the peaches to keep them from darkening. Stir in the berries. Arrange the fruit in the pastry shell, placing the peach slices more or less in concentric circles like the petals of a flower, with the blueberries scattered between. Bake the filled shell until the pastry is golden, 20 to 25 minutes. Let the fruit cool somewhat, then drizzle the remaining glaze (rewarmed, if it has jelled) over the peaches and then over the berries. Chill it well before serving.

MAKES ONE 9-INCH TART; 6 SERVINGS

Peach Cobbler

In a cobbler, biscuit dough is spread over a juicy fruit that moistens the dough during baking. It is often spooned on in mounds that look like cobblestones, hence the dish's name. Sometimes the topping gets heavy, so in this version it is rolled thin and cut in flower shapes, allowing the peach juice to bubble through.

3 pounds ripe peaches (about 8 peaches)
⅓ cup sugar, or to taste
2 tablespoons fresh lemon juice
1 tablespoon quick-cooking tapioca
Dash of ground cinnamon (optional)

FOR THE COBBLER DOUGH
2 cups all-purpose flour
3 tablespoons sugar
½ teaspoon baking soda
½ teaspoon salt
¼ cup (½ stick) unsalted butter, cut into pieces
1 large egg
¾ cup buttermilk

Peel, pit, and slice the peaches to measure about 6½ cups. In a large bowl, toss them with the sugar, lemon juice, and tapioca. If you like, add a little cinnamon. Turn the peaches into a large, shallow ovenproof pan, about 9 inches square, or any other shape of dish, and let it sit 15 minutes for the tapioca to work.

Meanwhile make the biscuit dough. Preheat the oven to 350°F. Mix together in a medium-size bowl the flour, sugar, baking soda, and salt. Add the butter and with a pastry blender, two knives, or your fingertips, quickly break up the butter into small pieces. Beat the egg into the buttermilk and stir into the dry ingredients to make a smooth, soft dough. Quickly knead the dough on a lightly floured board, no more than 1 minute, and roll it out to ⅓-inch thickness. With a flower- or star-shaped cookie cutter (or a plain circle will do fine), cut out the dough and lay the biscuits barely touching each other on top of the peaches.

Bake the cobbler until the topping is lightly browned and cooked through, about 45 minutes. Serve it warm with vanilla ice cream or whipped cream.

MAKES 8 SERVINGS

Peach Ice Cream

For homemade ice cream, peach is my hands-down favorite—a luxury to savor in season and to anticipate the rest of the year. Peach purée rather than chunks gives the best taste and texture.

3 large, ripe peaches
2 tablespoons orange juice
2 cups light cream
1 vanilla bean or ½ teaspoon pure vanilla extract
4 large egg yolks
⅔ cup sugar
1 cup heavy cream

Skin the peaches, pit and cube them, and purée the flesh to measure about 3 cups. Stir in the orange juice. Cover and chill thoroughly.

Scald the cream with the vanilla bean over medium heat in a small saucepan: heat it until little bubbles appear around the edges, but do not let it boil. Remove the vanilla bean and rinse it to use again.

In a medium-size bowl beat together well the egg yolks and sugar. Pour the scalded cream into the egg yolks in a slow, steady stream, beating continuously. Pour the custard back into the saucepan and stir constantly over low heat until the custard thickens enough to coat the back of the spoon; do not let the yolks curdle. Remove the pan from the heat and let it cool. If using vanilla extract, add it here. Cover the custard and chill thoroughly.

Whip the heavy cream to firm peaks, then fold it into the custard along with the peach purée. Freeze the mixture in an ice cream machine according to the manufacturer's directions or in a bowl, stirring from time to time to smooth the ice crystals. Allow the ice cream to mellow about 2 hours before serving.

MAKES ABOUT 2 QUARTS

PEARS

"The pear which comes from cultivated stock is one of our best fruits," wrote novelist and gastronome Alexandre Dumas *père* in his *Grand Dictionnaire de Cuisine*, published posthumously in 1873. "If we compare the small size, hardness and bitter taste of the wild pear with the huge size, sweetness and softness of many of our beautiful fruits, we realize what a marvelous influence cultivation has had."

"The finest varieties," he continued, "are divided into three classes: pears which 'melt in the mouth' (*poires fondantes*); pears which are crisp but sweet; and pears with firm or crisp flesh and impregnated with an astringent quality which even cooking fails to make disappear completely."

Dumas's remarks on pears reflect the French taste for *Pyrus communis*, especially in the seventeenth century, and their preference for it over its cousin, the apple. Consequently, many of our pears today have French names. American pears, grown from seeds first brought in the early seventeenth century, have further diversified varieties, but not nearly to the extent of the apple.

In the United States, there are four main varieties of pears with commercial significance, nearly all from California, Oregon, and Washington states. Except for the early-ripening Bartlett, their season is fall and winter. Bartlett is the most popular American pear, named after Yankee Enoch Bartlett, who brought it from England, where it is called Williams (the French call it Bon Chrétien, the Germans, Wilhelm). The Bartlett begins ripening in July. It is quite large, shaped like a bell, with white fine-textured flesh that is fragrant and juicy. The thin skin is usually yellow, but there is also a red variety. Besides catering to the American preference for red fruit, this red pear is hardier and more resistant to disease than the yellow. The Bartlett retains its shape in cooking, making it a useful all-purpose pear, but since it does not keep well, most of the crop goes to canning.

Anjou is the next most popular American pear, medium-large with a short stem set asymmetrically near its peak. The shape is plumper than that of most pears. Its skin color is yellowish green, although there is also a red variety. The flesh is cream-colored and juicy, best for eating fresh.

The tall Bosc pear is distinguished by its long tapered neck and russet skin even when ripe. Its creamy flesh has a crisp bite without graininess and an aromatic spiciness. The Bosc is equally good for cooking and eating. A winter pear, it keeps well.

If pears have an aristocratic individuality denied the sturdier apple, then the Comice is regal. Its exquisite fragility truly "melts in the mouth." The Comice is so sweet, delicate, aromatic, and succulent that nurserymen are loath to grow or ship it. The large, even fat, pear has thick yellow-green skin sometimes blushed with red, and ivory flesh. Fruit baskets and gift boxes often include it. Relatively expensive, the Comice is exclusively for eating.

Its small size, spicy aroma, and American pedigree differentiate the Seckel, which alone among pears keeps its quality when ripened on the tree. It has green to russet skin tinged with crimson. Even though Dumas could not have sampled a Seckel, it is of the "crisp but sweet" category he described. The Seckel's diminutive size makes it perfect for preserving whole.

Among other domestic varieties, the crisp Kieffer is excellent for preserves, but is declining in popularity. Winter Nelis, another firm late-season pear, is good for cooking and preserving. The early Clapp's Favorite is green and juicy. Packham's Triumph and Forelle are other pears with good flavor that can be hard to find. Asian pears, incidentally, which look like green, crisp, granular apples, are pears of a different species (see page 318).

Pears are one fruit that are best if picked mature but not fully ripe. When allowed to ripen on the tree, the grittiness in the texture becomes pronounced. At market choose firm pears without cuts or soft spots and let them ripen for a few days at room temperature. The flesh at the stem end will wrinkle slightly and soften, yielding also around the blossom end. Since pears ripen from the core outward, be careful not to let them soften too much: an overripe pear quickly turns to mush.

The pear's subtle flavor and silken or crisp texture make it perhaps more adaptable than the robust apple, but in the kitchen we tend to take the pear for granted. One variety or another is available most of the year, to be eaten, cooked, or preserved at its peak. Firm pears can be prepared in many of the same ways as apples, in chutneys, purées, and pastries. In eastern Europe, dried pears are braised with meat. Perry is pear cider and Poire Williams is the colorless *eau-de-vie* made from Bartlett pears.

Hollowed pear halves can make attractive boats for savory or sweet fillings. Pears make a natural partner to cheese, especially blue cheese, and a glass of port completes the perfect triangle. The fruit is elegant in simple cream or caramel sauces, with or without nuts. Whole peeled pears poached in red wine take on a beautiful crimson sheen. Bittersweet chocolate sauce on pears, if not overpowering, can make a marriage of opposites.

Pears are high in fiber, low in sodium. A medium-size Bartlett contains just under a hundred calories and a considerable amount of potassium.

Pears with Curried Crab Filling

This striking recipe comes from my friend Jane Whitten's artistic eye and imagination. For the first course of a dinner party, have everything done ahead but the final broiling.

3 large, firm pears such as Bartlett or Bosc
¾ cup fresh lemon juice
⅔ cup mayonnaise
1 large egg yolk
2 teaspoons curry powder, or to taste
Salt and freshly ground black pepper to taste
6 ounces lump crabmeat (about 1 cup), picked over for cartilage
¼ cup peeled, seeded, and chopped cucumber
3 scallions (green and white parts), thinly sliced
1 tablespoon peeled and minced fresh ginger
Watercress for garnish

Peel the pears, halve them lengthwise, and core them; drop them into a glass or ceramic bowl of cold water acidulated with ¼ cup of the lemon juice to keep them from darkening. Bring a large nonreactive saucepan half full of water to a simmer over medium heat and add ¼ cup of the lemon juice. Drop the pears into the pan, reserving the bowl of water, and poach them over low heat until just tender, 2 to 3 minutes. Return the pears to the reserved bowl of water and let them cool for 5 minutes. Remove them from the water, brush the pears with the remaining lemon juice, and drain on paper towels.

Adjust the broiler rack to 4 inches from the heat source and preheat. Whisk the mayonnaise, egg yolk, curry powder, salt, and pepper together in a bowl. In another bowl combine the crabmeat, cucumber, scallions, and ginger; fold in half the mayonnaise mixture. Fill the pears with the crab mixture, mounding it, and set them on the rack of a broiler pan. Broil until the filling is golden, 30 seconds to 1 minute—watch closely. Put the pears on a platter and garnish with watercress. Serve the remaining mayonnaise separately.

MAKES 6 SERVINGS

Baked Pears Stuffed with Chèvre, Leeks, and Walnuts

This unusual salad makes a beautiful first course. Leaving the peel on the red Bartlett pears helps them hold their shape and emphasizes their color.

4 ripe but firm pears, preferably red Bartlett
2 tablespoons fresh lemon juice
1 tablespoon butter
¼ cup chopped leeks (white part only)
¼ cup chopped walnuts, lightly toasted (see page 179)
4 ounces fresh mild chèvre cheese
Freshly ground black pepper to taste
3 tablespoons walnut or extra virgin olive oil

1 tablespoon sherry wine vinegar
Salt to taste
1 head redleaf lettuce torn into pieces

Preheat the oven to 350°F. Cut the pears in half lengthwise and core them, but do not peel. Place them cut-side down in a large, shallow nonreactive ovenproof pan and add the lemon juice and enough water to bring it to a depth of ⅛ inch. Bake the pears for about 12 minutes, depending on their texture, until they are tender but still firm; they must not get mushy. Pour off the water.

While the pears are cooking, melt the butter in a small skillet and cook the leeks over low heat, stirring occasionally, until softened, about 5 minutes. Take the pan off the heat, then stir in the walnuts and chèvre and season with a good twist of pepper. Carefully turn over the pear halves and divide the chèvre mixture among them, spreading it slightly in the cavities. Bake 5 minutes more.

Mix together the walnut oil, vinegar, salt, and some more pepper, then gently toss the lettuce in the dressing to coat each leaf lightly. Arrange the lettuce on individual serving plates and top with the pears.

MAKES 8 SERVINGS

Pickled Pears with Lime

This delicately spiced side dish, even better the day after it is made, balances the richness of roast pork, ham, or poultry.

2 cups sugar
1 cup fresh lime juice
Zest of 1 lime, cut into julienne
1 piece fresh ginger, about ¾ inch long, peeled and thinly sliced
6 whole cloves
20 firm Seckel pears (about 3 pounds), peeled but not cored or stemmed
1 cup boiling water

In a nonreactive saucepan just large enough to hold the pears, combine the sugar, lime juice and zest, ginger, and cloves. Bring to a boil, cover, and let boil over low heat until the sugar is dissolved, about 5 minutes. Add the pears and enough of the boiling water barely to cover them. Bring to a simmer and poach the pears, partially covered, until just tender, 5 to 7 minutes. Let them cool in the syrup.

Carefully remove the pears with a slotted spoon. Strain the syrup through a fine sieve into another nonreactive saucepan, saving the zest for garnish. Boil the syrup until it is reduced to 2 cups, then pour it over the pears.

Serve the pears warm or at room temperature, garnished with the reserved zest. The pears keep, covered and refrigerated, for several weeks. Bring them to room temperature before serving.

MAKES 20 SERVINGS

Spiced Pear Butter

Here's a good way to use a very ripe pear, delicious also on toast, waffles, or crêpes.

¾ cup (1½ sticks; 6 ounces) unsalted butter, softened
1 very ripe pear, preferably Bosc, cored and cubed but not peeled
2 tablespoons honey
1 teaspoon fresh lemon juice
¼ teaspoon grated lemon zest
¾ teaspoon ground cinnamon, or to taste
½ teaspoon freshly grated nutmeg, or to taste

Cream the butter in a food processor. With the motor running, add the pear cubes a few at a time through the feed tube, processing until smooth. Add the remaining ingredients and blend well, scraping down the workbowl once or twice.

Pack the spiced pear butter in a crock, cover, and refrigerate. Or roll it into a log, wrap in plastic wrap, and refrigerate. The butter will keep a week in the refrigerator, several months in the freezer. Serve the log cut into slices.

MAKES ABOUT 1½ CUPS

Pear Muffins

Delicious on their own or spread with Spiced Pear Butter (see the preceding recipe) to accent the fruit.

2 cups all-purpose flour
2 tablespoons baking powder
⅓ cup unprocessed bran
¾ cup sugar
½ teaspoon salt
1 large egg, lightly beaten
1 cup milk
3 tablespoons unsalted butter, melted and cooled

1 large, ripe but firm pear, peeled, cored, and shredded
¼ cup sliced almonds, lightly toasted (see page 179)

Preheat the oven to 400°F. Butter a 12-cup muffin tin and set aside.

In a large bowl sift together the flour and baking powder. Mix in the bran, sugar, and salt. In a smaller bowl combine the egg, milk, and butter.

Quickly stir the milk mixture into the dry ingredients, then fold in the grated pear and almonds, stirring just enough to combine them. The batter should be lumpy. Spoon the batter into the prepared muffin tin, filling each cup about two thirds full. Bake until they have risen and turned brown and test done, 25 to 30 minutes. Serve still warm from the oven with spiced pear butter.

MAKES 12 MUFFINS

Poires au Vin Rouge

(PEARS IN RED WINE)

This simple fall dessert is a fine way to use up red wine, spiced here with cardamom rather than the more usual cinnamon or clove. Whichever you use, whole spices are preferable, so they can be removed when the flavor is strong enough. Various other wines, such as port or white wine, are also delicious.

1½ cups dry red wine
1 cup sugar, or to taste
One 2-inch strip lemon zest
2 tablespoons fresh lemon juice
4 cardamom pods (preferably green), split open and tied in a muslin bag, or one 2-inch
   stick cinnamon, or 4 whole cloves
4 ripe but firm pears

First make the syrup. Combine the wine and sugar in a saucepan with the lemon zest, juice, and cardamom. Bring to a boil, cover, and let boil over low heat until the sugar is dissolved, about 5 minutes. Meanwhile, core and peel the pears, leaving the stems on and taking off as little flesh as possible. Take a slice off the bottom to make a stable base. Place the pears in the syrup and poach over low heat, turning them occasionally, until just tender, about 10 minutes unless they are very firm. Let the pears cool in the syrup, covered. Remove the cardamom or other spice when its flavor is strong enough. Chill the pears if you wish, turning them from time to time so they color evenly. (They can remain in the refrigerator for several days.)

To serve, put the pears in a glass serving bowl or dishes. Strain the syrup through a fine sieve (you can boil the syrup down to concentrate it if you like, although this is not necessary) and pour several spoonfuls over each pear.

MAKES 4 SERVINGS

Poires Belle Hélène

Escoffier's classic dessert honors Offenbach's comic opera about Helen of Troy.

3 cups sugar
3 cups water
8 firm pears, peeled and cored, but with the stems left on
Two 2-inch strips lemon zest
2 tablespoons fresh lemon juice
4 ounces bittersweet chocolate
1 teaspoon pure vanilla extract
Vanilla ice cream, homemade (see page 61) or storebought

Put the sugar and water in a large nonreactive saucepan and bring to a boil. Cover and let boil over low heat until the sugar is dissolved, about 5 minutes. Remove a slice from the bottom of each pear, if needed, so that they will stand upright. Drop the pears into the syrup with the lemon zest and juice and poach them over low heat, turning once or twice, for about 10 minutes, depending on the ripeness and variety of pears, until tender. Let them cool in the syrup. (This much may be done ahead.)

Gently melt the chocolate in the top of a double boiler over simmering water. Add ½ cup of syrup from the pears and stir to make a smooth thin sauce.

Make a bed of vanilla ice cream in eight glass serving bowls. Lift the pears by the stems from the syrup, drain them, and set them upright on top of the ice cream. Spoon some of the warm chocolate sauce on top and serve.

MAKES 8 SERVINGS

Caramelized Pear Porcupines

These spiny creatures are more inviting than forbidding, especially to children.

2½ cups sugar plus 2 tablespoons sugar for the caramel glaze
2½ cups water
6 ripe but firm pears, peeled, cored, and halved lengthwise
One 2-inch strip lemon zest
½ cup thinly sliced blanched almonds, lightly toasted (see page 179)

12 currants or raisins
Whipped cream lightly sweetened to taste, perhaps laced with a little sherry

Put 2½ cups of the sugar and the water in a wide nonreactive saucepan and bring to a boil. Cover and let boil over low heat until the sugar is dissolved, about 5 minutes. Drop the pear halves into the syrup with the lemon zest and poach them over low heat, turning once or twice, for about 5 minutes, depending on the ripeness and variety of pears, until barely tender. Do not let them get mushy. Let them cool in the syrup. (This much may be done ahead.)

Preheat the broiler. Drain the pears and lay them cored-side down in one layer in a shallow baking pan. Generously sprinkle each pear with the remaining sugar, about ½ teaspoon each. Briefly run them under the broiler, not too close, to caramelize the sugar—watch carefully so that the sugar doesn't scorch. When the pears are nicely browned, take them out and place them on serving plates, two halves each.

Stick the sharp end of the almond slivers into the pears so that they stick up at the same angle all over, to resemble porcupine quills. Make eyes near the stem end with the currants. Serve with whipped cream passed on the side.

MAKES 6 SERVINGS

Poires en Jalousie

This classic French pastry is named for the lattice openings—literally "Venetian blinds," a term which loses considerably in translation—that show off the voluptuous curves of the pears. Professional bakers use a special instrument to cut the slats, but you can achieve the same effect with a small pointed knife and a steady hand.

3 cups sugar
3 cups water
½ lemon
8 medium-size pears, peeled, halved, and cored to leave as much of the flesh as possible
1 package frozen puff pastry, thawed and chilled
¼ cup apricot preserves, homemade (see page 31) or storebought, strained through a sieve
1 large egg

To make a syrup, put the sugar and water in a large pot and bring to a boil. Peel two strips of zest from the lemon half and squeeze the juice, about 2 tablespoons. Add them to the liquid and boil over low heat until the sugar is dissolved, about 5 minutes. Add the pear halves and poach over low heat, turning once, until the pears are tender, about 8 minutes. Let them cool in the syrup, then remove them from the syrup to drain. (You can do this much well ahead of time.)

Preheat the oven to 375°F. Unfold the puff pastry sheets and cut off four strips along the folds. One at a time, rewrapping and refrigerating the other pastry strips, roll out each on a lightly floured board to measure 12 x 4 inches. Trim the edges slightly and lay two pastry strips on a cookie sheet. Brush the pastry with apricot jam to within a half inch of the edges. Lay the pear halves on top facing in alternate directions.

Make a latticework top by cutting alternating slits in the other two pieces of pastry nearly to the edges. Lay the cut pastry tops over the pears, opening the slits to emphasize the curves of the fruit. Moisten the edges of the bottom layer of pastry with water and press to seal top and bottom. Mix the egg with a tablespoon of water and brush it over the lattice topping, taking care not to let it run down. Bake the pastry until puffed and golden, about 20 minutes. Serve the pastry with crème anglaise (see page 155) or lightly sweetened whipped cream, perhaps topped with lighted toasted almond slivers.

MAKES 8 SERVINGS

Gateau Poires Belle Hélène

Serve this luxurious cake based on the classic ice cream dessert to chocoholic friends. If the parts are done ahead of time, it is truly simple to make. I have found that it is better assembled not too far ahead and then left at room temperature before serving.

1 chocolate sponge cake round (see page 73)

FOR THE PEARS
3 fairly small, firm pears
1½ cups sugar
1½ cups water
One 1-inch strip lemon zest

FOR THE CHOCOLATE GANACHE
6 ounces semisweet chocolate, broken up into pieces
¾ cup heavy cream
2 tablespoons Poire Williams liqueur or 1 teaspoon pure vanilla extract

Poach the pears ahead of time so they are cooled. Combine the sugar and water in a medium-size nonreactive saucepan and bring to a boil. Let it boil over low heat until the sugar is dissolved, about 5 minutes. Add the pears and lemon zest and poach over low heat until the pears are tender, depending on their firmness, about 8 minutes. Let them cool in the syrup. Drain the pears, carefully cut them in half lengthwise, and core them.

To make the chocolate ganache, combine the the chocolate and cream in a double boiler over gently simmering water. Stir until the chocolate melts and blends with the cream. When the mixture becomes glossy, stir in the liqueur. Keep the ganache warm.

Put the sponge cake on a cardboard round cut to fit and covered with aluminum foil. Split the cake across in half and spread the bottom half with a thin layer of the warm chocolate ganache. Replace the top half. Place the pears around the top with the stem ends toward the center. Spoon more ganache on top to cover the pears, and spread the remaining ganache with a spatula around the sides of the cake. Be sure to do this while the ganache is still warm; once cooled, it sets.

To serve the cake, cut wedges between the pears and pass whipped cream on the side.

MAKES ONE 8-INCH CAKE; 6 SERVINGS

Pear and Cranberry Tart

This pairing of two autumn fruits, stunning yet light, ends any dinner sumptuously. The tart should not wait long before being served.

1 cup sugar
3 cups water
2 cups cranberries, picked over
One 2-inch strip lemon zest
4 large, firm pears such as Bosc
One 9-inch pâte sucrée shell (see page 35), completely baked with a whole egg wash coating
Sprig of nontoxic greenery for garnish (optional)
Unsweetened whipped cream for garnish

Place the sugar and water in a medium-size saucepan and bring to a boil. Boil over low heat until the sugar is dissolved, about 5 minutes, then add the cranberries and lemon zest. Continue cooking over low heat until the berries have burst, about 5 minutes more. Pour the mixture through a fine sieve, pressing on the berries with the back of a spoon to extract the liquid. Discard the skins and seeds.

Put the cranberry syrup back in the pan with the pears; the liquid should just cover them. Poach them over low heat until tender, 15 to 20 minutes, depending on their firmness, turning them so they color evenly. Let the pears cool in the syrup. (This may be done ahead at your convenience.)

Remove the pears from the syrup and boil the liquid down by about half to a thick glaze. Let it cool somewhat but not completely. While it is reducing, carefully halve and core the pears, removing no more flesh than necessary. Slice the halves across into very thin slices. Holding each half together, angle the slices slightly to show the pale interior flesh. Carefully place each sliced pear half in the pastry shell with the stem ends toward the center. Before the reduced cranberry syrup cools completely and jells, skim off any scum, and spoon some of the syrup over and around the pears to form a glaze. Cool to set the glaze. Put a small sprig of greenery in the middle of the tart, and pass unsweetened whipped cream on the side.

MAKES ONE 9-INCH TART; 8 SERVINGS

Pear Crisp

This variation of an old American favorite is quick and easy to make with a food processor. If you like, bake only three pears and freeze half the topping for another time.

6 firm pears, peeled, halved, cored, and cut widthwise into ¼-inch slices
6 tablespoons (¾ stick) unsalted butter, cut into small pieces and chilled
½ cup all-purpose flour
⅓ cup firmly packed dark brown sugar
Grated zest of 1 lemon
½ teaspoon ground cinnamon
¼ teaspoon freshly grated nutmeg
⅛ teaspoon ground allspice
½ cup chopped pecans, lightly toasted (see page 179)
3 tablespoons bourbon

Preheat the oven to 350°F. Butter a 13 x 9 x 2-inch baking pan and angle the pear slices in the pan, covering the bottom.

Process the butter, flour, sugar, lemon zest, and spices in a food processor until the mixture resembles coarse crumbs. (Or with your fingertips or a pastry blender rub the butter into the flour, sugar, and spice mixture until crumbly, stirring in the nuts later.) Then stir in the nuts. Sprinkle the topping over the pears and drizzle them with the bourbon.

Bake in the center of the oven until the topping is brown and crisp, 15 to 20 minutes. Serve with vanilla ice cream, lightly sweetened whipped cream, sour cream, or yogurt.

MAKES 12 SERVINGS

Pear, Cranberry, and Port Sherbet

The rosy color and fruity flavor of this sherbet make it a family favorite in our house. I like to make it ahead and keep plastic bags of the frozen cubes on hand to whiz in the food processor for unexpected guests. The finished sherbet holds its smooth texture well.

1¼ cups sugar, or to taste
2 cups water
5 large pears, peeled, cored, and cubed

1 cup cranberries, picked over
3 tablespoons fresh lemon juice
One 2-inch strip lemon zest
½ cup port

Put the sugar and water in a large nonreactive saucepan. Bring to a boil and let boil over low heat until the sugar is dissolved, about 5 minutes. Add the remaining ingredients and continue cooking over medium-low heat until the berries pop and the pears are tender, about 5 minutes more. Pour the contents of the pan into a sieve set over a large bowl. Press on the solids with the back of a spoon to push the pears through and extract the cranberry juice; discard the cranberry skins. Since pears vary in sugar content, taste carefully for sweetness (the acid will dissolve any more sugar you stir in).

Cool the fruit syrup, then cover and chill it. Freeze the fruit syrup in a sorbetière or an ice cream machine according to the manufacturer's directions. Or freeze it according to directions on page 307.

MAKES 6 OR MORE SERVINGS

PERSIMMONS

Persimmon (*Diospyros virginiana*) comes from the Algonquian name, *pasimenan* or *putchamin*, for the fruit, which is native to North America. American Indians recognized the honeyed sweetness of the ripe fruit hanging like orange balls from the bare branches of the tree in late fall. They dried persimmons to eat during the cold winter or baked them into breads and puddings. From the Indians colonists learned how to bake persimmons, and in the Midwest and South the tradition continues where trees still grow.

Persimmons, until they are fully ripe, contain a great deal of tannin and taste extremely astringent, even savagely so. This characteristic has promoted the belief that they should never be picked until after the first frost, when freezing ripens them overnight. However strongly scientists assure us that persimmons can ripen just as well off the tree, these small, fragrant native fruit have never been cultivated for market, so that few of us have had an opportunity to taste their apparently superior flavor. Their nickname date plum describes their complex, rich, sweet taste that carries well in baking.

The persimmons that we buy at market, *Diospyros kaki*, were cultivated in Japan from native Chinese varieties and were brought here by Commodore Perry in 1856. These kaki persimmons, retaining their species name everywhere but in the United States, have been developed into many different varieties, mostly larger and seedless. Like the American persimmon, the color is a deep glowing orange, with a texture that turns soft and almost jellied, seemingly liquid within its thin skin, when it is at last ready to eat. Only the leaflike calyx around the stem needs to be removed before eating.

Persimmons are now grown on a commercial scale in California, as well as in southern Europe, northern Africa, and Chile. In American markets, the Hachiya is the variety most widely available, distinctive for its large size and acorn shape. Sharon fruit, bred in Israel from the Fuyu variety, is smaller and paler, with a rounded rather than pointed bottom, and no tannin even when firm. Persimmons are usually available in late autumn and winter, although Israeli and Chilean fruit are imported in spring.

Surely the persimmon's deep orange color, as well as its sweet plummy taste, enhances its appeal. The flesh is mellifluous, with a viscous quality, lending it well to sauces, puddings, creams, and purées that need little or no adornment. Its ability to retain moisture, especially the American fruit, makes it good for baking, when it may turn a rich glossy brown. The persimmon takes to many of the same simple flavorings as mango and papaya, so that a touch of citrus or ginger, as well as other spices, set it off. Persimmons sliced or cut open like a flower, particularly the firmer Sharon fruit, look stunning with meat, salad, or dessert.

To ripen persimmons, put them in a closed bag with a ripe apple or banana, whose natural ethylene gas will bring them to maturity faster. Similarly, Elizabeth Schneider recommends enclosing persimmons in a plastic container, stem-side up, and putting a few drops of alcohol, such as rum, brandy, or bourbon, on the calyx to hasten ripening. If you cannot use the fruit immediately when it reaches its peak, she suggests snipping off the pointed tip (if it is a Hachiya), wrapping it tightly, and freezing the persimmon for up to three months; use it as soon as it begins to thaw.

Persimmons vary considerably in size, but the Hachiya most often found in American markets weighs about half a pound. One of them yields approximately a half cup or slightly more of purée. To prepare persimmons, simply cut out the leaflike calyx in the stem end with a small knife or corer. For a purée, scrape the pulp off the very thin skin. Because persimmon flesh is corrosive, use nonreactive (nonaluminum) pans and sieves. Tightly covered, purée keeps well in the freezer for several months.

Persimmons contain large amounts of vitamin A, besides being a good source of fiber and potassium. They are fairly high in calories but very low in sodium.

Persimmon Slices in Caramel Nut Sauce

This dark, rich, nutty sauce goes well on many fruits, from peaches and plums to bananas and pineapple, adding a complementary depth and crunchiness. Make the caramel ahead without the nuts and store in a jar in the refrigerator, where it keeps indefinitely. Gentle heat makes it runny again.

½ cup sugar
⅔ cup water
1 tablespoon fresh lemon juice
¼ cup pecans or other nuts, lightly toasted (see page 179)
4 fully ripened Hachiya or other persimmons
Sour cream, plain yogurt, or crème fraîche (see page 155)

Put the sugar and half the water in a small saucepan and cook over medium heat without stirring to dissolve the sugar. Continue to cook, swirling or stirring occasionally, as the liquid evaporates and the syrup starts to caramelize around the edges. Watch to see that it doesn't go too far—the sugar will continue to darken after the pan is off the flame. When the color reaches a deep golden amber, in about 5 minutes, put the pan in the sink to avoid spatter burns and carefully add the remaining water and lemon juice. The caramel will "seize" (solidify) with the cold liquid. Put the pan back on low heat and stir to dissolve the caramel again. Thin with a little more water if necessary and keep warm. When the texture is smooth, stir in the nuts.

Remove the leaflike calyx from the persimmons. Slice them into very thin wedges and lay the slices attractively on serving plates. Just before serving, drizzle the warm caramel-pecan sauce over the persimmons and serve. Pass the sour cream on the side.

MAKES 4 SERVINGS

Persimmon Fool

Cream swirled rather than blended into the purée heightens the deep orange color without diluting the persimmon flavor.

2 fully ripened Hachiya or other persimmons
2 tablespoons fresh lemon, lime, or orange juice
½ cup chilled heavy cream
Ground cinnamon, ginger, or nutmeg for dusting

Remove the leaflike calyx from each persimmon and scrape the pulp off the skin. Purée the flesh in a food processor or by pressing it through a nonreactive sieve with the back of a spoon. Blend in the citrus juice and ladle the purée into glass bowls or cups. Whip the cream until it makes soft peaks and swirl some of it into each dish. Dust with a little ground spice and serve.

MAKES ABOUT 4 SERVINGS

Persimmon Pudding

Rum raisin ice cream (see page 123) makes an exceptional accompaniment to this traditional midwestern pudding—spicy, moist, and deep brown from baking.

2 fully ripe persimmons
4½ teaspoons fresh lemon juice
1 cup all-purpose flour
¾ cup sugar
1 teaspoon baking soda
Pinch of salt
½ teaspoon ground cinnamon
¼ teaspoon ground ginger
½ cup milk
2 large eggs, lightly beaten
¼ cup (½ stick) unsalted butter, melted and cooled
⅓ cup hazelnuts or other nuts, lightly toasted (see page 179)

Preheat the oven to 350°F. Butter and flour an 8-inch round cake pan and set aside.

Remove the calyx from the persimmons, scrape the flesh off the skin, and press the pulp through a nonreactive sieve with the back of a spoon to measure 1 cup. Put the persimmon purée in a medium-large bowl and stir in the lemon juice. In another bowl combine the flour, sugar, soda, salt, and spices. Stir the milk into the eggs, then add the butter. Alternately stir the dry and moist ingredients into the persimmon purée, making a smooth batter. Finally fold in the hazelnuts. Pour the batter into the prepared pan and bake until the pudding has risen, turned a rich brown, and pulled away from the sides of the pan, about 50 minutes. It should be quite moist in texture. Let the pudding cool somewhat on a rack before slicing it into wedges. Serve the pudding warm if possible with ice cream or whipped cream.

MAKES 6 SERVINGS

Persimmon Sauce

Once persimmons are fully ripe, their luscious flavor, deep orange color, and almost viscous texture help the puréed fruit to work well as a sauce. Serve it on ice cream or pound cake, or on fresh fruit, compotes, or puddings.

2 fully ripened Hachiya or other persimmons
2 tablespoons fresh lemon, lime, or orange juice
3 tablespoons bourbon or other whiskey, or to taste (optional)

Remove the leaflike calyx from each persimmon and scrape the pulp off the skin. Purée the flesh in a food processor or by pressing it through a nonreactive sieve with the back of a spoon. Stir in the citrus juice and bourbon. The fruit should be sweet enough on its own without added sugar. Cover and chill the purée until serving time.

MAKES 1 TO 1½ CUPS

Persimmon Sherbet

Just as delicious with lemon or lime juice and rum; or omit the spirit altogether.

⅔ cup sugar
⅔ cup water
6 fully ripened Hachiya or other persimmons
⅓ cup fresh orange juice
3 tablespoons orange-flavored liqueur (optional)

Combine the sugar and water in a small nonreactive saucepan and bring to a boil. Let it boil over low heat, covered, until the sugar is dissolved, about 5 minutes. Let it cool completely, covered.

Remove the leaflike calyx from the persimmons and scrape the pulp off the skin. Purée the flesh in a food processor or by pressing it through a nonreactive sieve with the back of a spoon. You should have about 3 cups of purée. Blend in the orange juice and liqueur. Stir the cooled syrup into the purée. Cover and chill thoroughly.

Freeze the mixture in a sorbetière or an ice cream machine according to the manufacturer's directions. Or freeze it according to the instructions on page 307.

MAKES ABOUT 1 QUART

PINEAPPLES

Europeans discovered the pineapple exactly five hundred years ago, on Columbus's second voyage to the New World. The fruit, native to Brazil but easily propagated from its crown, was already well-established in the West Indies. Indians hung it over their doorways as a sign of welcome, much as centuries later it became a symbol of hospitality to Europeans and Americans.

When Columbus introduced the pineapple to Spain in 1494, its novelty swept Europe by surprise. Charles V, king of Spain and Holy Roman Emperor, refused to taste a specimen for fear of being poisoned (his distrust tells more about political intrigues than his food preferences). A century later Louis XIV of France had quite the opposite impulse: he rashly bit into the strange fruit before it could be peeled and cut his mouth on the scaly skin, delaying its cultivation until Louis XV's succession.

In England, John Evelyn described Charles II eating a pineapple from Barbados, but confided to his diary that Oliver Cromwell had already been presented with one before the Restoration. Despite the famous portrait of Charles II being presented with the first English-grown pineapple, credit to king and gardener are probably a generation too late: John Tradescant the Younger very likely grew the first specimen for Charles I before he was beheaded, although no portrait commemorates the achievement. Indeed, pineapple cultivation in Europe spurred the development of the greenhouse. For wealthy aristocrats, growing the fashionable fruit became a fad.

Although the Spanish named the pineapple *piña* for its resemblance to the pine cone, Portuguese sailors did much for the fruit. They called it *ananas*, from a Brazilian Indian word meaning "excellent fruit," took it on long voyages for its ability to prevent scurvy, and unwittingly spread its range by discarding the crowns around the tropical world. Today Central America, Malaysia, Brazil, and Hawaii are the biggest producers of *Ananas comosus*, to use its botanical name.

The pineapple, though easily propagated in a tropical climate, takes two or three years to flower. The many blooms join together to develop into a multiple fruit outlined by the spirally arranged eyes. Like papaya and kiwi which contain similar enzymes, pineapple contains bromelin, which makes the skin tingle and, in raw fruit, counteracts the solidifying effects of gelatin. For this reason, you should use only cooked or canned pineapple in gelatin desserts. If you handle fresh-cut pineapple, your fingertips feel slippery afterward from the effect of the enzyme; for the same reason, pineapple workers must wear protective gloves.

Pineapples grow year-round, but spring is their high season. Most of those in American markets come from Hawaii, Puerto Rico, Costa Rica, and Mexico. Smooth Cayenne is the most common variety, with yellow flesh and a generous balance of acid and sugar, weighing from three to five and a half pounds. Red Spanish (used more often fresh than canned), Queen (smaller and milder), and Sugarloaf (large, sweet, delicately flavored) are other popular varieties. Since pineapples once picked cannot ripen further, the timing of harvest is crucial, and the crop must be delivered to markets quickly.

To choose a good pineapple, look for large, plump, heavy fruit with fresh, deep green plumage. The color can be green or gold, so go by scent, an excellent sign if the fruit is not too cold to give off its inimitable fragrance. Avoid specimens with dull yellow coloring, dry brown leaves, bruises and soft spots, watery eyes, and unpleasant odors. Chill the pineapple until you use it (45°F is ideal).

To cut pineapple spears or chunks, slice off the crown and bottom, then cut the fruit lengthwise into quarters with a large knife. Since the central core is tough and fibrous, trim off the core edges. Cut rows into the flesh all the way to the skin, crisscrossed if for chunks, then slip the knife just above the skin to cut it free. For pineapple rings, slice off the crown and bottom, stand the fruit upright, and cut downward along the skin with a heavy, sharp knife; then, on its side, slice across. A pineapple corer efficiently removes the central column of fiber. After peeling, use a spoon to scrape the juice from any flesh inside the skin. Remove pineapple eyes with the tip of a knife. In the Philippines, where it is an important crop, the fruit is commonly cut in spiral grooves to remove the eyes, even if it is then cut into chunks. Fresh pineapple is often sold already cut, for a price.

A perfectly ripe pineapple has a very high sugar and acid content. The flesh is delicious all by itself, perhaps with a splash of kirsch, rum, or other spirit. The fruit also combines well in compotes with other exotic fruit or those more prosaic. Remember that its acid will keep other cut fruits, such as apples and pears, from darkening from exposure to the air. Pineapple goes well with rich meats such as pork, ham, and duck, but beware that marinades can overtenderize meat, making it fall apart. The shell can make an attractive container, either halved lengthwise or stood upright and scooped out. For panache, you might want to oil the leaves for a glossy sheen.

Four ounces of pineapple contain about ninety calories. The pulp is high in vitamin C and offers a good amount of potassium and fiber.

Marinated Lamb and Pineapple

This makes a piquant starter for a barbecue or informal party. Also delicious with pork.

¼ cup soy sauce
¼ cup honey
¼ cup peanut oil
3 tablespoons Dijon mustard
1 clove garlic, minced
3 scallions (green and white parts), finely chopped
2 pounds lamb such as from the leg, cut into 1-inch cubes
½ pineapple, peeled, cored, and cut into large chunks

In a shallow baking pan mix together well the soy sauce, honey, oil, and mustard. Stir in the garlic and scallions. Put the lamb in the marinade, turning to coat all sides, and marinate for at least 3 hours or as long as overnight in the refrigerator, turning a few times.

Thread the lamb and pineapple alternately on skewers. Grill or broil them not too close to the source of heat, turning often and basting with the remaining marinade, until the lamb is crisp on the outside, but still juicy inside.

MAKES 8 FIRST-COURSE SERVINGS

Warm Curried Fruit with Rice

Ed and Susanna Tolini serve this as an unusual first course at their restaurant, Le Bocage, in Watertown, Massachusetts. They use whatever ripe but firm fresh fruit is at its seasonal peak, garnishing it with fresh berries. You may want to hold back at first on the curry powder to avoid overspicing: brands and palates vary. Serve the salad on colorful plates.

FOR THE RICE
1 cup uncooked long-grain white rice
2 cups milk
Pinch of salt

FOR THE FRUIT SALAD
½ cup peeled and cubed pineapple
½ cup peeled and cubed apple
½ cup peeled and cubed banana
½ cup cored and cubed pear
3 tablespoons golden raisins (sultanas)
1½ tablespoons unsalted butter
2 tablespoons curry powder, or to taste
1½ cups heavy cream
Fresh strawberries or raspberries for garnish (optional)

Put the rice, milk, and salt in a saucepan. Cover, bring to a boil, and stir with a fork. Turn the heat down very low, cover tightly, and cook until the rice is tender and the milk absorbed, about 18 minutes. It will be stickier than rice cooked with water. Toward the end you may need to add a little more milk or water. Let the rice steam for several minutes in the covered saucepan. Just before serving, fluff it with a fork.

Have all the fruit but the berry garnish cubed and ready. Melt the butter in a wide saucepan over low heat. Stir in the curry powder to make a paste and cook it for a minute or so until the curry's fragrance is released. Toss the fruit in the curry mixture to coat it on all sides. Add the cream and over high heat bring to a full boil. Stir and set aside, covered, off the heat.

To serve, mound some rice onto each individual serving plate. Spoon the curried fruit over or around the rice and garnish it with fresh berries and perhaps a sprig of fresh coriander or mint.

MAKES 4 FIRST-COURSE SERVINGS

Pineapple in Hot Buttered Rum Sauce

In early spring, made with a fragrantly ripe pineapple, this dessert is hard to beat. Consider adding raisins or diced dried apricots, plumped in brandy. This quick sauce is delicious on peaches and many other fruits.

¼ cup (½ stick) unsalted butter
¼ cup firmly packed dark brown sugar
¼ cup dark rum

½ teaspoon ground allspice
1 large pineapple, peeled, cored, and cut into bite-size chunks
Crushed macaroon crumbs or unsweetened shredded coconut, lightly toasted

In a wide nonreactive saucepan over low heat, heat the butter, sugar, rum, and allspice, stirring, until the sugar is dissolved and the syrup is thick and bubbly. Add the pineapple with any accumulated juices and baste it in the syrup to heat it through. Divide the pineapple among four serving dishes, spoon the sauce over, and sprinkle with the crushed macaroons or toasted coconut. Serve immediately.

MAKES 4 SERVINGS

Grilled Pineapple Rings with Coffee Ice Cream

The warm pineapple and melting ice cream mingle with the coffee liqueur to make a simple and sublime dessert—just right for a relaxed summer party.

1 fresh pineapple
Coffee ice cream or another flavor such as rum raisin (see page 123)
Ground cinnamon
Tia Maria, Kahlúa, rum, or other spirit

Cut the leaves off the top of the pineapple and remove the skin and eyes, leaving as much flesh as possible. Cut the pineapple across into ½-inch slices, one for each serving. With a pineapple corer, remove and discard the central core.

Put the pineapple rings on the grill over the glowing coals after the main course has been cooked (be sure to put them on a clean area of the grid). Let it cook just long enough to warm through, and turn once with tongs to grill the other side. If you want to make a crisscross pattern, make a quarter turn of the rings. Put the warm pineapple rings on serving plates with a scoop of ice cream in the center and dust with some cinnamon. Pour some spirit over it and serve at once.

MAKES ABOUT 6 SERVINGS

Pineapple with Praline

The dark crunchy taste of praline—caramelized sugar and toasted nuts crushed to a powder—makes a wonderfully rich contrast to the piquancy of pineapple. Add bananas, grapefruit, or other fruit if you like, and perhaps a scoop of good ice cream or sherbet. If you have praline on hand, this makes a great last-minute dessert.

Praline is often made with almonds, but various nuts, such as hazelnuts, pecans, and almonds, alone or in combination, can be used. To bring out their flavor, toast them first, skinned or not, sliced or whole. Nuts and sugar should be in equal weight or with a little more sugar. Store praline in a tightly covered jar in the cupboard for several weeks, or freeze indefinitely.

½ cup (3 ounces) whole almonds, lightly toasted (see page 179)
½ cup sugar
1 large pineapple, peeled, quartered, cored, and cut into bite-size pieces
2 to 3 tablespoons rum, bourbon, or liqueur

First make the praline. Lightly oil a cookie sheet or pan and set aside. Put the nuts and sugar in a heavy-bottomed pan over medium-low heat and heat until the sugar melts. Continue cooking, stirring often, until the sugar darkens and turns deep amber; do not let it burn. Whole almonds will make a quiet crackling noise as they toast. The caramel is very hot, so take care. Pour the mixture onto the cookie sheet and spread while still warm. Let it cool and harden. Break the praline into pieces and crush them to a powder in a mortar or food processor; do not overprocess. Store the praline powder in a tightly covered jar; it keeps indefinitely.

Sweeten the pineapple, if needed, and toss with the spirit. Spoon the fruit into serving dishes and at the last minute top with some of the praline powder.

MAKES ABOUT 4 SERVINGS; ABOUT 1½ CUPS PRALINE POWDER

Souffléed Stuffed Pineapple

When you need something showy but light, here is a simple dessert to serve with fanfare. If you like, omit the soufflé topping, pile more fruit into the pineapple shells, and garnish with fresh mint sprigs.

1 large pineapple
2 ripe bananas, peeled and sliced
1 cup fresh strawberries or other berries, hulled and sliced or left whole
2 tablespoons kirsch or other liqueur (optional)
2 large eggs, separated, at room temperature
2 tablespoons sugar

With a heavy sharp knife, cut the pineapple in half lengthwise, leaves and all. Leaving a half-inch border, cut around the shell without piercing the skin. Cut out and discard the core, and remove the pulp in pieces as large as possible. Scrape the inside of the shells to remove any juice, and freeze the shells wrapped in plastic bags. In a large nonreactive bowl set aside 2 cups pineapple flesh cut into bite-size pieces; set aside 3 tablespoons pineapple juice separately (save the rest of the pulp, about half, for another recipe). Add the bananas, berries (if fragile, add them at the last minute), and kirsch to the pineapple pulp, and sweeten to taste. Let the fruit macerate an hour or so before serving.

In the top of a double boiler, whisk together the egg yolks, sugar, and reserved pineapple juice. Over gently simmering water, whisk the mixture continuously until the yolks thicken; watch to see that they don't curdle. Set aside off the heat. This much can be done an hour or so ahead.

Shortly before serving, preheat the oven to 450°F. Set the frozen pineapple shells on a cookie sheet and fill the cavities with the fruit. Whip the egg whites until they hold gentle peaks, and fold the yolk mixture into them. Carefully mound the soufflé on top of the fruit, making little peaks. Put the sheet in the oven just long enough to brown the soufflé, about 4 minutes. Immediately place the pineapples on a serving platter, top to tail, and spoon the fruit into individual dishes at the table.

MAKES 6 SERVINGS

Pineapple Upside-Down Cake

You can use other fruits for this moist, rich upside-down cake, unskinned apricots and plums, for example. The important thing is to arrange the fruit attractively in the bottom of the pan, since that will become the top of the cake.

¼ cup (½ stick) unsalted butter
4 or 5 pineapple rings, fresh or canned, sliced ½ inch thick
½ cup firmly packed dark brown sugar
¼ cup rum (optional)
¼ cup chopped pecans or other nuts, lightly toasted (see page 179)
½ cup (1 stick; ¼ pound) unsalted butter, softened
½ cup white sugar
2 large eggs, separated
1½ cups all-purpose flour
2 teaspoons baking powder
¾ cup milk
Pinch of salt

Preheat the oven to 350°F.

Melt the ¼ cup butter in a 9-inch skillet (cast iron is fine) with a nonplastic handle and cook the fresh pineapple rings over low heat, carefully turning them once or twice, until they have given up their juice, 15 to 20 minutes. Do not let them brown. Carefully remove the slices to a plate. Swirl the butter left in the pan over the sides. Add the brown sugar and rum to the pan and cook over medium-low heat, stirring, until the sugar is dissolved.

(If using canned pineapple, omit the previous paragraph. Heat the canned pineapple juice with the butter, brown sugar, and rum and cook over medium-low heat, stirring, until the sugar is dissolved and some of the juice is evaporated.)

Arrange a layer of pineapple rings in the bottom of the skillet. When the cake is inverted, they will decorate the top of the cake. Scatter the pecans on top.

Cream together the softened butter and white sugar in a large bowl. Stir in the egg yolks one at a time. Mix together the flour and baking powder in a small bowl and stir into the butter mixture alternately with the milk to make a smooth batter. In a medium-size bowl, whip the egg whites with the salt until stiff peaks form. Stir a spoonful into the batter, then fold in the rest until no streaks of white remain. Spoon the batter over the pineapple rings, smoothing the top. Put the pan in the oven and bake until the cake shrinks from the sides of the pan and a skewer inserted into the center comes out clean, about 35 minutes. Take the pan out—leave the mitt on the handle to protect your hand from the retained heat as it gradually cools—and let it sit for a few minutes. Run a knife around the edge of the cake and turn it out onto a platter. Spoon any sauce in the pan on top and serve warm cut into wedges.

MAKES ONE 9-INCH CAKE; 8 OR MORE SERVINGS

Pineapple Parfait

Golden, creamy, yet light, this unusual and attractive dessert can be made ahead of time.

1 small pineapple (or ¾ of a medium one)
1 cup sugar
1 cup water
2 large egg whites, at room temperature
1 cup chilled heavy cream
2 tablespoons kirsch, Cointreau, or other liqueur

Peel, core, and slice the pineapple; scrape out and save the juice from inside the peel. Take about one third of the pulp and cut it into thin slivers to measure ¾ cup; add any accumulated pineapple juice and set aside until later. Purée the rest of the pineapple in a food processor, to measure about 2 cups.

Put the sugar and water in a saucepan and bring to a boil; let it boil over low heat until the sugar is dissolved, about 5 minutes. In a clean large bowl whip the egg whites until stiff peaks form. In a thin steady stream pour half the hot sugar syrup into the whites, beating continuously, until the meringue is thick, glossy, and cool. In another medium-size bowl whip the cream until it holds soft peaks. Quickly fold the pineapple purée into the meringue, then fold in the whipped cream. Divide the mousse mixture among six pretty glass goblets or bowls, cover tightly, and freeze for at least 2 hours.

Add the reserved pineapple and juice to the sugar syrup remaining in the saucepan. Simmer over low heat, uncovered, for about 20 minutes. Stir in the liqueur and allow the pineapple to cool completely. To serve, take the frozen parfaits out of the freezer to soften a bit. Spoon some of the slivered pineapple and dribbles of syrup over the parfaits.

MAKES 6 SERVINGS

Pineapple Strawberry Sherbet

When choosing a fully ripened pineapple for this recipe, try to find one with a panache of handsome, undamaged leaves. This recipe is perfect for a spring lunch party.

1 large pineapple
2 cups fresh strawberries, hulled
⅓ cup sugar, or to taste
3 tablespoons Cointreau or other orange-flavored liqueur
Whole strawberries and fresh mint sprigs for garnish

Split the pineapple in half lengthwise, leaves and all. Cut around the edge of one half without piercing the skin, then cut out and discard the tough central core. With knife and spoon cut out the pulp, leaving the shell intact. Scrape the inside with a spoon to get as much juice as possible. Repeat with the other half. Wrap the shells tightly in plastic wrap and if you are planning to serve the sherbet more than a few days away, freeze.

Cut the pineapple flesh into chunks and purée in a food processor with the strawberries. Add the sugar to taste, the amount depending on the ripeness of the pineapple, and flavor with Cointreau. Freeze the fruit purée in a sorbetière or an ice cream machine, according to the manufacturer's directions. Or pour it into a shallow bowl and stir every half hour or so to smooth the ice crystals. Or pour the purée into ice cube trays and freeze hard (you can keep the cubes, tightly wrapped in a plastic bag, ready in the freezer); then smooth the cubes in a food processor several at a time, breaking up the cubes and scraping down the sides with a rubber spatula two or three times. Cover tightly and let the sherbet ripen in the freezer for two hours or more.

Two hours or so before serving, scoop the sherbet into balls and put them back in the freezer to firm. Just before serving, unwrap the pineapple shells and place them top to tail on a pretty platter. Fill the shells with the sherbet balls and garnish with whole strawberries and mint sprigs.

MAKES ABOUT 1 QUART

Candied Pineapple

A beautiful garnish, candied pineapple also makes a sprightly addition to fruit cake and other holiday pastries.

Sugar
Water
Pineapple rings, either fresh or canned, about ½-inch thick

The amounts do not matter here so much as the proportion: use 1 cup of sugar to 2 cups water. Put the sugar and water in a wide pan just large enough to hold the pineapple rings, however many you wish to candy, in one layer without crowding. Make a syrup by bringing the water to a boil and letting it boil until the sugar is dissolved, about 5 minutes. Slip the pineapple rings into the syrup, which should cover them with room to spare. Simmer slowly over low heat until the rings become translucent; it should take about 30 minutes, depending on thickness. Carefully take the pineapple rings out and dry them on a rack for a few hours. Store them between sheets of waxed paper in a tightly closed tin, where they will keep for a few days.

PLUMS

When Little Jack Horner in the Mother Goose rhyme pulled out a plum and said what a good boy am I! he brought together several meanings for the word plum. It meant any dried fruit, not necessarily the European *Prunus domestica*, and that it was something choice and desirable, an unexpected treat. Indeed, the word plum has pleasant connotations in English. A plummy voice is rich, ample, mellow, and resonant. A sugarplum is a candied sweetmeat associated with Christmas fairies and fantastic visions. In the Middle Ages, fruits of many kinds—plums, raisins, dates, figs, apricots—were dried and saved for holiday desserts such as plum pudding and Jack's Christmas pie.

In addition to European varieties of plum, there is the American *Prunus americana* and Japanese *P. salicina*. (The Chinese plum *mei* celebrated in art and poetry is mistranslated as plum; this drupe is closer to the apricot.) Together they offer an enormous number of plum varieties, many of which have been crossed. Large or small, they have skin ranging in color from deep blue to purple-black, red, yellow, or green, with yellow or amber flesh. The sheer variety can be confusing, but the important thing to remember is a plum's sweetness. The savage astringency of some varieties makes them inedible raw, but that same quality tamed with sugar and cooking renders them intriguingly complex in soups and stews, preserves and pastries, compotes and brandies.

Plums, like peaches, are divided into freestones and clings. In the United States, where California grows most of the country's plums, both are sold for eating fresh. The Italian prune plum that separates easily from its pit and ripens late in the season is perhaps the best-known freestone. Red Beaut, Santa Rosa, Laroda, Friar, and Casselman are all good fresh varieties from California, ripening from May into October and peaking in late July and August. The beach plum, small, rosy, and tart, that grows wild on the northeastern Atlantic coast makes a fine jelly.

In Europe, the small, sweet, golden mirabelle is considered choice for its penetrating perfume. The French Reine Claude, called greengage in English, is also prized. The northern damson, small, dark, and tart, whose name derives from Damascus, makes a delicious jam or "cheese," an English preserve like fruit butter that is slowly reduced to a paste. Bullace and sloe are two wild plums whose unbridled tartness serves well in preserves and liqueurs. The French d'Agen is grown in Armagnac country, so the fruit and brandy are often paired in sweet and savory dishes. The quetsch plum of Alsace is distilled into a clear *eau-de-vie,* and in the Balkans slivovitz is a dry and slightly bitter plum brandy. In Eastern Europe, where prunes contribute to the popular sweet-and-sour dishes, there is even an eel soup with prunes, from Hamburg.

Not all plums can be prunes. High-sugar varieties, with pits still in, can survive the drying process without fermenting. Three pounds of fresh prune plums, ripened on the tree and dried in the sun without sulfites or sulfur dioxide (which are used with some dried fruits), make one pound of dried prunes. The variety called La Petite d'Agen, after the town in southwestern France where the best French prunes grow, was brought to California in 1856 by the Pellier brothers, who had failed in the Gold Rush but found their fortune in prunes. Today it dominates California production and supplies 70 percent of the world's prunes.

When marketing, choose plums that are fairly firm, perhaps softening near the tip, with good color for their variety. Avoid any that are very soft or shriveled, or have cuts, bruises, or punctures. Mature but not completely ripened plums will come to full fragrance and softness in a few days at room temperature (faster in a bag) and keep in the refrigerator for a few days. If you wish to remove the tart and tannic skins, immerse the plums in boiling water, as with peaches, before slipping off the skins. Dried prunes should be stored airtight in a cool, dry place.

For cooking prunes in dishes without stock, plump them first by steeping them in liquid; it will retain the fruit's nutrients and should be saved for another use. Just as many dishes for fresh plums are suitable for apricots and peaches, many of those for prunes are interchangeable with recipes for dried apricots.

Fresh plums are high in pectin, low in sodium, with some vitamins A, B, and C. A medium-size plum contains about thirty-three calories. Plums, especially dried, are well known for their laxative effect, as with all dried fruit. Rich in fiber, dried plums are very high in vitamin A, potassium, and iron, with little sodium and virtually no fat. A two-ounce serving (about seven prunes) has 150 calories and four grams of fiber.

Cock-a-Leekie Soup

This very old soup, a Scottish *poule au pot* (chicken in a pot), gains a depth of flavor from the prunes lightly poached in the broth. You can add most of the chicken meat, if you like, or save some for another meal. A perfect winter soup-stew.

One 5-pound chicken, preferably a mature stewing chicken
1 veal or beef bone, if possible
8 or more leeks
3 sprigs fresh parsley
½ teaspoon dried thyme

1 bay leaf
18 pitted prunes
Salt and freshly ground black pepper to taste

Put the chicken in a large pot with the veal bone and add fresh cold water to cover. Trim the roots and most of the green tops from the leeks. Set two leeks aside. Slit the others lengthwise in quarters and rinse under cold running water to remove any dirt. Chop these leeks coarsely and add them to the pot with the herbs. Bring to a boil and simmer over low heat, covered, until the meat is tender, about 2½ hours for a stewing chicken (less for a younger bird). Skim off the surface scum and fat. Take out the chicken and let it cool somewhat. With a slotted spoon, remove the veal bone (pick off any meat and add it to the chicken), leeks, and herbs, and discard. Taste the stock to see if it is concentrated in flavor; if not, boil it down.

About 15 minutes before serving, simmer the prunes in the broth over low heat. Cut the meat into neat pieces and the two reserved leeks into quarter-inch slices. Eight minutes before serving, simmer the leeks in the soup over low heat just to cook them through. Season, then ladle the broth into hot soup bowls, giving each portion some of the leeks, prunes, and chicken.

MAKES 6 TO 8 SERVINGS

Plum Salsa

Serve this fresh and zesty sauce with poultry, fish, or duck. If plums are unavailable, use melon, peaches, or grapes.

1½ cups ripe plums, pitted and diced or slivered
2 tablespoons fresh lime juice
1 tablespoon julienned lime zest
¼ cup chopped scallions (green and white parts)
3 to 4 tablespoons chopped fresh coriander (cilantro)
2 tablespoons peeled and minced fresh ginger
1 tablespoon peanut oil
A few drops of hot chile oil (optional; available in Oriental and specialty food stores)

Mix all the ingredients together in a small bowl and taste carefully to adjust the seasonings. Add the chile oil, if you like. Let the flavors mix and mellow for about half an hour before serving. This salsa can be kept for a day, but it is best eaten soon after it is made.

MAKES ABOUT 2 CUPS

Plum Preserves

Damson plums work best, if you can find them, because of their rich, tart intensity.

3 pounds ripe plums (damson, greengage, or Italian blue), stemmed and washed
½ cup water
Juice of ½ lemon
2¾ cups sugar

Put the plums in a nonreactive pot with the water and lemon juice, and cook slowly over low heat until the fruit is soft, about 20 minutes. Sieve the plums, pressing on them with the back of a spoon; discard the pits and skins and return the pulp to the pan. Add the sugar and stir to combine. Bring the mixture to a boil and simmer over low heat until the plum purée is reduced and thickened and falls off the spoon in sheets rather than drops (220°F on a candy thermometer), about 15 minutes. Toward the end be careful not to scorch it on the bottom of the pan. Spoon the preserves into warm clean half-pint jars and seal (see page 321).

    MAKES 5 TO 6 HALF-PINT JARS

Brandied Plum Sauce

This beautifully colored sauce, chilled or warmed, goes well on ice cream, pound cake, or pudding as well as over other fruit. Plums' sweetness varies according to variety and ripeness, so add more sugar only if they need it.

1 pound ripe purple plums, pitted and coarsely chopped
⅓ cup sugar, or to taste
¼ cup brandy
One 2-inch strip lemon zest

Place the ingredients in a small saucepan and bring the liquid to a boil. Cover and simmer over low heat, stirring several times, until the juices run red and the plums soften, 10 to 15 minutes. Remove them from the heat and let cool in the pan, covered; discard the lemon zest. Purée the fruit with the liquid, then pass it through a fine sieve, pressing on the purée with the back of a spoon to extract all the juice. Taste to see if it needs more sweetening. If the sauce is too thick, add a little more brandy or water. Chill the sauce in a covered container. (This may be made a couple of days ahead, and kept covered, in the refrigerator; it freezes well.)

    MAKES 2 SCANT CUPS

Autumn Compote

This compote cooks fall fruits—plums, apples, and blackberries—just enough to make their rich juices run and thicken.

¼ cup sugar, or to taste (depending on apple varieties)
¼ cup water
¼ cup dry red wine or port
2 tablespoons fresh lemon juice
Grated zest of ½ lemon
½ pound ripe purple plums, quartered, pitted, and sliced
2 crisp, tart apples, cored and cubed, with skin left on (try one red and one green apple, such as McIntosh and Granny Smith)
1 cup blackberries or raspberries

Place the sugar, water, wine, lemon juice, and zest in a small nonreactive saucepan and bring to a boil. Cover and let boil until the sugar is dissolved, about 5 minutes. Add the plums and cook until the liquid returns to a full boil. Take the pan off the heat, add the cubed apples, and stir to mix the fruits; then add the blackberries and stir just enough to distribute them. Cover the pan, let the fruit cool, then chill. The juices will turn darker and thicker as it cools. Serve the compote within half a day, spooned over ice cream or a slice of pound cake or simply on its own.

MAKES 4 SERVINGS

Plum and Madeira Compote

Any wine works in this syrup—port, sherry, brandy, leftover red or white, even ginger currant wine. Save the remaining syrup, perhaps sweetened a bit more, for drizzling over ice cream, for poaching peeled and sliced oranges, or for soaking sponge cake. If plums are past, then use fresh figs.

1½ cups sugar
2 cups water
2 pounds ripe Italian blue (prune plums) or other plums
½ lemon
½ cup Madeira or other wine
3 whole cloves

Put the sugar and water in a large saucepan and bring to a boil. Let boil over low heat until the sugar is dissolved, about 5 minutes. Meanwhile, prick the plums in two or three places to keep them from bursting. Peel the zest from the lemon and squeeze the juice, about 2 tablespoons. Add the plums, lemon zest, juice, wine, and cloves to the syrup, cover, and simmer over low heat for 5 minutes. Let the plums cool in the liquid.

When the plums are cool enough to handle, lift them out with a slotted spoon, make a slit to remove the pits carefully, but try to keep the plums whole. Place in a glass serving bowl. Discard the zest and cloves, boil the syrup down until thick and concentrated, and spoon some over the plums. Serve warm or chilled, garnished if you like with lemon zest cut into julienne.

MAKES 4 TO 6 SERVINGS

Plum Dumplings

Plums, lightly cooked and wrapped in pastry, make an attractive package with their own deep, rich, plummy sauce. This dessert is easy to make, and the little parcels are fun to look at.

4 large red or purple freestone plums (about 1 pound)
2 tablespoons sugar
2 tablespoons water
1 tablespoon unsalted butter
1 tablespoon marzipan or almond paste, quartered (optional)
1 sheet frozen puff pastry, thawed and chilled
1 large egg

Remove the plum pits by cutting halfway down the stem end of each plum along the natural line and prying out the pit. Close the plums up again, and set them stem-side up in a small saucepan just large enough to hold them in one layer. Sprinkle with the sugar and add the water and butter to the bottom of the pan. Cover and cook the plums over low heat until softened, about 15 minutes; they should not get mushy. Let them cool. Save the syrup in the pan. Roll four small knobs of marzipan between the palms of your hands into balls the size of a plum pit and insert them into the hollow; close the plums up. This may be done several hours or even a day ahead; cover and chill.

Preheat the oven to 400°F. On a lightly floured board roll out the puff pastry to about 12 inches square. Trim the edges and cut the sheet into four 6-inch squares. Set a plum in the center of each. Draw together two opposite corners of the pastry and tuck one tip under the other, as if tying a handkerchief around the plum; repeat with the remaining two corners, moistening the tips and tying them together. Press lightly to make sure the ends stay tied. Repeat with the remaining plums. Beat the egg with a tablespoon of water and brush a thin layer over the pastry. Set them in a lightly greased baking pan and bake them in the preheated oven for about 30 minutes, until the pastry is puffed and golden.

Set the dumplings on serving plates and spoon some of the reserved plum syrup around each.

MAKES 4 SERVINGS

Plum Walnut Tart

This uncomplicated tart has deep, rich, literally plummy flavors that make a perfect end to an early autumn dinner. If you have damson plum preserves (see page 248), use them instead of the currant jelly.

One 9-inch walnut pastry shell (see page 14), unbaked
1 pound Italian blue plums (prune plums), halved and pitted
2 tablespoons sugar
⅓ cup red currant jelly, homemade (see page 85) or storebought
2 tablespoons brandy

Preheat the oven to 400°F. Place the plums cut-side down on the tart shell, touching each other but not crammed together (they will shrink as they cook), and scatter the sugar on top. Bake the tart for 25 minutes, then lower the heat to 350°F and bake until the crust is golden brown and the plums tender, about 10 minutes more. Let the tart cool somewhat.

Place the currant jelly and brandy in a small saucepan over low heat until the jelly is melted; stir to combine them. Brush the warm glaze over the plums. Some of the glaze will slip off the skins, but it will mix with the plum juices and fill the cracks between the plums. Chill the tart before serving.

MAKES ONE 9-INCH TART; 6 SERVINGS

Italian Prune Plum and Port Sherbet

Rich and light at the same time.

1 pound Italian blue plums (prune plums), pitted and coarsely chopped
2 tablespoons fresh lemon juice
1 cup port
1 cup water
½ cup sugar

Put the chopped plums in a food processor and purée. Press the plum pulp through a fine sieve with the back of a spoon to remove any large pieces of skin. You should have about 1⅓ cups of purée. Stir in the lemon juice and chill.

Combine the port, water, and sugar in a small saucepan, bring to a boil, and simmer over low heat, covered, for 5 minutes. Cool the syrup and mix it with the plum purée. Chill thoroughly.

Freeze the sherbet in a sorbetière or an ice cream machine according to the manufacturer's directions. Or freeze according to the directions on page 307.

MAKES ABOUT 1 QUART

POMEGRANATES

The hardest fruit upon this planet/ Is easily the ripe pomegranate, wrote Ogden Nash. Although the pomegranate may be difficult to prepare, its myriad seeds have earned it a reputation as a fertility symbol. Indeed, the name itself means seedy apple. Its regal appearance—scarlet flower, calyx crown, ruby seeds cloaked in garnet tinged with gold— only emphasizes its nobility.

The legends of the ancient world attest to the pomegranate's stature. In a Greek myth, Bacchus turned a reluctant nymph, who believed she was going to wear a crown, into a pomegranate. In another, Pluto abducted Persephone, daughter of Demeter, goddess of fruit. Demeter obtained her daughter's release on condition that she eat nothing in Pluto's underworld realm. But Persephone could not resist a pomegranate, and the six seeds she had not spat out became the six months of winter she had to remain with Pluto. In the Old Testament, King Solomon sang of an orchard of pomegranates, and Moses assured the Israelites that they would find the fruit when they left Egypt for the promised land.

Tracing the pomegranate's migration east to the Orient and west to the Mediterranean, we find that the Moors took it from northern Africa to Spain. A bursting pomegranate is the symbol of their city of Granada, whose very name derives from it. Spanish sailors took the pomegranate to the New World, but it has never attained the same stature here. Virtually the only variety available in the United States is the large, red, sweet Wonderful, while in the Middle East there are many, ranging in color from purple to ruby, to gold, to green, even apparently to white. Wild ones are seedy and sour, offering refreshment in that dry climate, while there are cultivated seedless varieties that Persephone would have appreciated.

One look inside this unique fruit—*Punica granatum* is alone in its genus—tells why it is so special. Within the leathery skin are honeycombed chambers filled to bursting with seeds, each within a juicy red sac, or aril. Once these seed sacs are removed from the bitter surrounding membrane, their sweet-and-sour juice can be enjoyed along with the crunch. Look for pomegranates in autumn. Supermarkets increasingly offer them as a specialty, but Middle Eastern markets are a surer source. Choose specimens heavy for their size, indicating juiciness, with unbroken skin. Well chilled, they will last for two or three months.

To remove the seeds from a pomegranate, cut out the blossom end with an apple corer. Score the leathery skin lengthwise in sections without cutting through, then pull down the skin in sections. With your fingers, break out the chambers of seed sacs to free them from the pithy membrane, discarding the membrane. Wrapped tightly, the seed sacs freeze well.

To juice a pomegranate, roll it back and forth on the counter, pressing on it with the palm of your hand to crush the seed sacs inside. (Some people like to suck the freed juice through a straw poked into the fruit.) Cut the pomegranate across in half over a plate, and squeeze out the juice with a citrus reamer. Pour the juice through a sieve set over a bowl, adding the juice on the plate, and put any remaining seed sacs that are still whole in the sieve. Press lightly with the back of a spoon to extract the rest of the juice; discard the seeds and membrane, which are full of tannin. There should be about half a cup of juice.

In the Middle East, where the seeds are chewed almost like gum, the acid juice is used in cooking much as we add a few drops of lemon juice for flavor. Pomegranate juice makes an excellent marinade for pork and lamb stews and pairs well with walnuts, not only in Middle Eastern cooking. In the celebrated Mexican dish *chiles en nogada*, poblano chiles are stuffed with pork and covered in a sauce of walnuts and pomegranate seeds.

Since the fruit is more expensive in our part of the world and somewhat bothersome to prepare (though not so much as Ogden Nash would have us think), pomegranate sherbets and such are impractical for the home cook. Even so, dishes using less juice and the shimmering seeds can be delicious, attractive, and novel. The seeds add instant glamour to almost any dish, savory or sweet. A few do the trick and can be excavated and even frozen ahead of time. Baste Cornish hens with a little pomegranate juice, for instance, and garnish the roasted birds with seeds. Children are captivated by their red sparkle over a dish of ice cream or yogurt.

Pomegranates are extremely high in potassium, with some vitamin C and very little sodium. One pomegranate contains about a hundred calories. The red juice stains, so take the same precautions you would with other red fruit juices and red wine.

Grenadine

Grenadine is pomegranate syrup, but commercially bottled grenadine usually contains very little pomegranate juice. Make it yourself for more flavor and less expense.

Juice of 1 pomegranate, about ½ cup (see above)
½ cup sugar

Put the juice and sugar in a small saucepan and bring to a boil. Let it continue to boil over low heat for a few minutes until the sugar is dissolved.

Keep the syrup in a tightly closed jar in the refrigerator, where it will keep indefinitely and prove useful for flavoring and coloring cocktails and desserts.

MAKES ABOUT ¾ CUP

Pomegranate and Endive Salad

This elegant yet simple salad contrasts dark and light, bitter and sweet flavors.

2 small handfuls watercress
2 Belgian endives
¼ cup walnut or extra virgin olive oil
2 tablespoons raspberry or red wine vinegar
Salt and freshly ground black pepper to taste
2 tablespoons pomegranate seeds (see page 253)
2 tablespoons chopped walnuts, lightly toasted (see page 179)

Lay a bed of watercress on each of two salad plates. Take off a thin slice from the bottom of each endive, break off the larger leaves at the base, and spread them like fingers on the plates. Mix together the oil and vinegar and season with salt and pepper; drizzle the dressing over the salad. Top with a sprinkling of the pomegranate seeds and walnuts. Serve at once.

MAKES 2 SERVINGS

Pomegranate Marinade for Meat

This marinade is excellent for roasting or grilling lamb, pork, chicken, duck, or game. The pomegranate juice turns brown during cooking, but keeps its sweet-and-sour flavor. Otherwise you would never guess its presence, unless you add a few seeds for garnish.

1 pomegranate
2 tablespoons extra virgin olive oil
1 tablespoon honey
1 scallion (green and white parts) or shallot, chopped
1 clove garlic, minced
3 whole cloves
¼ teaspoon ground coriander
Salt and freshly ground black pepper to taste

Mix together all the ingredients in a pan. Marinate the meat in it in the refrigerator, turning to coat all sides, for at least 2 hours or as long as overnight. Turn the meat at least once during this period.

In the same pan with the marinade, roast the meat as usual, basting it a few times during cooking. To serve, spoon the pan juices over the carved meat and, if you like, garnish each serving with a few pomegranate seeds.

MAKES ABOUT ¾ CUP

Vanilla Ice Cream with Grenadine and Walnut Sauce

Exotic, colorful, simple: great for unexpected guests.

   Vanilla ice cream, homemade (see page 61) or storebought
   ½ cup grenadine (see page 254)
   ¼ cup chopped walnuts, lightly toasted (see page 179)

Scoop the ice cream into glass dishes and pour 2 tablespoons grenadine over each serving.
Top with the toasted chopped walnuts.

   MAKES 4 SERVINGS

PUMPKINS

That first winter in 1620, with the help of American Indians, the Pilgrims barely survived on the pumpkin, *Cucurbita pepo*, member of the large squash family. Their song commemorates it:

We have pumpkin at morning and pumpkin at noon.
If it were not for pumpkin, we would be undoon.

They knew sweet and fragrant melons, but had never seen these hardy cousins native to North America that the Indians grew as staples in between corn and beans. Cooking them into familiar breads, puddings, custards, and pies, the settlers brought pumpkins squarely into the tradition of English colonial cookery, from which too few of us have ventured in the centuries since. Because pumpkin pie is so much a part of that pantheon, pumpkin—botanically a fruit rather than vegetable—finds its place in this book.

Jack-o'-lanterns are an essential part of Halloween, the day before All Saints' Day on November first. This Christian holiday, like so many, combines a religious festival with a pagan parody, originally Celtic. Pumpkins grow in greater variety than the harvest-moon jack-o'-lanterns and in other colors too: white, peach, even blue and aqua. Sizes can range from petite to humongous. *National Geographic World* reported an 816-pound monster grown in Nova Scotia in 1990, where Peter in the nursery rhyme could have kept his wife fairly comfortably.

Fall, of course, is pumpkin season, and from spring into October a new sport for my family is pumpkin watching. The seeds sprout easily, as we learned when my young son brought home a seedling from school one year. As the vine threatened to take over the backyard, we learned to redirect its shoots into a spiral. Until the first frost, the great golden flowers opened to the sun each morning, only to wilt by sunset.

Just as the blooms' color is a pale yellow-orange, their mild taste is unmistakenly pumpkin too. The early male blossoms, those to pick for salads, sautéing, or stuffing, as Italians treat squash blossoms, soon drop off their slender stems. On the female blossoms, however, the stems below the wilted blooms swell into baby pumpkins. One of ours grew to green rotundity. We placed bets as to whether it would orange up by Halloween and turned it toward the sun. It did, just. After carving, we saved some of the seeds, whose sprouts are once again spiraling out of control.

The best pumpkins for eating are small varieties, weighing two to five pounds, often called sugar or pie pumpkins, with deep orange skin and flesh that is finer in texture and sweeter in flavor than those for feeding livestock or carving into jack-o'-lanterns. They should have firm, smooth rinds without blemishes, scars, or soft spots, and should feel heavy for their size. Good eating varieties are Small Sugar, Green Cushaw, and Golden Cushaw.

Once picked, pumpkins can keep for a week or perhaps a month or more, but do not put whole pumpkins in the refrigerator. Varieties differ, but they should be kept dry and stored in well-ventilated areas at about 50°F, chilled only if cut in chunks and put in plastic bags. To prepare pumpkin, scrape out all the interior seeds and membrane, saving the seeds if you plan to toast them. Peel the skin with a vegetable peeler. Canned purée tastes inferior to the freshness of homemade, but it is convenient, especially for breads and muffins where other flavors mask that of the pumpkin.

Too many of us think that this large vegetable grows in a can, but in fact its gastronomic tradition is surprisingly wide. Native Americans ate pumpkin blossoms sautéed, seeds roasted, and flesh stewed with game, corn, and chile peppers or baked with honey and bear fat. They also dried long strips of pumpkin flesh in the sun to keep for winter. In the Caribbean pumpkin is braised into spicy, fragrant stews with chiles, legumes, and sometimes meat. The French cook it into soup and serve it in a whole pumpkin tureen, like Cinderella's coach. In the Italian cities of Mantua and Ferrara, pumpkin is used to stuff pasta. In Turkey, pumpkin is baked into a sweetened pudding with chopped nuts and coconut, or candied as confectionery.

Pumpkin is a very good source of vitamin A, especially deeply colored specimens, with some vitamin C and B_1 and B_2. It also contains iron and potassium, lots of fiber, but little sodium and few calories. Pumpkin seeds (without oil or butter) contain sixteen calories an ounce.

Pumpkin Purée

To steam pumpkin, put 1½- to 2-inch chunks of seeded and scraped but unpeeled pumpkin in a colander over gently boiling water. Cover and steam until tender, about 20 minutes. Cool the pumpkin, then peel and purée it in a food processor or food mill or by pressing it through a sieve. Drain it again well.

To boil pumpkin, put 1½- to 2-inch chunks in a pot of boiling water to cover and boil until tender, about 10 to 12 minutes. Drain the pumpkin, let cool, then peel, purée, and drain again.

To bake pumpkin, put unpeeled chunks, quarters, or even halves of a small pumpkin cut-side down in a pan, and add a little water in the bottom to keep the pieces from scorching. Cover and bake in a preheated 350° to 400°F oven until the pumpkin is tender, 30 to 50 minutes (larger pieces take longer). The temperature and time can vary according to your convenience and whatever else you may have cooking. Cool, peel, purée, and drain.

Of these various methods, baking and steaming retain the most pumpkin flavor; boiling is quicker. Whichever method used, it is very important to drain the purée thoroughly in a sieve to get rid of excess moisture. According to Marian Morash in *The Victory Garden Cookbook*, a pumpkin weighing four pounds will give approximately two pounds of flesh which will yield about four cups of cooked and drained purée.

Toasted Pumpkin Seeds

These seeds make an excellent and healthful snack, like sunflower seeds, or a tasty garnish for soups and salads. Children love to make them in Halloween's aftermath.

> *Pumpkin seeds*
> *Vegetable oil*
> *Salt to taste*
> *Ground cumin to taste (optional)*

Save the pumpkin seeds from a jack-o'-lantern; remove the strings, wash, and dry the seeds. Lightly coat them with a little oil, and spread them on a cookie sheet. Bake the seeds in a very slow oven, about 250°F, for a long time, an hour or more, turning occasionally, until they dry out. When they start to color, watch to see they don't burn. Take them out when they have turned crisp and golden. Salt lightly, season with a little ground cumin if you like, and store in a tightly closed jar, where they keep indefinitely.

Pumpkin-Pear Bisque with Ginger

Ginger adds an unexpected touch of spice to this creamy (but creamless) soup, the pears a subtle fragrance and acidity.

> *2 tablespoons butter*
> *1 medium-size leek (white part only), trimmed, split, thoroughly rinsed, and coarsely chopped*
> *1 medium-size carrot, coarsely chopped*
> *2 tablespoons peeled and minced fresh ginger*
> *2 large cooking pears or apples, peeled, cored, and coarsely chopped*
> *1 small pumpkin (about 3 pounds), quartered, peeled, seeded, and coarsely chopped*
> *4 cups vegetable or chicken stock*
> *2 tablespoons fresh lemon juice, or to taste*
> *Salt and freshly ground white pepper to taste*
> *Toasted pumpkin seeds for garnish (see previous recipe)*

In a large saucepan, heat the butter over medium-low heat until it begins to foam, and cook the leek and carrot for 2 minutes, stirring from time to time. Add the ginger and pears and cook until the pears are translucent, stirring occasionally, about 5 minutes more; do not let them color. Stir in the pumpkin and stock, and bring to a boil. Cover and simmer over low heat until the pumpkin is tender, about 20 minutes.

Strain the stock through a sieve into a saucepan. Purée the solids in a food processor in batches, using some of the reserved stock as needed. For a finer, silken texture, press the purée through a sieve. The soup should be fairly thick, but not heavy. Season with the lemon juice, salt and pepper. To serve, ladle the soup into warm serving bowls and garnish with toasted pumpkin seeds.

MAKES ABOUT 6 CUPS; 6 SERVINGS

Pumpkin, Leek, and Ham Gratin

This grated fresh pumpkin dish makes a pleasing side dish or supper dish for fall. For more servings, simply multiply the ingredients.

1 small leek
3 tablespoons butter
2 cups peeled, seeded, and coarsely grated pumpkin (from ½ pound)
1 clove garlic, minced
¼ cup julienned ham
3 tablespoons heavy cream
Salt and freshly ground black pepper to taste
Generous ¼ cup grated cheddar cheese

Trim the roots and green tops from the leek. Cut it lengthwise into quarters nearly to the root and rinse under running water to remove the dirt. Dry the leek and slice it across thinly to make about 1 cup of julienne.

Over medium heat, melt the butter in a large skillet. When it begins to foam, add the pumpkin and cook, stirring, about 3 minutes. Add the leek and garlic and cook about 3 minutes more, stirring. The vegetables should be cooked through but not mushy. Mix in the ham, distributing it evenly. Stir in the cream, just enough to loosen the texture, and season with salt and pepper.

Preheat the broiler. Turn the mixture into a shallow baking dish, top with the grated cheese, and brown briefly under the broiler—watch closely to see that it doesn't scorch. You can prepare the dish ahead and finish it by baking it in a 400°F oven until golden brown, about 20 minutes.

MAKES ABOUT 4 SERVINGS

Pumpkin Cider Conserve

This jammy fruit butter is golden brown, subtle, and not too sweet—an excellent accompaniment to whole-grain breads and muffins. Although it takes time to cook down, the tedious part is peeling the pumpkin.

> *One 6-pound pumpkin, peeled, seeded, and cubed (about 12 cups; 3 pounds cubed pumpkin)*
> *1½ cups firmly packed dark brown sugar*
> *2 cups fresh sweet cider*
> *½ teaspoon ground cinnamon*
> *½ teaspoon ground coriander*
> *½ teaspoon ground allspice*

Put the pumpkin cubes in a large pot and toss them with the brown sugar. Let stand overnight to draw out the moisture. The next day, add the cider to the pot without draining off the liquid. Bring it to a boil, then simmer over low heat until the pumpkin turns tender and the liquid nearly cooks away, about 2 hours. Most of the pumpkin cubes will break up into a jam as you stir from time to time. Press any remaining chunks, if you like, with a slotted spoon. Toward the end, be sure to keep the heat low and watch closely so the bottom of the preserve doesn't stick and burn. Season with the spices, taste to see if it needs more sugar, and put up into warm half-pint jars. Sterilize them in a hot water bath and seal (see page 321). The conserve will keep for a year or more in the cupboard.

MAKES FOUR TO FIVE HALF-PINT JARS

Pumpkin Chutney

This warmly colorful chutney is a delicious way to use this autumn fruit whose versatility we rarely explore.

> *One 6-pound pumpkin, peeled, seeded, and cubed (about 12 cups; 3 pounds cubed pumpkin)*
> *Salt*
> *Water*
> *2 cups cider vinegar (at least 5% acidity)*
> *2 cups firmly packed light brown sugar*
> *1½ cups chopped onion*
> *1 cup golden raisins (sultanas)*
> *½ large red bell pepper, seeded and cut into small dice*
> *1 jalapeño pepper, seeded and minced*
> *One ½-inch piece fresh ginger, peeled and minced or grated*
> *One 2-inch stick cinnamon*
> *1 tablespoon mustard seed*
> *12 allspice berries*

Place the pumpkin cubes in a large bowl and sprinkle heavily with salt; toss the cubes to distribute the salt. Cover the bowl and let the pumpkin sit overnight or longer to draw the moisture out.

When you are ready to proceed, drain the pumpkin, rinse it well in fresh water, and drain again. Put the pumpkin in a large heavy-bottomed pot with the remaining ingredients. Bring the liquid to a boil and simmer over low heat, uncovered, for about 2 hours, stirring from time to time. Watch the pot toward the end so the bottom doesn't scorch. When the syrup is thick, discard the cinnamon stick and ladle the chutney into warm half-pint jars; sterilize them in a hot water bath (see page 321). Let it mature for at least a few weeks before opening.

MAKES ABOUT 8 HALF-PINT JARS

Pickled Pumpkin

This radiantly golden pickle will brighten your table during the cold winter months.

> One 6-pound pumpkin, peeled, seeded, and cut into 2 x 1 x ½-inch pieces (3 pounds pumpkin
>   pieces)
> Salt
> 4½ cups distilled white vinegar (at least 5% acidity)
> 4 cups sugar
> 4 to 5 cups water
> 1 tablespoon salt
> Zest of 1 orange, cut into julienne
> 12 allspice berries
> 6 whole cloves
> One 3-inch stick cinnamon
> One ½-inch piece fresh ginger, peeled

Put the pumpkin cubes in a large bowl and sprinkle heavily with salt; toss the cubes to distribute the salt. Cover the bowl and let the pumpkin sit overnight or longer to draw the moisture out. Drain, rinse well, and drain again.

In a very large, heavy, nonreactive pot, combine the vinegar, sugar, and water; bring to a boil. Add the pumpkin, salt, zest, and the spices tied in a cheesecloth bag so that you can easily remove them later. If necessary, add more water to cover. Return the liquid to a simmer and cook over low heat until the pumpkin turns tender and translucent, about 15 minutes. Fish out and discard the bag of spices. Remove the pumpkin and orange zest with a slotted spoon, and divide them among whatever size jars you wish. Boil down the liquid slightly and pour it into the jars so that it completely covers the pumpkin. Sterilize the jars in a hot water bath and seal (see page 321). The pickle will keep in the cupboard for about a year.

MAKES ABOUT 4 QUARTS

Spiced Pumpkin Bread

This spicy, moist pumpkin bread—almost a pumpkin gingerbread—is delicious with sweet butter or cream cheese for breakfast or tea. Or bake the batter in muffin tins filled two-thirds full for about 25 minutes. Wrapped in foil, the bread keeps well in the refrigerator for several days or in the freezer for several months. The idea for this recipe comes from my friend Liz Platts.

½ cup raisins, currants, or dried cranberries
3 cups firmly packed dark brown sugar
1 cup (2 sticks; ½ pound) unsalted butter, softened
4 large eggs, lightly beaten
2 cups pumpkin purée, homemade (see page 258) or canned (1 pound)
3 cups all-purpose flour
2 teaspoons baking soda
1½ teaspoons ground cinnamon
1½ teaspoons ground ginger
1 teaspoon freshly grated nutmeg
1 teaspoon ground allspice
1 teaspoon salt
⅔ cup buttermilk
½ cup broken pecans or walnuts, lightly toasted (see page 179)

Preheat the oven to 350°F. Pour boiling water over the raisins to cover and let them steep to plump up. Grease two loaf pans, each 9 x 5 x 3 inches; dust the sides with flour and shake out the excess.

In a large bowl, cream together the sugar and butter. Stir the eggs and pumpkin purée into the butter mixture. In another bowl, sift together the flour, baking soda, spices, and salt. Stir them into the pumpkin mixture alternately with the buttermilk. Drain the raisins well and stir them into the batter with the nuts. Pour the batter into the two loaf pans and bake until the bread tests done, about 1 hour. Cool the loaves for 10 minutes, then turn out to cool completely on a rack.

MAKES 2 LOAVES

Gingered Pumpkin Custard in Little Pumpkin Cups

These decorative little pumpkins don't hold much, so serve them at the end of a feast, when appetites are sated, or with another dessert such as mincemeat tartlets. You can also bake the custard in regular custard cups (this recipe is enough for six). For convenience, make them a day ahead.

> 8 to 10 mini pumpkins, about the size of a large squat apple
> 2 cups heavy cream
> 1 large egg, plus 2 large egg yolks
> ¼ cup sugar
> ½ cup pumpkin purée, preferably homemade (see page 258)
> 3 tablespoons ginger syrup from a jar of preserved stem ginger (available in Oriental or
>   specialty food stores)
> 1 tablespoon dark rum (optional)
> ¼ cup preserved stem ginger, diced

Preheat the oven to 325°F. Wash the pumpkins and cut a lid from each. Remove the seeds and string, and scrape the insides well. Put the lidded pumpkins in a baking pan and cook them for 15 minutes.

Meanwhile, make the custard. Scald the cream in a small, heavy saucepan: cook it over medium-low heat until little bubbles appear around the edges, but do not let it boil. In a bowl, whisk together the eggs and sugar. In a slow, steady stream, whisking constantly to keep the eggs from scrambling, pour the scalded cream into the egg mixture. Add the pumpkin purée, ginger syrup, and rum, and whisk to blend the ingredients.

Carefully ladle the custard into the warm pumpkins to just below the lids. Set the tops beside each pumpkin (so you can match them later). Pour a little water in the bottom of the pan to keep the pumpkins from scorching, and return to the oven. Bake, uncovered, for about 35 minutes, until the custard is set: insert a knife near the edge to see if it comes out clean. Take the pumpkins from the pan, top each custard with the diced ginger (which will sink slightly into the custard), and put the lids on to keep skins from forming as the custard cools. Serve the pumpkins chilled or at room temperature.

MAKES 8 TO 10 SERVINGS

Pumpkin Maple Walnut Pie

A walnut or pecan crust adds a nice texture to this traditional custard pie. You might also place some whole walnuts or pecans on the surface of the pie halfway through cooking.

> One 9-inch walnut pastry shell (see page 14), unbaked
> 3 large eggs

1½ cups pumpkin purée, preferably homemade (see page 258)
½ cup pure maple syrup
1 cup heavy cream
2 tablespoons dark rum (optional)
¾ teaspoon ground cinnamon
½ teaspoon freshly grated nutmeg
½ teaspoon ground ginger
¼ teaspoon salt

Preheat the oven to 425°F. Prick the pastry shell and chill it well; line it with aluminum foil, weight it with pie weights or dried beans, and bake it for 10 minutes. Remove the foil and weights and bake 6 to 7 minutes longer. Remove the shell from the oven and let it cool. Lower the heat to 350°F.

While the pastry is baking, in a bowl beat together the eggs and pumpkin purée. Stir in the remaining ingredients. Make sure they are well blended. Pour the pumpkin custard into the partially baked pie shell, and put it back into the oven, taking care to keep it level. Bake the pie until set around the edges but still barely liquid in the center, about 35 minutes. Cool the pie on a rack, where the rest of the pie will solidify by retained heat as it cools.

MAKES ONE 9-INCH PIE; 6 SERVINGS

Pumpkin Orange Pie

This pumpkin pie, a variation on the Pumpkin Maple Walnut Pie above, is lighter in texture, flavor, and calories than the traditional custard.

One 9-inch pâte brisée pastry shell (see page 16), unbaked
3 large eggs
2 cups pumpkin purée, preferably homemade (see page 258)
½ cup white or firmly packed brown sugar
1 cup milk
2 tablespoons orange juice
Grated zest of ½ orange
¾ teaspoon ground cinnamon
½ teaspoon freshly grated nutmeg
½ teaspoon ground ginger
¼ teaspoon salt

Preheat the oven to 425°F. Prick the pastry shell and chill it well; line it with aluminum foil, weight it with pie weights or dried beans, and bake it for 10 minutes. Remove the foil and weights and bake 6 to 7 minutes longer. Remove the shell from the oven and let it cool. Lower the heat to 350°F.

While the pastry is baking, in a bowl beat together the eggs and pumpkin purée. Stir in the remaining ingredients. Make sure they are well blended. Pour the pumpkin custard into the partially baked pie shell, and put it back into the oven, taking care to keep it level. Bake the pie until set around the edges but still barely liquid in the center, about 45 minutes. Cool on a rack, where the rest of the pie will solidify by retained heat as it cools.

MAKES ONE 9-INCH PIE; 6 SERVINGS

QUINCES

To the contemporary American, the quince is a quaint and homely fruit that looks like a knobby, misshapen pear. But this neglected autumn pome, too hard and astringent to eat from the tree in our climate, was prized in ages past—a golden love apple symbolic of fertility at ancient and medieval weddings.

The quince originated in the Caucasus, like its apple and pear cousins. In the warm Persian climate it can develop sweetness and succulence, so its cultivation spread to other parts of the Mediterranean even before the apple. Cydonia on Crete grew such fine quinces that it gave the fruit its botanical name, *Cydonia oblonga*, from which our word quince derives. The Romans preserved it with honey in a jam called *melimelum* (honey apple), and spread the fruit throughout Europe. Medieval Portugal was renowned for its superior quince, called *marmelo* (a corruption of *melimelum*), and the marmalade made from it, although the word was translated to bitter orange preserves in the eighteenth century. Today marmalade can mean any jam, but the term goes back to the Roman preserve.

English colonists brought the quince to America early on. Pastries and preserves of quinces were popular in all the colonies, and quince trees were common in family orchards. A charming, narrow cobblestone street in the center of old Philadelphia still bears the fruit's name, testimony to its favor. In this century the quince sharply dropped in popularity in North America, probably because it needs long cooking, but in Latin America it remains a favorite.

Quinces can be found as a specialty item in some supermarkets. A more likely source is farm markets in fall. Look for large, unbruised specimens. Unripe green quinces keep long and well in a cool, dark place. Leave them at room temperature to ripen: it may take a long time, a week or even several, but the skin will gradually turn yellow and the fragrance develop until it permeates the room.

To prepare quinces for cooking, peel and quarter them, then cut out the tough granular core. You can use the peel and core tied in cheesecloth, especially for preserves and dishes where you want their pectin, discarding them later. Slice or cube the firm flesh as directed. It holds its shape amazingly well and does not disintegrate. Quinces require long, slow cooking, with generous amounts of sugar or other sweetening for desserts; this probably accounts for the fruit's current neglect. But its unique flavor, distinctive and yet elusive, amply rewards the patient. Not only does the aroma develop during long cooking, the pale ivory flesh deepens into a delicate coral and then a beautiful rich amber.

Quinces are very high in pectin, which explains their traditional use in jellies, jams, and preserves of all kinds. They are also delicious in pies and pastries, perhaps with spices and nuts. A quince added to apple and pear dishes gives an intriguing flavor, scent, and color. Since pears are low in pectin, the addition of quinces in pear preserves makes technical sense. In savory dishes, the quince's astringency complements rich meat and fowl. Greek, Armenian, Persian, and Turkish cooking often include quinces in stews of beef, lamb, and other meats, a tradition that reaches back to the fruit's origins.

Nutritionally, quinces are high in fiber, with some vitamin C and potassium, and few calories.

Baked Quince Cups

This recipe, which can be made ahead and rewarmed before serving, makes an unusual accompaniment to roast lamb or pork. Or add a little minced meat to the filling for a light lunch or supper dish.

4 large quinces
3 tablespoons honey
2 tablespoons fresh lemon juice
¼ cup diced dried apricots
2 tablespoons raisins
1 tablespoon olive oil
¼ cup chopped onions
½ cup cooked rice, barley, or bulgur
2 tablespoons pine nuts, lightly toasted (see page 179)
¼ tablespoon ground allspice, or to taste
Salt to taste

Preheat the oven to 350°F. Peel, halve, and core the quinces. Hollow the core to make a cup, taking care to remove all the hard center with a small sharp knife or apple corer. Place the quinces cut-side down in a baking pan. Mix together the honey and lemon juice and drizzle half of it over the quince. Pour in a little water to cover the bottom and keep the quinces from scorching. Bake until tender, about 30 minutes.

While the quinces are cooking, pour boiling water over the diced apricots and raisins and let them steep for 15 to 20 minutes to plump up. Heat the olive oil in a small pan and cook the onion in it over low heat, stirring, until it is softened but not browned, about 3 minutes. Drain the dried fruit and stir it into the onions along with the rice, pine nuts, allspice, and salt. Taste and adjust the seasonings. Turn the quince halves over and spoon some of the mixture into each cup. Drizzle the remaining lemon juice and honey mixture on top, add a little more water to the bottom of the pan, and bake for 30 minutes longer. Baste once or twice during the baking with the liquid in the pan. Serve hot or warm.

MAKES 8 SERVINGS

Quince Jelly

Make quince jelly and quince jumbles together from one batch of fruit, using the liquid for the jelly and the pomace for the jumbles. The clear jelly is a delicate shade somewhere between pink and coral, the flavor similarly ambiguous. Serve this delicious jelly with meats as well as breads.

> 2½ pounds quinces, cored, quartered, and coarsely chopped, but unpeeled (if you are not making jumbles from the pomace, don't bother to core them)
> Grated zest and juice of ½ lemon
> 6 cups sugar

Place the quinces, zest, and sugar in a large pot with enough water to cover. Cover and bring to a boil, then lower the heat and simmer until the fruit is very soft, about 40 minutes. Put it in a jelly bag or a fine-holed colander lined with a triple layer of cheesecloth moistened in water and squeezed out, and let the liquid drip through without pressing it (this eliminates the fruit solids that will cloud the jelly). Set aside the quince pomace for the jumbles.

Measure the quince liquid. For each 2½ cups of liquid, measure 2 cups (1 pound) of sugar: you will have about 7 cups of liquid to 6 scant cups of sugar. Combine the liquid and sugar in a clean pot that is large and heavy-bottomed. Slowly bring to a boil over medium heat, stirring occasionally to dissolve the sugar. Boil hard until the syrup has reached the jelling point (220°F on a candy thermometer). If you spoon some onto a cold saucer and push your finger through it, the jelly will wrinkle. Skim any scum or bubbles from the surface and ladle the jelly into warm, clean half-pint jars. Cover, sterilize in a hot water bath (see page 321), and store on a cool cupboard shelf for a year or longer.

MAKES ABOUT 7 HALF-PINT JARS

Quince Jumbles

Make these from the fruit pomace left over from the quince jelly in the previous recipe. Jumbles are a traditional confection that keep well for months, if properly stored, and make charmingly old-fashioned presents at holiday time.

2¼ pounds quince pulp (see headnote and previous recipe)
4½ cups sugar

Purée the quince pulp, including the peel. Using a food processor or food mill is infinitely easier than trying to force it through a sieve. Weigh the purée (you should have about 2¼ pounds) and measure an equal or nearly equal weight of sugar (2 to 2¼ pounds, 4 to 4½ cups). Put the purée in a large heavy-bottomed pan with high sides. Over low heat gradually add the sugar, stirring with a long-handled spoon to dissolve it. Cook the quinces over low heat for an hour or more, keeping close watch and stirring often as the sauce thickens and reduces into a paste. Eventually it sputters and spits, so protect your forearm with a mitt. Stir constantly toward the end to avoid scorching the bottom. When the paste is thick enough to show the bottom of the pan when you draw the spoon across it, like the parting of the Red Sea, it is done.

Spread the paste in large, flat pans, such as jelly-roll pans, lined with waxed paper or aluminum foil. The layer should be very thin, ¼- to ⅓-inch thick. Let it cool, then cover lightly with a cloth that will allow ventilation (not plastic). Let the paste set for several days, until dry and firm.

Stamp out shapes with cookie cutters or cut into the traditional diamond shape (less waste) with a knife. Roll the shapes in sugar and store between sheets of waxed paper in airtight tins. The jumbles will keep indefinitely.

MAKES SEVERAL DOZEN, DEPENDING ON SIZE OF CUTTERS

Candied Quince Chips

These candied quince chips make a festive holiday present or after-dinner sweetmeat. Their deep amber color and almost pineappley flavor are quite unusual. Their preparation, though simple, takes time, so make them while doing another task in the kitchen.

1 pound quince (about 4), peeled, cored, and thinly sliced
2 cups (1 pound) sugar plus more (about another pound, which can be reused) for sand sugar,
  for rolling slices
1 cup water
1 thin slice fresh ginger, peeled
One 2-inch strip lemon zest

Put the quince slices in a large, heavy pot and cover with boiling water. Boil for 10 minutes, then drain. Using the same pot, add the sugar and 1 cup water and stir to combine. Add the drained quinces, ginger, and lemon zest, and slowly simmer over low heat for a very long time, almost 2 hours, stirring occasionally, until the slices turn a deep red color and become almost translucent. After about half an hour, take out and discard the ginger and lemon zest.

Remove the quince slices with a slotted spoon and put them on plates to drain the thick syrup. If necessary, transfer them to fresh dry plates. When the syrup is well drained, roll the slices on a clean dry plate of sugar (you will need a fair amount), coating all sides. Let them dry overnight covered lightly with a dish towel. Shake off the excess sugar (use it for desserts), and store the candied slices in an airtight tin in single layers separated by sheets of waxed paper, where they will keep several months or longer.

MAKES ABOUT 1 POUND

Poached Sliced Quinces

Whether or not you eat them with a runcible spoon, put these slices of quinces over vanilla ice cream or serve them in bowls with a dollop of sour cream or yogurt in the middle. To please jaded palates, add raisins and curry powder for an unusual and delicious compote. Chopped preserved stem ginger (available in Oriental or specialty food stores) or dates also make an excellent garnish.

3 large quinces, peeled, cored, and thinly sliced
2 cups sugar
½ teaspoon ground ginger
½ teaspoon ground cinnamon
Two 2-inch strips orange zest, cut into julienne

Put the quince slices in a pot with the sugar, spices, and enough water barely to cover the fruit. Cover and simmer over low heat, stirring occasionally, until the flesh is tender and the syrup rosy pink, about 40 minutes. Serve warm or cold garnished with the orange zest.

MAKES 6 SERVINGS

Quince Tart

The custard topping on this tart can be omitted altogether, the quince slices baked like the French Apple Tart with apricot jam (see page 31). The custard is also delicious on pear, apple, or peach tart.

1 cup sugar
1 cup water
3 large quinces, peeled, cored, and thinly sliced
One 9-inch almond tart shell (see page 14), unbaked
1 cup heavy cream
1 large whole egg plus 1 egg yolk
¼ cup sugar
½ teaspoon ground ginger, or to taste

Preheat the oven to 350°F.

Place the sugar and water in a pot and bring to a boil; let boil over low heat until the sugar is dissolved, about 5 minutes. Add the sliced quinces and poach over low heat until tender, 20 to 30 minutes; let the slices cool in the syrup. (This may be done well ahead.) Drain the quince slices and lay them in the crust overlapping each other in a pretty pattern. Bake the tart for 20 minutes. If the crust darkens too much, cover it with aluminum foil.

While the quinces are baking, beat the cream, eggs, sugar, and ginger together well with a fork until the mixture forms ribbons when you lift the fork over the bowl. Very carefully, pour the custard mixture over the quinces and with a steady hand put the tart back in the oven. It is important not to spill the custard over the rim of the tart. Bake the tart until the custard is just set, about 25 minutes more. Cool the tart slightly and serve.

MAKES ONE 9-INCH TART; 6 SERVINGS

RASPBERRIES AND BLACKBERRIES

The members of the large bramble family are just as tangled and thorny as their long-reaching canes. The raspberry and blackberry are the best-known members of the clan having the genus name *Rubus*, but there are hundreds and thousands of others, some deliberate hybrids, others accidental crosses. Their lineage confuses even breeders and botanists.

Within this brier patch glistens the jewellike berry, colored brilliant ruby (the red raspberry gives the genus its name), as well as other varieties in yellow, amber, purple, mauve, and black. It is actually a composite fruit, the berry's many little juicy seed sacs surrounding a central core. In the blackberry, that core remains within the berry after it is picked. In the raspberry, the ripe fruit slips off the core to form a tiny cup.

The blackberry grows wild in profusion, especially in cool, damp northern regions. In Britain it is much loved. Hedgerows, thickets, and cottage gardens are favorite haunts, and many simple country recipes celebrate it. "Flopsy, Mopsy, and Cotton-tail," wrote Beatrix Potter in her timeless *Tale of Peter Rabbit*, "went down the lane to gather blackberries." At the end of her story those good little bunnies, unlike their brother Peter, were rewarded with "bread and milk and blackberries for supper."

Compared to its country cousin, the raspberry, although also found wild, is more cultivated, refined, and genteel. It is grown in rows, the old canes trimmed back each year, and most of the thorns bred out. With small seeds and no hull once picked, it tastes best raw. The French delight in the raspberry unlike the Italians, who largely ignore it, probably because the Mediterranean heat is too strong. In haute cuisine the raspberry often appears in pastries, fruit compotes, alone adorned with crème fraîche or custard of some sort, or in sauce where its crimson color and spicy perfume bathe other fruits.

Because the sheer number of *Rubus* berries is confusing, here is a quick overview. The red raspberry, of course, is most popular and best known. The black raspberry, distinguished from the blackberry by its hollow cup shape, tends to be smaller and seedier than the red raspberry, but distinctly aromatic. Though unusual, the golden yellow raspberry, sometimes having an amber blush, is not a brand-new fruit, but has recently come back into favor. It is far more than a novelty berry: the taste is unusually sweet and fine.

The blackberry is often called bramble in Britain. Among hybrid crosses, the loganberry, named after Judge James Logan of Santa Cruz, California, is deep red, juicy, large, conical in shape, and abundant; its parentage has never quite been clear. The garnet tayberry is another large, sweet, odoriferous blackberry cross named after its breeder, as were the luscious boysenberry and the youngberry. Southern California's fragile olallieberry is enjoyed close to home and rarely travels.

The bulk of the domestic raspberry crop comes from California, Oregon, and Washington, and, to a lesser degree, from Michigan and New York. A small supply is sold at specialty markets sporadically throughout the year, rising in June through October. The peak of the commercial crop comes in late June and again in early September. In December and February some fresh raspberries are imported from Chile. Blackberry supplies are greatest in June and July, diminishing in the summer heat but continuing in smaller volume through September, when they find their way into autumn dishes and preserves.

In July native raspberries are can be found at local farmers' markets and farm stands at affordable prices. Then again, from September up to the first frost, late-bearing bushes offer their exquisite fruit. Unless you have a patch in your own backyard, this is the best time to enjoy them. Blackberries and some of the crosses are often sold at farm markets too.

Wherever you find your raspberries or blackberries, look for plump, brightly colored, well-scented fruit with no signs of mold. You should use them as soon as possible after picking or purchase, that same day if you can. Avoid baskets with juice stains at the bottom. Sometimes stores sell day-old raspberries at reduced prices, but these should be regarded with skepticism.

Keep your berries well chilled in open baskets to allow ventilation. Handle them as little as possible, since they are so perishable, but remove at once any moldy berries that might spoil the whole batch. Because raspberry caps fill with water that rinses off the perfume, do not wash them at all if you can avoid it and, if you must, only right before using.

The best way to eat raspberries is plain, possibly with a sprinkling of sugar and cream of some kind. Other fruits make good companions, as does fine pastry. The tartness of raspberries widens their range, making them suitable for savory meat dishes and allowing them to stand up to dark chocolate. Since raspberries' summer season is so short, preserves such as jam and vinegar prolong it. Unlike raspberries, blackberries take well to cooking, often with other fruits, since they tend toward seediness in "unimproved" strains. Jams and preserves take advantage of their high pectin content. Remember that the juice of these berries stains.

A cup of fresh raspberries contains about seventy calories, lots of vitamin C, some iron, but very little sodium. A cup of blackberries also contains a generous amount of vitamin C, potassium, and calcium, and about eighty-four calories.

Smoked Chicken Salad with Raspberries and Walnuts

Serve this elegant salad on a steamy night when you can't bear to cook at all. The dark flavors of the smoked chicken and walnuts balance the sweetness and acidity of the berries.

4 handfuls bitter lettuce, such as frisée (curly endive)
1 smoked chicken breast or smoked turkey or plain poached chicken breast (about ½ pound), skinned, boned, and thinly sliced
1 cup fresh raspberries
¼ cup chopped walnuts, lightly toasted (see page 179)
2 scallions (green and white parts), thinly sliced

FOR THE VINAIGRETTE
¼ cup walnut oil or extra virgin olive oil
2 tablespoons raspberry vinegar (recipe follows), or to taste
Salt and freshly ground black pepper to taste

Spread the lettuce on four serving plates to make a bed. Lay the smoked chicken slices on the lettuce, and scatter the raspberries, walnuts, and scallions on top attractively. Mix together the vinaigrette ingredients and drizzle over the four dishes. Serve at once.

MAKES 4 SERVINGS

Raspberry Vinegar

This fruit vinegar is excellent for salads, sauces, glazes, and marinades, especially when used with raspberries or other fruit. For a refreshing summer drink, pour a little into an ice-filled glass with a spoonful of syrup and fill with soda water. This vinegar works well with many other fruits such as currants, gooseberries, cranberries, strawberries, cherries, and plums.

2 cups fresh raspberries
2 tablespoons sugar
1½ cups good white wine vinegar

Put the raspberries into a large glass jar, crush a few of them, and sprinkle with the sugar. Pour the vinegar on top to cover. Close the jar and let the vinegar steep for at least one month, stored in a cool, dark cupboard. Strain the raspberry vinegar through a fine sieve and pour the liquid into a fresh bottle or bottles. (Use the strained raspberries that have kept their shape in a savory duck or pork dish, as in the Orange Sauce for Roast Duck, page 184, substituting the berries for the oranges.) If you like, put in a few pristine berries for decoration. Cork it well. In a cool, dark cupboard, the vinegar will keep up to a year.

MAKES ABOUT 1½ CUPS

Raspberry Jam

The fresh, fruity flavor of homemade jam is so much better than storebought that the effort, especially in small quantities, is well worthwhile. It will be runnier than storebought jam. Remove the seeds, if you like, by passing the jam through a fine sieve.

2 pounds fresh raspberries (about 3 pints)
4½ cups sugar (2 pounds)

Pick over the raspberries to remove any stems or leaves. Put them in a large, heavy-bottomed nonreactive pot and heat over low heat to soften the fruit. Add the sugar, stir to dissolve it, and bring the liquid to a boil. Cook until the jam has reached the jelling point, 220°F on a candy thermometer, taking care not to let the bottom scorch. Or put a little jam on a cold plate to cool; if it wrinkles when you push it with your finger, it's ready. Put the jam into warm, clean half-pint jars, seal, and sterilize (see page 321). If you prefer not to bother with boiling hot water baths, close the jars, refrigerate, and give them away as presents (remember to tell them it's not sterilized). This jam should be eaten within six months.

MAKES ABOUT 6 HALF-PINT JARS

Raspberry Gratin

This simple, beautiful dessert shows off raspberries at their best. If you like, use a combination of fruits, such as several berries or sliced peaches and berries. Sour cream, yogurt, or crème fraîche, or a mixture of any of the three, can be used in place of yogurt.

1 cup fresh raspberries
½ cup plain yogurt
1 to 1½ tablespoons dark brown sugar, lumps broken up

Spread the raspberries in two small ovenproof dishes. Spread the yogurt over the top, allowing some of the fruit to show through. Scatter the brown sugar over that. You can leave the dishes just so on the counter for some time while you eat the main part of your meal. The acid in the yogurt will begin to dissolve the sugar.

Arrange the broiler rack 6 inches from the heat source and preheat. Immediately before serving, run the dishes under the flame for about 3 minutes to caramelize the sugar. Watch closely to see that it does not burn. Serve right away.

MAKES 2 SERVINGS

Summer Pudding

For this sumptuous English pudding, once a country dish, use whatever juicy fruits you can find—raspberries, currants, strawberries, loganberries, blueberries, blackberries, peaches, plums. Unless you have a farmers' market or garden nearby, frozen berries do well. The point is to have a variety of lush fruits that saturate the bread lining with their glorious juices.

2 cups strawberries, hulled and quartered
2 cups blueberries
3 cups raspberries
1 cup blackberries
¾ cup sugar, or to taste
½ loaf stale firm-textured white bread, thinly sliced and crusts trimmed

Put the strawberries and blueberries in a large nonreactive pot and soften over low heat. As the juices start to run, stir in the remaining berries and sugar. Heat only to make the mixture runny, not to make the fruit disintegrate. Remove from the stove and taste for sweetening, adding as much sugar as needed. (The softened fruit is delicious as it is, served over pound cake.) Pour the fruit into a sieve set over a bowl, reserving the juices.

Cut the bread to fit a 6- to 8-cup pudding mold or bowl with steep sides. Put a round piece on the bottom with fan-shaped pieces around the sides; try to make the pieces even. Once fitted, dip both sides of the bread in the reserved juice, then fit each piece back in place. Fill any holes with leftover bread to completely line the bowl. Spoon the fruit into the mold nearly to the top. Trim any bread that extends over the sides, and cover the top of the pudding with bread.

Cover the pudding in plastic wrap and set a saucer on top that just fits inside the bowl. Place a heavy object on top to weight the pudding down and force the juice into the bread. Refrigerate at least overnight, weighted. Save the remaining juices in a covered container and chill.

To serve the pudding, run the tip of a knife around the edge of the pudding, invert the bowl onto a platter, and jerk it down once or twice to unmold it. Pour the reserved juice over the bread to cover any pale spots and bathe the pudding in its rich color. A few whole fruits, perhaps with green leaves still attached, make a pretty garnish but are not necessary. Pass heavy cream or lightly whipped cream on the side.

MAKES 8 TO 10 SERVINGS

NOTE: Summer pudding *must* be made a day or two ahead. If you are lucky enough to have a glut of summer fruit, make an extra pudding or two for the freezer.

Summer pudding can also be made in individual servings. Use 6-ounce Pyrex custard cups or molds with slanted sides and line them with very thinly sliced bread (so the proportion of bread to fruit won't be too high) and proceed as above.

Blackberry Bread and Butter Pudding

This old-fashioned, homey pudding can be made with any tart berry, such as currants, raspberries, cranberries, and blueberries. It always makes me think of Flopsy, Mopsy, and Cotton-tail, those good little bunnies in Beatrix Potter's *Tale of Peter Rabbit*, who had blackberries and milk for supper.

> 8 thin (½ inch thick) slices white bread
> 3 tablespoons unsalted butter
> 2 cups blackberries or other tart berry (for smaller berries, use 1 cup)
> 3 large eggs
> ⅓ to ½ cup sugar
> ½ teaspoon pure vanilla extract
> ½ teaspoon freshly grated nutmeg
> 2½ cups milk

Butter an 8-inch-square baking pan that is fairly deep. Trim the slices of bread, removing the crusts, so that four slices just fit together in the pan in one layer. Butter the bread on one side and place the slices buttered-side down in the pan. Scatter the blackberries over them, then lay the remaining 4 slices of bread on top with the buttered-side up. In a medium-size bowl, beat together the eggs, sugar (the amount depending on the tartness of the berries), vanilla, and nutmeg. Stir in the milk until the mixture is well blended, then pour over the bread. Let it sit for an hour, pressing down on the bread occasionally, so that the bread absorbs some of the liquid.

Preheat the oven to 325°F. Bake the pudding until it puffs up and turns golden brown, 50 to 60 minutes. Let it cool somewhat. Serve the pudding warm, cut into rectangles.

MAKES 4 TO 6 SERVINGS

Raspberries in Orange Zabaglione

This elegant sauce must be made at the last minute, but the expectant pause at time of serving makes for a grand entrance. In addition to raspberries, it is wonderful with all kinds of fruits and puddings, and you can substitute other liqueurs for the orange.

2 large egg yolks
2 tablespoons sugar
1 teaspoon grated orange zest
¼ cup Grand Marnier or other orange-flavored liqueur
2 cups fresh raspberries

Put the egg yolks in the top of a double boiler with the sugar and orange zest. Over gently simmering water (be sure the upper pan is not touching the water), beat the egg yolks. As they begin to mount up with incorporated air, gradually add the liqueur. Continue beating until the yolks increase in volume and form a soft billowy custard cooked by the heat, about 5 minutes. Be careful—if gets too hot, the eggs will scramble. Serve the zabaglione warm: as it cools it deflates. Place the raspberries in elegant serving dishes, such as saucer champagne glasses, spoon the zabaglione over, and serve.

MAKES 4 SERVINGS

VARIATIONS: This recipe can easily be doubled or tripled to serve more people. To turn it into its stabler French cousin *sabayon*, continue beating the mounted cooked custard over a bowl of ice to cool it down and keep it from deflating; chill it before serving. If you like, fold the finished *sabayon* into two egg whites whipped to stiff peaks or into ¾ cup of heavy cream whipped to stiff peaks. To stabilize it into a Bavarian cream, soften ½ envelope unflavored gelatin in ¼ cup orange juice, dissolve it over simmering water, stir into the sabayon cream, and chill.

Raspberry Sauce

This simple raspberry sauce is beautiful with many desserts. In Peach Melba (see page 211) Escoffier put it on poached peaches and vanilla ice cream to honor the great soprano, Dame Nellie Melba. In another sublime pairing of the two fruits, pêche cardinale combines skinned but uncooked peaches with raspberry sauce, brilliantly colored like a cardinal's robes, to give the dish its name.

2 cups fresh or frozen and thawed raspberries
¼ cup sugar, or to taste
1 teaspoon fresh lemon juice or 1 tablespoon fresh orange juice
1 to 2 tablespoons orange-flavored liqueur, kirsch, or other liqueur (optional)

Purée the raspberries in the food processor or simply crush them in a bowl. Pass the purée through a fine sieve to remove the seeds, pressing on the solids with the back of a spoon to force through as much of the fruit as possible. Stir in sugar to taste, sharpen with a little citrus, and flavor with liqueur. The sauce, covered and chilled, keeps well for a week and can be frozen for several months.

MAKES 1 GENEROUS CUP

Fresh Peaches and Raspberries

These two fruits brighten the market at the same time every summer. Together they are eloquent in their simplicity.

3 large, ripe peaches
2 cups fresh raspberries
Superfine sugar to taste
2 to 3 tablespoons Grand Marnier or other orange-flavored liqueur (optional)

Peel, pit, and slice the peaches. Gently toss with the raspberries and sugar. Drizzle on the liqueur and serve.

MAKES 4 SERVINGS

Fresh Raspberry Tart

The berries in this exquisite tart shimmer like jewels. Be sure to use a good-quality shell with thin, buttery pastry, since heavy dough will ruin it. If you prefer, make several small tartlets or one large one in any shape you choose. It is also excellent made with strawberries, preferably small ones.

½ cup red currant jelly or seedless raspberry jam, homemade (see page 85 or 276) or storebought
1½ tablespoons kirsch, crème de cassis, or port
One 9-inch pâte sucrée tart shell (see page 35), baked
2 cups fresh raspberries

In a small, heavy-bottomed pan, gently heat the currant jelly with the liqueur over low heat until it is melted. Brush a thin layer over the bottom of the tart crust. Before the jelly has cooled, set a layer of raspberries close together in the jelly in concentric circles. Heat the jelly again if it has solidified and brush it over the berries to make them glisten. Serve the tart at room temperature soon after it is made, no more than a few hours, with lightly sweetened whipped cream or crème fraîche (see page 155).

MAKES ONE 9-INCH TART; 6 TO 8 SERVINGS

Raspberry Frangipane Tart

This tart is sublime after a large or special dinner, when you need something spectacular yet restrained that is completely made ahead. Unlike the other raspberry tart, this one needs no gilding. It should be served fairly soon after it is put together.

About ½ cup seedless raspberry jam, homemade (see page 276) or storebought
1 tablespoon raspberry or other flavored liqueur (optional)
1 frangipane base (recipe follows)
2 cups fresh raspberries

In a small heavy-bottomed saucepan, melt the jam over low heat. Stir in the tablespoon of liqueur. Spread a smooth layer of the melted jam over the surface of the frangipane. Set the raspberries into the jam, starting at the circumference and working into the center. Chill slightly to set it.

MAKES ONE 9-INCH TART; 6 TO 8 SERVINGS

Frangipane Tart

This frangipane (as with the amandine base on page 36) can be made ahead, wrapped, and frozen. It makes an excellent base for many special fruit tarts.

One 9-inch pâte sucrée tart shell (see page 35) in a false-bottom pan, unbaked
6 tablespoons (¾ stick) unsalted butter, softened
¼ cup plus 2 tablespoons sugar
1 large egg yolk
3 ounces almonds, finely ground (about ¾ cup ground)
3 tablespoons all-purpose flour
Grated zest of 1 large lemon
2 large egg whites, at room temperature

Preheat the oven to 375°F. Prick the pâte sucrée shell with a fork and chill well. For the filling, cream together the butter and sugar until light, then stir in the egg yolk. In a small bowl, mix the almonds, flour, and lemon zest together. Beat the egg whites until stiff peaks form; fold most of the egg whites into the butter-and-sugar mixture alternating with the almond mixture. Add the remaining egg white at the last moment for lightness. Spread the amandine in the tart shell and bake for 20 to 25 minutes. The top should not brown (if it starts to color or puff up, lower the heat to 325°F). Cool the tart on a rack and remove it from the tin.

MAKES ONE 9-INCH TART

Linzertorte

This torte from the town of Linz in Austria is celebrated for its pastry, aromatic with spices and textured with nuts. The dough is extremely rich, virtually a butter cookie, so it is hard to handle. If it breaks apart as you work with it, simply push it back together again and perhaps chill it. Instead of raspberry jam, similar fruits such as cranberries and currants can be used.

¾ cup blanched whole almonds (or almonds and hazelnuts), lightly toasted (see page 179) and
    cooled
⅓ cup sugar
Grated zest of 1 lemon
½ teaspoon ground cinnamon
¼ teaspoon ground cloves
1 cup all-purpose flour
½ cup (1 stick; ¼ pound) unsalted butter, chilled and cut into small pieces
1 large egg plus 1 yolk
1¾ cups raspberry jam, homemade (see page 276) or high-quality storebought
2 tablespoons fresh lemon juice
Confectioners' sugar (optional)

First make the crust. Place the almonds, sugar, zest, cinnamon, and cloves in a food processor and process until the nuts are finely chopped but not pulverized. Add the flour and quickly combine. Finally, add the butter and eggs, and process until they are distributed and a ball is just beginning to form on the blade. Divide the dough into two portions, two thirds and one third (wrap and chill it at this point if you wish). Pat the larger portion of dough ¼-inch thick into a 9-inch false-bottom tart pan, or roll the dough between two sheets of plastic wrap or waxed paper and then fit it into the pan (you do not roll this dough out on a floured board as with most tarts). Give the tart high rims. Cut the smaller portion of dough into eight pieces and roll them into ropes on the counter for the latticework. Wrap and thoroughly chill all the dough with plastic wrap.

Preheat the oven to 425°F. Bake the pastry shell on a cookie sheet for 10 minutes; don't let it brown. Halfway through, prick the pastry, which is very likely puffing up. Take it out and let it cool. Lower the heat to 375°F. Mix together the raspberry jam and lemon juice and spoon it into the shell. Lay the pastry ropes on top, with the upper layer traditionally crossing the bottom at a 45-degree angle. Cut the ends off neatly just inside the rim. Return the tart to the oven until the pastry is browned and the jam bubbling, about 30 minutes. Cool thoroughly, remove from the outer rim, and put it on a serving platter. Serve the Linzertorte at room temperature with confectioners' sugar sifted around the edges.

MAKES ONE 9-INCH TART; 8 SERVINGS

Katherine Maloney's Cake

This birthday cake has become a favorite in our house, thanks to the inspiration of Sarah Boardman's mother, Katherine Maloney. Ice cream and cake come together with sherbet, for simplicity, and all made ahead.

> Two 8-inch vanilla sponge cakes (recipe follows)
> ½ cup sherry
> ¾ cup seedless raspberry preserves or red currant jelly, homemade (see page 276 or 85); or storebought
> Vanilla ice cream, homemade (see page 61) or storebought, softened
> Raspberry sherbet, homemade (see page 285) or storebought, softened
> 1 cup heavy cream
> Confectioners' sugar to taste
> 1 tablespoon chopped pistachios (undyed and unsalted)
> Fresh raspberries for garnish

Early on the day of the party, split each layer cake in two. Place three halves, cut-side up, in each of three cake tins. Sprinkle each cake half with a third of the sherry, then spread with a third of the jelly. Cover them and freeze. Now spread two of the cake halves each with a half inch of ice cream, and the third cake half with a half inch of raspberry sherbet. Stack the layers in an 8-inch springform pan so that the ice cream cake layers sandwich the raspberry sherbet layer in between. Set the last cake half on top. Cover all in plastic wrap and freeze for 2 hours.

Whip the cream to firm peaks, sweeten it lightly with confectioners' sugar, and spread it over the cake in a pretty, swirling manner. Decorate with chopped pistachios, and freeze again. Shortly before serving, take the cake out and garnish it with fresh raspberries.

MAKES ONE 9-INCH CAKE; ABOUT 12 SERVINGS

Vanilla Sponge Cake

This simple, light cake is the basis of many desserts. It also makes a quick substitute for the classic French génoise (see page 302).

5 large eggs, separated, at room temperature
¾ cup sugar
2 tablespoons milk
1 teaspoon pure vanilla extract
½ cup all-purpose flour
½ teaspoon baking powder
Pinch of salt

Lightly butter and flour two 8-inch cake pans or a 16 x 11 x 1-inch jelly-roll pan lined with aluminum foil or waxed or parchment paper; shake out the excess flour and set aside. Preheat the oven to 375°F.

In a large bowl, beat together the egg yolks and sugar until the yolks turn paler and the sugar dissolves; stir in the milk and vanilla. In another bowl, sift together the flour and baking powder, then gradually stir them into the eggyolk mixture. In a large bowl, beat the egg whites with the salt until stiff peaks form. Fold a spoonful into the batter, then quickly and deftly fold in the rest of the whites. Pour the batter into the prepared pans and bake until the cakes have risen high and turned golden and the edges of the cake shrink away from the pan, about 22 to 25 minutes for the 8-inch pans, 15 for the jelly-roll pan.

For the two round cakes, take them out of the oven, run a knife around the inside edges, and let cool somewhat. When they have deflated slightly but are still warm, turn the cakes in the pans upside down, to keep their volume. When completely cooled, turn the cakes out of the pans. If you are not using them right away, enclose them in plastic wrap or bags and refrigerate or freeze.

For the sheet cake, loosen the edges as soon as you take it out of the oven. After it has cooled for a few minutes, put a tea towel on top and carefully turn the cake over onto the towel. Lift off the pan, peel away the paper or foil, then roll the cake up along the long side in the towel. Be sure to do this while the cake is still warm. Keep covered so it will stay moist.

MAKES TWO 8-INCH CAKES OR 1 SHEET CAKE

Raspberry Charlotte Royale

This dessert looks spectacular with the cake spirals outlined in crimson, the center filled with mousse, and a raspberry purée for accent, but it is quite simple to make. All the parts can be done ahead at your convenience, the whole assembled and frozen. Just take it out of the freezer to soften a little beforehand.

1 sheet vanilla sponge sheet cake (see previous recipe)
½ cup seedless raspberry jam, homemade (see page 276) or storebought
2 cups heavy cream
¼ cup confectioners' sugar, or to taste

1½ to 2 cups raspberry purée, lightly sweetened (recipe follows)
¼ cup crème de cassis

First make the vanilla sponge cake in a jelly-roll pan. When the cake is cool, unroll it, trim the two long edges, and spread the cake with a thin layer of the raspberry jam. Roll the cake back up again and slice it into ¾-inch rounds. Place the rounds close together in a 2- or 2½-quart mold to line the entire mold. Tightly cover the cake with plastic wrap and chill.

Whip the cream in a large bowl until stiff peaks form and sweeten with confectioners' sugar. Mix ½ cup of the raspberry purée with the crème de cassis and quickly fold it into the cream. It should be delicately pink in color and raspberry flavored; add more purée if you like. Spoon the cream mixture into the lined mold until level with the top. Cover the mold with plastic wrap and freeze for several hours or overnight.

To serve, thaw the royale for 1 hour at room temperature or longer in the refrigerator. Unmold by inverting it onto a serving plate and surround it with the remaining raspberry purée. Cut the royale into thin wedges and spoon some of the sauce beside them.

MAKES UP TO 16 SERVINGS

Raspberry Purée

Two 12-ounce packages frozen unsweetened raspberries, thawed
⅓ cup sugar, or to taste
2 tablespoons orange or lemon juice

Purée the raspberries in a food processor and pass them through a fine sieve, pressing with the back of a spoon to extract as much liquid as possible. Discard the seeds. If the berries are not already sweetened, add sugar to taste and the citrus juice. Stir well before using. (This can be made a couple of days ahead, covered, and chilled.)

MAKES ABOUT 2 CUPS

Raspberry Sherbet

The best of all sherbets, especially served in Chocolate Pecan Tulipes (recipe follows).

2 cups fresh raspberries, or two 10-ounce packages frozen raspberries in syrup, thawed, omitting
    any additional sugar
2 tablespoons fresh lemon juice
⅔ cup sugar, or to taste
1¼ cups water

Purée the raspberries in a food processor and press the pulp through a fine sieve with the back of a spoon to strain out the seeds. Mix in the lemon juice and sugar; the acid will soon dissolve the sugar. Stir the water into the raspberry purée and chill well. Freeze the fruit syrup in a sorbetière or an ice cream machine according to the manufacturer's directions. Or freeze it according to the directions on page 307.

MAKES ABOUT 1 QUART

Chocolate Pecan Tulipes

A scoop of raspberry sherbet is exquisite in these chocolate tulipes. Garnish them if you like with a few fresh berries and a mint sprig. You can fill the tulipes with any other sherbet, ice cream, or mousse.

1 cup sugar
¾ cup coarsely chopped pecans
¼ cup sifted unsweetened cocoa powder
¼ cup all-purpose flour
4 large egg whites
½ teaspoon pure vanilla extract

Preheat the oven to 425°F. Generously grease two cookie sheets. Put the sugar and pecans in the food processor and process for about 15 seconds, until the nuts are finely ground. Transfer to a small bowl and mix in the cocoa and flour. Blend in well the egg whites and vanilla; the batter will be quite loose.

Spoon 2 tablespoons of the batter on the front half and also the back half of a cookie sheet, with plenty of space between the two. With the back of a spoon spread each mound into a 5-inch round. Repeat on the other cookie sheet. Bake the rounds until the edges just begin to brown, about 7 minutes.

Removing the sheets one at a time, carefully lift each cookie with a spatula and place it over a small bowl. With your fingertips quickly ruffle the edges like a flower and form a cup shape by carefully pushing the cookie down into the bowl. If the pastry cools and stiffens, put it back in the oven to soften. Repeat until all 8 tulipes are made. Store the tulipes in a cool, dry place, well protected as they are fragile. If you are keeping them for more than a few hours, store them wrapped in plastic wrap in the freezer or in airtight tins.

MAKES 8 TULIPES

RHUBARB

Rhubarb, indigenous to northern Asia, thrives in cold climates: it has been found growing wild in such forbidding regions as Siberia, Mongolia, and the Himalayas. For gardeners in North America, the crinkled leaves and pink shoots pushing up through the soil are one of the first harbingers of spring. The edible stalks of the *Rheum* plant, botanically a vegetable rather than a fruit, have enjoyed popularity largely because they make some of the earliest desserts of the season, sweetened with plenty of sugar and cooked into pies, puddings, preserves, compotes, and fools.

Rhubarb first came to the West as a medicinal plant, its rhizome root used as a purgative. It was introduced into England in the late sixteenth century, but only after 1800 did growers discover that blanching the astringent stalks—shielding them from light—made them tender, juicy, and pink. The Victorians experimented widely in forcing rhubarb and developing new varieties, until rhubarb dishes became almost a fad. At Harrogate in Yorkshire, England, there is a botanical garden, a rhubarb museum, if you will, that has collected and preserved over one hundred varieties for researchers and breeders of the present and future.

Rhubarb came to the United States in the early nineteenth century. Easy to grow, the perennial soon acquired the sobriquet "pie plant" for its usefulness to settlers. But its apparent homeliness, like so much fashion, has recently reversed itself. Once ignored in French restaurants, rhubarb assumed a previously unimagined style with nouvelle cuisine, when it accompanied meat and fish dishes. Current interest in rhubarb comes with the vogue for old-fashioned desserts, pairing nostalgia for the farms and homesteads of our memory (or fantasy) with our recently acquired taste for exotic sour fruits.

Besides America, rhubarb is popular in Britain, Scandinavia, Switzerland, northern Germany, and Iran. In these cuisines, rhubarb often goes with meats such as pork and lamb, where its puckery tartness balances the meat's richness, much like apples with pork and gooseberries with mackerel. That same sourness helps make rhubarb into a successful sherbet, its pale shade of pink-mauve as refreshing as its taste on a hot summer day. In traditional pies, pastries, chutneys, and jams, ginger and orange are natural complements to rhubarb, as well as strawberries, which come into season at the same time.

Hothouse rhubarb arrives in markets early in the new year, with thin, tender, bright pink stems, sweeter than the garden variety, and yellowish leaves which have usually been

287

removed. Unforced rhubarb comes into season in April or so and continues through the summer, its green leaves unfurling to enormous size. The stalks should be eaten only as long as they remain red. As they grow greener and thicker, they become stringier, sourer, and coarser. Rhubarb leaves, especially the ribs, contain oxalic acid, which is poisonous, and should not be eaten at all.

Trim the stalks at the ends, removing any brown spots. Refrigerate them and use soon after purchase or picking. To cook rhubarb, cut the stalks across into ½- to 1-inch chunks and stew (or bake) them with plenty of sugar. Recipes often recommend removing the outer stringy peel from field rhubarb, but I have never found this necessary or desirable, since the rosy color, which sugar helps retain, is in the peel. Simply choose thinner stalks and slice them into short segments. Rhubarb cooks very quickly, fiber and sugar dissolving into a puddle of syrup; cook it no longer than necessary.

Rhubarb without added sugar contains only twenty calories per cup. It is a natural laxative, which is why folk medicine has long considered it a spring tonic.

Rhubarb Pie

The early colonists made so many pies from the hardy rhubarb, which adapted well to the cold New England climate, that they called it pie plant.

> *Double pastry for a 9-inch pie (see page 35)*
> *1½ pounds rhubarb, cut into ½-inch lengths (about 5 cups)*
> *1½ cups white or firmly packed brown sugar, or to taste*
> *3 tablespoons quick-cooking tapioca*
> *1 tablespoon grated orange zest*
> *½ teaspoon ground allspice or other spice*
> *1 tablespoon unsalted butter, cut into small pieces*

Preheat the oven to 400°F.

Roll out half the pastry to ¼-inch thickness and fit it in the bottom of a pie plate. Toss the rhubarb in a bowl with the sugar, tapioca, orange zest, and allspice. Pile the rhubarb mixture into the pie shell and dot with the butter. Roll out the top crust and lay it over the rhubarb. Trim the edges and crimp them together to seal the pie. Cut vents in the top crust to allow the steam to escape. If you like, brush the surface with an egg glaze (1 egg beaten with a little water), or with milk, or simply scatter a little sugar on top: none of these embellishments is necessary. Bake until the crust is golden brown and the rhubarb thickly bubbling through the vents, about 1 hour. Cool the pie and serve it with a jug of heavy cream passed on the side.

MAKES ONE 9-INCH PIE; 6 TO 8 SERVINGS

Rhubarb Strawberry Tart

Concentric circles of rhubarb and strawberries shimmer under a glaze that holds the tart for a day.

10 ounces rhubarb, cut into 1-inch slices
⅓ cup sugar
½ envelope unflavored gelatin
2 tablespoons water
½ cup red currant jelly or seedless raspberry jam, homemade (see page 85 or 276) or storebought
One 9-inch pâte sucrée shell (see page 35), baked
1 cup medium-size fresh strawberries, sliced lengthwise
Whipped cream or crème fraîche (see page 155)

Preheat the oven to 350°F. Place the rhubarb slices in one layer in a wide pan, strew the sugar over them, cover, and bake until the chunks are just tender, about 20 minutes. Let the rhubarb cool undisturbed.

Make the fruit glaze. Sprinkle the gelatin over the water in a cup to soften for 5 minutes. Melt the currant jelly over low heat in a small saucepan. Add the softened gelatin, heat it until dissolved, stirring, then bring to a boil. Set the glaze aside to cool somewhat. Spread a scant half of the glaze over the bottom of the pastry shell and chill to firm it.

Arrange a row of the fattest rhubarb segments in a ring around the outside of the tart shell. Lay a circle of strawberry halves inside the rhubarb. Continue with concentric circles of fruit, finishing with one upright strawberry in the center. Rewarming it if necessary, spoon or brush the remaining glaze over the fruit. Chill the tart until 15 minutes before serving time. Serve with whipped cream or crème fraîche on the side.

MAKES ONE 9-INCH PIE; 6 SERVINGS

Rhubarb Mousse

I like to freeze this mousse in a ring mold, thawing it in the refrigerator the day before serving, and fill it with whole strawberries.

½ envelope unflavored gelatin
¾ cup fresh orange juice
½ pound rhubarb, cut into ½-inch slices
¾ cup sugar, or to taste
2 large egg whites, at room temperature
1 cup chilled heavy cream
Fresh strawberries or mint sprigs for garnish

Soften the gelatin in the orange juice for about 5 minutes, then put it in a small nonreactive saucepan with the rhubarb and sugar. Bring the liquid barely to a boil, cover, and simmer over low heat until the gelatin and sugar are both dissolved and the rhubarb soft, about 5 minutes. Cool and purée in a food processor or blender.

Whip the egg whites in a medium-size bowl until stiff but not dry. In another bowl with a clean, dry mixer or whisk, whip the cream until it hold peaks. Swiftly fold the egg whites into the rhubarb purée, then fold in the whipped cream. Spoon the mixture into a 4½- or 5-cup mold, cover, and chill for at least 3 hours.

To unmold, run the tip of a knife around the edge and dip the mold into hot water for a few seconds. Place the serving plate on top and invert; while holding mold and plate together, jerk downward. You may need to repeat this: be patient. When unmolded, wipe away any melted cream and garnish with fresh whole strawberries or sprigs of garden mint.

MAKES 6 TO 8 SERVINGS

Stewed Rhubarb

This homey dessert of early springtime, when few fruits have yet appeared, can be embellished with strawberries or orange juice as the season progresses. It is also delicious simply spooned over sponge or pound cake. Thinned with water, the same rhubarb compote becomes a refreshing punch for an unseasonably hot spring day. Reducing the sugar turns it into a nouvelle cuisine sauce for rich pork or mackerel.

Alternatively, you can bake rhubarb in its own juices, without water, in a covered dish in a 350°F oven for about 20 minutes; but since stovetop rhubarb is so simple and quick I generally prefer it.

1 pound rhubarb, sliced into 1-inch lengths
1 cup sugar, or to taste

Put the rhubarb in a pot and add water just barely to cover, then the sugar. Bring to a boil and simmer over low heat until the rhubarb is tender, about 5 minutes. Taste to see if it needs more sugar; if so, stir it in—it will dissolve without further cooking. Cool and serve the rhubarb in glass bowls.

MAKES 6 SERVINGS

Rhubarb Strawberry Fool

All kinds of berries and fruit can be made into a fool, a name which captures the fanciful pairing of rich cream and fruit purée. Spring rhubarb and strawberries combine happily, as in this updated fool sparked with orange. If you cook the fruits together, the strawberries will lose their integrity.

> 2 cups fresh strawberries, hulled and sliced
> 3 tablespoons orange-flavored liqueur (optional)
> 2 oranges
> ½ pound rhubarb, cut into ½-inch pieces
> ¾ cup plus 2 tablespoons sugar, or to taste
> ½ cup or more heavy cream, lightly whipped if you wish

Toss the sliced strawberries with the liqueur to macerate. Cut the zest of one orange into fine julienne, and squeeze the juice from both oranges. Put the rhubarb in a nonreactive saucepan with the orange juice and enough water nearly to cover the rhubarb. Add the sugar, bring to a boil, and let boil over low heat until the sugar is dissolved, about 5 minutes. Let the rhubarb cool and stir to break up the chunks; you may purée it in a food processor or blender, but this is not necessary. (This may be done ahead, the fruit covered and chilled.)

To serve, spoon the rhubarb into four dessert bowls, preferably glass. Swirl the cream into the purée, pile the strawberries in the middle, and top with the reserved orange julienne.

MAKES ABOUT 6 SERVINGS

Rhubarb Brown Betty

This old-fashioned dessert can be made with rhubarb and various other fruit as well as the more usual apples. Use white or whole-wheat bread, as you like.

> 1½ pounds rhubarb, cut into 1-inch segments and halved if thick, so that they are about the same size
> 1 cup firmly packed dark brown sugar, or to taste
> 2 large knobs preserved stem ginger (available in Oriental or specialty food stores), minced, or 1 teaspoon ground ginger or other spice
> ¼ cup dark rum (optional)
> 2 cup fresh bread crumbs
> 6 tablespoons (¾ stick) unsalted butter
> ¼ cup chopped pecans or other nuts, lightly toasted (see page 179)

Preheat the oven to 350°F. In a large bowl, combine the rhubarb with the brown sugar, ginger, and rum, stirring to mix them well. In another bowl, mix together the bread crumbs, butter, and nuts. Spread one third of the crumb mixture in the bottom of a buttered 6-cup casserole or deep pie plate. Cover with half the rhubarb mixture. Repeat with another layer of half the remaining crumbs, then the remaining rhubarb, and finally top with the rest of the crumb mixture. Cover the dish loosely with aluminum foil. Bake the brown betty for 25 minutes. Uncover and bake about 25 minutes more, until the crumbs are browned. Serve warm or at room temperature with vanilla ice cream or lightly whipped cream.

MAKES 6 SERVINGS

Rhubarb Sherbet

The refreshing tartness of rhubarb and almost iridescent shadings of color help turn it into an intriguing sherbet. In early spring it is appealing served in scooped-out lime cups, the pale pinks and mauves of the rhubarb showing against the green skin.

½ pound rhubarb, cut into ½-inch slices
1 cup sugar, or to taste
2½ cups water
2 tablespoons fresh lime juice

Put the rhubarb and sugar in a pot with the water, bring to a boil, and simmer, covered, until the sugar is dissolved and the rhubarb tender, about 5 minutes. Cool and purée in a food processor or blender. Add the lime juice and chill thoroughly. Freeze the rhubarb syrup in a sorbetière or an ice cream machine according to the manufacturer's directions. Or freeze according to the directions on page 307. A sprig of mint makes a pretty garnish.

MAKES ABOUT 1 QUART

STRAWBERRIES

The strawberry that we know came about in the eighteenth century after a French spy on a mission to Chile smuggled the large scarlet berry *Fragaria chiloensis* home to France. In King Louis XV's garden at Versailles, the New World berry was crossed with another, *F. virginiana*, which Virginian colonists had sent back to England. The resulting strawberry astonished the king with its increased flavor, size, and fertility, just as its descendants delight us.

"Strawberries, scarlet strawberries!" cried the English street hawkers, whose conical baskets, called pottles, kept the berries from being crushed. At the time of the French Revolution, English gardeners took over strawberry cultivation, growing them outside London to supply the eager market. Strawberries with cream remains the quintessential spring refreshment in England, traditional even today at Wimbledon. In the United States, California breeders expanded the berry's season when they developed the Shasta berry at the turn of the century, suitable for mass production and transportation. But to the connoisseur, the intensity and scent of the wild strawberry remain unsurpassed.

In season, strawberries are best eaten in the patch—lush, juicy, and warm from the sun. Failing a backyard bed or pick-your-own farm, try to find locally grown berries. Their savor and sweetness is balanced by a pleasing acidity lacking in the woolly berries we often tolerate out of season. The peak supply from California and, to a lesser extent, Florida comes in March through June; from November through February supplies are lowest.

Whatever time of year, choose berries that are scarlet, shiny, plump, and fragrant, with fresh green caps. The tiny green seeds mounted on the outside, unique among fruit, give a certain texture. Small berries may have more flavor than large ones, but white shoulders or tips show they have not had enough sun to ripen thoroughly. Also avoid baskets with berries that are spotty, soft, or dull, since one bad berry can quickly spoil the whole batch.

When you get the berries home, chill them in well-ventilated baskets so they can breathe. If they are not fully ripe, you can leave them out overnight to sweeten a little further, but only if they are completely dry. Wash them just before using, if at all, and remove the stems and hulls after, not before, washing. Fresh strawberries do not keep well and should be eaten soon.

A natural complement to strawberries is cream in various forms, whether whipped into clouds, slightly soured as in crème fraîche, clotted as in Devonshire cream, enriched with egg into a custard, or a low-fat substitute such as yogurt. Also on the lighter side, a touch of wine—dry or sweet, still or bubbly, white, red, or fortified—goes uncommonly well. So does a spark of citrus juice or zest. The mellow acidity of a few drops of balsamic vinegar can do wonders for bland berries.

Strawberries go sublimely with all other spring and summer fruits, indeed, with virtually any fruit. They are irresistible with most pastry, whether tart, biscuit, puff, or short-cake. To decorate desserts, the berries' appearance is so beautiful in itself that you need not glaze their top, though no one would complain if you did. Whole berries on stems are perfection dipped in white or dark bittersweet chocolate. To extend strawberry season, you can preserve the fruit in compotes, jam, or vinegar, or freeze berries whole or puréed for later use in ice cream, sherbet, sauce, and other concoctions.

One pint of fresh strawberries, weighing nearly a pound, holds twelve large to thirty-six small berries. That pint yields about three and a half cups of whole berries, two and a quarter cups of sliced berries, and one and two-thirds cups of purée.

Strawberries are very high in vitamin C, with a good amount of potassium and some iron. One cup contains about fifty-five calories.

Kissel

This traditional dessert of tart red fruit from the Baltic region appears in Polish, Russian, and Scandinavian cuisines. Flavored with a little sugar and wine and thickened with corn-starch, it makes a most refreshing summer dessert. It is delicious with other juicy berries and fruits such as blueberries, cranberries, currants, and rhubarb.

2 tablespoons cornstarch
1½ cups water
1 cup dry white wine
¼ cup sugar, or to taste
One 2-inch stick cinnamon
4 cups fresh strawberries, hulled
2 tablespoons fresh lemon juice
2 tablespoons grated lemon zest
2 tablespoons Curaçao or other orange-flavored liqueur (optional)
Crème fraîche (see page 155) or unsweetened whipped cream
Slivered almonds or chopped pistachios (undyed and unsalted), lightly toasted (see page 179),
*   for garnish*

Moisten the cornstarch in a pot with 2 tablespoons of the water, just enough to make a paste. Stir the rest of the water together with the wine and sugar in a large nonreactive saucepan. Put the cinnamon stick in the pot, cover, bring to a boil, and cook for 1 minute. Stir the mixture, which will have thickened. Let the mixture cool somewhat, then discard the cinnamon stick, and add the strawberries. Purée in the food processor with the lemon juice and zest; you may have to do this in batches. Taste carefully for balance and add a touch more sugar if needed. Chill thoroughly, covered.

Shortly before serving, stir in the Curaçao. Ladle the Kissel into attractive glass bowls. Swirl a little crème fraîche into each and serve garnished, if you like, with a few nuts toasted just long enough to bring out their fragrance.

MAKES 6 SERVINGS

Strawberry Jam

This traditional recipe makes a fairly runny jam that is full of the fragrance of fresh strawberries. Wait until peak season, then use the best berries you can find. This jam should be eaten within six months.

> 6 cups fresh strawberries, hulled and halved, quartered if large
> Juice of 1 lemon
> 4 cups sugar (scant 2 pounds)

Combine the strawberies and lemon juice in a large, heavy nonreactive pot. Cook over low heat, stirring occasionally, until a lot of juice runs from the strawberries, enough to float them. Add the sugar, stir to dissolve it, and bring the liquid to a boil. Cook until the jam reaches the setting point, 220°F on a candy thermometer, about 15 minutes, stirring as it boils to avoid scorching. Cool the jam slightly, skim off the scum, and spoon it into warm, clean half-pint jars. Sterilize in a hot water bath (see page 321) and store in a cool, dry cupboard.

MAKES ABOUT 6 HALF-PINT JARS

Strawberries in Strawberry Sauce

To turn this into strawberry shortcake, slice the whole strawberries into the purée and serve on rich biscuits (see page 54), split and lathered with whipped cream.

4 cups fresh strawberries
2 tablespoons sugar, or to taste
3 tablespoons kirsch or other liqueur, or to taste (optional)

Hull the strawberries, cutting the largest into halves or quarters. Set aside a third of them, choosing those that are misshapen or ugly, including the white shoulders of any that did not ripen thoroughly. Purée these by whizzing them in the food processor, pressing them through a sieve, or mashing them with a fork. Stir the sugar and liqueur into the purée and taste to see if it needs more.

Put the whole strawberries in a pretty crystal serving bowl and pour the purée over them to macerate. Serve them with a touch of fresh mint leaves and pass cream on the side.

MAKES 6 OR MORE SERVINGS

Meringue Cups

Serve fresh strawberries, as in the preceding recipe, on these tender meringue cups and drizzle strawberry sauce around or on top. These meringues are handy for holding scoops of ice cream or sherbet, or for poached or mixed fruit of all sorts. Top with grated chocolate, toasted nuts, caramel, or another contrasting sauce. Make them when you have extra egg whites and save them for when you need something unexpectedly or don't feel like cooking.

4 large egg whites, at room temperature
Pinch of salt
1 cup sugar
1 teaspoon pure vanilla extract

Preheat the oven to 225°F. Butter and flour two cookie sheets and set aside.

Put the egg whites in a large bowl and add a pinch of salt. Beat on high until the whites make soft peaks. Gradually add ¾ of the sugar a little at a time, and beat until the meringue makes stiff, satiny peaks. Continue beating until the sugar has dissolved: pinch the meringue to see if you can feel the crystals. For a tender meringue, fold in the remaining sugar at the end with the vanilla.

Put the meringue into a pastry bag fitted with a grooved or rosette tip. Pipe the meringue onto the sheets in 4- or 5-inch spiral rounds, and make a raised edge. Bake in the preheated oven for about 45 minutes (longer if the day is humid), until the meringues are very pale beige. Turn the heat off and let them dry out for at least 15 minutes in the oven. Carefully remove the meringues and store them in tightly closed tins.

MAKES ABOUT 8 CUPS

Strawberries with Banana Yogurt Cream

Bananas puréed with yogurt make a topping for strawberries that is creamy and smooth, yet light and refreshing.

3 cups fresh strawberries, hulled
Sugar to taste (optional)
1 teaspoon grated lemon zest
1 very ripe banana, peeled and sliced
½ cup plain yogurt

Toss the strawberries gently in a bowl with a little sugar, if desired; set aside at room temperature. Put the lemon zest in a food processor along with the banana and yogurt. Combine thoroughly, scraping down the sides once or twice with a rubber spatula. The purée should be the consistency of heavy cream. Cover and chill if time allows.

   Divide the hulled strawberries among four serving plates and spoon the banana yogurt mixture on top, as for cream.

   MAKES 4 SERVINGS

Strawberries Romanoff

Especially at the beginning of the strawberry season, the simplest ways to serve them often taste the best. This one is hard to improve upon.

2 cups fresh strawberries, hulled and halved, quartered if large
1 tablespoons sugar, or to taste
1 teaspoon grated orange zest
1 tablespoon fresh orange juice
2 tablespoons Curaçao or other orange-flavored liqueur, or to taste
Crème fraîche (see page 155) or whipped cream lightly sweetened with confectioners' sugar

Toss all the ingredients together in a bowl except for the crème fraîche. Leave at room temperature if you are going to serve them within an hour or two, or chill for longer. Serve with crème fraîche or crème Chantilly, that is, lightly sweetened whipped cream.

   MAKES 3 TO 4 SERVINGS

   SERVING IDEAS: Serve the strawberries Romanoff, if you like, with a simple lemon cookie (see page 150) or a slice of pound cake. If you have any leftover crêpes (see page 23), ruffle them like flowers in muffin tins and dry them in the oven just long enough to crisp them (10 minutes at 350°F); right before serving dust the crêpes with confectioners' sugar, then spoon the strawberries into the flower cups. Garnish with leaves of fragrant mint or rose geranium.

Strawberries and Custard

This comforting nursery dish is simple and beloved, but a touch of liqueur on the berries turns it into something more sophisticated. Use 2 cups of milk and 2 whole eggs if you prefer, but the custard will not be as tender.

4 large egg yolks
½ cup sugar
Pinch of salt
1½ cups milk
½ cup cream, preferably heavy
1 teaspoon pure vanilla extract
1 teaspoon grated orange zest
2 cups fresh strawberries
2 tablespoons orange-flavored liqueur (optional)

Preheat the oven to 325°F. Beat together in a bowl the egg yolks, all but 2 tablespoons of the sugar, and the salt; stir in the milk, cream, vanilla, and orange zest. Set 6 unbuttered ramekins or custard cups in an ovenproof dish big enough to hold them without touching each other. Pour the custard mixture into the cups and add boiling water to the pan to reach halfway up the sides of the cups. Carefully set the pan in the oven and bake until a knife inserted in the center comes out clean, about 50 minutes. Take out the custards and let them cool completely. (This much can be done a day ahead.)

A few hours before serving, hull the strawberries and halve or quarter them if they are large. Toss them with the remaining sugar and the liqueur, and let the berries macerate for 30 minutes or longer. Do not chill the berries if you plan to serve them soon. Shortly before serving, run a knife around the edges and invert the custards onto individual serving plates. Spoon the strawberries around and serve at once.

MAKES 6 SERVINGS

Coeur à la Crème

Coeur à la crème is a French country dessert that is rustic, simple, and charming. Farmer's cheese (fresh cream cheese) is mixed with cream, lightened with egg whites, packed in a special heart-shaped mold with little holes that allow the whey to drain off, and served with strawberries (or other berries) and French bread. For our health-conscious times, this light version made with low-fat cottage cheese and ricotta is delicious, with a fraction of the calories.

You will need a *coeur à la crème* mold (this recipe is for a large 3½-cup mold, but several smaller ones will do). If you don't have a *coeur à la crème* mold, drain the cheese in a large sieve lined with cheesecloth and then pack the cheese into a mold of any shape, heart or otherwise, before unmolding.

1 pound low-fat cottage cheese
1 pound low-fat ricotta
2 tablespoons sugar, or to taste (optional)
Small pinch of salt
2 large egg whites, at room temperature (optional)
Fresh strawberries (preferably small ones)
Confectioners' sugar for dusting
French bread

Process the cottage cheese in a food processor until it is smooth and light. Add the ricotta, sugar, and salt, and continue processing until the cheeses are well blended and creamy. Beat the egg whites in a medium-size bowl until stiff peaks form, and fold them into the cheese mixture until evenly distributed; do not mix them in the food processor. (You can omit the egg whites entirely if you like.)

Cut a large piece of cheesecloth folded double, big enough to cover the *coeur à la crème* mold with several inches to spare. Rinse the cloth in cold water and squeeze it dry. Lay it over the *coeur à la crème* mold with the sides overlapping. Spoon the cheese into the mold and wrap the cloth over on top to enclose it. Set the mold on a plate, cover, and refrigerate it overnight (or for a couple of days) to let the whey drain off.

To serve the *coeur à la crème,* unwrap the top of the cheesecloth and unmold the heart onto a serving plate, removing the cheesecloth neatly so that its crisscross pattern doesn't smear. Surround the cheese with strawberries—whole if small, halved if large. Sift confectioners' sugar on top and provide slices of good French bread for the cheese.

This dessert is excellent for a large informal party or picnic, especially one with an indefinite number of guests. The amount here will serve any number from eight to sixteen. Just be sure to have enough strawberries—can you ever have too many?

Fresh Strawberry Tart on Puff Pastry

This pastry tart, when made with storebought puff pastry, is more impressive than difficult. The pastry base is baked ahead, cooled, and lined with pastry cream, topped with strawberries and other fresh fruit if you like, then glazed with currant jelly. Although the pastry and cream can be made ahead, the tart should be assembled as close to serving time as possible.

>   1 sheet frozen puff pastry, thawed and chilled
>   1 large egg beaten with 1 tablespoon water
>   1 recipe pastry cream (recipe follows)
>   4 quarts perfect fresh strawberries
>   ½ cup red currant jelly, homemade (see page 85) or storebought
>   1 to 2 tablespoons water or liqueur of choice

On a lightly floured board, cut the pastry sheet in half lenthwise. Wrap one half in plastic wrap and chill. Roll the other out to about 12 x 7 inches and trim the edges. Cut off a half-inch strip in a straight line around the outside. Moisten the edges of the pastry, place the strips along the edges to make a rim, and press firmly into place. Make little notches along the outside edges by pressing the flat of a knife at half-inch intervals around the periphery. Prick the inside of the pastry well with a fork. Brush the tops of the edges with the egg wash, taking care not to let it run down the sides, which would keep the pastry from rising. Cover with plastic wrap and chill the prepared pastry. Repeat with the second piece of pastry and chill.

Preheat the oven to 375°F. Place the pastry shells on an ungreased cookie sheet moistened with a little water. Bake until puffed and golden, about 20 minutes. Take the pastry out and, if the center is puffed up, press down the inside of the shells with a spatula to deflate it. Let it cool.

Shortly before serving, spread a layer of pastry cream on the inside of each pastry shell. Arrange the strawberries and any other fruit, whole, halved, or sliced, in a pleasing pattern on top. Melt the currant jelly in a small saucepan over low heat with the water, stirring. Lightly brush a layer of the preserves over the berries to glaze them. Chill to set. To serve, slice the pastries into rectangles or squares.

MAKES 2 TARTS; 8 TO 12 SERVINGS

Pastry Cream

(CRÈME PATISSIÈRE)

This sturdy custard is invaluable for filling tarts, cream puffs, and other pastries without making them soggy. You can flavor it with coffee, chocolate, or liqueur; lighten it with whipped cream or egg whites; or use it to make a hot soufflé. For even better flavor, steep a vanilla bean in the hot milk, then dry and save the bean for use again.

>   1⅓ cups milk
>   2 large egg yolks

¼ cup sugar

2 tablespoons all-purpose flour

1 teaspoon pure vanilla extract or liqueur of your choice

In a small saucepan over medium-low heat bring the milk barely to a boil. In a medium-size bowl, beat together the egg yolks and sugar until thick and pale. Stir in the flour, then whisk the hot milk into the egg-yolk mixture until it is smooth. Return the mixture to the pan and, whisking constantly, bring it to a boil; lower the heat and cook 2 to 3 minutes, until the flour is cooked. Stir in the vanilla extract and cool. The pastry cream, covered and refrigerated, will keep for a few days.

MAKES ABOUT 2 CUPS

Strawberry Mousse Cake

This strawberry extravaganza is for a special celebration—when you need something sumptuous yet practical, made ahead, and large enough to serve a crowd. Most of its parts can be made ahead, so that the liqueur-soaked layers of cake assembled in a springform pan are filled with whole strawberries and berry mousse (really a Bavarian cream), chilled up to a day ahead until set, removed from the springform pan, and then decorated with whipped cream, fresh berries, and mint leaves.

⅔ cup sugar

⅓ cup water

3 tablespoons orange-flavored liqueur

4 cups fresh strawberries, preferably smaller, regular ones, plus another 4 cups for the mousse
  (since they will be puréed they can be irregular)

1 recipe Strawberry Bavarian Cream (see page 304)

Two 8-inch vanilla génoise cakes (recipe follows) or sponge cakes (see page 302)

1 cup chilled heavy cream

Confectioners' sugar to taste

To make a syrup, combine the sugar with the water and liqueur in a small saucepan. Bring to a boil, let boil over low heat, covered, until the sugar is dissolved, about 5 minutes. Let the syrup cool. (The syrup can stored indefinitely in a jar in the refrigerator.)

Hull the small, regular strawberries, set them on their stem ends not quite touching each other on a plate, and cut their shoulders if necessary so they stand at the same height. These berries will stand between the two cakes. Wash and hull the remaining less perfect berries, and purée them with any trimmings in the food processor. The purée should measure 1½ cups. Keep the regular berries refrigerated for garnishing the finished cake right before serving.

Make the strawberry Bavarian cream and before it has set, assemble the cake, anywhere from six to twenty-four hours before you plan to serve it.

With a long thin knife, cut each cake across in half as evenly as possible. Choose the flattest for the top of the cake; keep track of how the cakes fit together and which belongs on top.

Put the bottom of the four cake layers centered in an 8-inch springform pan (with the side buckled in place) and spoon a quarter of the liqueur syrup over the surface. Spoon a little of the strawberry mousse evenly over the layer, letting some of it spill over the outside edge. Fit the next layer of cake on top and spoon more of the syrup over. Stand the reserved berries on top of thé cake, close but not touching each other, and carefully spoon a thick layer of mousse between and up to the tops of the berries. Let some of the mousse spill over the sides of the cake. Set the third layer of cake down so that the berries support it. Spoon over some of the syrup and a thin layer of mousse. Set the last layer of cake on top and spread the remaining mousse over the surface. If you have extra mousse let it spill over the sides. Smooth the mousse over the top, put plastic wrap over without touching, and refrigerate for at least 4 hours.

To complete the cake before serving, run a knife around the inside of the springform pan between the mousse and the metal, and carefully remove the side. Whip the heavy cream until stiff peaks form, adding confectioners' sugar to taste. With a pastry bag, pipe rosettes or whatever decoration you like around the sides and top of the cake. Cover any imperfections with decoration and use more cream if you wish, but be sure to let some of the pink mousse show through. Hull some of the remaining strawberries and place them on and around the cake, halved if flat, whole if standing, in a pretty pattern accented by fresh mint leaves. Refrigerate until serving time. Slice the mousse cake into thin wedges for serving.

MAKES ONE 8-INCH CAKE; 15 TO 16 SERVINGS

Vanilla Génoise Cake

This classic French cake, rich and elegant, makes an excellent base for all kinds of creamy and fruity toppings.

6 tablespoons (¾ stick) unsalted butter
6 large eggs, at room temperature
⅔ cup sugar
1 teaspoon pure vanilla extract
1 cup all-purpose flour

Preheat the oven to 350°F. Butter and flour two 8-inch cake pans, tapping out the excess. Melt the butter in a small pan over low heat without letting it color or separate; allow it to cool again without solidifying. Have all the other cake ingredients measured and ready.

Put the eggs in a deep bowl with the sugar and vanilla. Place the bowl in a warm spot, such as on top of the stove or over hot water, to slightly warm the ingredients. With an electric beater mix them together on low speed. As the eggs become frothy with incorporated air, turn the beater to medium speed, then high. Beat for 10 minutes or more, until the batter turns pale in color, forms ribbons, and at least doubles in volume. As the air bubbles gradually get very small, the batter will become billowy. If in doubt, keep on beating. Gradually sift the flour into the egg batter, folding it in with a circular motion. Similarly fold in the butter in a slow, steady stream, until it is just incorporated. Pour the batter into the two prepared cake pans, and bake them in the preheated oven until the cake leaves the edges of the pans, 25 to 30 minutes. Let them cool for 5 to 10 minutes, then turn them out onto racks to cool completely. Wrap the cakes separately in plastic wrap and store in the refrigerator for a few days or in the freezer for longer.

MAKES TWO 8-INCH CAKES

Strawberry Trifle

This British classic, infinitely varied, layers sherry-laced sponge cake, creamy custard, and colorful fruit. I prefer seasonal fresh fruit and purée to preserved or candied fruit, but suit your imagination. The one essential is to assemble the trifle at least eight hours ahead, preferably overnight, to allow the cake to absorb the different flavors. This is a good place to use broken sponge cakes or imperfect yet fully ripened fruit, but never second-rate ingredients. Made with good-quality custard, sponge, and fruit, it deserves its place of honor among British puddings.

> *2 cups fresh strawberries*
> *Sugar to taste*
> *2 vanilla sponge cake rounds (see page 283)*
> *½ cup sherry, or to taste*
> *1 cup raspberry sauce or purée (see pages 279 or 285); if you prefer, use fruit of a contrasting color*
> *1 recipe crème anglaise (see page 17)*
> *¾ cup heavy cream*
> *Confectioners' sugar to taste*

Saving several perfect fresh strawberries for garnish, hull and slice the rest. Put them in a bowl with a little sugar, stir, and allow to macerate.

Slice the sponge cakes across as evenly as you can to make 4 thin layers and douse each with some of the sherry. Put one in the bottom of a large, deep, steep-sided glass dish, trimming the sides of the cake as needed to make it fit. Spoon half the raspberry purée over the cake and spread a third of the custard on top, allowing some of the purée and custard to dribble over the side for effect if you like. Place another layer of cake on the custard, then spread with half the sliced strawberries and another third of the custard. Repeat with the third layer of cake and the remaining raspberry purée and custard. Top with the last layer of cake and the rest of the sliced strawberries with their juice. Cover the trifle with plastic wrap and refrigerate for at least 8 hours, preferably 24.

Shortly before serving, whip the cream to firm peaks, sweeten it with confectioners' sugar, and spoon or pipe it over the top of the trifle to make it look pretty. Garnish with the reserved strawberries, perhaps some chopped nuts or angelica or fresh mint leaves.

MAKES 8 OR MORE SERVINGS

Strawberry Bavarian Cream

This wonderful mousse dessert can be chilled in a Bavarian cream mold with all the fanciful turrets and towers that look like a castle of King Ludwig. Or pile it into a soufflé dish with a paper collar tied around to resemble a hot soufflé risen high (you can even dust a little praline powder, page 239, on top to look like the oven's browning). Or chill half of the mousse in a ring mold to be filled with fresh berries, and the other half in individual ramekins, to be frozen and saved for a later occasion.

1 envelope unflavored gelatin
¼ cup orange-flavored liqueur
1 cup milk
4 large egg yolks
½ cup sugar
1½ cups strawberry purée (made from 1 quart hulled berries)
3 large egg whites, at room temperature
1 cup chilled heavy cream
Fresh strawberries and mint leaves or other greenery for garnish

Soften the gelatin in the orange liqueur for at least 5 minutes. Then heat the mixture over low heat, stirring, until the gelatin is completely dissolved.

To make the custard, scald the cup of milk in a pan over medium-low heat, until little bubbles appear around the edges (do not let it boil). Beat together the egg yolks and sugar in a medium-size bowl. Stirring the yolk mixture continuously to keep the eggs from scrambling, pour the heated milk into the yolks in a slow, steady stream. Pour the custard back into the saucepan. Over low heat stir the custard just until it thickens (any longer will scramble the eggs) and coats the back of a spoon. Take the pan off the heat and continue beating a little longer until the custard cools somewhat. Stir the gelatin mixture and the strawberry purée into the custard.

Whip the egg whites in a medium-size bowl until they make stiff peaks. In a large chilled bowl and with a clean beater or mixer, whip the heavy cream into soft high peaks. Quickly fold the egg whites into the custard mixture until no streaks of white remain. Then fold it into the whipped cream until it too is evenly distributed. Pour the mixture into a 7- or 8-cup mold, cover, and chill well until the gelatin is set, at least 4 hours. You can freeze the Bavarian cream a week or even a month ahead of time and thaw it overnight in the refrigerator before serving.

To serve, run a knife inside around the rim, dip the mold in hot water for a few seconds, and invert onto a serving platter with a good jerk or two. Center the mousse on the platter while still in the mold. Mop up any melted cream and garnish with fresh whole berries and mint leaves, strawberry purée, whatever you fancy. A little garnish goes a long way here.

MAKES ABOUT 7 CUPS OF MOUSSE; 8 OR MORE SERVINGS

Strawberry Sablés

Sablés are nothing more than French shortbread cookies, named for their sandy texture. Whole strawberries are sandwiched in between two fluted rounds, with purée and whipped cream to moisten them. Of course, you can use other fruit such as raspberries, peaches, apricots, or plums instead.

FOR THE SABLÉS
½ cup (1 stick; ¼ pound) unsalted butter, cut into pieces
½ cup sugar
2 large egg yolks
¼ teaspoon pure vanilla extract
Pinch of salt
1⅓ cups all-purpose flour

FOR THE STRAWBERRY TOPPING
5 cups small fresh strawberries
¼ cup sugar
2 tablespoons orange-flavored liqueur

TO COMPLETE
Confectioners' sugar for dusting
Whipped cream

First make the sablés. Cream the butter and sugar together in a food processor for about 1 minute, stopping to scrape down the sides with a rubber spatula. Blend in the egg yolks, vanilla, and salt. With the machine running, gradually add the flour through the feed tube and mix just to incorporate it. Divide the dough in half, wrap each tightly in plastic wrap, and flatten into disks. Chill the dough for several hours or overnight.

Preheat the oven to 350°F and butter cookie sheets. Because this dough is so rich and crumbly, roll out one disk between two sheets of waxed paper to ⅛-inch thickness. Cut out 6 rounds with a 3½- to 4-inch fluted cutter. Transfer them with a spatula to a cookie sheet and chill. Repeat with the remaining dough, making 12 rounds in all. Bake the sablés until pale golden, about 8 minutes. Cool on racks.

Setting aside 6 perfect strawberries for garnish, hull the remaining berries. Set aside 3 cups of berries of equal size. Purée the remaining berries in the food processor with the sugar and liqueur. Put the purée in a bowl, cover, and chill.

Just before serving, set one sablé on each of six dessert plates. Dividing the 3 cups of strawberries evenly among the plates, arrange them stem-side down on the sablés (to make them fit evenly, you may need to halve a few for the middle). Sift confectioners' sugar on top of the remaining 6 sablés and set them on top of the strawberries. Put the 6 reserved strawberries on top of the sablés, fanned if you like. Surround the sablés with the strawberry purée and pass whipped cream separately.

MAKES 6 SERVINGS

Quick Strawberry Ice Cream

This ice cream is surprisingly delicious, considering how little time and effort it takes. The berries must be frozen individually rather than in a block, and the cream must be very cold. It is best if eaten soon after it is made. Soften any leftovers in the refrigerator before serving. You can make this ice cream with other berries and cubed fruit so long as they are frozen in individual small pieces.

2½ cups very cold light cream or half-and-half
½ cup sugar
2 tablespoons fresh lemon juice
One 1¼-pound package unsweetened strawberries individually frozen, still frozen (preferably berries on the small side)

Put all the ingredients in the food processor and process until combined, the cream and strawberries forming a soft billowy cream with bits of berry visible. Scrape down the sides once or twice with a rubber spatula. Put the ice cream in the freezer in a covered container to firm up a little before serving.

MAKES 6 TO 7 CUPS; ABOUT 6 SERVINGS

Strawberry Sherbet

The high proportion of berries makes this sherbet intensely fruity. Call it a sorbet, if you prefer, to use the French term; sherbet is the English term and usually excludes milk. You can stir in a little beaten egg white or Italian meringue during the final freezing for a smoother texture and greater volume, but it changes the taste and color. Experiment to see which method you like best.

1¼ cups sugar
1¼ cups water
4 cups fresh strawberries
3 tablespoons fresh lemon juice

First make a simple syrup by combining the sugar and water in a pot and bringing to a boil; let boil over low heat, covered, until the sugar is dissolved, about 5 minutes. Let the syrup cool. You should have about 2 cups of this simple syrup.

Hull the strawberries and purée them by whizzing them in a food processor or by pressing them through a sieve with the back of a spoon. You should have about 3½ cups of purée. Add the lemon juice and cooled syrup. Cover and chill thoroughly in the refrigerator.

Freeze the sherbet in a sorbetière or an ice cream machine according to the manufacturer's directions, or in a bowl in the freezer, stirring the sherbet from time to time to keep ice crystals from forming. Or spoon the sweetened purée into ice cube trays (you will need about four) and freeze solid; whiz several cubes at a time in the food processor, breaking up the cubes and scraping down the sides with a rubber spatula several times; keep the smoothed and finished batches in the freezer until all the sherbet is made. Sherbet made by this method is best served within 2 to 4 hours but holds well for several days in the freezer, softened slightly in the refrigerator shortly before serving. Sherbert with higher fruit content will stay softer.

MAKES 2 SCANT QUARTS

WATERMELON

If watermelon refreshes us on a hot summer's day, imagine how it must taste to someone lost in the African desert during a drought. The aptly named melon originated on that great continent, where the explorer David Livingstone found large stretches of them growing wild in the Kalahari Desert. Each melon, 92 percent water, is an oasis in itself.

Long before Livingstone's discovery, African slaves brought the seed to this continent, and by 1629 it was growing in Massachusetts. The giant melon prefers a hot, dry climate and sandy soil, so the deep South is where it thrives in the United States. The little town of Hope, Arkansas, latterly renowned as the birthplace of Bill Clinton, has the right combination of climate, soil, seed, and tradition to produce champion melons. Heavy rainfall made the vines grow so fast one year, a native related, that they had to put roller skates under the watermelons to keep them attached. But the 1991 *Guinness Book of World Records* gives the prize to a 279-pound specimen grown in 1988 by Bill Rogerson of Robertsville, North Carolina. Dr. Livingstone, I presume, would agree that that's a thirst-quencher.

The watermelon, *Citrullus lanatus*, belongs to a different genus than other melons, which are distant relatives. Botanically it is close kin to the cucumber, another gourd: gardeners know they must plant the two far apart to avoid cross-pollination and muddled flavors. Watermelon shapes come small and round or large and oval, and melons weigh anywhere from five pounds up to thirty or forty pounds, or many times higher for the giants. Small melons are handier for most households, but large ones have a higher proportion of edible flesh.

Smooth green skin and scarlet flesh punctuated with black seeds add to the watermelon's appeal. Depending on variety, the skin can vary from deep solid green to lighter green with darker wavy or mottled stripes. Yellow-fleshed varieties, ranging from orange to pale yellow, now seen on the market are more novel than new: the yellow watermelon has actually been around for a while. Some people may like it, but for me the vibrant red is part of the melon's attraction on a hot summer day.

Of the four basic types of watermelon commercially available, the picnic is large and oblong (fifteen to forty-five pounds; Charleston Grey, Jubilee, Peacock, and Allsweet are leading varieties), with red or yellow flesh. The round Sugar Baby and Ice-Box varieties (five to fifteen pounds) are convenient for ordinary households. Seedless (ten to twenty-five pounds) is oval or round, with the obvious advantage of no seeds. Crimson Sweet is another round to oval melon (sixteen to thirty-five pounds) with deep red flesh. Yellow Flesh (ten to thirty pounds) is oblong, with a yellow interior. Some other varieties can have yellow flesh too.

The best way to choose a good whole melon is to choose a good grocer. Aside from cutting out a plug, look for firm, even, symmetrical melons with a waxy sheen on the skin. The underside is yellowish (not white or very pale green) where it sat on the ground, but otherwise the skin should have the green markings typical of its variety. Cut watermelons should have strong color and flesh that is crisp, not mealy, dry, or watery. Seed color can vary from black to gray to white.

Watermelons need to wait about a week after picking for best flavor. Uncut melons kept at room temperature can improve in flavor, so don't chill yours until soon before you plan to serve it. Once picked, the sugar content (8 percent) of a ripe watermelon will not actually increase, although it may seem sweeter, but the color will deepen. The flesh of cut watermelons should be covered with plastic wrap and chilled.

In Greece watermelon seeds are toasted as a snack, much as we eat sunflower or pumpkin seeds. In Italy the rind is candied, in contrast to Americans' pickled rind as a savory condiment. Italians also like to make watermelon puddings, particularly the *gelu u muluni* of Sicily, made with ground almonds, chocolate, and cinnamon. Americans prefer simpler watermelon desserts, such as fruit cups, melon balls, or ices. On a hot summer day nothing beats a slice of fresh watermelon.

As for nutrition, watermelon is high in vitamin C, fairly good in vitamins A and B, with some potassium. It has so much water that there's little room left for calories (eighty per ten ounces)—just the thing for dieters, marathoners, and lost explorers.

Watermelon Rum Cocktail

The color and scent as much as the flavor of watermelon add to this drink's summery appeal.

> *4 ounces watermelon juice*
> *2 ounces light rum*
> *2 ounces soda water*
> *Juice of ½ lime*
> *Ice cubes*
> *Lime slice for garnish*

Pass the watermelon juice through a fine sieve to remove any seeds and fiber. Pour it into a tall glass with the rum, soda, and lime juice. Add ice cubes and top with the slice of lime.

MAKES 1 SERVING

Watermelon Rind Pickle

Alum gives watermelon rind its special crunch, but you can make very good pickles without it.

  3 pounds watermelon rind, preferably from a thick-skinned melon, cut into manageable
     pieces (about 5 pints)
  1 tablespoon alum (available at drugstores; ask the pharmacist)
  ¼ cup salt
  1 gallon water
  1 quart cider vinegar (at least 5% acidity)
  6 cups (3 pounds) sugar
  One 2-inch stick cinnamon
  12 whole cloves
  12 allspice berries
  1 lemon, sliced and seeded

Remove any pink flesh from the watermelon rind and peel the skin. Cut the white rind
into bite-size pieces about 1 inch square. Put the alum and salt in a large pot with the
water and stir to dissolve them; soak the watermelon rind in it overnight, covered. The
next morning rinse the rind thoroughly in clear water to remove the alum and salt, and
drain well.

   In a large pot, make a syrup with the vinegar and sugar: bring the liquid to a boil
and let boil until the sugar is dissolved, about 10 minutes. While the sugar is dissolving,
tie the spices securely in a cheesecloth or muslin bag, so you can remove them later. Drop
the bag of spices and sliced lemon along with the watermelon rind into the syrup. Return
the syrup to a boil, then simmer over low heat until the rind becomes tender and translucent,
30 to 40 minutes. Remove and discard the bag of spices and lemon. With a slotted spoon
ladle the watermelon rind into clean, warm preserving jars. Boil the syrup up again, pour
it over the rind, jiggling the rind to release all the air bubbles and making sure the rind is
covered. Seal the jars and sterilize them in a hot water bath (see page 321). Store in a cool,
dark cupboard. Let the pickles mature for at least a week before opening; refrigerate after
opening.

   MAKES ABOUT 4½ PINTS

Spiked Watermelon

For an adult picnic this makes a festive finale, but be sure to tell your guests that the melon
is spiked.

1 whole watermelon

½ cup or more liquor (rum, gin, Curaçao, white wine, or other liquor), depending on the size of the melon, the strength of the liquor, and your guests' taste and tolerance; a very large "picnic" melon will take a whole bottle of white wine

Cut a 1-inch round plug from the top of a whole watermelon (if it is very large, cut two or three holes). Reserve the plug. Slowly pour the liquor into the hole, as much as the melon and your judgment will allow, and replug. Let the watermelon sit for half a day for the liquor to be absorbed throughout the melon. Chill it before serving, and cut the melon into thin slices.

Fresh Fruit Compote in Watermelon Shell

If you like carving a Halloween pumpkin, here is a summertime equivalent that can be as simple or ambitious as you like.

1 small round watermelon
Juice of 1 lemon
¼ cup sugar, or to taste
3 large ripe peaches, peeled, pitted, and sliced
½ pound fresh Bing cherries, pitted (about 1 cup)
2 kiwi, peeled, halved, and sliced
2 cups fresh strawberries, hulled and halved or quartered if large
1 cup fresh raspberries
3 tablespoons chopped fresh mint

Decide on the design of your watermelon shell. Zigzag edge, rounded scallops, acanthus leaves, basket with handle, or swan with arching neck and ruffled wings are all attractive designs that can be elaborated if you wish. The most complicated need not be best.

First cut a thin, flat slice off the bottom of the melon to make a stable base. For a zigzag (perhaps the simplest), with a short sharp knife cut along the equator of the melon, or at a latitude slightly north, making sure you come out right at the end. Whatever you decide, pencil markings help ensure accuracy.

Scoop out 3 cups of melon balls with a melon baller, pressing the large scoop deep into the flesh until the juice comes out the hole in the bottom of the baller; twist to cut a whole ball and remove. Remove any seeds and toss the melon balls with the lemon juice and sugar. Scoop out the rest of the watermelon, leaving a thin red liner; drain well (use the rest of the flesh for granita or one of the other recipes, and the rind of the top for pickles). Put the melon balls in the shell, and stir in the remaining fruit, the fragile berries last. Aim for contrasting shapes, colors, and flavors. Cover the melon in plastic wrap and chill. Shortly before serving, stir in the fresh mint. Serve the fruit in the watermelon, spooning it into bowls at table.

MAKES 8 SERVINGS

Watermelon Granita

Granita is like water ice or sherbet, but less sweet and smooth, with an intentionally grainy texture from the ice crystals—a perfect refresher for hot summer weather. This is an excellent way to use up very ripe (but not overripe) watermelon left over from recipes such as the compote above. Call it slush and children will want to make it with you.

4 cups seedless watermelon purée
½ cup sugar, or to taste, depending on the sweetness of the melon
Juice of 1 lemon

Put the watermelon purée in a bowl, add the sugar (hold some back to avoid oversweetening) and lemon juice, and stir until the sugar has dissolved. Cover and chill thoroughly.

Pour the watermelon mixture into a wide shallow pan and set it in the freezer. As it begins to freeze, stir from time to time to break up the ice crystals, but do not try to smooth them as for sherbet. The granita takes about 3 hours to freeze in an ordinary home freezer. To serve, spoon into bowls.

MAKES ABOUT 1 QUART

EXOTIC FRUITS

ASIAN PEAR

Also called Nashi, Chinese, and Oriental pear, among other names, the Asian pear is distantly related to ordinary pears. It exists in many different varieties which can look unlike each other, but in general resembles a very round, firm apple with a green, yellow, or brownish skin. It is grown in Japan and on the West Coast and available in late summer through fall. Select those with the most scent. It needs no ripening after purchase and keeps for a long time in the refrigerator.

The Asian pear is immensely crisp, crunchy, and yet juicy all at once, and you can cut one into extremely thin slices that hold their texture. With a mild fragrance, the taste of the raw fruit is faintly sweet and acid—in other words, bland but refreshing. Cooked, the flavor becomes somewhat stronger, but the texture remains crisp. You can cook Asian pear by all the usual methods, but it requires more time and, in fact, seems almost indestructible. Its elusive flavor disappears when mixed with other assertive fruits.

A medium-size Asian pear contains about sixty calories. It supplies some vitamin A and C and a small amount of fiber.

ATEMOYA

This fruit is a recent cross between the cherimoya (see page 314) and the sugar apple, two tropical American fruits of the *Annona* genus. The outside looks like "a distorted, slightly melted, Stone Age artichoke," as Elizabeth Schneider wryly describes it. The heart-shaped fruit has pale green skin and bumps that look like leaves that didn't quite emerge. Ripened at room temperature, the skin yields to gentle pressure, starts to split open, and turns dark. Inside, the cream-colored flesh is sweet, smooth, soft, and rich, tasting like nothing so much as custard, punctuated by dark, flat, shiny seeds.

Cultivated in Florida, atemoya is available from August to November. Try to purchase fruit that has not yet cracked open from ripeness. When it reaches that point at home, wrap or cover it. Keep it at room temperature until ripe, and only then refrigerate it. It will keep for a few days more, the skin darkening harmlessly in the cold like that of banana.

To eat atemoya, simply cut it in half and spoon out the pulp. It is also delicious in fruit compotes, sherbets, mousses, and puddings, especially mixed with or set off by other tropical fruits.

Atemoya is rich in vitamins C and K as well as potassium and is fairly high in calories, one third of a cup containing about ninety-four calories.

CARAMBOLA

Carambola is perhaps better known by its descriptive common name of star fruit: cut across, it forms a five-pointed star. About four to five inches long and some two inches across, the shape is oval. The thin, smooth skin ripens to yellow (white in two varieties, both sweet), and the pale yellow flesh is translucent, crisp, and juicy, with occasional seeds. The taste can be acidic or sweet, depending on the variety. In general, the fruit with thicker ribs are of the sweeter varieties, those with thinner ribs tarter.

Carambola (pronounced with the emphasis on the penultimate BO syllable) comes from Malaya in Southeast Asia and is increasingly available in American markets, especially those in Latin American and Caribbean neighborhoods. Florida produces most of those we see in continental American markets.

Star fruit's main season is fall and winter and it is available between August and March. Choose shiny, plump, firm fruit without brown discoloration. If green and still unripe, allow it to ripen at room temperature until golden and fragrant. It keeps well in the refrigerator, up to a week. If the edges of the ribs turn brown, simply shave them off with a vegetable peeler. No further peeling is necessary. Slice the fruit across thinly into stars. You can remove any seeds with the tip of a knife. Like kiwi, the flesh will not turn dark until long after it is cut.

The tropical carambola, with its gently refreshing acidity, goes well with all manner of foods, savory and sweet, and can be puréed into puddings and sherbets. But the shape is what makes it extraordinary, so play it up—but for greatest effect with restraint. Flash slices in a pan to heat them through for poultry and seafood dishes. Add slices to vegetable salads, fruit compotes, pickles, chutneys, and other preserves. Serve with eloquent simplicity in a light syrup, or adorn the surface of a tart with a single layer of slices. At the time of the winter solstice, equally appropriate for Christmas, Hanukkah, and New Year's Eve, a golden star on anything makes a festive and glamorous garnish.

Carambola contains ten calories per ounce, or forty calories per medium-size fruit. As for nutrition, sweet and sour varieties both offer vitamin C, potassium, and fiber.

CHERIMOYA

This South American fruit, also known as a custard apple, has pale green skin that gradually ripens to grayish then brownish green. It looks slightly like a large artichoke or pine cone with closed scales and comes in various sizes weighing from a half to two pounds. The flesh inside is creamy and custardlike, juicy and smooth, but with a slightly grainy texture and fibrous core. Its flavor has overtones of several tropical fruits and lots of dark seeds like those in watermelon. Because of new cherimoya varieties and hybrids such as the atemoya (see page 313), there is more and more confusion as the fruit becomes better known.

Cherimóya is available from late November through May, increasingly grown in California. Because it is very sensitive to cold temperatures, avoid fruit with blotchy skin. Ripen it at room temperature for a few days up to a week, out of direct sunlight and turned often, like an avocado, until it gives to gentle pressure and turns brownish green. Chill after, not before, it turns ripe. To eat cherimoya, cut it lengthwise in half and scoop out the flesh with a spoon, perhaps pouring on a little cream. It makes a fine addition to tropical fruit salads and compotes and works well puréed into sauces, sherbets, puddings, and mousses. Citrus sets off its rich smoothness.

Full of fiber, cherimoya contains a moderate amount of vitamin C, iron, and niacin and is fairly high in calories.

FEIJOA

The feijoa belongs to the aromatic myrtle family and is native to South America. As an attractive evergreen with scarlet blooms, it is sometimes grown as an ornamental. The fruit looks like a large plum, oval and up to 3 inches long, with jade green to dull olive skin sometimes touched with red. Inside the thin skin, the flesh is creamy pale gold with tiny edible seeds in a central cavity, soft but granular in consistency.

Fruit found in American markets from March through June comes from New Zealand. A smaller crop from California is available from September through January. The feijoa (pronounced fay-YO-ah) is sometimes marketed as pineapple guava or even (incorrectly) as guava, which is confusing. Leave the fruit in a cool room to ripen; to hasten the process, enclose it in a paper bag with an apple. Immature, the taste is tart, even bitter. As the fruit ripens, its perfume grows rich, the flesh tender. Ripe fruit can be stored briefly in the refrigerator. You can keep purée in the freezer.

Feijoa has an assertive aroma which can overwhelm other fruit, but combines well with tropical flavors and spices. Like many tart-sweet fruits, its ambiguity suits both sweet and savory dishes. Raw, sautéed or poached, sliced or puréed, preserved in jellies and chutneys, baked or frozen, feijoa is surprisingly versatile.

Feijoa contains plenty of vitamin C and potassium.

GUAVA

Guava, native to Brazil, is found all over Latin America. Disseminated by sailors and birds, it now grows in tropical and semitropical regions around the world. Guava takes diverse shapes—pear, oval, round—and colors—green, white, yellow, red—but because it is vulnerable to fruit flies, virtually the only guavas commercially produced in the United States come from Florida.

These domestic guavas are oval and green maturing to yellow. For determining ripeness, follow your sense of smell. An immature guava will give off a somewhat unpleasant odor (described as "zoo-ish" by Elizabeth Schneider). In a few short days at room temperature that odor will become a heavenly sweet tropical fragrance that wafts throughout your kitchen. The flesh will soften too. You can refrigerate such a guava for a day or two once it is ripe—never before—but use it soon, before the texture becomes gravelly.

The inside of a Floridian guava has white to coral or carnelian pink flesh with many small stony seeds that need to be strained or picked out. Depending on how you plan to use it, you will probably want to peel the skin and slice or purée and strain the flesh. The pulp is dense and viscous, tart yet sweet, musky and highly aromatic.

Guava can be prepared in a wide variety of ways. The purée makes a good sauce for rich meat and poultry, as well as a base or filling for mousses, puddings, fools, sponge cakes, and dessert sauces. Some people like to stew guavas in syrup to flavor fruit compotes and sherbets, perhaps serving the poached guava slices separately. Guava nectar makes a luscious tropical drink, and guava liqueur is even more exotic. *Goyabada,* from the original Caribbean name, is a Brazilian fruit paste, like apricot leather, made from guava purée and served with lamb and other meats, with creamy cheese for dessert, or with coffee as an after-dinner sweetmeat. Sour guavas make a luscious jelly, but Elizabeth Schneider considers it highly unpredictable to make at home. Guava jelly is so delicious that I suggest buying it ready-made.

Feijoa (see page 315), although similar in size and shape, is sometimes misleadingly and mistakenly marketed as guava.

Nutritionally, a guava offers a wealth of vitamins A and C, some potassium, but only about forty-five calories.

KIWANO

This fruit is a brilliant golden orange oval about five inches long, with spikes all over. Its appearance, at once startling and droll, is like a comic-book creature in neon colors from either the deep sea or outer space. The kiwano, in fact, is an ancient fruit native to Africa and now cultivated in New Zealand and California. Common names are horned melon or horned cucumber. The green pulp inside, gelatinous and juicy, holds lots of white seeds like those of melons. The kiwano keeps at room temperature for up to six months and is available year-round. Its flavor is very subtle, many would say bland. Since the fruit is very expensive, choose it for its charmingly disarming looks.

LYCHEE

Lychee or litchi is the fruit of a tall evergreen native to tropical Southeast Asia. A favorite in Chinese cuisine for thousands of years, canned lychees are served for dessert in many

Chinese American restaurants. Oriental markets sometimes import fresh lychees from the Far East, but increasingly the fruit is shipped to American markets from Florida and Mexico for a month in early summer.

The red bumpy covering, thin but leathery, turns brown as it loses its freshness, so try to choose ruddier lychees. Inside the translucent ivory fruit, tasting like sweetly scented grapes, surrounds a smooth brown inedible seed. Fresh lychees keep for some weeks in the refrigerator, the skins quickly turning brown, the perfume gradually dissipating. Serve the white edible lychee pulp either by itself or mixed with other tropical and soft fruits.

Lychees are high in vitamin C and potassium, with three and a half ounces (about ten lychees) containing approximately sixty-six calories.

PASSION FRUIT

If you think that passion fruit is a potion for erotic pleasures, an elixir of love, you should know that this Brazilian fruit is named for the religious symbolism suggested by its elaborate blossom. To early Spanish Jesuit missionaries in the South American wilderness, it represented Christ's crucifixion. Various parts of the magnificent white, gold, and purple flower represent the crown of thorns, the three nails, the five wounds, the twelve apostles, and so on.

There are many varieties of passion fruit. The fruit of the variety primarily available in this country is downright plain. Also called granadilla, meaning "little pomegranate," for its many seeds, it looks like a large, purple-brown egg dried and wrinkled on the outside and filled with seedy ochre-colored pulp. The lemony taste, however, is fragrant, intense, and potent, and a little goes a long way. Most of the passion fruit sold in American markets, from New Zealand (February to July), Florida (July to March), or California (November), is dark and dusty, but varieties from tropical rather than subtropical climates have red or yellow skins.

Choose fruit that feels heavy for its size and keep at room temperature until the skin is dimpled. Refrigerate it up to a week or freeze it whole in a plastic bag for longer keeping. To use the fruit, wipe the skin if it has become moldy. Cut into it with a short, sharp knife over a bowl to catch any of the slightly sticky juice. You can sieve out the many edible crunchy seeds if you wish. Use this very expensive fruit diluted with syrup or cream as a sauce, mixed into drinks and punches, or in sherbets, custards, and mousses. The seeds retain the powerful perfume, so you can use them for effect.

Passion fruit contains vitamins A and C, and three and a half ounces—a large amount—contain ninety calories.

PEPINO

Pepino, which means cucumber in Spanish, has many common names—pepino melon, melon pear, and mellowfruit. All of them hint at its delicate, elusive flavor. The small oval fruit, slightly pointed at one end, is yellow with purple stripes that look like quick brushstrokes of paint. The thin skin is very smooth, like that of its relative the eggplant. Inside, the flesh is golden with edible seeds, silky smooth and juicy, but less sweet than melon.

Pepino melon originally came from South America, but those found in American markets in late winter and spring are imported from New Zealand. When ripe it should yield to gentle pressure and smell sweet and fragrant. Elizabeth Schneider observes that in riper pepinos the yellow background of the skin should be more golden or even pinkish in color. Prepare pepino as you would melon.

Pepino melon contains a generous amount of vitamin C and some vitamins A and B. Low in calories, three and a third ounces of fruit contain only twenty-two.

PRICKLY PEAR

The prickly pear, also called cactus pear and a variety of other names, is indeed a cactus, with sharp spines as proof (they are usually removed before reaching market). Native to Central America and the American Southwest, where most of them are still grown, it is an extremely popular fruit in Mexico and the Mediterranean because it is refreshing.

Ranging up to five inches in length, the color variation is almost like the rainbow: green, chartreuse, pale yellow, pink, red, magenta, and purple, depending on the variety. The interior flesh varies similarly in color, with black seeds that can usually be ignored. Prickly pear tastes like watermelon and is similarly refreshing.

Prickly pears can be found in fall, winter, and spring. Look for fruit that is soft but not flaccid or mushy. Firm fruit can be ripened in a few days at room temperature, then refrigerated. It must be peeled before use. Even though the fruit in American markets have been debarbed, Elizabeth Schneider suggests impaling it on a fork. Then slice a half inch off each end and make a lengthwise incision a quarter inch deep. Insert the point of the knife underneath the thick double-layered skin and pull it off all the way around.

Take advantage if you can of the more brilliantly colored varieties of prickly pear. For fruit salads and compotes, chill the raw flesh and serve it sliced or cubed with a generous dash of citrus or combined with other soft fruits. You can purée the flesh and strain out the seeds through a sieve to make beautiful drinks and cocktails, sauces, and sherbets. Southwesterners like to make it into jelly, jam, or fruit butter.

Prickly pear offers a generous amount of vitamin C, potassium, calcium, and fiber, with only about forty-five calories in an average-size fruit.

TAMARILLO

This fruit, native to Peru, was called tree tomato until New Zealand promoted it heavily as the tamarillo. The red, amber, or golden fruit looks like a slim plum tomato and has a rich coral or golden interior with swirls of small black seeds. Tamarillos come onto the market in summer through fall. Choose heavy fruit and ripen at room temperature until scented and soft like a plum, when it can be refrigerated for a week or more.

Tamarillo tastes something like a spicy tomato with fruity overtones, and this androgynous identity carries over into cooking. With strong, somewhat bitter, dense flesh, the tamarillo is better cooked than eaten raw, and it may be more successful if treated as a vegetable rather than a fruit. Some people consider the yellow varieties superior for their milder, sweeter flavor. In cooking, tamarillo benefits from added sugar and acid. The fruit makes a good accompaniment to meat and works especially well in chutneys and relishes. Because of its dominant flavor, use tamarillo carefully in fruit compotes. The skin should be removed with a vegetable peeler before cooking. Since the flesh stains, watch out for wooden boards as well as clothing.

Tamarillo contains vitamins A and C, with about fifty calories in a half cup.

Appendix

PRESERVING AND PICKLING

The making of jellies, jams, marmalades, and preserves is one of the more technical aspects of cooking with fruit. By trial and error, people learned how to make preserves many centuries ago, but a general discussion may help you avoid some of those trials and errors.

Fruit itself contains the sugar, acid, and pectin that need to be present in the proper proportions for the chemical bonding that we call a "set" to take place. Sometimes more is added to ensure a good set. The best-tasting preserves have a high ratio of fruit to sugar. Commercial pectin, often added to low-pectin fruits (pears, peaches, raspberries, strawberries, blueberries, cherries, figs, grapes, and pineapple), requires a large amount of sugar to work, thus reducing the fruity flavor of the preserve. The preserves in this book call for no commercial pectin, but sometimes a high-pectin fruit (apples, citrus, quinces, currants, gooseberries, plums, and cranberries) is combined with a low-pectin fruit to bring about the desired set. It should be added that high-pectin fruit past its prime may give you trouble.

When you are making preserves, be sure to use a large, heavy-bottomed pot and, if possible, a candy thermometer. Follow the directions in the recipe for cooking the fruit with water, sugar, and probably some added lemon juice. Pectin needs to be extracted from the fruit to combine with the sugar and acid. When the mixture is brought to a rolling boil and the temperature reaches 220°F (105°C) at sea level (218°F at 1,000 feet, 216°F at 2,000 feet, 214°F at 3,000 feet altitude), the correct proportion of acid to sugar to pectin has been achieved. You can check this temperature on a candy thermometer. Other techniques are to put a little of the preserving liquid on a cold saucer, wait a few seconds for it to cool, and then push your finger through it: if the liquid wrinkles, it will achieve the desired set when cool. Or you can lift a spoon from the mixture and watch the liquid drop off the edge back into the pot: if two or three drops combine and slowly fall off together in a sheet, it will achieve a set. When checking by any of these methods, it is important to remove the pan from the heat so the mixture (if it has reached 220°F) does not overheat. If the liquid is not yet hot enough, return the pot to the heat, continue boiling, and test again in a few minutes.

When the preserve has reached the setting temperature, take it off the heat and skim off any scum or foam from the surface. If solid fruit is in the preserve, wait a few minutes before putting it in jars, so the solids will not rise to the surface but rather distribute themselves evenly.

To put up the preserve, have thoroughly clean, warm preserving jars ready. Spoon the preserve into the jars to within a quarter inch of the top. Wipe the top and the threads on the sides of the jar with a clean, damp cloth. Place the clean lidded disk on top and screw the ring on securely but not as tightly as you can.

To sterilize the preserves in a hot water bath, put a rack in the bottom of a large, wide, heavy-bottomed pot or a boiling water canner, and fill it with water deep enough to cover the jars standing on the rack by one inch. Bring the water to a full boil and carefully immerse the jars in the pot with tongs. They should stand on the rack without touching each other. Return the water to a boil, lower the heat to a steady gentle boil, and boil for ten or more minutes to sterilize the contents. Carefully lift the jars out with tongs onto a towel or rack.

Leave the jars undisturbed to cool for twelve to twenty-four hours. This is a good time to label them with their contents and the date. When the lids suddenly make the sound of a pop and turn concave, they are sealed and the vacuum inside the jars will keep the preserve free of bacteria during storage. (If your jars fail to seal properly, and this does happen from time to time even if you have done everything correctly, you can start over with fresh jars or, more simply, store them in the refrigerator for your family's immediate use.) Check the seal of the lids (you can remove the rings if you wish) and store the jars in a cool, dark, dry cupboard or pantry shelf. The preserves will keep for several months, depending on the particular recipe, or as long as a year. Although preserves can keep longer, it is a good idea to use them within that time. Once the jar has been opened, the contents are vulnerable to mold, so unless you plan to finish the jar quickly, store the preserve in the refrigerator, where it will keep for several weeks or longer.

It should be added the United States Department of Agriculture has recently changed its directives on sterilizing preserves to make them stricter. The use of paraffin is no longer advised. In England, where preserving sometimes seems to be a national pastime, recipe directions for storage are far less stringent. Bear this in mind when using English cookbooks.

PICKLING

Pickles and chutneys are preserved in acid, usually vinegar (at least 5 percent acidity), which keeps bacteria from growing in the jar. To prevent unfavorable reactions with the acid, use jars with glass lids rather than metal. When you have followed the recipe for pickling, fill the warm, clean jars to within a half inch of the top or the space specified in the recipe. Make sure there are no air bubbles in the jar by running a knife between the jar and the food to dislodge any. You may need to tuck the pieces of fruit under the shoulder of the lid to make sure they are immersed in the liquid. Wipe the threads of the jar and put on the clean tops according to the manufacturer's directions.

Sterilize the pickle or chutney jars in a hot water bath as described on the previous page and store them in the same manner as preserves. Pickles and chutneys may last for several months or up to a year. Once opened, it is a good idea to keep them in the refrigerator unless you plan to finish the jar very soon.

Selected Bibliography

Bacon, Josephine. *The Citrus Book*. Boston: Harvard Common Press, 1983.

Bianchini, Francesco, and Corbetta, Francesco. *The Complete Book of Fruits and Vegetables*. New York: Crown Publishers, Inc., 1976.

Davidson, Alan, and Knox, Charlotte. *Fruit: A Connoisseur's Guide and Cookbook*. London: Mitchell Beazley, 1991.

Forsell, Mary. *Berries: Cultivation, Decoration and Recipes*. New York: Bantam Books, 1989.

Grigson, Jane. *Jane Grigson's Fruit Book*. New York: Atheneum, 1982.

Grigson, Jane, and Knox, Charlotte. *Exotic Fruits & Vegetables*. New York: Henry Holt and Co., 1986.

Hathaway, Carolyn, ed. *The Packer: 1992 Produce Availability & Merchandising Guide*. Overland Park, KS: Vance Publishing Corp., 1992.

Root, Waverley. *Food: An Authoritative and Visual History and Dictionary of the Foods of the World*. New York: Simon and Schuster, 1980.

Schneider, Elizabeth. *Uncommon Fruits & Vegetables: A Commonsense Guide*. New York: Harper & Row, 1986.

Shere, Lindsey Remolif. *Chez Panisse Desserts*. New York: Random House, 1985.

INDEX